International Political Economy Series

General Editor: **Timothy M. Shaw**, Professor and Director, Institute of International Relations, The University of the West Indies, Trinidad & Tobago

Titles include:

Hans Abrahamsson
UNDERSTANDING WORLD ORDER AND STRUCTURAL CHANGE
Poverty, Conflict and the Global Arena

Morten Bøås, Marianne H. Marchand and Timothy Shaw (*editors*)
THE POLITICAL ECONOMY OF REGIONS AND REGIONALISM

Sandra Braman (*editor*)
THE EMERGENT GLOBAL INFORMATION POLICY REGIME

James Busumtwi-Sam and Laurent Dobuzinskis (*editors*)
TURBULENCE AND NEW DIRECTION IN GLOBAL POLITICAL ECONOMY

Elizabeth De Boer-Ashworth
THE GLOBAL POLITICAL ECONOMY AND POST-1989 CHANGE
The Place of the Central European Transition

Bill Dunn
GLOBAL RESTRUCTURING AND THE POWER OF LABOUR

Myron J. Frankman
WORLD DEMOCRATIC FEDERALISM
Peace and Justice Indivisible

Helen A. Garten
US FINANCIAL REGULATION AND THE LEVEL PLAYING FIELD

Barry K. Gills (*editor*)
GLOBALIZATION AND THE POLITICS OF RESISTANCE

Richard Grant and John Rennie Short (*editors*)
GLOBALIZATION AND THE MARGINS

Graham Harrison (*editor*)
GLOBAL ENCOUNTERS
International Political Economy, Development and Globalization

Patrick Hayden and Chamsy el-Ojeili (*editors*)
CONFRONTING GLOBALIZATION
Humanity, Justice and the Renewal of Politics

Axel Hülsemeyer (*editor*)
GLOBALIZATION IN THE TWENTY-FIRST CENTURY
Convergence or Divergence?

Helge Hveem and Kristen Nordhaug (*editors*)
PUBLIC POLICY IN THE AGE OF GLOBALIZATION
Responses to Environmental and Economic Crises

Takashi Inoguchi
GLOBAL CHANGE
A Japanese Perspective

Jomo K.S. and Shyamala Nagaraj (*editors*)
GLOBALIZATION VERSUS DEVELOPMENT

Dominic Kelly and Wyn Grant (*editors*)
THE POLITICS OF INTERNATIONAL TRADE IN THE 21st CENTURY
Actors, Issues and Regional Dynamics

Sandra J. MacLean, Sherri A. Brown and Pieter Fourie (*editors*)
HEALTH FOR SOME
The Political Economy of Global Health Governance

Craig N. Murphy (*editor*)
EGALITARIAN POLITICS IN THE AGE OF GLOBALIZATION

George Myconos
THE GLOBALIZATION OF ORGANIZED LABOUR
1945–2004

John Nauright and Kimberly S. Schimmel (*editors*)
THE POLITICAL ECONOMY OF SPORT

Morten Ougaard
THE GLOBALIZATION OF POLITICS
Power, Social Forces and Governance

Jørgen Dige Pedersen
GLOBALIZATION, DEVELOPMENT AND THE STATE
The Performance of India and Brazil Since 1990

Markus Perkmann and Ngai-Ling Sum
GLOBALIZATION, REGIONALIZATION AND CROSS-BORDER REGIONS

Marc Schelhase
GLOBALIZATION, REGIONALIZATION AND BUSINESS
Conflict, Convergence and Influence

Herman M. Schwartz and Leonard Seabrooke (*editors*)
THE POLITICS OF HOUSING BOOMS AND BUSTS

Leonard Seabrooke
US POWER IN INTERNATIONAL FINANCE
The Victory of Dividends

Timothy J. Sinclair and Kenneth P. Thomas (*editors*)
STRUCTURE AND AGENCY IN INTERNATIONAL CAPITAL MOBILITY

Fredrik Söderbaum and Timothy M. Shaw (*editors*)
THEORIES OF NEW REGIONALISM

Susanne Soederberg, Georg Menz and Philip G. Cerny (*editors*)
INTERNALIZING GLOBALIZATION
The Rise of Neoliberalism and the Decline of National Varieties of Capitalism

Ritu Vij (*editor*)
GLOBALIZATION AND WELFARE
A Critical Reader

Matthew Watson
THE POLITICAL ECONOMY OF INTERNATIONAL CAPITAL MOBILITY

International Political Economy Series

Series Standing Order ISBN 978-0-333-71708-0 hardcover
Series Standing Order ISBN 978-0-333-71110-1 paperback

You can receive future titles in this series as they are published by placing a standing order. Please contact your bookseller or, in case of difficulty, write to us at the address below with your name and address, the title of the series and one of the ISBNs quoted above.

Customer Services Department, Macmillan Distribution Ltd, Houndmills, Basingstoke, Hampshire RG21 6XS, England

Health for Some

The Political Economy of Global Health Governance

Edited by

Sandra J. MacLean
Simon Fraser University, Canada

Sherri A. Brown
Simon Fraser University, Canada

and

Pieter Fourie
Macquarie University, Australia

palgrave
macmillan

First published 2009 by
PALGRAVE MACMILLAN

Palgrave Macmillan in the UK is an imprint of Macmillan Publishers Limited, registered in England, company number 785998, of Houndmills, Basingstoke, Hampshire RG21 6XS.

Palgrave Macmillan in the US is a division of St Martin's Press LLC, 175 Fifth Avenue, New York, NY 10010.

Palgrave Macmillan is the global academic imprint of the above companies and has companies and representatives throughout the world.

Palgrave® and Macmillan® are registered trademarks in the United States, the United Kingdom, Europe and other countries.

ISBN: 978–0–230–22424–7 hardback

This book is printed on paper suitable for recycling and made from fully managed and sustained forest sources. Logging, pulping and manufacturing processes are expected to conform to the environmental regulations of the country of origin.

A catalogue record for this book is available from the British Library.

A catalog record for this book is available from the Library of Congress.

10 9 8 7 6 5 4 3 2 1
18 17 16 15 14 13 12 11 10 09

Printed and bound in Great Britain by
CPI Antony Rowe, Chippenham and Eastbourne

Contents

Tables

Figures

Foreword

This book is published at a crucial moment in global economic development. The 2008 calendar year saw an economic crisis develop, the like of which had not been seen for decades. There are those who argue Marx is vindicated; this is the 'collapse of capitalism'. Others suggest that now is the time for Keynesian economic policies to be revisited. The economic turmoil is taking place in a globalized world. Unless there are some dramatic new developments, either an economic turnaround or a new political order, then the Millennium Development Goals are unlikely to be met.

In this book globalization is defined as the remarkable rapidity with which impacts and events take place. In the first chapter MacLean and Brown argue: 'global health issues are those health issues that have emerged as the result of changes in relations and behavior of states, businesses and people, and these changes are determined by the recent dominance and contradictions of global neoliberalism' (p. 12).

The book is a collection of papers presented in 2007 and updated for publication. On reading it, there are three themes that I found particularly striking. These are: the relative importance of global health; the concept of long waves; and the changes in global heath architecture, including the new role of public–private partnerships.

Global health is distinguished from international health as being consequential within the context of global changes in the political economy. However, this begs the question. Is it considered important by policymakers and governments whether they are in the developed or the developing world? The evidence presented here is equivocal.

Communicable diseases get attention when they are framed as threats to global (read rich world) security. Increasingly it is clear that most such diseases do not have this status – the exceptions being SARS and avian flu. The book has several interesting sections on Canada and the Canadian role in global health (Chapter 4 particularly). This may be because, of all the developed nations in the world, the Canadians appreciate the dangers of new epidemics as a result of their SARS experience.

Chronic diseases in the developing world are ignored. This is well discussed in the chapters on the political economy of global health research (Chapter 11) and discussions of pharmaceuticals, access prices and patents (Chapters 12 and 13), but it is a constant theme. Of great concern is the lack of priority given to health by the developing world governments. The Abuja declaration saw African leaders pledge to allocate at least 15 per cent of annual budgets to the improvement of the health sector. Most countries have fallen far short of this and there seems little likelihood that they will meet these goals. Equally, in the developed world, the commitment to allocating 0.7 per cent of GDP to official development assistance seems increasingly distant. Global health is not a priority; the challenge is to make it one.

The AIDS epidemic is the best example of a 'long-wave' health event and this is well captured by Fourie (Chapter 5). Achieving global health will require long-term investments and a vision of what long-wave events are. Indeed, deterioration of health is, at the community or national level, also a long-wave event. The good news is that health is resilient; the bad news is that improving it will take time and investment. There are simple basic interventions that can have massive benefits, such as attended births and iodizing salt, but in the long run, as this book demonstrates, it is the political economy that needs to change.

As is well illustrated, the global health architecture is changing. Schrecker looks at the G8, globalization and the needs for a global health ethic in the second chapter. Hein and Kohlmorgen discuss transnational norm-building in the health and non-state actors in Post-Westphalian politics (Chapter 7). The role of philanthropic foundations and global health is the theme of Moran's chapter (8), and he describes 'venture philanthropy' and 'social entrepreneurship'. Here a concern is that the role and influence of these organizations may result in a skewed agenda.

The case studies: the Global Fund (Chapter 9) and World Bank Multi-country programme (MAP), Global Fund and President's Emergency Plan for AIDS Relief (Chapter 10) are deeply interesting. There seems to be huge redundancy in global health financing, with countries being overwhelmed by organizations that both set the agenda and have stringent reporting requirements. The conclusion is that 'making the money work' is difficult and again needs changes in attitude and governance.

One way forward might be through Public–Private Partnerships, as discussed in Chapter 7. These have become particularly numerous in global health. They bring opportunities, but the question is: to whom are they answerable? This is one area to watch with interest.

Ultimately this book shows two things. The first is that global public health is at a moment when there will be change. Its importance may be questioned and ignored. The challenge is to make it really 'public' in a global sense. Given the 2008 economic crisis this may not be easy. Secondly, there needs to be a fundamental realignment of global politics and economics. Ironically, the events of 2008 mean that this is closer to being possible than has been the case recently. There are opportunities for those of us concerned by ensuring the world has a healthier population to intervene and influence, as this book has the potential to do.

Alan Whiteside
Director, Health Economics and HIV/AIDS Research Division,
University of KwaZulu-Natal, Durban, January 2009

Abbreviations

AAI	Accelerating Access Initiative
ACHAP	African Comprehensive HIV/AIDS Partnerships
ARV	antiretroviral
ASAP	Aids Strategy and Action Plan
BIO	Biotechnology Industry Organization
CCGHR	Canadian Coalition for Global Health Research
CCIC	Canadian Council on International Cooperation
CCM	Country Coordinating Mechanism
CEO	Chief Executive Officer
CFP	Canadian foreign policy
CGPA	Canadian Generic Pharmaceutical Association
CHAT	Country Harmonization and Alignment Tool
CIDA	Canadian International Development Agency
CIHI	Canadian Institute for Health Information
CIHR	Canadian Institute for Health Research
CMH	Commission on Macroeconomics and Health
CoATS	Coordinating AIDS Technical Support database
CPTech	Consumer Project on Technology
CRADA	Cooperative Research and Development Agreement
CSDH	Commission on the Social Determinants of Health
CSIR	Council for Scientific and Industrial Research
CSO	civil society organization
DAC	Development Cooperative Directorate
DCD	Development Assistance Committee
DDA	Doha Development Agenda
DFAIT	Department of Foreign Affairs and International Trade
DFID	UK Department for International Development
DND	Department of National Defence
DOTS	Directly Observed Therapy Short-course
DTC	direct-to-consumer
EFPIA	European Federation of Pharmaceutical Industries
ESC	economic, social and cultural
EU	European Union
FAO	Food and Agriculture Organization (FAO)
FBO	faith-based organization
FDA	Food and Drug Agency
FDI	foreign direct investment
FCTC	Framework Convention for Tobacco Control
FTA	free trade agreement

G7	Group of Seven (of the OECD)
G8	Group of Eight (of the OECD)
GAO	Government Accountability Office (US)
GATS	General Agreement on Trade in Services
GATT	General Agreement on Tariffs and Trade
GAVI	Global Alliance for Vaccine and Immunization
GBC	Global Business Coalition on AIDS, TB and Malaria
GEF	Global Environmental Facility
GF	Global Fund (to Fight AIDS, Tuberculosis and Malaria)
GFATM	Global Fund to Fight AIDS, Tuberculosis and Malaria
GIST	Global Implementation Support Team
GNI	Gross National Income
GNP	Gross National Product
GNP	The Global Network of People Living with HIV/AIDS
GPA	Global Programme on AIDS (WHO)
GPEI	Global Polio Eradication Initiative
GPG	global public good
GPHIN	Global Public Health Intelligence Network
GPPP	Global Public–Private Partnership
GTT	Global Task Team on Improving AIDS Coordination among Multilateral Institutions and International Donors
HAI	Health Action International
HHS	Health and Human Services (US Department of)
HIPC	Heavily Indebted Poor Countries
HIV/AIDS	Human Immunodeficiency Virus/Acquired Immune Deficiency Syndrome
ICASO	International Council of AIDS Service Organizations
ICESCR	International Covenant on Economic, Social and Cultural Rights
IAVI	International AIDS Vaccine Initiative
IDA	International Development Association
IDPL	Indian Drug and Pharmaceutical Laboratories
IDRC	International Development Research Council
IFPMA	International Federation of Pharmaceutical Manufacturers and Associates
IGO	intergovernmental organization
ILO	International Labor Organization
IMF	International Monetary Fund
ICASO	International Council of AIDS Service Organizations
IP	intellectual property
IPPPH	Initiative for Public–Private Partnerships in Health
IPE	International Political Economy
IPR	intellectual property rights
IPS	International Policy Statement

IR	International Relations
LFA	Local Fund Agent
LMIC	low- and mid-income countries
LSHTM	London School of Hygiene and Tropical Medicine
MAP	Multi-Country HIV/AIDS Programme for Africa
M&E	monitoring and evaluation
MD	Managing Director
MDGs	Millennium Development Goals
MDRI	Multilateral Debt Relief Initiative
MMV	Medicines for Malaria Venture
MNC	multinational corporation
MSF	Médecins Sans Frontières
NAC	National AIDS Coordinating Authority
NCE	new chemical entity
NEPAD	New Partnership for Africa's Development
NIH	National Institutes of Health (US)
NIHR	National Institute for Health Research
NSERC	Natural Sciences and Engineering Research Council
ODA	Official Development Assistance
OECD	Organization of the Economic Cooperation and Development
OGAC	Office of the Global AIDS Coordinator
OIE	Office International des Épizooties
PAHO	Pan American Health Organization
PDUFA	Prescription Drug User Fees Act
PEPFAR	President's Emergency Plan for AIDS Relief
PhRMA	Pharmaceutical Research and Manufacturers of America
PDP	product development partnership
PHC	Primary Health Care
PMPRB	Patented Medicine Price Review Board
PPP	public–private partnership
PR	Principal Recipient
PTI	Press Trust of India
PTO	Patent and Trademark Office
RF	Rockefeller Foundation
RNA	ribonucleic acid
Rx&D	Canada's Research Based Pharmaceutical Companies
SARS	Severe Acute Respiratory Syndrome
SDH	social determinants of health
SPP	Security and Prosperity Partnership
SRP	Screening Review Panel
SSHRC	Social Science and Humanities Research Council
TAC	Treatment Action Campaign
TB	tuberculosis
TNC	transnational corporation

TNCM	Tanzanian National AIDS Coordinating Authority
TSF	Technical Support Facilities
TRIPS	Trade-Related Aspects of Intellectual Property Rights
TWG	Transitional Working Group (TWG)
UN	United Nations
UNAIDS	Joint United Nations Programme on HIV/AIDS
UNICEF	United Nations Children's Fund
UNCTAD	United Nations Conference on Trade and Development
UNDP	United Nations Development Programme
UNEP	United Nations Environment Programme
UNFPA	United Nations Population Fund
US	United States
USPTA	United States Patent and Trademark Office
USTR	United States Trade Representative
WIPO	World Intellectual Property Organization
WHO	World Health Organization
WTO	World Trade Organization

Contributors

Sonja Bartsch is Research Fellow at the GIGA German Institute of Global and Area Studies in Hamburg. Her areas of research include global governance, civil society organizations, policy networks, international organizations, global public health and development policy. At present she works on global health governance and the role of public–private partnerships. She was co-leader of a research project on 'Institutional Changes in Global Health Governance' at the GIGA and Fellow of the 2007 Wall Summer Institute for Research on 'Civil Society and Global Health'. She has authored articles on various topics of Global Politics and Health Governance; her most recent publication is *Global Health Governance and the Fight against HIV/AIDS* (2007, Palgrave Macmillan), edited with Wolfgang Hein and Lars Kohlmorgen.

Sherri A. Brown is a PhD Candidate, 2007 Trudeau Foundation Scholar and SSHRC Canada Graduate Scholar in the Department of Political Science at Simon Fraser University. Her doctoral dissertation investigates the architecture, roles, and behaviour of global institutions and non-state actors in health governance, with a focus on the political economy of access to essential medicines in sub-Saharan Africa. Her research interests are in health, political economy and development, particularly the interfaces between globalization, gender, and health.

Eowynne Feeney has an Honours Degree in International Development Studies from McGill University and is currently directing the African Support Program at the Institute of Cultural Affairs Canada. Her honours thesis was on access to medicines under Trade-Related Aspects of Intellectual Property Rights (TRIPS).

Pieter Fourie teaches Politics at Macquarie University in Sydney, Australia. He has a PhD in Public Policy and a Master's in International Political Economy. Pieter pursued formal studies at the Universities of Stellenbosch, Johannesburg, London (King's College) and Paris (Sciences Po), and he is a fellow of La Trobe University's Institute for Advanced Study. In 2003–4 he worked for UNAIDS on a scenario project regarding the future of AIDS in Africa, and he remains involved in a number of AIDS-related projects. His book *The Political Management of HIV and AIDS in South Africa: One Burden Too Many?* (Palgrave Macmillan) appeared in 2006.

Wolfgang Hein is Head of the Research Programme 'Transformation in the Process of Globalization' at GIGA German Institute of Global and Area Studies and Professor of Political Science and Development Studies at the Institute for Political Science at the University of Hamburg. He is author of a number of edited volumes and monographs in the field of development, globalization and the interfaces between global and national health politics. Recently he co-published a volume on *Global Health Governance and the Fight against HIV/AIDS* (Palgrave Macmillan).

Siri Bjerkreim Hellevik is a Norwegian political scientist and a PhD student working at the Norwegian Institute for Urban and Regional Affairs, Oslo, Norway. Her PhD project is on efforts towards coordination of national HIV/AIDS programmes at the global, national and local levels. Her main research interest is in HIV/AIDS politics and governance, the linkages between national and local level responses to HIV/AIDS in African countries, and decentralization reform.

Carmen Huckel Schneider is a research associate at the Centre for International Studies/Peace and Conflict Research, at the University of Tuebingen in Germany, and a member of the Research Training Group Global Challenges: Transnational and Transcultural Solutions. She has published on the role of non-state actors in the global political economy, public–private partnerships and global health governance.

Lars Kohlmorgen is senior research fellow and lecturer at the Institute of Political Sciences, University of Hamburg and associated research fellow at the GIGA German Institute of Global and Area Studies. His main research interests are in the fields of International Relations, globalization, global governance, global social policy, civil society and politics of intellectual property rights.

Rodney Loeppky is an Assistant Professor and Associate Chair of the Department of Political Science, York University, Canada. His research interests include the political economy of biomedical innovation and advanced industrial development strategies, advanced industrial social policies, US domestic and foreign policies.

David R. MacLean is Adjunct Professor, and founding Dean, of the Faculty of Health Sciences, Simon Fraser University. His main areas of research include chronic disease prevention and control; health promotion and disease prevention; and health system and health policy development. His numerous publications draw on an extensive academic research agenda as well as practical experience as a physician clinician, public health officer and consultant to the World Health Organization as well as provincial and federal governments.

Sandra J. MacLean is an Associate Professor of Political Science at Simon Fraser University, British Columbia, Canada. Her research is concerned with global governance in areas of health, human security, and development. She is the author of several chapters and journal articles on these topics and is co-editor with Timothy Shaw and David Black of *A Decade of Human*

Security: Global Governance and New Multilateralisms (Ashgate, 2006) and with Fahimul Quadir and Timothy Shaw of *Crises of Governance in Asia and Africa* (Ashgate, 2001).

Michael Moran has degrees in political science and public policy and is a PhD candidate at the University of Melbourne, Australia. His PhD examines the influence of private philanthropic foundations in the global governance system. Recently he co-published a volume on *Global Health Governance and the Fight against HIV/AIDS* (Palgrave Macmillan).

Colleen O'Manique is an Associate Professor of Politics and Women's Studies at Trent University in Peterborough, Canada. She holds a PhD in Political Science from York University, and has been teaching at Trent since 2001, after working for a number of years as an international development consultant both in Canada and overseas. Today, her research focuses on the global political economy of health, in particular on the intersections between specific features of globalization, HIV/AIDS, and gender relations. Her publications include *Neoliberalism and HIV/AIDS Crisis in Sub-Saharan Africa: Globalization's Pandemic* (Palgrave, 2004).

Shree Mulay is a Professor and the Associate Dean of Community Health and Humanities Division in the Faculty of Medicine, Memorial University, St John's Newfoundland. She has published over 60 peer-reviewed scientific papers. More recently she has turned her attention to the impact of liberalization and international trade regimes on access to medicines and health services by vulnerable populations in rural India.

Valbona Muzaka recently finished her PhD in international trade and intellectual property regulation at the Department of Politics, University of Sheffield, UK. She has been teaching and lecturing on global political economy issues, globalization, and comparative political analysis at the same department for the last 3 years. Her research interests include economic and human development, globalization, trade, human rights, public health and poverty eradication.

Ted Schrecker is a scientist and Associate Professor in the University of Ottawa's Department of Epidemiology and Community Medicine, and a principal scientist at the University's Institute of Population Health. He is a political scientist with more than 20 years of professional experience as a legislative researcher, academic, and consultant to a variety of government agencies and civil society organizations. Professor Schrecker is a co-author of *Fatal Indifference: The G8, Africa and Global Health* (University of Cape Town Press, 2004), the first normative report card on the health impacts of G8 policies, and numerous subsequent publications on globalization and health. He also acted as Hub coordinator for the Globalization Knowledge Network of the WHO Commission on Social Determinants of Health. For more details and links to selected recent publications and presentations: http://www.globalhealthequity.ca/about/schrecker.shtml.

Daya R. Varma is Professor of Pharmacology and Therapeutics, McGill University, Quebec, Canada. He has published over 200 scientific papers, including over a dozen on the effects of the Union Carbide gas disaster in Bhopal, India, in 1984 on pregnant women and their offspring.

Part I

Introduction

1

Introduction: The Social Determinants of Global Health: Confronting Inequities

Sandra J. MacLean and Sherri A. Brown

Health, at a population level, is largely socially determined; consequently, rich countries and communities tend to have significantly better health outcomes than poor ones. In the current era, this observation is critical, given that globalization has been implicated in producing economic convergence within and between some countries, but appreciably greater socioeconomic gaps in others (Farmer, 2003; OECD, 2008). To grasp the nature of health and disease in the world today, therefore, entails understanding not only biological phenomena, but also who wins and who loses as a result of the recent changes in global political economy. Moreover, to be effective, global health governance must address the underlying structures of political economy that are primary sources of social inequalities and inequities and thus contributors to negative health outcomes (CSDH, 2008).

Over the past two to three decades, several health problems with worldwide implications have emerged to spawn an explosion of interest in 'global health'. The burgeoning literature on the subject has produced important and informative research on a set of issues. However, there are problems with the current situation in global health analysis. First, there are conceptual problems. The notion of global health is not often clearly defined; it is frequently used, for instance, in ways that do not distinguish it from the long-established concept of international health. Second, the weights given to the range of issues addressed are skewed; in particular, much of the attention is focused on infectious disease to the detriment of research on chronic disease as a global health issue. Third, while interdisciplinarity is a welcome feature of global health scholarship, emerging bridges between public health and international political economy (IPE) and international relations (IR) are still inadequately constructed[1]; few public health scholars address health through a meaningful engagement with the causal issues of political economy, while many IPE and IR scholars focus mainly on health as a security issue, paying little attention to the compelling social determinants of health literature. Finally, while the global health governance literature has been preoccupied with new governance forms, such as public private partnerships (PPPs), the majority of the analyses to date have been essentially descriptive accounts of the nature and form of an emerging governance architecture; there has been insufficient attention paid to the way that these novel arrangements conform to, much less challenge, structural inequalities in the global economy.

This collection, which comprises edited and updated versions of papers originally presented in September 2007 at the Sixth Pan-European Conference on International Relations in Turin, Italy, is an attempt to stimulate discussion and debate on these still undertheorized areas. It seeks to disaggregate the two overarching themes – (i) the impact on health of political economy changes associated with globalization, and (ii) emerging forms of global health governance – by identifying the major players responsible for framing, and thus controlling, the current global health paradigm; by exposing the nature and extent of inequalities that are emerging in areas of global health; and by analyzing the potentials and problems of current forms of global health governance. Because the problems of global health (and the potential solutions) are embedded in social dynamics, as much as or more than in biological determinants or technical innovation, there is a compelling need for interdisciplinary approaches in the analysis of global health, drawing especially, but not only, on IPE and IR. Consequently, the proposed volume includes contributions from scholars in the fields of Public and Population Health as well as IR IPE. Furthermore, as senior and junior scholars representing several countries/geographic areas and different analytical approaches, the contributors bring comprehensive and nuanced analyses of global health/global health governance, an area in which there is a growing, but still nascent and inchoate, literature.

Conceptualizing global health

The political economy of global health

The term 'global health' is not entirely new (there are occasional references to it in the literature at least as far back as the 1950s), but in the past two decades the use of the term has escalated noticeably (Brown et al., 2006). Given that most aspects of human life are now being re-evaluated within the context of globalization, it is not unexpected that the critical area of health would be scrutinized as a 'global' issue. But what exactly is *global* about global health?

Global phenomena may be defined as events and experiences having worldwide reach or impact, as in global warming affecting the entire world. Thus, by this definition, global health involves health issues that are experienced in all areas of the world and/or those that derive from phenomena that have global reach. However, this definition does not address causal factors or provide any insights regarding what has changed to allow us to now regard global health as a new disciplinary focus. What, for instance, distinguishes global health from international health? In IR and IPE literatures, to reflect the transformational nature of globalization, global phenomena tend often to be defined by comparison with international events and processes. Some scholars view globalization as intensified international relations: greater interconnectedness occurring at an 'accelerated pace' (McGrew, 2006, p. 22). Interconnectedness implies that the events and practices in one area impact upon people and communities in other parts of the world. However, as this feature applies to both international and global orders, globalization is distinguished by the remarkable rapidity with which the impacts are felt around the world. Moreover, the interconnections are vertical as well as horizontal, and the local–global interface has become an important terrain of economic, political and social interaction. Also, according to Jan Aart Scholte (2000), an essential feature of globalization is deterritorialization, meaning that the increasing social interactions occurring around the world rely less than previously, and sometimes not at all, on geographical space and boundaries.

While globalization involves transformations of social and cultural as well as economic and political relations, political economy (defined here as the inseparable integration of politics and economy) is the essential driver of the changes (see, for example, Cox, 2000). As Ronen Palan (2000) observes, all perspectives of political economy have been interested traditionally in the themes of 'state, firm, capital, power [and] labour'. Over the past two to three decades, a preoccupation of many, especially critical, scholars in the field has been to map and explain the changes in relations among these sets of actors under the dominance of neoliberalism. Core features of the transition from predominately international to increasingly global relations in the neoliberal order are: the transnationalization of production and finance (Scholte, 2000); the role of technology as both product and driver of changes in production and distribution; and the loss of bargaining power of labour vis-à-vis the state (Tabb, 2004, pp. 22–3). The role of the state in this transformation is both critical and complicated. While transnational capital is identified as the leading force in globalization (Gill, 2008), states are viewed as actors that have been complicit in support of these changes as well as respondents to, and sometimes victims of, the transformations (Sørensen, 2002). Another important feature of the changing political economy not identified in Palan's list is the increasing importance of civil society organizations as central members in the contemporary nexus of relevant governance actors (Cox, 1999; O'Brien et al., 2000). As with the state, civil society actors can assist or resist globalization, although resistance activities have been the most frequently documented (e.g., see Broad, 2002; Gill, 2008).

The concept of global health, then, as distinct from international health, is consequential only within the context of these global changes in political economy. The term 'international health' has been widely used for several decades to refer to interventions by health organizations such as the World Health Organization (WHO) and personnel (usually health professionals from the North) in other countries (usually in the South) to produce health improvements (MacLean, 2007). The main foci of the international health agenda have been the control and reduction of infectious disease, maternal and child health, and, to a somewhat lesser extent, the health of workers and health-related trade. All of these issues continue to be important considerations within a global health paradigm, but it is the impact of globalization processes upon these and other health issues that makes the concept of *global health* meaningful. In other words, global health can be understood as health conditions and outcomes that are determined by changes in relations among state, business, labour and civil society resulting from increased interdependence and deterritorialization of social relations. This conceptualization of global health provides a theoretical framework for exploring the cause and nature of the changes. To date, other definitions of global health, while useful, have been mainly descriptive, as, for instance, is the following from Lee and Collin (2005, p. 3), who assert that a global health issue is one '...where the determinants circumvent, undermine or are oblivious to the territorial boundaries of states and, thus, beyond the capacity of individual countries to address through domestic institutions'.

The transition from international to global health

After the Second World War, it was thought that the international spread of infectious disease had been brought under control within a health governance framework led by the WHO (MacLean, 2007). However, any complacency that accompanied this perceived success began to dissolve in the 1980s following outbreaks of lethal, highly contagious, infectious diseases such as Ebola and the rapid worldwide spread of HIV/AIDS. The range and speed of transmission of HIV, in particular, but also the resurgence of old diseases such as drug-resistant malaria and tuberculosis, provided clear evidence of the high degree of interdependence in the contemporary world, and also demonstrated that, with advances in transportation and increasing transnational movements of people, threats to health were becoming rapidly transnationalized, and beyond the capacity of established national and international mechanisms to control effectively. When the short-lived but deadly epidemic of Severe Acute Respiratory Syndrome (SARS) broke out in 2002–3, the responses by WHO as well as various non-governmental actors prompted David Fidler (2003; 2004a; 2004b) to exclaim that an important milestone in global health governance had been reached, namely that post-Westphalian governance had replaced the traditional state-based system. Since then, the impending threat of a worldwide avian flu pandemic has brought together an unprecedented mix of national, international, state and non-state actors in 'emerging governance modalities' around infectious disease (Neubauer, 2005). In summary, a defining moment in the transition from international to global health involves the emergence of new infectious diseases, their rapid transnationalization and the development of new governance arrangements to address their national as well as human costs.

The shift from international to global health has been demonstrated by worldwide alterations in chronic disease patterns as well, although the global health aspects of chronic disease are not yet as well documented as are those associated with infectious disease (Strong et al., 2006, p. 492). Since the late 1990s, more deaths in the world each year have been caused by chronic diseases, so that currently 'chronic' or 'noncommunicable' diseases such as cardiovascular disease and diabetes account for 60 per cent of deaths worldwide (MacLean and MacLean, 2008); and, except in the African region, 'chronic diseases kill and disable more people than HIV/AIDS, tuberculosis, and malaria' (Spinaci et al., 2006, p. 32). Eighty per cent of these deaths occur in low and middle-income countries (Daar et al., 2007, p. 494). In sub-Saharan Africa, infectious diseases still claim more deaths in the region (mainly because of AIDS) than chronic diseases, but a rapid increase in chronic disease rates in the region means that Africa is now wrestling with a double health burden (Mufunda et al., 2006).

The global epidemiological transition is due in part to demographic shifts (many populations are aging and thus are more susceptible to chronic diseases), but especially in Southern countries, where the diseases manifest more in middle age than in old age as in the North, global political economy forces are largely responsible for the transition. Increased urbanization, which encourages changes in lifestyle associated with the new global division of labor and/or cultural shifts in diet or exercise patterns, are partly responsible, as are lifestyle changes encouraged by trade and/or global marketing (especially increased smoking rates) (Brown, 2002; Popkin, 2006).

Influential international organizations such as the WHO (2005a) and the World Bank (Adeyi et al., 2007) have begun campaigns to raise awareness about the discrepancies in global health burden associated with the epidemiological transition. In response to the growing global tobacco epidemic, for instance, the WHO enacted its first international health treaty, the Framework Convention for Tobacco Control (FCTC), which came into force on 27 February 2005. The FCTC reflects the WHO's concern with the growing global epidemic of tobacco use and tobacco's harmful health, social, environmental, and economic effects. Furthermore, it heralded growing interest in the increasing chronic disease burden, which has been largely neglected to date. Indeed, chronic diseases were overlooked in the preparation of the Millennium Development Goals (MDGs) and have yet to be specified as other health issues have been in this major global initiative.

Increased rates of chronic disease as well as emerging infectious diseases help to expose the impacts of changes in the global political economy on social conditions and welfare. For instance, one of the major impacts on chronic disease rates has been global trade. Some effects of increased trade may be positive, such as in possible advancements for diagnosing disease, or greater foreign investment in health sectors (Blouin, 2007a). However, to date, many of the effects have been negative, as in the lessening of states' ability, independently, to control and develop their national health policies (Bettcher et al., 2000), decreased access of many people, especially in the South, to affordable drugs (Mulay et al., in this volume), increased availability of unhealthy products such as tobacco (Bettcher et al., 2001) or processed foods with high salt and/or fat content (Popkin, 2006) and increased challenges to worker health and safety (Brown, 2002).

In addition to new endemic and pandemic infectious diseases (and the securitization of these diseases), the emerging worldwide 'epidemic' of chronic diseases and various trade-related health issues, there are several other global health issues. These include the drug trade, the transnational trade in people for prostitution and/or slavery, the health problems of refugees, the rapidly expanding, illegal trade in organs and the emergence of 'surgery vacations' where patients travel to countries to receive cut-rate plastic surgery or cardiovascular treatments. In most if not all of these global health issues disparity is a notable feature; poor people, communities and countries carry a significantly greater burden of global disease and a sizably reduced level of health (CSDH, 2008). In this volume, we argue that the distinguishing feature of these issues as global health items, and their differential impacts, is their source and/or embeddedness in the political economy of globalization. In other words, global health issues are those health issues that have emerged as the result of changes in relations and behaviour of states, businesses and people, and these changes are determined by the recent dominance and contradictions of global neoliberalism.

Global health governance

The inability of the established international health governance system to deal effectively with global health issues prompted Andrew Cooper et al. (2007, p. 3) to declare emphatically that '[g]lobal health is in crisis'. Also, although new governance architecture is emerging to deal with the various issues, the verdict is still out on how effective the new arrangements will be to deal with the health problems of the global era. In particular, structural changes in the neoliberal organizations and principles that have dominated in setting the current global health agenda are unlikely to occur quickly, even if the neoliberal system has entered a crisis phase. Although the current architecture of global health governance will no doubt be altered by the crisis (especially in terms of the respective power of central players), the extent is still uncertain.

To date, the global health governance architecture has conformed, generally, to the pattern of nascent global governance structures in that it involves a range of actors that interact over several levels from the local through national, international and global. James Rosenau (2005) has described this framework of global governance as involving 'multiple spheres of authority' that interact within an arrangement of 'disaggregated complexity'. In the new complexity, the World Health Organization continues to be a central player in health governance, as it was in the international era. However, it is now only one of several key players in the health governance nexus. Many of the newly engaged actors have not previously been involved, or have been involved only marginally, in health. One of these is the WTO, as noted above. The World Bank is also a relatively new, and highly influential, actor in global health governance and, unlike the WTO, this organization has become involved specifically to influence health outcomes. Since acknowledging in the *World Development Report 1993* that health plays a critical role in economic development, the World Bank has increased its expenditures on health appreciably so that now it is one of the main funders. Between 1990 and 2004, the Bank 'lent nearly $20 billion and disbursed $15 billion' to the health sectors of developing countries and it supports 11 global health partnerships (Lele et al., 2004, xiv). Yet, the Bank's role in global health is decidedly contradictory; while it shares the centre of global health governance authority with the WHO, and although it has committed significant resources to solve global health problems, it has also been a major contributor to global social inequities. Indeed, as David McCoy (2007, p. 1500) argues, the Bank's recent decision to devote more of its attention to health sector reform may be 'cause for alarm':

> while the Bank's strategy contains much to agree with, its claims to expertise and credibility in the field of health systems are troubling. Indeed, structural adjustment programmes and health sector reforms inspired by the Bank have underpinned many of the current problems in poor countries [and] ... the Bank's continued promotion of proprivate market-oriented policies and its view that health care can be reduced to a set of tradeable commodities and services raises important concerns.

Similarly troubling and controversial is the growing importance of the G8 group of the Organization of the Economic Cooperation and Development (OECD) at the centre of global health governance. Some view the G8's role as constructive. For instance, according to John Kirton and Jenevieve Mannell (2007, p. 115), in the wake of failure of the WHO to deal effectively with global health issues, the G8 'has taken up the challenge' to provide effective leadership through a variety of initiatives. Kirton and Mannell give credit to the G8 for several high-profile global health initiatives, including the Global Fund to Fight AIDS, Tuberculosis, and Malaria, founded in 2001, the G8 Africa Action Plan and the G8 Health Action Plan, as well as specific programmes on infectious diseases such as HIV/AIDS and polio (ibid., pp. 115–16). Kirton and Mannell's generally positive view of the G8's role in global health governance is not shared by everyone, however. Indeed, others (Schrecker et al.; O'Manique) in the same volume are much less sanguine about the G8's role. As Colleen O'Manique (2007, p. 216) observes, any contributions that the G8 makes to global health governance need to be evaluated '...in the context of the collateral damage caused by its members' attachment to the specific policies governing the global political economy and their enforcement by the IFIs [international financial institutions]....'

While dominant organizations within the neoliberal order, such as the G8 and World Bank, are among the more prominent players in emerging global health governance, other international organizations are also contributors to the new health order. The United Nations General Assembly is one such organization. While it was not much concerned with international health in the past, it became a significant player in global health governance by adopting the Millennium Declaration in 2000, since three of the eight Millennium Development Goals established by the Declaration deal directly with health, while the remaining five target social determinants of health.[2] The UN Security Council also became involved in global health governance when it identified HIV/AIDS as a significant international security issue in 2000, thus marking the first time that a health issue had been securitized by the major international security body (Holbrooke, 2000). Various other organizations – UNICEF, UNDP, UNFPA, ILO, IMF[3] – are also featured in global health governance, although as second-tier players that are less prominent than central organizations such as the WHO or World Bank (Dodgson et al., 2002, p. 22).

Bilateral relations are also an important part of the emerging global health governance architecture. Most of, if not all, the major industrialized countries now commit resources individually to research and project initiatives under the rubric of 'global health' (see the MacLean and MacLean chapter in this volume). Among these, the United States wields probably the greatest influence in setting the global health agenda, since it is the most significant state donor of funds to global health projects and research (see the chapter by Rodney Loeppky). For instance, when the President's Emergency Plan for AIDS Relief (PEPFAR) was launched in 2003, committing $15 billion over 5 years to the fight against HIV/AIDS, it was 'the largest commitment ever by a single nation toward an international health initiative' (PEPFAR website). By 2005, PEPFAR was providing 70 per cent of the US$3 billion per year being transferred by all actors engaged in the fight against HIV/AIDS (Bernstein and Sessions, 2007). Some scholars have argued, however, that PEPFAR is designed primarily to serve US domestic interests and that the US involvement in global health generally is motivated as much or more by concerns to protect national interest (or regime interest) than by humanitarian, human rights or human security objectives (e.g., see Stuckler and McKee, 2008). Motivation is impossible to discern with certainty, and it is probable that mixed motives are driving policy. However, it is clear that a central theme in US government publications on global health is the threat of emerging diseases to American security, as recent realignments of US foreign policy include increased spending on response preparedness against increased threats from bioterrorism and emerging infectious diseases, including HIV/AIDS (HHS, 2001).

Many of the most influential non-state actors in global health are also largely concentrated in the US. Within the business sector, this includes pharmaceutical companies, which have been among the most controversial of global health actors. For instance, they have come under heavy criticism for taking financial advantage of the global market while neglecting diseases of the South, including chronic diseases. As Trouiller et al. (2001, p. 946) assert:

> Today drug development is confined almost exclusively to a consolidated and highly competitive multinational drug industry driven by profit and subject to the laws of a globalized market economy. Market forces inevitably skew the direction of drug R&D [research and development] towards those diseases and patients (customers) that assure the highest financial returns (Sachs, 1999). In 1999, North America, Europe and Japan accounted for 82.4 per cent of the world pharmaceutical market (valued at US $337 billion), while Africa and Asia, representing more than two-thirds of the world population, only accounted for 10.6 per cent of the market....

Another major concern expressed about pharmaceuticals is the pressure they exert to keep drug costs high – prohibitively so for many individuals in the South. The most widely publicized case involved the attempt by a group of companies in the late 1990s to block South Africa's compulsory licensing of generic drugs (Kumaranayake and Lake, 2002, p. 88). Intense opposition led by the South African coalition, Treatment Action Campaign (TAC), and supported by powerful international NGOs as well as the WHO and some Western European countries (see TAC website) eventually persuaded the pharmaceutical companies to withdraw their petition. Buoyed by this success, the campaign to make antiretroviral drugs more widely available continued to expand[4] and witnessed some success in the adoption in 2001 of the Doha Declaration on the TRIPS Agreement, which supported '...WTO Members' right to protect public health and, in particular, to promote access to medicines for all' (WTO, 2001, p. 1). A subsequent General Council Decision in 2003 approved an amendment to the 2001 Declaration (the Pérez-Motta text) to facilitate '...effective use of compulsory licensing by Members with no or insufficient manufacturing capacities in the pharmaceutical sector' (UNCTAD/WTO, 2005, p. 1). The following year, Canada's Bill C-9 was the first national legislation to enact compulsory licensing to export essential medicines to countries that could not produce their own (Government of Canada, 2004).[5]

Although the greater flexibility introduced into the WTO patent regulations has helped somewhat to increase the availability of needed drugs, as Roy Love (2007) points out, it has not solved all problems of access. He points out that the regulatory framework is onerous and many developing countries do not have the capacity to put 'TRIPS-compliant legislation' in place easily or soon (p. 11). Also, despite lower prices of drugs under the improved arrangements, '...even the lowest quote of about US$140 per annum (mid-2005) [for a common ARV drug] remains out of reach of most households in the developing world' (ibid., p. 212). Finally, as others have observed, there is inadequate infrastructure capacity and/or political will to distribute drugs in some countries, even when cheaper drugs are available (Richey, 2008).

Despite lingering problems, the ongoing efforts to resolve the continuing problems with developing countries' access to drugs indicate potentially hopeful aspects of emerging global health governance; that is, the increasing role of socially responsible civil society organizations. This role tends to be complicated, as the interactions are national–international–grassroots, as João Biehl (2007) explains in his detailed account of the events and processes by which Brazil was able to introduce free retroviral treatment for the country's HIV/AIDS victims. In this age of intense power and influence of pharmaceutical companies ('pharmaceuticalization', as he terms it), he argues that '[a]gainst all odds, Brazil invented a public way of treating AIDS' (p. 1084). This 'public way' was a 'state-society synergy' that emerged within the dialectics of the 'political economy of pharmaceuticalization' and culminated in the state's decision and ability to deliver free HIV/AIDS drugs (p. 1094).

The increasing involvement of civil society organizations and movements and the partnerships between state and non-state actors is one of the defining characteristics of global health governance. Some NGOs stand out as significantly influential actors. As noted above, TAC in South Africa is one example in the local/national arena, but there are myriad local/national NGOs and faith-based organizations contributing to the debates and practices. (For example, Biehl (2007, p. 1091) indicates that there are 500 AIDS NGOs, alone, registered in Brazil.) Likewise, there are numerous international NGOs now contributing to global health governance. To illustrate with one well-known example: MSF has worked since the late 1990s to establish a coalition of state and non-state actors to provide greater and cheaper access to medicine; it 'now has more than 60 000 people on treatment for HIV/AIDS in 32 countries around the world'; and in 2006 it launched the Drugs for Neglected Disease Initiative for delivering not-for-profit drugs (Orbinsky, 2007, pp. 34–5).

Major initiatives of global health governance now, almost invariably, are characterized by leadership that includes mixed actor coalitions. Prominent examples of these are the Global Fund to Fight AIDS, Tuberculosis and Malaria, the Roll Back Malaria Partnership, the Stop TB Partnership, the International AIDS Vaccine Initiative (IAVI) and the Global Alliance for Vaccine and Immunization (GAVI). The phenomenal growth in numbers of these various public private partnerships (PPPs) has stimulated considerable analytical attention over the past decade, and it is the focus of several chapters in this volume. Yet, while such partnerships have generated exceptional attention to and resources for global health, their efficacy remains open to question. Several disquieting issues include: agenda setting (powerful business members of the partnerships may be motivated more by profit than by human rights and needs or global public goods); coordination (problems arise in managing actors from different sectors; also with multiple players now in the field both redundancies and gaps exist in programming); and accountability (current legal structures are inadequate to regulate these new forms of governance). Until these issues are resolved, questions will remain about the efficacy of PPPs. As the organizers of a recent conference on PPPs in global governance asked: 'What are they all about, and do they represent a critical, lasting strategy?' (Global Health Council, 2008).

Philanthropic individuals and organizations have become increasingly important actors within the new private–public governance arrangements. Some, such as personalities like Bono, have 'public appeal [that] can influence, if not shape, international political agendas' (Orbinsky, 2007, p. 37), while others, especially major financial donors like the Bill and Melinda Gates Foundation, can shape as well as influence. The influence of the Gates Foundation in global health, already well established, was enhanced significantly in 2006 with the infusion of US$37 billion from financier Warren Buffett. With assets now of approximately US $60 billion, the Foundation's annual donation of around $3 billion to global health research and aid makes it a major player in global health (Okie, 2006, p. 1084). Media coverage of the Gates' contributions has been extensive and almost invariably positive; however, other actors within the global health field are less sanguine. Indeed, as David Fidler (2007, p. 2/18) observes, '...governing Bill Gates may prove as challenging in its own way as governing the United States in terms of global health' (Fidler, 2007, p. 2/18). The main concern is that the amount of funds donated by the Foundation gives it disproportionate power to influence the directions of the global health research and policy agendas (*The Economist*, 2008). The Foundation's main interest has been in technical solutions to health problems, and excessive emphasis on the biotechnical approach to health distracts from addressing social determinants. The Gates Foundation recently announced support for an anti-tobacco initiative,[6] which may indicate a new direction for the organization, but to date the Foundation has provided few funds for social determinants. It has been criticized, for instance, for not funding projects to investigate and/or develop capacity in national governments for delivering health services and promoting healthy communities. Generous donations of funds for biotechnical solutions may be counterproductive, and are certainly administered inefficiently, in developing countries that lack capacity to absorb and manage large sums (Ramiah and Reich, 2005).

The myriad actors, their complex interactions, and the range of problems as well as possibilities are features that define the emergence of global health governance. David Fidler (2007, p. 15) argues that 'the sheer expanse of international relations in which global health now features undermines the feasibility of achieving all-encompassing architecture for global health governance'. And, indeed, the picture of global health governance that emerges is more consistent with Rosenau's description of 'multiple spheres of influence' in a 'disaggregated complexity' than it is with any discretely organized governance structure. This complex, multi-actor, multi-layer, multidimensional arrangement of global health governance that is emerging can offer unprecedented possibilities and opportunities for innovation as well as cooperation to improve health outcomes throughout the world. However, unless the dominant actors begin to put more emphasis on the social determinants of global health, the potentials of the system will not be realized. The emerging structures of global health governance, in themselves, point to important dimensions of social determinants that call for better understanding. Global health issues are largely socially determined, the result of recent changes in global political economy and the shift from a predominately international to an increasingly global order. Similarly, the global health governance architecture that is developing is dominated, but not determined entirely, by the most powerful actors in the global political economy. Conditions of inequality and inequity are among the main determinants of the current pattern of disease burden in the world, and the unequal disease burden, in which those who shoulder the heaviest burden receive the lowest amount of resources, severely challenges the logic and authority of the dominant order.

The chapters in this volume question the ways in which that order is influencing health outcomes. In all, the underlying concern is to add to current debates about the concepts and problems of global health, the major players currently involved and the types of governance arrangements that are emerging in the global health area. Specifically, they address the political economy of global health by examining how hegemonic actors and contemporary conditions in a globalizing world order are contributing and/or responding to global health and disease.

Structure of the book

Part II examines the roles and responses of state and interstate actors in the global health nexus. Ted Schrecker begins by examining the G7/G8 as one of the major players in global health governance. He argues that, since the increasing commodification of health in a global marketplace is undermining health equity, the G7/G8 governments and electorates who place them in office have 'redistributive obligations' and he identifies specific 'policy entry points' where responsible action could begin. However, as Rodney Loeppkey's chapter points out, the ability to take advantage of the policy entry points by any actor is compromised by power inequalities among the major actors. Loeppky observes that the United States, in particular, exerts profound effects on global health through the powerful health 'complex' that is emerging in that country. Given that powerful actors such as the US and the G7/G8 have considerable control over the governance framework and agenda, weaker states are in a position of having to respond to conditions and exigencies that stronger players are able to manipulate. However, Colleen O'Manique argues that a national government need not only maneuver, but can also to some extent influence behaviour within the emerging global health governance complex. Her case study of Canadian foreign policy on global health examines the contradictory roles the country plays by promoting the commodification of global public goods while also supporting initiatives such as the Global Fund for HIV/AIDS, Tuberculosis and Malaria. Meanwhile, Pieter Fourie's case study from a Southern perspective explores the South African state's ability to respond to the HIV/AIDS epidemic. He argues that, although evidence does not support the assumption that HIV/AIDS necessarily contributes to state fragility, it does create a profound governance challenge, and thus a 'moral imperative...for states and individuals to maintain a sense of urgency and purpose'. In turn, this reinforces the need for prominent global health actors to address the social determinants along with the biological imperatives of disease.

Part III of the volume explores transformative factors in the transition from international to global health governance. The chapter by Wolfgang Hein and Lars Kohlmorgen explores the expanding role of non-state actors in global health governance. Based on a study of the pressure that civil society organizations (CSO) exerted on the Doha Declaration on the TRIPs Agreement and Public Health, Hein and Kohlmorgen conclude that CSOs 'successfully use their discursive power to push for the implementation of these norms'. The subsequent chapters in the section investigate various issues involving what Carmen Huckel Schneider refers to as the 'innovative forms of governance' that have emerged in global health. In seeking to uncover the origins of the contemporary development of PPPs, as one of these innovative forms, Huckel Schneider highlights five discourses of public health governance that provide historical rationales for the contemporary development of PPPs. An increased role for private philanthropic foundations has been a feature of the recent innovations, and Michael Moran's chapter investigates this role though a case study of the Rockefeller Foundation's support for Product Development Partnerships (PDPs) throughout the 1990s and early 2000s. Sonja Bartch explores the critical issues of legitimacy and effectiveness in global health governance. Through a case study that regards the operations of the Global Fund to Fight AIDS, Tuberculosis and Malaria (GFATM) from the perspective of Southern partners, Bartch argues that Southern participation enhances the legitimacy of the GFATM, but that effectiveness is compromised to some extent by the partnership model. Siri Bjerkreim Hellevik's chapter extends the investigation into the issue of effectiveness. She argues that, in areas where engagement is now occurring, a continuing lack of coordination among the various donors – despite efforts to alleviate the problem – is a serious impediment to efficiency. Focusing on global HIV/AIDS programmes operating in Africa, she argues that, in fact, there is a 'crisis of implementation'.

Part IV explores several practical implications of current global health governance. The first chapter in this section, by Sandra MacLean and David MacLean, explores the present state of global health research, and argues that business interests dominate in setting the research agenda, which is much more directed towards biotechnical innovation than social determinants. Business interests also underscore Valbona Muzaka's chapter, which is concerned with the production of pharmaceutical products. Muzaka examines TRIPs as both a legal structure and an international norms setter and considers the effects of TRIPS on the public health of developing countries. Shree Mulay, Eowynne Feeney and Daya R. Varma continue the investigation of trade issues and global health. According to these authors, as the result of changes in WTO rules in 2005, treatments for neglected global diseases are potential growth industries for the South. However, in order for the medicines produced to be affordable to poor members of populations, national governments must step up efforts to produce policies that enhance complementarity between social need and global opportunity. Sherri Brown examines the ethical dimensions that arise from the business of global health through an examination of practices of three types of global PPPs operating in Africa (African Comprehensive HIV/AIDS Partnership, International AIDS Vaccine Initiative and Accelerated Access Initiative).

The contributors to this volume approach the issue of global health from different methodological frameworks and theoretical perspectives. Yet, the authors are united in a common concern to highlight the health inequalities and inequities that characterize global health in the contemporary period. Also, the authors, through different lenses, expose how political economy factors are both contributing to current global health problems and supporting governance arrangements that produce inadequate solutions.

Notes

1. Progress is being made in developing more effective interdisciplinarity; refer to the Oslo Ministerial Declaration as one example (see http://www.diplomatie.gouv.

fr/en/france-priorities_1/health_1102/events_2135/oslo-ministerial-declaration-march-20-2007_8924.html).

2. Goals 4, 5 and 6 deal directly with health and are, respectively, to 'reduce child mortality', to 'improve maternal health' and to 'combat HIV/AIDS, malaria and other diseases'. The other goals are to 'eradicate extreme poverty and hunger', to 'achieve universal primary education', to 'ensure environmental sustainability' and 'to develop a global partnership for development' (see http://www.un.org/millenniumgoals/).
3. These are acronyms for, respectively, the United Nations Children's Fund, the United Nations Development Programme, the United Nations Population Fund, the International Labour Organization and the International Monetary Fund.
4. As well as legislative developments to promote better access to antiretrovirals, there have been several other initiatives to facilitate the delivery of these drugs. One of the most highly developed is WHO's '3 by 5' initiative, established to provide antiretroviral treatment (ART) to 3 million by 2005 (WHO, 2003). The target was not met by 2005 (only 1.3 million were receiving treatment), although some scholars note that 'treatment centres and programmes report good initial responses' (Gilks et al., 2006, p. 505).
5. This legislation was prompted by fears of a pending global epidemic of avian flu and the realization that Hoffman-LaRoche's patent for Tamiflu would limit supplies of this drug, deemed to be the most effective treatment for the disease.
6. The Foundation announced that it would provide financial support to the Bloomberg Initiative to Reduce Tobacco, founded by the New York mayor, Michael Bloomberg (see the Foundation's website, http://www.gatesfoundation.org/press-releases/Pages/bloomberg-gates-tobacco-initiative-080723.aspx)

Part II

Globalization, the State, and Global Health

2

The G8, Globalization, and the Need for a Global Health Ethic

Ted Schrecker

Introduction: why study the G8 and global health?

In 2001, colleagues and I[1] began the first 'report card' on how the actions and policies of the G7/G8[2] affected population health, in particular the health of populations outside the high-income countries (Labonté and Schrecker, 2004; Labonté et al., 2004). The focus on the G7/G8 was and is justified for at least two reasons.

First, the G8 countries 'account for 48 per cent of the global economy and 49 per cent of global trade, hold four of the United Nations' five permanent Security Council seats, and boast majority shareholder control over the International Monetary Fund (IMF) and the World Bank' (Corlazzoli and Smith, 2005, p. 5).[3] They provide roughly 75 per cent of the world's development assistance; their deep pockets, organizational resources and superior bargaining power provide them with formidable advantages in trade negotiations and dispute resolution proceedings; and firms located within their borders have until recently been the primary sources of outward foreign direct investment (FDI).[4] The decisions their governments make, individually and jointly, have unavoidable impacts on literally billions of people outside their own borders, whether or not those impacts are intended.

Second, although the G8 came into existence (as the G6) in response to a number of shocks in the international economic environment and initially were concerned mainly with macroeconomic policy coordination, annual Summits and periodic ministerial meetings – in particular, meetings of finance ministers – subsequently emerged as comparably important in a variety of social and economic policy fields. According to researchers with the University of Toronto's G8 Research Group, Summits 'have value in establishing new principles in normative directions, in creating and highlighting issue areas and agenda items, and in altering the publicly allowable discourse used' (Kirton et al., 2006, p. 3). Acknowledging both the dominant role of the G8 in the global economy and the function of Summits as 'the only forum where heads of the major governments routinely meet'

(Collier, 2007, p. 13), development economist Paul Collier presented his important book *The Bottom Billion* as a development policy agenda for the G8. Whatever normative questions surround the legitimacy and accountability of G8 Summits and ministerial meetings, which are briefly addressed in the concluding section of this chapter, the facts of G8 influence on global affairs are beyond serious dispute.

The report card work initially addressed commitments made at the 1999 through 2001 Summits, although subsequent publications updated the analysis to include the 2005 Summit at Gleneagles, which arguably represented the zenith of G8 interest in development issues as of mid-2008 (Labonté and Schrecker, 2005; Labonté et al., 2005; Labonté and Schrecker, 2006; Schrecker et al., 2007; Labonté and Schrecker, 2007a). We first considered the extent to which G8 countries had lived up to their Summit commitments. However, we examined not only commitments that directly referred to health, but also commitments in a variety of other policy fields that affect social determinants of health (SDH): the conditions that make it relatively easy for some people to lead long and healthy lives, and all but impossible for others. These policy fields included education and nutrition; development assistance; trade policy and market access; macroeconomic policy and poverty reduction; and debt relief.[5] Furthermore, we examined not only the extent to which the G8 had fulfilled or complied with their commitments, but also the *adequacy* of those commitments when measured against the nature and scale of unmet needs and the *appropriateness* of commitments, based on what is known about influences on health outcomes. In other words, we were and are concerned not only with whether the G8, individually and collectively, have done what they said they would do but also with whether they committed themselves to doing enough, and doing what the evidence indicates is necessary.

Globalization, development and health

Describing the health implications of Summit commitments and G8 policies outside the health care field requires that researchers 'work backward' from what is known about the elements of daily life that increase probability of illness or injury, while simultaneously 'working forward' from different bodies of evidence relevant to how policy choices and dynamics at the national and international level influence those elements. For much of the world's population, the most important influence on those elements of daily life is undoubtedly transnational economic integration (globalization): societies rich and poor alike are becoming part of the global marketplace, in various ways and on various terms.

Globalization influences social determinants of health by way of multiple pathways that are often complex and contested (Labonté and Schrecker, 2007b). For instance, controversy surrounds globalization's implications for economic growth and poverty reduction. Over the long term, and with considerable variation at any given income level, richer societies are healthier (World Bank, 1993; Deaton, 2003) and socio-economic gradients in health are present in societies rich and poor alike, with the relatively poor exhibiting poorer health (see Figure 2.1). If globalization could be shown to be reliable and effective in increasing growth rates and reducing poverty, then a strong initial presumption would exist that measures to promote globalization, such as trade liberalization, should be embraced for their health benefits (Feachem, 2001).

However, the evidence that globalization contributes either to economic growth or to poverty reduction is at best equivocal, depending *inter alia* on how one assesses the extent to which national economies have been integrated into the global marketplace; how poverty is defined; and how many uncertainties about data quality one is willing to live with or overlook (Milanovic, 2003; Satterthwaite, 2003; Reddy and Pogge, 2005; Kawachi and Wamala, 2007; Woodward and Abdallah, in press). Between 1981 and 2005, while the value of the world's economic output quadrupled, only modest poverty reductions were recorded based on the World Bank's poverty lines, which were updated in August 2008 (Chen and Ravallion, 2008).[6] Worldwide, the number of people living on $1.25 per day (at 2005 prices, adjusted for purchasing power parity) or less declined from 1.9 billion to 1.4 billion, but this decline was entirely attributable to drastic poverty reductions in China.

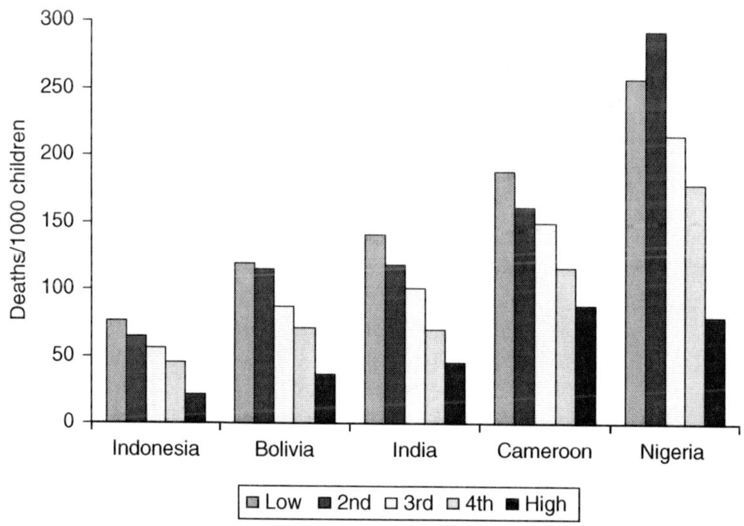

Figure 2.1 Socio-economic gradients in under-5 mortality, by household wealth quintiles, selected countries

Source: Data from Gwatkin et al., 2007.

Outside China, the number of people living below the $1.25 per day threshold actually increased, mainly because of a near-doubling of the number of poor people in sub-Saharan Africa. Worldwide, the number of people living on $2.50 per day or less (stated on the same basis) increased from 2.7 billion to 3.1 billion, with reductions in China offset by a substantial increase in India and sub-Saharan Africa (Chen and Ravallion, 2008).

Indeed, at least during the post-1980 period, economic growth proved remarkably ineffective in reducing poverty (Woodward and Simms, 2006); an innovative econometric study completed in 2007 suggests that globalization may actually have reduced the extent to which the growth that does occur is translated into improvements in health status (Cornia et al., 2008). Even globalization's enthusiasts concede that there may be substantial numbers of losers within national economies. Thus, the only responsible answer to questions about globalization and poverty reduction is that 'the net effects of globalization on the poor can only be judged on the basis of "context-specific" empirical studies' (Nissanke and Thorbecke, 2006, p. 1340).

Even if the connection between globalization and growth were stronger, promoting globalization would not fulfil the commitment made by the G8 in 2001 to 'make globalization work for all [their] citizens and especially the world's poor' (G8, 2001, ¶3). Once almost heretical, this perspective has now entered the mainstream of development policy discourse – notably, by way of a number of recent research syntheses and consultative processes. The International Labour Organization's World Commission on the Social Dimension of Globalization (2004) organized its recommendations around the idea of 'fair globalization' and addressed *inter alia* the need for reform of trade, the international financial system, labour standards, and development financing. In its 2005 report, the UN Millennium Project, established as an advisory body to the Secretary-General, mustered a prodigious amount of evidence to support its arguments for organizing development assistance, trade policy, and scientific research around the imperative of achieving the Millennium Development Goals (MDGs) derived from a resolution passed by the United Nations General Assembly in 2000.[7] Also in 2005 the multinational Commission for Africa, convened by the British government as part of the lead-up to the 2005 G8 Summit, argued for similar reforms with specific reference to the development needs of sub-Saharan Africa (Commission for Africa, 2005). The United Nations Development Programme (through annual Human Development Reports) and the UN's Department of Economic and Social Affairs, although somewhat marginalized within the UN system, nevertheless continue to demonstrate the incomplete and unequally distributed benefits of globalization. In this they are joined by a growing number of social scientists who recognize the 'disequalizing' dynamics of the global marketplace and the 'asymmetrical' distribution not only of its benefits, but also of the ability to influence its rules and institutions (Birdsall, 2006a; Birdsall, 2006b).

As production has been reorganized across multiple national boundaries (Dicken, 2007), genuinely global labour markets have emerged. National and subnational jurisdictions can be played off against one another based on labour costs and 'flexibility', and redistributive policies are constrained by the possibility of disinvestment and capital flight (Williamson, 2004; Evans, 2005; Mosley, 2006). Cerny has described this dynamic in terms of pressure for policy convergence toward the competition state, focused on 'promotion of economic activities, whether at home or abroad, which will make firms and sectors located within the territory of the state competitive in international markets' (Cerny, 2000, p. 136). The rise of the competition state is accompanied by far-reaching redefinition of citizenship rights, which even in formal democracies are increasingly held not by individuals as members of a polity but rather by transnational corporations (TNCs) and players in the global financial markets. 'These markets can now exercise the accountability functions associated with citizenship: they can vote governments' economic policies in or out, they can force governments to take certain measures and not others' (Sassen, 2003, p. 70; see generally Sassen, 1996). A parallel development, albeit structurally related, is the infusion of the logic of the marketplace into domestic economic and social policy. Individuals and households, like sectors of national economies, are expected to 'earn their keep' in the new global environment. Social policies are organized around the anticipated return on investment in 'human capital' (Giddens, 1998; Jenson and Saint-Martin, 2003; Molyneux, 2007) and citizenship is redefined within national borders in terms of effective participation in the domestic and global marketplace as a producer or consumer.[8]

The G8 and health: challenges

The assessment presented here concentrates on official development assistance (ODA), debt relief, trade policy and support for health systems. These are by no means the only areas of G8 policy that are relevant to population health, but taken together they strongly influence both the volume of resources available to meet basic health-related needs such as those related to income, nutrition and education in much of the developing world and the policy environment for meeting those needs, to the point where shortcomings in these areas are unlikely to be offset by initiatives in others.

An immediate need exists for increased resources to support national health systems (Schieber et al., 2007; Ooms et al., 2008). Despite substantial increases in development assistance for health in recent years, publicly financed health systems in low- and some middle-income countries remain drastically underfunded relative to the costs of 'a rather minimal health system', estimated by the World Health Organization's Commission on Macroeconomics and Health (Commission on Macroeconomics and Health,

2001) as $34 per capita ($40 in 2007 dollars). By comparison, annual per capita health spending from all sources, public and private, in the Least Developed Countries (as defined by the United Nations) where 770 million people live is $15 (World Bank Health, 2007). To provide basic health care, such countries will need to rely on infusions of external resources well into the future. Jeffrey Sachs, who chaired both the Commission and the Millennium Project, estimates that poor sub-Saharan countries might be capable of generating US$50 per capita in total annual public revenue, out of which '[t]he health sector is lucky to claim $10 per person per year out of this, but even rudimentary health care requires roughly four times that amount.... Foreign aid is therefore not a luxury for African health. It is a life-and-death necessity' (Sachs, 2007). His argument is not relevant only to sub-Saharan Africa: think for example of Haiti, the poorest country in the Western Hemisphere, or Vietnam, where public sector spending on health care was just US$4 per capita as recently as 2001 (United Nations Country Team Viet Nam, 2003).

A similarly savage arithmetic applies to the need for development assistance more generally. The Commission for Africa and the Millennium Project each argued that approximate doubling of the industrialized world's development assistance spending *circa* 2005 was needed and justified within a relatively short time frame. Each body acknowledged recurring (and legitimate) concerns about the effectiveness of aid, but emphasized *donor* rather than recipient policies and practices as constraints on aid effectiveness, the Millennium Project noting *inter alia* that 'the notion of taking the [Millennium Development] Goals seriously remains highly unorthodox among development practitioners' *because of* a lack of financial support from the industrialized world (UN Millennium Project, 2005, p. 202; see also p. 59). If nothing else, these and related findings (see, for example, Collier, 2006a; Collier, 2006b) should have shifted the burden of proof to the aid sceptics: those who claim that improvements in health can be achieved without substantial and predictable increases in aid flows. They do, however, leave open an important question about whether aid's effectiveness should be assessed primarily with reference to its contribution to economic growth, or rather with reference to its contribution to meeting basic needs. While the Millennium Project emphasized the importance of using aid more effectively in support of the MDGs, the effectiveness of aid is frequently equated with its contribution to economic growth; indeed Killick (2005, p. 19) argues that *less* attention should be paid to the MDGs and poverty reduction, and more to 'promoting the development of directly productive sectors'. Here, as elsewhere, the need exists for an explicitly normative perspective on development policy choices.

External debt has been recognized for at least two decades as undermining developing countries' ability to meet basic needs (Cornia et al., 1987; Cheru, 1999). One of the most serious constraints on aid's effectiveness is that 'dozens of heavily indebted poor and middle-income countries are forced by creditor governments to spend large parts of their limited tax receipts on debt service, undermining their ability to finance investments in human capital and infrastructure. In a pointless and debilitating churning of resources, the creditors provide development assistance with one hand and then withdraw it in debt servicing with the other' (UN Millennium Project, 2005, p. 35; see also Figure 2.2). With this observation, the Millennium Project reinforced numerous earlier critiques by academic researchers and civil society organizations. Debt relief does not automatically bring about increased expenditure on basic needs, although this has happened in some countries following the past decade's multilateral initiatives (Gupta et al., 2002). Much more needs to happen, not least because of the relatively modest increase that even complete debt cancellation would provide in the revenues available to many governments in low-income countries (Schieber et al., 2007). Like increased development assistance, easing the debt burden of developing economies is best viewed as a necessary rather than a sufficient condition for improving access to basic needs.

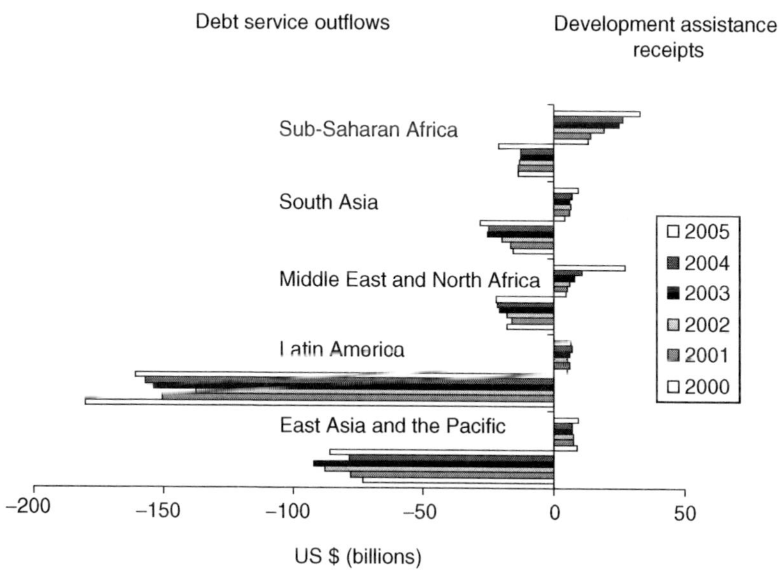

Figure 2.2 Debt service and development assistance, by region, 2000–2005

Source: World Bank, World Development Indicators [on-line], accessed March, 2008. Note that 'spikes' in development assistance for the Middle East and North Africa and sub-Saharan Africa in 2005 reflect one-off debt cancellation offered to Iraq and Nigeria, which counts as development assistance. As noted in the text, development assistance figures for 2006 and preliminary figures for 2007 show a reversion to pattern.

Then there is trade. Development policy protagonists who disagree about much else agree that improving market access for developing country exports is indispensable for growth, poverty reduction and associated improvements in social determinants of health. Researchers and many developing country governments attach special importance to eliminating agricultural subsidies that lower world prices and limit developing country export opportunities (Watkins and Fowler, 2002; Commission for Africa, 2005), although the actual magnitude and distribution of benefits from agricultural trade liberalization remain uncertain (Wise, 2004; Birdsall et al., 2005; McMillan et al., 2006). Within the industrialized countries agricultural subsidies are often justified in populist terms, yet they mainly benefit the richest agricultural producers and agribusiness firms (Commission for Africa, 2005, pp. 279–84; UNDP, 2005, p. 130). Both within and outside the agricultural sector, a source of special concern is the tendency of industrialized countries to apply much higher tariffs (tariff peaks) to labour-intensive exports, which are of special importance to many developing countries, than they do to raw or semi-processed commodities (IMF Staff, 2002). The irony is bitter because some developing countries have destroyed domestic industries by opening their markets to imports, accepting the resulting social dislocations as the price of global integration (Jeter, 2002; Atarah, 2005). The research literature does not appear to include a systematic inventory of such cases, suggesting an important area for future research.

A further dimension of the relation between trade and SDH, one widely neglected in the country-specific research literature, involves the effects of tariff reductions. Tariffs are an important source of revenue for many low- and middle-income countries, as they were for today's high-income countries before and during the early stages of their transition to industrialization.[9] The best available research shows that many middle-income countries, and especially low-income countries, have been unable to make up from other sources more than a fraction of the tariff revenues lost from trade liberalization (Baunsgaard and Keen, 2005; see also Aizenman and Jinjarak, 2006).[10] Commitments under the General Agreement on Trade in Services (GATS) or in a proliferation of bilateral and regional trade agreements may open up health care as well as services such as water and sewage treatment to private investment, 'locking in' privatization and its associated barriers to access to services by the poor and economically insecure. Finally, despite an interpretation of the Agreement on Trade-Related Aspects of Intellectual Property (TRIPs) that apparently preserves flexibility in response to crises such as the AIDS epidemic, it is far from clear that intellectual property rights have been removed as a barrier to ensuring access to essential medicines 'on the ground' in developing countries (Haakonsson and Richey, 2007; Kerry and Lee, 2007; United States Government Accountability Office, 2007; Correa, 2008).

The G8 and health: responses

The G8 Gleneagles commitment to double development assistance to Africa by 2010, a promised annual increase of $25 billion, was driven primarily by the European Union (EU). Although aid spending in 2005 increased, it included major one-off debt cancellations for strategically important and oil-rich Iraq and Nigeria. The industrialized world's overall development assistance spending fell by 5.1 per cent in 2006, and by a further 8.4 per cent in 2007 (OECD Development Assistance Committee, 2007; 2008). The OECD's Development Assistance Committee warned in April 2008 that 'most donors are not on track to meet their stated commitments to scale up aid; they will need to make unprecedented increases to meet their 2010 targets' (OECD Development Assistance Committee, 2008).

Provision of health care and public health interventions is likely to be one casualty of failure. The Global Fund to Fight HIV/AIDS, Tuberculosis and Malaria is the G8's flagship global health initiative, established in recognition of the need to mobilize additional resources and to find more effective ways of delivering those resources. Although the G8 claimed at the 2001 Summit that the Global Fund would 'make a quantum leap in the fight against infectious diseases and...break the vicious cycle between disease and poverty' (G8, 2001, ¶15), the Fund lacks a stable, long-term financing mechanism; it relies instead on periodic replenishment meetings where it essentially passes a hat among donors. Over the 2005–8 period, the G8 failed to make commitments that would provide a long-term funding base for the Global Fund. It could be argued that the 2007 promise to 'provide predictable, long-term additional funding in the ongoing replenishment round' (G8, 2007) was partly met at the September 2007 replenishment meeting, which elicited pledges of $9.7 billion for the period 2008–10: an improvement over previous commitments, but this amount is still far below the Fund's anticipated resource needs of $12–18 billion for the period (GFATM, 2007d). Furthermore, former UN Special Envoy on AIDS Stephen Lewis warned in 2006 that 'what is happening, in a very insidious way, is that African governments are being discouraged from asking for what they really need from the Global Fund. The word is out, and it's often reinforced by Western diplomats at country level – don't ask for too much, because the Global Fund just doesn't have the resources.' Consequently, 'governments are reluctant to ask for what they really need, lest their whole proposal be turned down. They undershoot the level, in order to accommodate the G8 refusal to fund the Global Fund at the levels required' (quoted in Cook, 2006).

The inadequacy of the resources available to the Fund is dramatized by a proposal to expand the Fund's mandate beyond three specified diseases to financing comprehensive country health programmes, thereby responding to a frequent claim that disease-specific programmes undermine already fragile national health systems. In order to ensure the availability of the $40 minimum per capita cost of a basic health care system, as per the Commission on Macroeconomics and Health estimate, the Fund would need to be prepared to disburse US$28 billion per year, *even if* it did not provide any funds to countries where spending on health already exceeds that level and even if all recipient countries committed 3 per cent of GDP to public spending on health care – something many low-income countries are far from doing (Ooms et al., 2008).

The G8 record on debt relief is one of gradual and grudging, but consequential, response. Starting in the 1999 G8 led the industrialized world in partially cancelling the debts of up to 40 countries, 32 of them in Africa, under the enhanced Heavily Indebted Poor Countries (HIPC) initiative. '[T]he amount of debt relief...was determined by eligibility thresholds which (according to public statements by [International Monetary] Fund and [World] Bank officials) were based on initial analysis...and then modified to suit political compromises amongst G7 creditors, balancing the need to include strategic G7 allies and their desire to keep costs down'(Martin, 2004, p. 17). Eligibility thresholds are based on a ratio of anticipated export earnings to debt service obligations; partly because of undue optimism about export performance, HIPCs' progress toward meeting basic needs and reducing debt burdens has been inadequate (United Nations Secretary-General, 2006). Many saw only modest decreases in their debt service obligations; three – Mali, Mozambique and Bolivia – had actually experienced *increases* in these obligations as of 2005 (United Nations Department of Economic and Social Affairs, 2005, p. 148). Eligibility for debt cancellation was and is accompanied by the requirement that macroeconomic policies be approved by the World Bank and International Monetary Fund, creating what some observers view as a destructive reprise of earlier conditionalities aimed at integrating national economies into the global marketplace (Cheru, 2000; Cheru, 2001; Gore, 2004; Gaynor, 2005).

At Gleneagles, the G8 agreed to cancel an additional US$40–56 billion of debts owed by HIPCs to the World Bank, IMF and the concessional arm of the African Development Bank once they have reached their 'completion point' under the earlier initiative. This Multilateral Debt Relief Initiative (MDRI) was welcome and overdue, yet it is incomplete and compromised. Development assistance to recipient countries will be reduced by some or all of the amount of additional debt relief provided under MDRI (Joint World Bank/IMF Development Committee, 2005; Tomitova, 2005). The shell game may enter a new round if donor countries, mainly the G8, do not fully fund the requisite levels of debt relief through the World Bank, thus reducing the budget of the International Development Association (IDA), the branch of the Bank that offers grants and below-market loans (Hurley, 2007). No mechanism exists to require participation of private sector creditors in multilateral debt relief initiatives. In addition, debt relief will not be extended to many countries that are not statistically desperate enough to qualify, despite high levels of poverty (only a minority of the world's poor live in HIPCs; see Labonté and Schrecker, 2004, pp. 1665–6) and high external debt burdens (Hanlon, 2000; Pearce et al., 2005).

The G8 have consistently failed, at least for public consumption, to address two fundamental questions. First, what justifies the definition of sustainability of external debt for purposes of determining eligibility for debt relief, and what is the ethical justification for the criteria chosen? The current criterion, based on a country's ability to service its debts from export earnings, prioritizes the interests of creditors. An alternative definition of sustainability instead prioritizes the ability of governments to undertake public expenditure to meet basic needs or achieve the MDGs, and then works backward to determine how much of the public budget, if any, should be devoted to debt repayment. Calculations using this approach indicate a need for far more extensive debt cancellation, for a much larger number of countries, than available under MDRI (UN Millennium Project, 2005; United Nations, 2005; Mandel, 2006).

Exemplifying this approach is the New Economics Foundation proposal to structure debt cancellation around ensuring that debtor countries have available the resources needed to raise the living standard of their poorest residents to an 'ethical poverty line' of $3 per person per day, as contrasted with the World Bank poverty thresholds. On this basis, a total of 136 countries would require either complete or partial debt cancellation with a net present value of between $424 and $589 billion – that is, a fivefold increase relative to the amounts of debt cancellation available under the combined enhanced HIPC and MDRI initiatives, for a much longer list of countries (Mandel, 2006).

Second, should 'odious debts' incurred by repressive or corrupt governments without the consent of their subjects be regarded as collectable under international law (Khalfan et al., 2003)? The Commission for Africa cited an estimate 'that stolen African assets equivalent to more than half of the continent's external debt are held in foreign bank accounts' (Commission for Africa, 2005, p. 150); other estimates of capital flight from sub-Saharan Africa yield an even higher figure (Ndikumana and Boyce, 2003). In 2005, the G8 committed themselves to '[w]ork vigorously for early ratification of the UN Convention Against Corruption and start discussions on mechanisms to ensure its effective implementation' (G8, 2005), although as of July 2008 Germany, Italy and Japan had yet to ratify the Convention. The Convention is potentially valuable because it binds parties to implement mechanisms to seize and repatriate illegally appropriated assets. Its effectiveness will depend on the commitment of governments whose subjects have been victimized; this is by no means assured (Rice et al., 2007), although the G8 could provide encouragement in several ways.[11] Even if ratified by all members of the G8 the Convention cannot substitute for a systematic initiative to define odious debts; to develop multilateral mechanisms to preclude their collection (by either public- or private-sector creditors); and to ensure that cancelling debts run up by brutal and unaccountable regimes cannot be counted as development assistance, as is now the case.

On trade, although substantial opportunities exist to reshape trade policy in a way that is simultaneously and synergistically development-friendly and supportive of improvements in health, the challenges are formidable. The G8 claimed in 2002 that: 'The launch of multilateral trade negotiations by World Trade Organization (WTO) members in Doha...placed the needs and interests of developing countries at the heart of the negotiations' (G8, 2002). Similar rhetoric in following years culminated in the 2006 Summit's call 'for a concerted effort to conclude the negotiations of the WTO's Doha Development Agenda (DDA) and to fulfill the development objective of the Round' (G8, 2006, ¶1). Only days later, negotiations reached an impasse over the issue of agricultural subsidies, and a similar collapse terminated a subsequent round of talks in July 2008 (Castle and Landler, 2008). Expectations for the Doha round may always have been too high (Ricupeiro, 2006), and the failure is perhaps not surprising, since introducing development goals into trade policy would mean a fundamental shift in the self-interested character of negotiations as they now exist (Stiglitz and Charlton, 2005). Nevertheless, the continued impasse underscores the need for G8 leadership – assuming, that is, that the rhetoric of commitment to integrating development objectives into trade policy is to be taken seriously. Collier has recommended that, if the OECD countries as a whole were interested in unblocking WTO negotiations, they might jointly and unilaterally offer improved access to certain sectors of their markets, in order to revitalize the negotiating process by way of an upfront incentive to developing country governments that is not conditional on subsequent bargaining – in other words, adding an explicitly redistributive component (Collier, 2006c). No evidence to date suggests that this proposal has been taken seriously by the G7. On other trade issues, the lack of concrete proposals relating to the effects of intellectual property protection on access to essential medicines, and the fact that the United States has sought stronger, 'TRIPs-plus' intellectual property protection in its bilateral and regional trade agreements (Fink and Reichenmuller, 2006; United States Government Accountability Office, 2007), are not reassuring.

Conclusion: whither (or wither?) the G8 and global health?

How much can be expected from the G8 in terms of policies that improve population health? Many international relations scholars think it unrealistic to expect that the foreign policies of powerful national governments will ever be driven by considerations other than national economic[12] and geopolitical interest. On this view, the G8 can be expected to adopt measures favourable to the health of those outside the industrialized world only when these will generate domestic political payoffs or enhance the competitive advantage of national economies and firms within their borders (Cerny's competition state).

It could therefore be argued that the most productive route for advocacy involves appeals to enlightened self-interest, notably by linking health with security. Unfortunately, the claim that 'better health for anyone, anywhere on earth, benefits everyone else' (Global Forum for Health Research, 2002, p. 35) is vacuous. Although such developments as rapid, low-cost air travel and the global reorganization of food production have increased possibilities for disease transmission, direct danger to most people in high-income countries is probably limited to a small range of diseases, such as SARS and influenza, which can be easily transmitted through casual contact before symptoms develop. Not surprisingly, the 2006 Summit statement on infectious diseases was mainly concerned with planning for an influenza epidemic in the industrialized world. Arguably, a more serious travel- and migration-linked threat is spread of resistance to antimicrobial drugs, which compromises treatments for a wide range of diseases (Okeke et al., 2005a; Okeke et al., 2005b; Zhang et al., 2006); control of antimicrobial resistance may be one of the few true global public goods for health. However, only the occasional intrepid adventure traveller or tropical disease researcher is likely to be exposed to malaria. Most G8 residents have nothing to lose from the HIV epidemic in developing countries, from the social conditions that contribute to vulnerability to tuberculosis or HIV infection (Bates et al., 2004; De Vogli and Birbeck, 2005), or from the rapid increase outside the industrialized world in the prevalence of non-communicable diseases that were once mistakenly thought to be diseases of affluence (Adeyi et al., 2007). The global distribution of health risks, in other words, parallels and reflects the distribution of economic (dis)advantage that is characteristic of contemporary globalization. Appeals to self-interest on this score are unlikely to be credible either to leaders or to G8 electorates that understand, at least in general terms, the nature and extent of their risk exposure.

More fundamentally, the legitimacy of the G8 as a forum for making decisions that affect the health of the entire world is challenged with increasing frequency. For instance, a 2008 *Lancet* editorial called it 'preposterous and unjust to allow the leaders of eight countries that command 65 per cent of the Gross World Product and represent only 13 per cent of the world's population to assume the mantle of governance about issues that concern the entire world's economy, environment, health, and security' (MacDonald and Horton, 2008, p. 100, citations omitted). Ash has proposed building on the informal and partial inclusion of additional countries in recent Summits by adding China, India, Brazil, Mexico, South Africa and Indonesia to the club (Ash, 2008). Former Canadian Prime Minister Paul Martin and several international relations scholars (English et al., 2005; Thompson, 2005) have advocated further expansion into an L20 (or Leaders' 20), building on an existing forum for finance ministers by adding to the list of countries above Argentina, Australia, South Korea, Saudi Arabia and Turkey.

Bradford (2005) enthuses about this proposal as a way of overcoming 'global economic apartheid', but it might in fact deepen the gap between excluded and included states by leaving out (for example) all the Nordic countries and all of Africa except South Africa, a country that some argue now has a 'sub-imperial' relationship with the rest of the continent (Bond, 2004). Furthermore, the record of several countries proposed for inclusion, notably China, India and South Africa, with respect to health disparities and SDH within their own borders is far from reassuring. China has marketized much of its system for providing health care, leading to increased difficulties in access for many and exacerbating problems associated with the rapid increase in economic inequality (see, for example, Akin et al., 2005; Office of the World Health Organization Representative in China, 2005; Dummer and Cook, 2007; Wong et al., 2007). The main trade union congress in the United States, admittedly not a disinterested party, has documented a pattern of extremely long working hours, lack of labour standards, and hazardous working conditions leading to accidents that kill 140,000 workers every year (AFL-CIO, Cardin, and Smith, 2006). India actively displaces slum dwellers in order to create space for commercial development (Appadurai, 2000; Dupont, 2008), and its policy priorities have prompted the United Nations Development Programme (2005, pp. 30–1) to observe that: 'Were India to show the same level of dynamism and innovation in tackling basic health inequalities as it has displayed in global technology markets, it could rapidly get on track for achieving the MDG targets'. South Africa's government for a long time fiercely resisted publicly funded provision of antiretroviral therapy, and its macroeconomic policies have resulted in devastatingly high, and persistent, unemployment and poverty rates (Koelble, 2004; Streak, 2004; Kingdon and Knight, 2005).

It can be argued that the situations described are no worse than those that obtained in the G8 countries at comparable stages of development – and, further, that they represent in part responses to the constraints created by globalization. Domestic politics come into play as well, and governments in countries rich and poor alike respond to the preferences of domestic constituencies roughly in proportion to the political resources those constituencies can deploy – resources that are, of course, augmented or diminished by globalization. The point here with respect to G8 reform is simply that expanding the club will not necessarily change the orientation of its member governments to issues of equity and distribution as they affect population health, either within or across national borders.

These observations are made without the detailed explication they deserve, but nevertheless suggest that progress toward policies that generate widely shared improvements in population health is likely to depend on effective advocacy, in the first instance at least at the level of domestic politics, of some form of global health ethic that is explicit about the need for priorities other than those of the global marketplace. Obligations related to the health of people outside a country's borders are recognized with increasing frequency (Labonté and Schrecker, 2007a), based on an expanding body of philosophical argument most closely associated with Thomas Pogge (Pogge, 2002; 2005; 2007), but see also Moellendorf (2002). In my own view, the obligations in question must reflect the problematic nature of resource 'scarcities' for basic health-related purposes such as saving the lives of six million children under the age of five in developing countries every year (Bryce et al., 2005), against a background of unprecedented abundance (Schrecker, 2008). As Sachs has said, 'in a world of trillions of dollars of income every year, the amount of money that you need to address the health crises is easily available in the world' (Sachs, 2003).

One example suffices to illustrate the heuristic value of such a critical approach to scarcity. The author of a thoughtful critique of the politics behind the 2005 Gleneagles Summit characterized as 'astonishing' the US$169 billion in additional funds over the 2005–10 period that would be needed to bring the G7's development assistance spending up to the 0.7 per cent of Gross National Income that has been a non-binding United Nations target since 1970 (Payne, 2006, p. 926). Subsequent developments underscore the hypocrisy of the rhetoric of making poverty history that permeated the 2005 Summit, and, as noted earlier, development assistance is only one of several channels of global redistribution, and its effects must be assessed in the context of overall global resource flows. Yet Norway, Denmark and Sweden have consistently met or exceeded the 0.7 per cent target for two decades, and the amounts in question fade to insignificance beside the G8's annual military spending. A less familiar comparison breaks down the amounts needed to bring each G7 country's development assistance spending to the 0.7 per cent target in terms of Big Macs per person per year, using *The Economist's* annual price comparison of that common gastrocommodity (Figure 2.3). The resulting amounts are modest, suggesting along with previously cited comparisons that astonishment is in the eye of the beholder, and beholder perceptions tend to vary widely among national contexts.

Philosophers do not make public policy, which is probably a good thing, and even using the language of global ethics often incurs the derision of one's colleagues. That derision may reflect a pragmatic appraisal of today's political climate, which, at least within the Anglo-American countries with which I am most familiar, could hardly be less hospitable. Although 'solidarity' is routinely invoked even by governments of the centre-right in discussing access to health services in continental Europe, a recent content analysis did not even find the term in Canadian health policy reform documents (Flood et al., 2002; Giacomini et al., 2004). Further research is needed on the reasons for these international contrasts, their relation to globalization

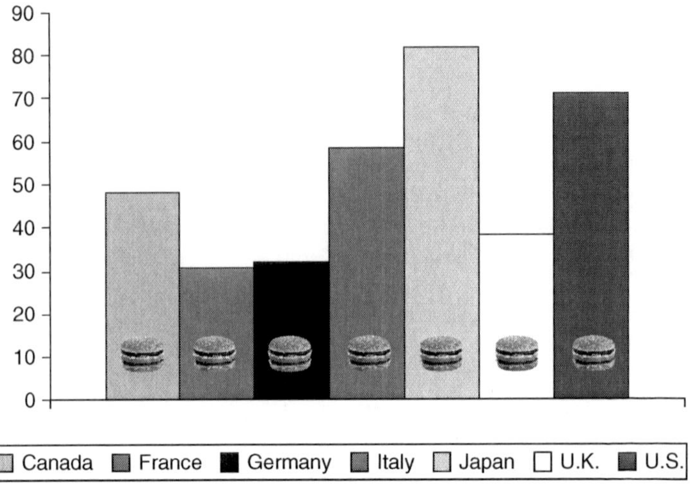

Figure 2.3 Additional cost to the G7 nations in 2007 of spending 0.7 per cent of GNI on development assistance, in Big Macs per capita

Source: OECD Development Assistance Committee, 2008; Big Mac prices from *The Economist* (2007, p. 74).

as mediated by domestic class structures and political allegiances, and the consequences for foreign policy as it affects health. Meanwhile, against the derision must be counterposed a long tradition of rigorous, engaged scholarship by such authors as Richard Falk and Susan George who insist on applying ethical standards to foreign policy and international relations.[13] Those of us who are committed to some form of global redistribution as ethically imperative based on its role in improving population health must draw strength from their examples and others', maintaining optimism as advocates and humanists while often undertaking a willing suspension of disbelief as social scientists.

Notes

1. This chapter draws on findings from several years of research collaboration with Ronald Labonté and David Sanders. I am indebted as well to many members of the Globalization Knowledge Network (Labonté et al., 2007) of the WHO Commission on Social Determinants of Health, for which I acted as Hub coordinator. All views expressed and conclusions drawn are exclusively my own unless attributed to cited authors.
2. The Russian Federation achieved partial membership of the Group of 7 industrialized countries, making it the G8, in 1998 and full membership in 2003. However, Russia still does not participate in the periodic meetings of finance ministers that have become an important element of the Group's activities. Thus, some references in this chapter are to the G7, as appropriate to the context.

3. This quotation is from introductory matter for which authorship is not attributed.
4. Signs that this may be changing include the acquisition in 2006 of Canadian mining giant Inco Ltd. by Brazil's Companhia Vale do Rio Doce; the acquisition in 2008 of Ford Motor Company's Jaguar and Land Rover brands by India's Tata Motors; and an emerging pattern of Chinese direct investment in mining and oil and gas extraction. A valuable discussion of the emergence of world-scale transnational corporations based in developing countries is provided by Goldstein (2007).
5. The importance of SDH, well established in the research literature (Evans and Stoddart, 1990; Marmot and Wilkinson, 2006), was recognized in 2005 by the World Health Organization's establishment of a multinational Commission on Social Determinants of Health (CSDH, 2008).
6. These are used to assess the extent of poverty worldwide, based on household surveys, with reference to incomes of US $1.25 and $2.50 per day (in 1995 dollars, at purchasing power parity). Readers are likely to encounter references to the Bank's earlier $1 per day and $2 per day poverty lines in the literature; these have now been superseded by the new poverty thresholds, based (according to the Bank) on improved data on price comparisons among countries.
7. Three of the MDGs are explicitly health-related, and four others directly address crucial social determinants of (ill) health. The MDGs have numerous shortcomings as policy objectives (Pogge, 2004; Gwatkin, 2005; Moser et al., 2005), yet have the merit of recognizing at least implicitly 'that many of the most devastating problems that plague the daily lives of billions of people are problems that emerge from a single, fundamental source: the consequences of poverty and inequality' (Paluzzi and Farmer, 2005, p. 12).
8. For an eloquent description of this process as it has unfolded in Chile, based on extensive fieldwork, see Schild, 1998; Schild, 2000; Schild, 2007 and also Cooper, 1998.
9. This is why smuggling was both a capital offence and a frequent axis of class conflict at the local level in eighteenth-century England (Winslow, 1975).
10. Baunsgaard and Keen (2005) found that middle-income countries had been able to recover 45–60 cents of each dollar lost in tariff revenue, while low-income countries had recovered 30 cents or less of each dollar lost. Against the background realization that the revenue base in most such countries was already insufficient to support public provision of basic needs, the impact of such revenue losses can best be understood by way of a thought-experiment in which national general government revenues in a high-income country like Canada or Sweden were reduced by somewhere between 40 and 70 per cent over a relatively short period of time. Who would lose first, and worst, from the resulting cutbacks in service provision?
11. Perhaps, in some cases, by linking eligibility for debt relief to specific asset repatriation initiatives. It is, of course, difficult to envision the implementation of such conditionalities in the absence of ratification of the Convention by all members of the G8.
12. In the context created by globalization, in which domestic economic interests are increasingly fragmented, it is more accurate to refer to the economic interests of politically decisive national pluralities or coalitions.
13. Falk has epitomized the adherents of this position for two generations, from a crucial volume that condemned the conduct of US military forces in Vietnam (Falk et al., 1971) to more recent work on the relevance of human rights in

international relations (Falk, 2000) and the need for 'a regulatory framework for global market forces that is people-centred rather than capital-driven' (Falk, 1996, p. 18). Scholar–activist Susan George, who first achieved international acclaim for a study of the political economy of hunger and nutrition-related illness (George, 1976), received the International Studies Association's first Outstanding Public Scholar award.

3

The Accumulative Nature of the US Health Complex

Rodney Loeppky

Introduction

In the midst of increasing interest in both conceptual and practical questions of 'global health', a critical source of change remains strangely underexplored: the evolving nature of the United States' total approach to health. On a range of topics, from biotechnology to the HMO industry, US 'interests' are regarded as having profound effects on outcomes across a broad spectrum of global health issues. However, understanding (and possibly forecasting) these effects will be difficult without more extensive renditions of the entire US system, particularly in politico-economic terms. In order to evaluate global transformations of public/private configurations, forms of health governance, or even definitions of health 'crises', the specificities of the most powerful protagonist in this sphere need to be comprehensively understood.

To this end, this chapter argues that the United States is now inhabited by what might be termed a 'health-industrial complex'. Moreover, the goal of participants within this complex is to maintain the guise of efficient market relations, while orchestrating 'certainty' for its dominant market actors. In arguing this, the chapter begins with a brief discussion of the political economy of certainty that invests this health complex. It then turns to a discussion of the biomedical industry, the regulatory sphere, and the implications for health care delivery. While not the focus of this paper, this more complete array of US domestic interests, deeply devoted to the increasing expansion of a robust health industry, needs to be carefully linked to trade, health 'reform' agendas and even security concerns. Ultimately, such work will contribute to a richer understanding of the politico-economic pressures that invest health, from which analyses on both national and global health questions could draw support and insight.

The health-industrial complex

The United States has, without a doubt, the largest health-related market in the world. It has been estimated that by 2011 the US market in health will approach a volume of US$3 trillion, comprising some 17 per cent of US gross domestic product (Heffler et al., 2002, p. 207). With such an enormous volume of interaction, it behoves analysts to find a way to characterize both the immensity and flavour of this system. The most obvious manner in which to do this would be to highlight the United States as the most developed private health sector in the world. There is more than a grain of truth to this designation, as private actors inhabit virtually every corner of the system, from research to health care delivery. Most illustrative of this, health care delivery is predominantly inhabited by private firms, typified by an extensive and complex separation between producers and providers, and the state plays a predictably supportive role that undergirds the profitable continuance of this system.

It is, of course, incumbent upon any student of health to understand analytically why such structures can hold so soundly and uniquely within the United States. In this respect, political economy elucidates a broader picture of US health dynamics in a manner that ties together its disparate elements, each of which is often the subject of social struggle and political strife. Thus, it is valuable to take seriously the notion of a 'health-industrial complex', adapting Dwight Eisenhower's famous terminology. This should not take on a conspiratorial tone like so many discussions of the military-industrial complex. Rather, the reference to a 'complex' simply captures the structural imperative that prevails in virtually every corner of the health sector either to maintain or to enhance accumulative capacities. Importantly, individual sections of the health arena (drug companies, regulatory bodies, health maintenance organizations) are often dissected and criticized as discrete social phenomena, but it is important to note their interrelation within a system that demonstrates consistent accumulation imperatives across its many component parts. These imperatives play themselves out in interesting ways throughout the US politico-economic terrain, but each moment is, most importantly, marked by a dual necessity: to valorize market relationships, on the one hand, while, on the other, to attempt systematically to evade their uncertain outcomes.

In relation to market dynamics, it is fair to say the United States fits within a historical trajectory of capitalist development that can loosely be designated as Anglo-American. State structures have, across a range of venues, been positioned in a manner that is largely subservient to capitalist civil society. From antitrust legislation to 'contracts with America', the institutions and actors of the US political scene have shaped a regulatory structure that is either minimized or highly conducive to strengthened accumulation dynamics for American corporations. This politico-economic disposition is anything but a coincidence, and needs to be understood, first and foremost, from the particularity of American transition to capitalism. For Ellen Wood (1991), US capitalism needs to be seen through the lens of original transition circumstances in England. For Wood, the contemporary facets of

British capitalism – facets she later relates to the US – are a function of that state having fully absorbed an indigenously emergent capitalism, with the result that state structures were subordinated to the 'supremacy of "civil society"'. Wood links the American experience to the British, in that '... they have both been most responsive to the pure logic of capitalism and to the imperatives of mass consumer markets ... [T]hese two less adulterated capitalisms have been more susceptible to the demands of short term profits' (ibid., p. 106).

The politico-economic terrain within the US, then, remains highly disposed toward conditions shaped for the enhanced possibility of profit accumulation. In relation to biomedical and health issues, this implies the clearing of space for private actors to capitalize on the production and sale of commodities or services. In keeping with the liberal adage that removing the spectre of governmental control and restraint spurns healthy competition, the US Congress, federal agencies and local state authorities have worked in lock-step over the past two decades to unleash the benefits of market efficiencies. For instance, on the recent issue of 'follow-on biologics' – a term referring to the second generation of complex biotechnology-derived therapies or treatments – Senator Charles Schumer captures a tone consistent throughout governmental policymaking: 'we don't want a law that stifles innovation, by making biologic drugs unprofitable. That would make no sense whatsoever' (US Senate, 2007a). Indeed, as will be elaborated below, corporate actors, policymakers and regulators alike take advantage of most, if not all, possibilities to foster innovative practices *via* a perceived instantiation of competitive market dynamics. This tendency resonates as much in biomedical research as it does in health care delivery.

Paradoxically, the second necessity grafted onto this tendency is a desire to control – usually in some competitively advantageous way – the rampant uncertainty of market dynamics. Uncertainty should, *perforce*, play a predominant role in all sectors subject to market scenarios, particularly in areas where actors rely on or participate in innovation, always trying to outpace competitors' access to and utilization of knowledge. But, in keeping with the contradictory tendencies in capitalist societies, competitive uncertainty brings with it a relentless desire to *foster certainty*. In the case of a growing US health sector, this translates into the strategic securing of avenues for enhanced accumulation, largely by circumventing, to the greatest extent possible, the imperatives of market competition. And shaping certainty within uncertainty is no passive affair – it demands consistent and proactive struggle around public discourse, legal terrain and policymaking trajectories. This relentless series of attempts to secure certainty in every corner of health demonstrates the manner in which the US health arena needs to be understood as an industrial complex. Like nowhere in the world, there exists an extensive imbrication of interests among corporate health actors, policymakers and regulators, as well as a deeply engrained *laissez-faire* ideology cohabiting with a highly structured and supported 'market'.

Nowhere are the contradictions of this dual necessity more prominent than in the US Congress, where policy, regulation and public affairs are reviewed by all players in a political space of confrontation and struggle. In understanding how the health arena has progressed in the United States, it is critical to gain a sense of how such players attend to their interests in this conflictual political space. Here it becomes abundantly obvious that certain modes of understanding win out, time and time again. Across the range of activities related to health – biomedical research, regulatory safety and health care delivery – accumulation potential is prioritized, often with actors in different spheres interweaving their interests *vis-à-vis* one another. This common maximization of potential, while not requiring outright collusion, does demand a common understanding that the politico-economic terrain for enhanced accumulation needs to be kept open on the best possible terms.

Biomedical production

The US biomedical industry is flourishing well beyond that in any other OECD state, and this has not been a function of chance. There is, on a *per capita* basis, far more spent on biomedical investment than anywhere else in the world, a funding scenario with roots in both the public and private sectors. As a product of the deliberate association of the biological sciences with practical, socio-economic applications – led early on by the Rockefeller Foundation – the United States has fostered an impressive array of production sources related to health. At the centre of this stands the National Institutes of Health (NIH), the Bethesda campus on which so much biomedical research in the United States depends. More than a series of institutes, the NIH extends external (extramural) grants out to the university and private sector, creating the foundation for 'basic', cutting-edge research in the biomedical sphere. The NIH has been the golden centrepiece of US research, and this has not gone unnoticed by either policymakers or corporate players, who have long since understood this 'jewel' to be the 'envy of the world'.

In fact, it is true to say that the NIH, along with the range of (corporate and non-corporate) laboratory benches it supports, has typically been harnessed for national objectives. At no time has this been more true than in the aftermath of the neoliberal turn of the late 1970s and early 1980s. Starting with the Stevenson–Wydler Technology Transfer Act and the Bayh–Dole Act of 1980, the US Congress, in cooperation with successive presidential administrations, has acted in a concerted fashion to enlarge and accelerate NIH research while also ensuring its robust commercial transfer. There has been a concerted push to ensure that the NIH, along with all funding associated with it, moves away from a pure disease 'mission'. Instead, the onus would be on the NIH and researchers to promote 'consortium formation, exchange of research personnel between government laboratories and industrial firms, special technology transfer programmes of federally owned laboratories, and transfer of patent rights to government grantees and contractors' (US Congress, Office of Technology Assessment, 1988, p. 167). Thus began a long line of industrial–academic agreements, intended to carry 'pure' research out of the laboratory and into biomedical applications within the broad sphere of US health (Kenny, 1986). This has proven as true for pharmaceuticals as it has for biomedical instrumentation, although the former has certainly received the most dramatic 'boost' along the way.

Such state-structural support does not occur in a social vacuum, and corporate actors have been central in driving this process from the start. In particular, the pharmaceutical industry in the United States has made, since the 1970s, a strenuous effort both to reinfuse energy into its own industrial dynamics and to protect and foster its privileged position among American economic sectors. The pressure felt on pharmaceutical corporations had precisely to do with the danger that their product lines would be subject to *normal market forces*. The problem, that the industry as a whole was producing fewer products which could be subject to the political protection of the 20-year patent, constituted a form of rallying cry for both affected firms and their prominent trade association, the Pharmaceutical Research and Manufacturers of America (PhRMA). Thus, we find that pharmaceutical corporations were among the first to foster the groundswell around biotechnology and heightened biomedical research as a potential dynamic lead sector in the US economy. Between 1976 and 1985, large firms provided 56 per cent of the funds invested in new biotechnology outfits (Chang, 1998; Gambardella, 1995). The subsequent rush to capitalize on decades of research stemming from biotech firms, university laboratories and NIH research has been evident in the flurry of public–private contracts with the NIH (Cooperative Research and Development Agreements or CRADAs), gargantuan funding agreements between pharma and biotech, and waves of takeovers, buyouts, alliances and mergers between and within biotech and pharmaceutical sectors.

The results are now plain to see: a biomedical productive sector attached to the American economy, which is the most highly capitalized in the world. Even the research stemming from public research funding has reflected this, as NIH-backed research grew to a remarkable $28 billion last year (US House, 2003). In 2006, the seemingly impervious US biotechnology sector reached a market capitalization of almost $400 billion, and grew, and increased its revenues by 14 per cent (Ernst and Young, 2007, p. 18). Big pharma continues its extraordinary presence in the US, the predominant sales market, with sales in 2006 of US$252 billion. Profitability in this industry is much higher than average within Fortune 500 firms, averaging a rate of 17 per cent against revenue (Pattison et al., 2003). With much to lose, these industries vigorously pursue their interests in political venues, constantly emphasizing their value not only to patients but also to the US economy. Corporations and trade associations fight at every turn to ensure that legislation, policy and regulation are tailored in such a way that profitability is not hampered and is possibly even extended. As such, Billy Tauzin, Chief Executive Officer (CEO) of PhRMA, consistently reiterates in an oft-heard sentiment from the biomedical industry: '[in] order to foster these much-needed medical breakthroughs, we must continue to pursue public policies that provide...opportunity to recoup and secure the benefits of their significant investments' (US Senate, 2007b). The Biotechnology Industry Organization (BIO) echoes this by asserting that '[b]iotechnology product development is also fraught with high risk, and the vast majority of experimental biotech products fail to ever reach the marketplace. Investors will invest in capital-intensive, long-term, and high-risk research and development endeavours only if they believe there will be a return on their investment' (US Senate, 2007c).

While accumulation objectives are well entrenched in the political and corporate health landscape, the extent to which predominant actors seek a 'free market' remains strictly limited. As we will see below, along with the desire for unbridled realization of profits comes the concomitant imperative to control structures and procedures which might affect the unique context of accumulation in the United States. This involves consistently ensuring that state structures play an active role in the preparation of much-needed infrastructural features of biomedical development. Infrastructural outlay is the first condition that the 'internationalized state' needs to fulfil, in order to round out its self-imposed conditions as a competitive state. In the case of US biomedical production, current infrastructural endeavours have seen the Bush Administration and Congress double the funding of the NIH in this current round of biotechnological frenzy (US House, 2003). Previous to this, Congress and several administrations went out of their way to validate and underwrite the execution of the Human Genome Project, largely an infrastructural endeavour to provide genetic cartography to the burgeoning biotechnology and pharmaceutical industries (Loeppky, 2005a). The next round of support has long since started with the progressive exploration of proteomics, an attempt to map out the vastly complex terrain of the human protein complement. Finally, even Project Bioshield – supporting research on terrorist-associated vaccines and therapeutics – exhibits a similar tendency, ensuring guaranteed funding (and markets) for therapies that are reasonably rare in form, but *may* yield commercial value (Cooper, 2006; Loeppky, 2005b).

In short, at the heart of the US health-industrial complex lies an intensive regime of bioaccumulation.[1] This involves the mobilization of research capacities in the United States and beyond, as a means to isolate and target population-wide health conditions, with an eye to commercial value. The biomedical industry as a whole, however, while highlighting the necessity of such a mobilization, remains unwilling to foster the prerequisite conditions. In order to keep the accumulative potential of current biomedical production churning, industry demands and receives vast portions of 'burnable' research capital, directed through public channels. This affords a degree of certainty of access to productive infrastructure and knowledge rarely afforded to other industrial sectors. However, making certain the viability of production across new biomedical sciences lays the foundation for, but does not complete, the kind of assurance pursued within the health-industrial complex. Instead, it is necessary to control both the channels through which health commodities must travel to realize profit in the market and the disposition of market participants themselves. And it is to these two spheres, regulatory and health care, that this paper now turns.

Regulatory outcomes and certainty

In the context of very large investments in health-related research, on the part of both corporations and states, the regulatory conditions for production have become the subject of considerable scrutiny. Here, remarkably, virtually all players – corporate, state and institutional–academic – are invested in a similar outcome: ongoing enhancement of the production–provision–profit cycle. This could be interpreted as a serendipitous confluence of objectives, a situation in which societal consensus fosters beneficial results in a frictionless policy arena. Such a scenario, however, should more properly be interpreted as problematic in relation to regulatory questions. The difficulty is one of proximity: how close can advocates of a particular social objective (enhanced biomedical production and its profitable realization in the market) be linked to the regulation of that same objective? Examining two prominent examples in the regulatory landscape, the Patent and Trademark Office (PTO) and the Food and Drug Agency (FDA), it seems evident that heightened proximity has become an integral feature of the US health-industrial complex.

PTO

Health represents an industrial arena marked by a considerably accommodating regulatory environment, aimed primarily at fostering and reproducing dynamic biomedical development. Following the investment upswing of the late 1970s and 1980s, a shift in the regulatory 'mood' has been discernible, with recurring assessments of the patenting system in the United States. This is logical, since the first regulatory step with commercial transfer in the biomedical sciences involves securing intellectual property rights.

Throughout the earlier years of the biotechnology frenzy, actors from all sides put the US Patent and Trademark Office under pressure to review and approve patents with greater urgency. Indeed, in the wake of considerable patent backlogs, and a largely underfunded PTO, Senator Jim Kerry summarized a strongly felt Congressional sentiment, by emphasizing that '[t]his is a real problem to [researchers and corporations] and it is slowing down the process of commercializing. Thus, it is one more instance in which we seem to shoot ourselves in the foot with respect to our own productivity and commercialization' (US Senate, 1989, pp. 58–9). Particularly once the Human Genome Project was in full swing, it became evident to advocates that commercial transfer was going to require a stepped-up effort on the part of regulators at the PTO. The backlog was addressed by creating a special group within the PTO, known as Group 1800, to devote attention solely to biotechnology-related patent applications (Patent and Trademark Office, 1994). In the current context, this has dramatically decreased the amount of time pending for biomedical patent applications, and it occasioned the substantial increase in commercial language to understand the PTO's public tasks. Indeed, the then PTO Commissioner, Bruce Lehman, highlighted the importance of public hearings, to understand 'where our *customers* stand on the important issues in the patent system. This is particularly true for the biotechnology industry which is particularly dependent on effective and meaningful patent protection' (ibid., emphasis added).

But, while adding patent examiners has eased some of the political pressure on the PTO, it has certainly not eliminated the prominence of discourse concerning better performance for industrial needs. In fact, much of the attempted revision and upgrading of the PTO in the mid-1990s (then understood to be facing pressure from the burgeoning biotechnology arena) was aimed at ensuring that examiners understood the PTO's role as 'the patent office, not the rejection office' (B. Lehman, quoted in Thompson, 2001, p. 9). Industry and its associations have been relentless in ensuring that the PTO is under constant scrutiny to clarify and accelerate its procedures. Its current strategic mission over the 2007–12 period emphasises a 'quality-focused, highly productive, responsive USPTO that supports a market-based intellectual property system' (USPTO, 2003, p. 14). In addition to previous reform, one of the office's main objectives is still to address the issue of speed. It intends to 'control patent and trademark pendency, reduce time to first Office action, and recover…investments in people, processes and technology' (ibid.). Here, we find not only the promise to create a 'rocket-docket' (12-month) application process available for purchase, but also the not-so-coincidental determination to reduce substantially the number of hired patent examiners. All of this fits squarely with a vision of an internationalized state, whereby institutions are made 'lean' but also highly responsive to their 'customer base'. Along these lines, regulatory capture starts to blend in with wider state objectives, to extend development prospects to an entire industry, particularly one willing to extend co-payment (or full payment) for its own governmental supervision.

Despite this intensification of an already industry-friendly environment, health-related trade associations struggle to push this governmental amenability to commercial transfer as far as it will go. BIO, for instance, cautions that 'many of the underlying assumptions of the plan are either unclear or uncertain', and that the PTO needs to 'ensure that existing protections are not weakened or undermined and will also ensure that certain industry sectors are not disproportionately impacted' (BIO, 2006, p. 3). The reason for such tenacious behaviour on the part of biomedical sectors is not hard to see: intellectual property (IP) offers the mechanism by which successful corporate bodies can evade the ravages of the market and accelerate accumulation to the widest possible scope. This process is often depicted in biomedical corporate circles as pricing their commodities at a level according to 'what the market will bear'. This latter terminology is, excusing the pun, patent nonsense, and a more accurate description would read: 'what political access will afford'. The strict enforcement of advantageous patent regulations is the primary vehicle through which a range of biomedical corporations (devices, biotech, pharma) have been able to *politically constitute* their position within the wider American political economy. Importantly, patents render multiple results, only one of which is accentuated profit margins, although that is clearly one of their significant attributes. Beyond this, however, they also section off knowledge from other players – they are overwhelmingly instruments of exclusion. In this sense, for the applicable corporate actor, they create legal and behavioural certainty in relation to other actors that could not otherwise be achieved in the 'free marketplace'.

While it will be touched on further below, it is precisely in this sense that we should understand the extension of US patenting rules to international fora, such as the World Trade Organization (WTO). Orchestrated entirely by corporate actors (with Pfizer taking the lead), the extension of patent law worldwide does more than secure profits abroad – indeed, there may be little profit within many of the regions in question. It excludes the possibility of competitive behaviour or even the incremental improvement of knowledge, blocking out even the potential for countervailing competitive behaviour. This is why the PTO's strategic plan cannot and is not limited to the American domestic scene – it highlights repetitively the need to enter into and enhance bilateral and multilateral agreements around intellectual property (USPTO, 2003, pp. 4, 5, 7 and 12). In terms of certainty, the global propagation of 'harmonized' patent regulation places this political constitution of profit accumulation in the US domestic market on a more solid footing. Above all, worldwide control of patent regulation must be seen as precedent control – defiance of politically constituted pricing abroad would erode the legitimacy of such practices within the American market, a situation that is anathema to biomedical producers.

FDA

Even more than the PTO, the FDA garners widespread understanding as a regulatory institution of public trust, particularly in relation to human health questions. It carries the responsibility for regulatory review of the biomedical commodities now under production in the United States and abroad, ostensibly with a priority to public safety and health. The FDA, in other words, operates in line with the public interest as a gatekeeper for medical devices, pharmaceuticals and biologics. In view of the heavy civic burden placed on this agency, it would accord with common sense to find that the critical distance between regulators and industrial and/or state advocates remains considerable. At a foundational level, however, this proves largely untrue. The Congressional oversight bodies that give life to the FDA's mandate are the same ones that support and bolster the health industry in its 3-decades-long expansion within and beyond the American market. One result of this is a contradictory plea from policymakers and regulators alike: maintain rigorous standards for regulation while facilitating robust industrial development. Thus, we find that even one of the staunchest Congressional critics of the pharmaceutical industry, Sherrod Brown, qualifies his comments on the FDA, by stating that Congress's 'objective in looking at these issues is not to dismantle legitimate incentives and rewards for innovative drugs and biologics' (US House, 2001a). Ultimately, on the all-important question of regulation, the production–provision–profit cycle is never *fundamentally* questioned.

In fact, the FDA forms one of the central arenas in which the 'fuzzy' boundary between state regulation and industrial advocacy is most evident. Increasingly, the very power source that afforded the FDA relative autonomy from the industry it regulates – its governmental funding source – is being drastically eroded. In 1992, under enormous pressure from biomedical industries (as well as patient advocacy groups) to step up approval times, Congress passed the Prescription Drug User Fees Act (PDUFA). Under this legislation – subject to review every 5 years – corporations pay a user fee for their drug and biologics approval applications. The legislation ensures that the funds are used only for this purpose and that certain benchmarks (set out by Congress) are met. PDUFA continues to meet with overwhelming support in Congress, heralded as the source of patient well-being, regulatory streamlining and a boon to US competitive practice. Throughout periods in which the act is being reviewed, policymakers state incessantly how obvious it is that Congress must 'ensure quick, clean, reauthorization', and that such actions will 'guarantee patients' continued access to innovative drugs, and meet our country's gold standards of safety and efficacy' (US House, 2002a). More than just a 'pet project' of Congressional members, however, the results of the PDUFA are touted by FDA officials as signposts of American competitive success. Indeed, the criterion for evaluation of this programme, from the standpoint of administrative personnel, is *how quickly* the FDA is able to accelerate processing times. In testimony, the agency's Deputy Commissioner goes so far as to link the PDUFA to global competition:

> We now have 8 years of data on our efforts to achieve PDUFA goals. During this period the FDA faced a total of 73 performance goals. We met or exceeded 71 of those goals. If you add procedural goals to that total, the Agency met or exceeded 86 out of 92 PDUFA goals. The result has been a dramatic reduction in product approval times. Drugs are now reviewed in the U.S. as fast or faster than anywhere in the world, without compromising the very stringent standards that Americans have come to expect. With the enactment of PDUFA, U.S. companies have overtaken their European counterparts, and now have a commanding lead in world markets. A July 2001 report found that the European share of the world pharmaceutical market fell by 10 percent over the past decade, while the U.S. market share rose by more than 10 percent. (US House, 2002b)

The unabashed support for *accelerated approval* times is regularly linked to the competitive position of the American economy, and the FDA has fallen under critical eye for such practices only from *outside* sources. While there are no existing systematic studies, strong anecdotal evidence suggests that the FDA has grown far too close to the industries that it ostensibly regulates. This has fostered an atmosphere in which safety precautions are downloaded on physicians; extraordinary pressure is placed on a revolving door of drug reviewers (even the Director of the Center for Drug Evaluation and Review admitted publicly to a 'sweatshop' environment); and a prevailing 'basic message to approve'.[2]

The result of this 'cooperative' (rather than strictly regulative) relationship can be said to go well beyond the acceleration of approval times. It reaches, instead, into a range of industry-friendly policies designed to maintain or improve upon conditions for accumulation. Of these, several can be offered up as examples. Certainly the disastrous recall cases of the last 15 years could be placed within consequential orbit of this act. This is not because of the number of cases as much as it is about the apparent disregard for mounting evidence of public health harm when weighed against the industrial interest backing the product in question. Vioxx, Redux and Prozac stand out as prominent but not exclusive examples of this phenomenon. Direct-to-consumer (DTC) advertising, allowed by the FDA since 1997, could be understood to exacerbate problems around drug safety and appropriate usage. Importantly, the FDA's capacity (and apparent willingness) to punish exaggerated or false claims on the part of manufacturers has been greatly constrained. Indeed, the agency admits publicly that the pressures emanating from the objectives of the PDUFA have made it necessary to redirect funds that might otherwise be used to monitor DTC practices.[3] The effects of DTC advertising, although not studied conclusively, seem to indicate enhanced use of 'ethical drugs' (the term used by industry to denote prescription drugs) (Aiken et al., 2004). Additionally, the willingness of the FDA to close loopholes stemming from Waxman–Hatch legislation of 1984, which allows manufacturers huge patent and exclusivity extensions based on either approval times or patent litigation, remains limited. And there are few in Congress who are seriously willing to challenge such *laissez-faire* agency practices. In fact, the Chair of the Energy and Commerce Committee, Billy Tauzin, who would later become CEO of PhRMA, has resisted such pressure by maintaining that Congress must 'keep things in perspective' and that the '1984 act has been a resounding success' (US House, 2001c). Finally, one could look at the consistent resistance put forward on the part of the FDA to allow drug reimportation by state Medicaid and Medicare programmes, despite the fact that safety concerns have been grossly fabricated. While state budgets, low-income citizens and senior citizens are failing to find reasonable access to prescription drugs, the FDA has chosen blatantly to defend the pricing practices resident in the US market (Connolly, 2003).

All of this must be understood as something which goes well beyond the question of 'regulatory capture', a situation in which state agencies come to identify too closely with the groups they regulate. Instead, we find an interlocking dynamic of policymakers, regulatory officials, corporate players and extremely sophisticated industrial lobby groups. In a characteristic moment of candour, Sherrod Brown describes this total relationship: 'when the drug industry wants us to move quickly to ensure that the FDA doesn't hold their products up from getting to the market, we move with lightning speed to do their bidding' (US House, 2002c). Such statements, however, meet largely with silence in policy terms, as the FDA is understood presently to be occupied with a public–private partnership that *facilitates* the competitive position of the US health industry. The objective for all parties, in relation to an industry with extraordinary, politically-constituted accumulation levels, is to foster certainty and fend off destabilizing threats. Fittingly, when the FDA considered utilizing its authority in limited cases to require manufacturers to switch drugs from prescription to over-the-counter status, detractors argued that 'to allow such a practice would create uncertainty and unnecessarily complicate the already highly risky business of drug development. New research and development would be chilled as a result' (US House, 2001d). This final threat summarizes the endgame in most regulatory debates related to US health: innovation is equated with quality of care for US citizens, and the spectre of endangering the former is always the material and discursive thread that reproduces consensus within the health-industrial complex. Regulatory institutions ensure that health-related production is enabled far more than it is hampered, making growing investment and pursuit of blockbuster product circulation a worthwhile endeavour.

Conclusion

The interrelated character of US health politics, from its production advocates through to its political backers, exhibits all the tendencies of an industrial complex. This complex is now so deeply engrained in American political circles that participants no longer think there is anything particularly unique about it. When two prominent members of Congress responsible for the negotiation of the Medicare Modernization Act – Billy Tauzin and Jim Greenwood – announced their future positions heading PhRMA and BIO, respectively, they were criticized only for their timing (they had not yet left their public duties!). It is a powerful symbol of an interlocking health-industrial complex when Washington insiders are unproblematically and seamlessly transforming themselves into lobbyists for the most powerful trade associations on Capitol Hill. The complete nature of this politico-economic arrangement ensures that few critical questions are asked of the structural features that foster oligopoly-level bioaccumulation; conducive regulatory environments; and enhanced market-based health care outlets.

Ominously, the wider instantiation of a production–provision–profit model can be forecast *via* the successful recent attempts by both the biotechnology and pharmaceutical industries to reformulate IP and trade policy in this area. PhRMA's 2005 Special 301 submission to the United States Trade Representative (USTR) steps well outside IP policy concerns, directly into areas associated with public health delivery. Countries can be placed on the 301 list for the maintenance of 'price control' and 'market access' health care regulation, now understood as trade barriers for innovation-based industry (PhRMA, 2006). Germany's attempt, for instance, to get health care spending under control is said to 'distort the marketplace, limit market access for US research-based pharmaceutical companies, and deny patients the most effective medicines' (PhRMA, 2006, p. 16). In turn, the USTR's Special 301 Report reproduces this industry language, indicating a dramatic shift in government policy. The report, mandated to deal with IP issues, now focuses attention on

> regulatory barriers that impede [industry's] ability to sustain the cycle of innovation and may inhibit the availability of new, ground-breaking products. These types of regulatory barriers include, for example, non-transparent administrative regimes; decision-making that lacks a scientific basis; and cumbersome and lengthy drug listing and other administrative processes. (USTR, 2005, p. 10)

On top of the judicial enforcement possibilities of the WTO, none of this bodies well for the many biomedical and healthcare configurations in states that seek or have settled TRIPS+ bilateral trade arrangements. Global health, modelled on the US complex of production–provision–profit, will turn out poorly for the overwhelming majority of populations who cannot afford such heightened costs.

Notes

1. Here the term is adapted, without apologies, from Michel Foucault's 'biopolitics'. In the author's opinion, bioaccumulation stands at the core of biopolitics, a process whereby populations, and in particular their biological functions, become the subject of measurement, surveillance, and optimization. A biopolitics without bioaccumulation at the centre remains an empty exercise in control. For a more extensive discussion of biopolitics, see Foucault (1997).
2. See Willman (2002) 'How a New Policy Led to Seven Deadly Drugs', *Los Angeles Times*, 20 December. The quoted text cites Dr Solomen Sobel, former Director of the FDA's metabolic and endocrine drugs division. See also Harris (2004) 'At FDA, Strong Drug Ties and Less Monitoring', *New York Times*, 6 December; 'Study Condemns FDA's Handling of Safety', *New York Times*, 23 September 2006.
3. See testimony of Janet Woodcock (Director, Center for Drug Evaluation and Research) in US House (2001b).

4

Palliative Interventions: Canadian Foreign Policy, Security and Global Health Governance

Colleen O'Manique

Introduction

Thirty years ago, 134 representatives of member states of the World Health Organization (WHO) gathered in Alma Ata in the former Soviet Union, and drafted and unanimously adopted the Alma Ata Declaration, 'Health for All by the Year 2000.' The much publicized declaration called for 'the attainment by all citizens of the world by the year 2000 of a level of health that will permit them to lead a socially and economically productive life', and the cornerstone of achieving health for all, the implementation of a broad-based primary health care vision. What happened next? Certainly some gains in some places were made. But, in the 3 decades that followed, the governance of global health shifted away from the state and World Health Organization (WHO); first toward the World Bank (WB), whose 1993 report *Investing in Health* signalled its growing interest in global health policy. Over the years a much broader network of state and non-state actors – civil society organizations and the G7/G8 – have taken on a more important role in the governance of global health. As neoliberal policies of structural adjustment eroded public health care systems, the discourse of Primary Health Care was replaced with that of economics (cost recovery, willingness to pay, technical efficiencies, opportunity costs); single-disease, vertical interventions became more fashionable, and the understanding of health as a basic right gave way to health as a commodity provided by the market, poor health increasingly disengaged from its social and political roots.

Through these decades, Canada emerged as a significant actor in global health governance, active through both bilateral and multilateral channels, and as part and parcel of the G7/G8. Viewed historically as a nation that 'does the right thing', Canada provided leadership in 2001 to set up the Global Fund for HIV/AIDS, Tuberculosis and Malaria; was a major instigator of the WHO's '3 by 5 Initiative' to provide antiretroviral treatment to

3 million people with HIV/AIDS; and in 2005 passed a bill to make less expensive generic drugs available to developing and least developed countries. Canada's International Policy Strategy of 2005 identified health as a programming priority in Canada's development cooperation programme, consistent with Canada's recent history of health-related development assistance. But a closer examination challenges Canada's reputation as a leader in global health governance. This paper argues that Canada has deviated little from promoting a global health research and policy agenda that focuses on the global health priorities of the G8, while Canada's overarching foreign policy agenda can be shown to undermine the health and security of communities outside Canada's borders.

The HIV/AIDS pandemic, a resurgence of infectious diseases, bioterrorist threats, tainted food scandals, and mounting controversies over trade-related intellectual property rights and access to medicines have put public health more firmly on the foreign policy agenda (Fidler and Drager, 2006, p. 687). Canada claims to be a leader in promoting a foreign policy that has human security as one of its pillars, human security being a broad concept that places the individual at the centre of security, understood as 'freedom from want and freedom from fear', and shifting the focus away from state-centric notions. Rosalind Irwin argues that, in Canada and elsewhere, much of the human security agenda is incommensurable with national security agendas which reflect the unequal Westphalian divisions of political sovereignty and global structural inequalities in power and wealth (Irwin, 2001). It is in this context that Canada's role in global health can be seen as a complicated mix of national 'self-interest' (defined broadly within the parameters of neoliberalism) and 'doing the right thing'; its role consistent with the country's self-image as a middle-power state and its rhetorical commitment to human security and human rights. This chapter begins to examine some of the contradictions between Canadian foreign policy goals and Canada's role in global health governance, focusing on Canada's official development assistance (ODA) in health (including Canada's role in responding to the HIV/AIDS pandemic) and the Canadian government response to the new 'global threats' of SARS and avian influenza.

Canadian foreign policy: a snapshot

Mainstream accounts circulating in policy circles give an uncritical view of Canada as a 'moral leader' on the international stage, our foreign policy fostering the conditions for human security abroad while ensuring the security of Canadians at home. Canada's post-war foreign policy has been shaped, at least in part, by an ambiguous and shifting concept of human security. Prior to the Second World War, Canadian foreign policy (CFP) closely mirrored Britain's, but Canada's post-war engagement with the creation of international institutions cemented its reputation (at least in the eyes of the Canadian public) as an enlightened and able middle power. In the post-war years CFP has been conditioned by Canada's proximity to the United States and the country's heavy dependence on foreign investment, Laura MacDonald (1997, p. 175) and others arguing that its history has been, to a large extent, the story of successive attempts to manage economic integration with the United States while maintaining some degree of independence. The deliberate strategy of strengthening Canada's middle-power status was a means of establishing a degree of autonomy from the superpower next door; it was not radical, and, while criticisms of US foreign policy existed, they tended to be muted. The emergence of Canada as an able middle power may well have been shaped by the vision and ideals of its political leaders and a Canadian public who were forming a national identity as 'the world's helpful fixer', a vision of their country more perceived than real, in Chapnick's (2005, p. 152) view. The active attainment of middle-power leadership was also strategy of preventing Canada's legacy as a British colony from falling into its destiny as an American one.

In Canada, the notion that state security rests with broader peace and prosperity outside its borders is not new, its antecedents going back to 1944 and Mackenzie King. In his words, 'Security from war is indeed essential, but real security requires international action and organization in many other fields – in social welfare, in trade, in technical progress, in transportation, and in economic development' (ibid., p. 84). But it was Lester Pearson who has been largely credited with solidifying Canada's image as a state that promotes human security on the world stage. Pearson's reputation as an international peace broker and peacekeeper emerged from his instrumental role in the formation of the UN, tenure as President of the UN General Assembly, and his Nobel Peace Prize in 1957 for his proposal to create a peacekeeping force during the 1956 Suez Crisis. Political leaders have since linked human security to national security as a principle of Canadian foreign policy. Former Prime Minister Pierre Trudeau stated in a 1969 speech that 'It is in our national interest to reduce the tensions in the world, tensions which spring from the two-thirds of the world's population who are poor whereas the other third is rich and the tensions which spring from this great ideological struggle between the East and the West.' Lloyd Axworthy's time as Minister of Foreign Affairs (beginning in 1996), under Jean Chretien's tenure as Prime Minister, marks Canada's central roles in the campaign to ban anti-personnel landmines, the creation of the International Criminal Court and Canada's chairship of the Kimberly Process in 2004. Axworthy was also instrumental in drafting the blueprint for the 'Responsibility to Protect' and in the establishment of the International Commission on Intervention and State Sovereignty (ISCC). He was an active campaigner against the use of child soldiers and the international trade in light weapons.

During the decade of the 1990s the concept of human security became more popular in the discourses of global development, promoted by civil society organizations, policy and research institutes and western governments alike. Strong civil society organizations in Canada have been instrumental in pushing the human security agenda, a logical extension of 'Canadian values' that are said to be reflected, for example, in Canada's universal health care system and welfare state policies of redistribution. With regard to ODA, Cranford Pratt (2001) has argued that an important determinant between 1966 and 1975 was the government's increased responsiveness to poverty at home, this responsiveness a result of the strong and active campaigning of human rights, social justice and church groups. But he adds that the government's central preoccupation with advancing Canadian international economic and political interests has historically diluted the humanitarian focus on Canadian aid, reversing an earlier trend that suggested increasing government responsiveness to human values (ibid., p. 73). Other critical commentators view Canada's high-profile activities on the international stage as 'quick wins' that have served to increase Canada's status and prestige both at home and abroad. David Black (2006, p. 55) characterizes the discourse of human security as palliative and system-maintaining; although Canada's iteration of human security encompassed both 'freedom from fear' and 'freedom from want', which were encapsulated in the UNDP's discourse-shifting global report of 1994, by 1999 the Department of Foreign Affairs and International Trade (DFAIT) had dropped 'freedom from want' in favour of a narrower 'freedom from fear' approach. In the same year, Canada adopted 'projecting Canada's values and culture' as one of the three pillars of its foreign policy platform, the other two being ensuring global security and the security of Canadians, and promoting the prosperity of Canadians and global prosperity. Kyle Grayson (2004, p. 54) makes the argument that the discourse of human security has provided Canada with 'brand recognition'; that the issues that Canadians have focused on – anti-personnel landmines, child soldiers, small arms transfers – are not divisive, require no sacrifice, and are shared by people across the political spectrum: '...while the Canadian human security agenda has been able to brand itself as transformative, the ways in which it has conceptualized contemporary security issues has done far too little to address the underlying global, political, social and economic inequalities that make these possible.'

But, as Canada's foreign policy has distanced itself from 'freedom from want', little has changed in the discourse of enlightened internationalism. Canada's most recent International Policy Statement (IPS), under the title 'A Role of Pride and Influence in the World,' released in April 2005 as the government's first integrated international policy framework, lays out the 'vision' and 'action plan' in four areas (diplomacy, development, defence, and commerce) to guide the activities of DFAIT, the Canadian International Development Agency (CIDA) and the Department of National Defence (DND). Canadian civil society groups have responded to the contradictions contained in the documents. Far from an 'integrated' approach, it is only within the development document that human security is mentioned at all: 'The obligation to address poverty is seen as subsidiary and instrumental to the pursuit of Canada's particular interests in promoting its own prosperity, reducing threats to global terrorism, and responding to regional insecurity,' states the Canadian Council on International Cooperation (CCIC). With the election of the Conservatives and Stephen Harper as Prime Minister in January 2006, the IPS guides only the parts of CFP consistent with a stronger relationship and harmonization of foreign policy with that of the United States. Under Harper, any pretence of embedding human security in CFP has been further eroded by an agenda that shifts the focus to antiterrorism and support for Canadian business interests overseas. Agencies involved in border control, antiterror and security have received budget increases while Canada's military role in Afghanistan has become the government's flagship foreign policy issue, eating up a significant proportion of Canada's ODA. Between 2001 and 2004, about 28 per cent of total new aid resources was targeted at Iraq and Afghanistan, with Afghanistan in 2007 the single largest recipient of bilateral aid.

The geopolitical and domestic context of CFP began to shift long before the Harper government took power, however. On the domestic front, change began around the early 1990s, with successive provincial and federal governments overhauling welfare states and promoting economic and political restructuring along neoliberal lines. While acknowledging its achievements, Canada's human security agenda has directed little attention to the political and economic forces that undermine human security; it has essentially been 'system maintaining', in Black's words, viewed in isolation from national security agendas, and the changing global distribution of wealth, resources, and life chances. It is in this context that health has recently become securitized, defined as a threat to global order. Global health has been mentioned explicitly as an issue in Canadian foreign policy in the 2002 Romanow Commission Report on the Future of Health Care in Canada. The Report states that health promotion in other countries has been an afterthought in Canadian foreign policy, but that now 'we have an opportunity to ensure that access to health care is not only part of our own domestic policy but also a prime objective of our foreign policy as well' (Romanow, 2002, p. 240) and that Canada should use its leadership role in the world to help improve health and health care around the world. Tony Clement, Canada's Federal Minister of Health, had these words for the meeting of the World Health Assembly on 14 May 2007:

> When it comes to global health, more and more we talk in terms of health security. And in Canada's view, our strongest asset is shared knowledge, cooperation our smartest strategy... Whether it comes to continuing our work internationally to safeguard our societies from a pandemic; contribute to the drive for developing desperately needed vaccines; or sharing

> our success in developing new policy to protect our people and environment, Canada will always stand as a ready, willing and compassionate partner, as we work together, toward a healthier and more secure world for all. (Canada's Statement to the World Health Assembly, 2007)

Global health and Canada's ODA

Many Canadians remain committed to a strong national public health care system, and to the legacy of Canada in the world (whether perceived or real) as an enlightened middle power committed to social justice. ODA is the normative arm of foreign policy, a mechanism for revealing 'Canadian' values and the underlying humanitarianism of CFP, yet the Canadian government is explicit in its articulation of the links between Canada's ODA and 'security' and prosperity at home. The stated mandate of the Canadian International Development Agency is 'To support sustainable development in developing countries in order to reduce poverty and contribute to a more secure, equitable, and prosperous world; to support democratic development and economic liberalization in the countries of Central and Eastern Europe and central Asia; and to support international efforts to reduce threats to international and Canadian security' (CIDA, 2006). And the benefits to Canadians? 'The aid program plays an important role in Canada's global reach and influence; provides a concrete expression of values Canadians cherish, such as humanitarianism, democracy and human rights; provides security, control of population movements and immigration, as well as protection from global diseases; builds long-term relationships with some of the fastest-growing economies in the world; and helps make the world more secure for Canadians' (ibid.).

David Morrison's (1998) comprehensive review of Canadian development assistance captures the contradictory mix of humanitarian, commercial and political goals that have been pursued by foreign aid. Canada extended international cooperation to all parts of the developing world under the leadership of Maurice Strong in 1966–70, and since that time aid has ebbed and flowed, with the 1980s budget crisis marking the beginning of cutbacks and downsizing to CIDA. Geopolitical and economic context has always shaped the aid regime in Canada and elsewhere, but in contradictory ways. State preferences and policy orientations have not been fixed. The turn toward neoliberalism translated into a greater emphasis on private sector development and a drop in Canada's aid budget; at the same time donor programmes and projects have responded to the various crises induced by austerity measures, adding a 'human face' to adjustment in the 1980s, and today ensuring that even the most marginalized can share in the 'benefits of globalization'. Morrison rejects the deterministic flavour of accounts of development assistance that view it as always deferring to corporate hegemony, demonstrating instead that officials within CIDA and Canada's strong voluntary and NGO sectors have pushed hard to promote poverty alleviation and sustainable development. Beginning in the 1980s, the discourses of poverty reduction, women and development, environment and human rights became prominent in CIDA and they have continued to shape interventions, to greater or lesser extents. Bill C-293, which was passed in the House of Commons in 2007, established that Canada's ODA must contribute to poverty reduction, take into account the perspectives of the poor, and be consistent with international human rights standards. It is too soon to tell what kinds of changes might emerge from the bill, but the January 2007 Senate Report on CIDA fixes Canada's aid reform securely within the parameters of market liberalism.

Klaudia Dmitrienko and Anne-Emannuelle Birn's (2006) account of the recent history of Canadian development assistance in the health sector in Latin America reflects some of the contradictions and inconsistencies between the 'national interest' and 'human security'. They argue that the role of Canadian aid has been multifold; to forge an independent foreign policy without challenging traditional US hegemony, to develop cordial relations, and to support the general goals and values of the Canadian government. Canada initially distanced itself from Latin America, not wanting to challenge US intervention and hegemony in the region. Involvement in Latin American health was 'more symbolic then substantive'; health aid consisting mostly of the provision of medical equipment and public health training which grew steadily from the mid-1950s and through the 1960s. It was not until 1971 that Canada became a member of the Pan American Health Organization (PAHO), only after attacks on Canada's reputation as a generous nation, and its late decision to join was ultimately based upon whether Canada would benefit from the $500,000 a year membership. Pierre Trudeau's 1968 foreign policy review called for the strengthening of ties to Latin America, leading to an increase in technical assistance in a variety of sectors: rural water and sanitation, nursing and dental health education, health worker training, development of food and drug standards, and emergency preparedness (Dmitrienko and Birn, 2006, pp. 12–18). For Dmitrienko and Birn (2006, p. 12), given Canada's limited economic and military clout, health aid has been a diplomatic tool in the context of bilateral relations, giving the country a voice in the region. 'Providing health and development assistance [was] a means of engendering international prestige and goodwill as well as securing national interests' (ibid.).

Canada was also able to distance itself from American foreign policy in the region by providing aid to Cuba and to Nicaragua. But, in 1980, Canada declined to support Nicaragua for a seat on the PAHO executive, citing that a possible 'shift to the left' in PAHO could have negative effects on policies in the region (ibid., p. 16). Though Canada's approach to Cuba was radically different from that of the United States, John Kirk and Peter McKenna (1997, p. 4) argue that this was because both Canada and Cuba 'were disconcertingly vulnerable to the twitches of the U.S.', and had a common vested interest in devising strategies to strengthen the sovereignty of each country *vis-à-vis* Washington. Trade dominated bilateral ties and the main reason to pursue bilateral relations was, and has been, to respond to Canadian business interests (ibid., p. 159). During the Trudeau years Canadian aid was granted, but all CIDA programmes were halted in May 1977 with the exception of a few essential medical and scientific programmes administered by the International Development Research Centre, a Canadian crown corporation at arm's length from the government (ibid., p. 112). The official face-saving rationale was that 'CIDA was putting greater emphasis on poorer countries,' when in fact the cuts were in opposition to Cuba's military support to Angola and to guerrilla training for the war against Rhodesia's white minority; relations also cooled as a result of Cuba's support for the Sandinista government and for the FMLN in El Salvador. In 1993, when 'the storm of the century', compounded by the abrupt end of the Cuba-Soviet relationship and sharp downturn in the economy, resulted in a massive humanitarian crisis, a $250,000 proposal by CIDA for medicines and hospital supplies was rejected by the Secretary of State for External Affairs. The decision to provide the (rather paltry) basket of assistance was eventually made after persistent lobbying from Canadian NGOs and church groups and led, in 1994, to an opening of a variety of CIDA avenues in NGO division, industrial cooperation division, and bilateral support.

Today, health tops the list of Canada's most recent stated priorities for ODA, with the focus on prevention and control of high-burden, communicable, poverty-linked diseases, especially HIV/AIDS, improving infant, child and maternal health, improving water and sanitation, and strengthening health systems (CIDA, 2006). The four other priorities are basic education, governance, private sector development, and tsunami relief and construction, while gender and the environment are considered 'cross-cutting' issues. The 2005–06 budget breakdown put disbursements to multilateral development institutions at the top of CIDA's health spending; $450.3 million (43.6 per cent of CIDA's Multilateral Program aid disbursements) was spent on health. Health spending constituted 16.1 per cent of the Partnership branch's $41.2 million budget, which was disbursed through 750 Canadian civil society and private sector organizations overseas. Bilateral aid stood at $218.1 million, with almost half of that – $98.3 million – targeted to African countries, and 20.1 per cent going to health.

Compared with Latin America, Canada's role in global health in Africa has generated a higher public profile, in large part owing to the severity of the HIV/AIDS pandemic in SSA. HIV/AIDS has dominated donor assistance in Africa over the last decade (ibid.). In 1987 CIDA began funding HIV/AIDS programmes, disbursing over $135 million to HIV prevention, education and care between 1987 and 1999, aid largely concentrated in sub-Saharan Africa with some activities in the Caribbean, and through multilateral channels such as the World Health Organization Global Programme on AIDS (WHO/GPA) and UNAIDS. The initial Canadian response was heavily tilted toward support for biomedical and behavioural programmes, consistent with the global response to AIDS emerging from WHO and then UNAIDS. But soon enough it embraced all the hallmarks of the global multisectoral approach of the 1990s: of gender-sensitive training, 'local ownership', 'mitigating local impacts' and a variety of other AIDS initiatives tied to a 'community base'. The Southern African AIDS Training Program, implemented by the Canadian Public Health Association, was first funded for $13 million by CIDA in 1990, with subsequent disbursements of $24.3 million, and then, in 2002, $31.5 million for 5 years. The programme was viewed as successful and a model to emulate. HIV/AIDS moved deeper into the Canadian spotlight with the appointment of Stephen Lewis in 2001 as the UN Envoy for AIDS in Africa, and with civil society pressure to ramp up aid, especially to SSA. Canada's aid was a drop in the bucket given the severity of the pandemic.

Health aid from Canada to countries in Africa deviates little from the list of global priorities set out at G8 meetings and multilateral forums. The Millennium Development Goals (MDGs) were adopted in 2000 at the UN Millennium Summit, and have become the central benchmarks around which the global donor agenda is to revolve until 2015. As host of the G8 Summit in Kananaskis, the Canadian government gave itself credit for getting the G8 to embrace the New Partnership for Africa's Development (NEPAD) and the G8 Action Plan in 2002, a policy framework to place Africa on a path of sustainable development emerging from 15 African heads of state and supported by G8 leaders. Aspects of NEPAD have been praised, particularly those relating to conflict resolution and the alleviation of poverty. But it has come under criticism from African civil society organizations for a lack of democratic consultation in its formulation, as well as for fixing its vision uncritically on increased global integration and unregulated markets (Saul, 2004, p. 4). The MDGs have faced similar criticism. Of the eight goals, three are related directly to health: to reduce infant mortality by two-thirds and maternal mortality by three-fourths, and to stop the spread of pandemic disease (AIDS, malaria and tuberculosis); while four other goals address health's social determinants: to reduce extreme poverty by half, achieve universal primary education, promote gender equality and empower women, and promote environmental sustainability. The eighth goal is to 'develop a global partnership for development, the first principle of which declares the development of "an open trading and financial system that is rule-based, predictable and non-discriminatory, includes a commitment to good governance, development and poverty reduction – nationally and internationally"' (UN MDGs). The MDGs do represent a break from the Washington Consensus, an acknowledgement that human needs cannot be guaranteed through growth alone; that 'public goods' and 'social empowerment' are critical to development and poverty alleviation.

But the partnership becomes synonymous with liberal economics and the externally imposed 'good governance' agenda consistent with the range of development declarations of the new millennium (such as the Monterey Consensus for the financing of Development, and the Paris Declaration), all which reaffirm commitments to trade liberalization, and are unquestioning of the macroeconomic policies that and have been unresponsive to human needs.

A number of high-profile funding mechanisms have emerged to support NEPAD and the MDGs. At the national level, Canada established the $500 million Canada Fund for Africa to support NEPAD; 22 per cent of which is allocated to health, another 28 per cent for agriculture, environment and water, 15 per cent for peace and security, and ICTs 7 per cent (CIDA, Canada Fund). Health initiatives supported by the Canada Fund include $50 million for AIDS vaccine research and development, $50 million for polio eradication through immunization, $12 million for HIV prevention and care targeted at youth, and 1.5 million for childhood development through sport in refugee camps. Since 2000, Canada has committed more than $800 million to global HIV/AIDS, but most of this is through high-profile Global Public–Private Partnerships, consisting of multilaterals such as UNICEF, IFIs, foundations such as Bill and Melinda Gates, the pharmaceutical industry, and public health institutions. Canada has disbursed $550 million to the Global Fund to Fight AIDS Tuberculosis and Malaria (60 per cent of which goes to HIV/AIDS); $100 million to the WHO '3 by 5 initiative' (a programme to provide three million HIV-positive people with ARVs by 2005, which ultimately missed its target), of which Canada was the first and largest donor; and 67.4 million to the UNPF, including over $58 million to sexual and reproductive health and HIV/AIDS among women and girls. $100 million was earmarked for 'gender based responses to HIV/AIDS' and $15 million for the International Partnership for Microbicides. Canada also supports the Global Polio Eradication Initiative (GPEI), and has been among the top five donors since its formation in 1988, providing a total of $152 million. The Global Alliance for Vaccines and Immunization (GAVI) has received $200 million between 2001and 2005 from the Canadian government.

In many countries the government is not capable of managing the scale-up of AIDS treatment due to lack of health care infrastructure, limited financial resources and human capacity, and evidence suggests that high levels of aid have compromised the quality of local governance. The Global Fund, created to finance 'a drastic turn around in the fight against AIDS, tuberculosis and malaria', has disbursed $8.4 billion in 136 countries since its inception. It is a financing instrument that works through 'country coordinating mechanisms' to ensure 'local ownership' and 'participatory decision-making'. Public and private sector organizations can serve as principal recipients of grants (Global Fund website). Like other PPPs, it has been criticized for its narrow focus on treatment and specific technical interventions, and in some instances for undermining the conditions needed for a sound public health system, and for deflecting attention away from the social determinants of health. Often it is the case that grants from large global funds exceed national health budgets, and the uncoordinated nature of the aid regime creates problems of competition between health personnel working in the beleaguered public system and the aid regime. Governing institutions are challenged by the task of coordinating the complex web of development projects, oftentimes competing, at other times complementary.

While the Canadian government has supported multilateral initiatives to scale up treatment in Africa (to much public fanfare in 2004, changes were introduced to the *Patent Act* and the *Food and Drugs Act* to allow developing countries to obtain more affordable drugs from Canadian generic manufacturers), another arm of its foreign policy has involved the recruitment of health personnel from countries in the global South. Even the WB admits to the desperate shortage of doctors, health care workers and researchers, and the chronic lack of basic health services. The entry of private sector recruitment agencies and the growth of targeted bilateral recruitment schemes have accelerated the pace of specialized labour migration, many from countries at the bottom of the UN scale who show the lowest ratios of per capita health workers and have the most critical health worker shortages. Canada has been a destination country for health professionals who offset the domestic shortage of health workers in Canada. Historically Canada has recruited and received a large number of health workers from the global South, trained at the expense of their governments (Blouin, 2007b).

Supportive donors and effective policies no doubt play a role in improving public health, and this discussion is not meant to paint all Canadian aid with one brushstroke. There is an obvious need for the delivery of health services, including essential medicines. The point is that aid for global health has ambiguous and mixed results, and is palliative to the extent that it fails to address the structural drivers of poor health, and in some cases serves to undermine the governance structures that are needed to improve it. When we turn to Canada's role in pandemic preparedness, national security goals are more explicit, and the disjuncture between human security and national security goals becomes more obvious.

Pandemic preparedness

Canada's recent experience of SARS removed any notion that Canadians were somehow immune to the effects of pandemic disease. When the virus landed in the city of Toronto in 2003, the cracks in Canada's public health system were exposed. The economic impact of SARS in Toronto was tiny compared with that in the Asia Pacific Region, estimated at $40 billion. In Canada, 438 people became infected and 43 died, costing the local economy almost half a billion dollars, and the health care system about CAN$793 million (Osterholm, 2005, p. 28). Given that the Ontario health care system had difficulty coping, it is hard to imagine anything less than a global disaster if a more virulent pathogen was not immediately stopped in its tracks. Global pandemic preparedness has been part and parcel of the merging of security agendas with global health; a potential global pandemic viewed by commentators on both sides of the political spectrum as a potential destabilizing force. Avian influenza has been under the spotlight as the next coming pandemic, and its potential mutation is being closely watched.

Canada's experience of SARS, and its negative impact on the economy, led to the Canadian state's deeper mobilization around pandemic preparedness. On the international front, Canada has contributed $1 million to support the United Nations System Influenza Coordination; over $15 million over 5 years to the WHO, Food and Agriculture Organization (FAO) and the Office International des Épizooties (OIE) (or World Organization for Animal Health) to support collaborative work on avian and human influenza pandemic preparedness; and over $18 million to projects in SE Asia and China to improve surveillance and outbreak investigation, strengthen laboratory systems, and develop capacity for risk communications and public education. It has also contributed, through PAHO, resources to support the development of national influenza pandemic preparedness plans. Canada's overall contribution totalled $105.5 million as of July 2006 (DFAIT, 2008). Canada is also home to the Global Public Health Intelligence Network (GPHIN), an internet-based early warning system that tracks significant public health outbreaks and disseminates information globally, in seven languages. The GPHIN is managed by the Public Health Agency of Canada's Centre for Emergency Preparedness and Response, which was created in 2002 as the country's central coordinating point for public health security. States the website: 'It tracks topics such as disease outbreaks, infectious diseases, contaminated food and water, bio-terrorism and exposure to chemical and radio-nuclear agents, and natural disasters. It also monitors issues related to the safety of products, drugs and medical devices' (Public Health Agency of Canada).

Tracking is of critical importance. But who would be the beneficiaries? Neil Ferguson postulates that a virus similar to the one that caused the 1918 pandemic would likely cause a death toll of 62 million, but only four per cent of those deaths would be in the industrialized world (Ferguson, 2006, pp. 2187–8). At this point, access to vaccines, antiviral and other drugs for the most vulnerable groups does not exist, and biological and social co-factors (malaria, HIV infection, malnutrition and compromised immunity) would render certain people more susceptible to contracting the virus. Living conditions in the burgeoning slum areas, overcrowding, and lack of basic hygiene would also augment viral spread. Even if a global stockpile of antivirals were created, it is not clear today how and under what conditions it would be deployed (WHO Media Centre). And, though new global health regulations oblige countries to report suspicious clusters of novel diseases, a real disincentive to poor country reporting is the devastating socio-economic effects of quarantine that might follow. Little evidence exists to suggest that the first affected countries would be assisted by the international community. The Canadian government has placed far more emphasis on the North American pandemic plan, through the new Security and Prosperity Partnership (SPP) between Mexico, the US and Canada, which is evolving in a less than transparent manner. The website assures us that 'The SPP provides the framework to ensure that North America is the safest and best place to live and do business. It includes ambitious security and prosperity programs to keep our borders closed to terrorism yet open to trade.' The North American approach to pandemic preparedness is to prevent or slow the spread of a strain to North America, sustain infrastructure, and mitigate impact on the North American economy. North America will not be alone in developing a bunker mentality if and when a new pandemic emerges. The new discourses of interdependence and 'mutual vulnerability' that have accompanied threats of SARS and avian influenza have yet to lead to any significant shifts in global health policy. While they have become a more central feature of the foreign policy of nation states, chronic, persistent poor health, malnutrition, access to health's social determinants, and the fragile state of public health systems are not high up on the global public health agenda. And the health impacts of the current governance of the global political economy are not even on the radar screen.

Some concluding thoughts

Canadians may be committed to human security abroad, but are also interested in the maintenance of their own prosperity and standard of living, and their competitive position in the global economy. They are also, in the post 9/11 era, concerned about their personal security and 'threats out there'; the preoccupation with the 'war on terror' nurturing a climate and economy of fear and deflecting attention from the forces that shape human insecurity at home and abroad. A question, then, is to what extent Canada's 'good deeds' are cancelled out by Canada's role in the governance of global trade, investment, environment, and military policy. It is not within the scope of this paper to answer this question, apart from raising a few issues that require further exploration. But my point is that foreign policy in the health arena does not operate separately from other domains of foreign policy, and this is where the analysis becomes more complex.

A common incantation is that nothing can be done about the structural drivers of global health disparities; that the critique remains polemical while lives are being saved though development assistance and access to life-saving medicines, despite the shortcomings of the current regime governing global health. But strategic and well-selected demands on the Canadian government, the G8 and multilateral institutions can be made. If Canada is serious about global health, then it can reverse its policy on asbestos; it continues its opposition to adding asbestos to the Rotterdam Convention, which restricts trade in toxic substances. Canada is one of the world's leading exporters of asbestos, a clear carcinogen that is banned in Canada, with more than 90 per cent of these exports going to the global South. While the European Union and Australia support the addition of asbestos to The Rotterdam Convention, Canada 'continues to lobby hard against such a move, anxious to protect a lucrative niche selling a highly toxic carcinogen to the world's poor' (McQuaig, 2007, p. 233). It can support Kyoto and rethink Tar Sands development; it can play a leadership role in developing global standards and mandatory codes of conduct on occupational health. It can channel its development assistance toward strengthening public health care systems, and increase its aid budget. It can provide genuine assistance to countries that have little or no pandemic preparedness.

That being said, it is also important to illuminate the pathways between the current governance of global health and other policies that impact health and to ask the question: governance for whom? The unquestioned growth trajectory that is destroying ecosystems and economies on which human life depends is increasingly being challenged. Mark Duffield (2005, p. 155) describes the current order as '... a fragile biopolitical equilibrium that enables a small part of the world's population to live through consuming beyond its means while a larger part is allowed to die chasing the mirage of self-reliance.' Development assistance, for the most part, manages, rather than seeks to remove 'this life-chance lottery' (ibid.). When one measures Canada's performance on the global health stage in this context, its reputation as global champion of human security seems ambiguous at best.

But we may eventually reach the point at which we can insulate ourselves no longer.

5
The Relationship between the AIDS Pandemic and State Fragility*

Pieter Fourie

Introduction

On 5 June 1981 the Centre for Disease Control (CDC) in the United States (US) published its *Weekly Morbidity and Mortality Report*, chronicling for the first time the symptoms amongst a few urban gay men of what was set to become the most deadly plague known to humanity. That was over 25 years ago, and the AIDS pandemic has since then killed around 30 million individuals worldwide. More than 40 million people are currently infected globally; of these, 25 million live in Africa south of the Sahara, making this continent the most infected and worst affected region in the world (UNAIDS, 2006c).

According to the global report published by the Joint United Nations Programme on AIDS (UNAIDS) in mid-2006, some data for the proximate Southern African region can be summarized as shown in Table 5.1 (UNAIDS, 2006c, pp. 505–40).

In terms of mortality this translates into more than 3,000 deaths amongst Southern African Development Community (SADC) states' citizens *every single day* – and this number is steadily increasing. To put this in comparative perspective, these numbers mean that SADC experiences the equivalent of a 9/11 attack every day of the year, all year round.

To make matters worse, epidemiologists tell us that the AIDS epidemic (since it results from HIV, a *lentivirus*, meaning that it acts slowly) is a 'long-wave event'. Amongst other implications, this means that we are faced with an insidious phenomenon that might take up to 130 years to play itself out (Barnett, 2006, p. 304). The conventional parameters of such an event and the programmatic responses to such a 'crisis in slow motion' are simply unknown. Long-wave events share a number of distinguishing features (Barnett, 2006, pp. 302–3):

- One is usually unaware of their starting point;
- Once awareness is there, it is difficult to stop and turn the progress and impact of the long-wave crisis/event around;

- People with power (such as politicians) find it difficult to face such crises, since their own terms in office are normally for a much shorter time, and it is difficult to mobilize the appropriate amount of resources to counter the crisis;
- There are few precedents for such events, which means that there is little experience or 'best practice' to fall back on – leading to a sense of fatalism and impotence;
- Such events tend to threaten any realistic impact that any governmental administration might have to oppose them;
- Short-term responses taken in haste may act as band-aid solutions that work counter to more effective, longer-term changes in the long run; and
- A holistic response to such long-wave events requires long-term thinking that challenges the contemporary short-term way of doing things among current epistemic and political elites.

Simply put, humanity has never experienced anything comparable to this, and we simply do not know what the long-term impact of the pandemic will be. How does one respond to such a threat in an effective and appropriately scaled way? One key response has been to polemicize the epidemic; a master narrative has been created to 'securitize' AIDS. By making appeals to *states'* security, and by crafting AIDS as an 'enemy' that needs to be 'battled' and 'defeated' (note the securocratic register or the language of

Table 5.1 HIV/AIDS prevalence levels in Southern Africa

Country	Adults and children living with HIV	HIV prevalence rate (%) in adults aged 15–49	AIDS deaths (adults and children) in 2005	Number of orphans (0–17 years) due to AIDS
Angola	320,000	3.7	30,000	160,000
Botswana	270,000	24.1	18,000	120,000
DRC	1,000,000	3.2	90,000	680,000
Lesotho	270,000	23.2	23,000	97,000
Madagascar	49,000	0.5	2,900	13,000
Malawi	940,000	14.1	78,000	550,000
Mozambique	1,800,000	16.1	140,000	510,000
Namibia	230,000	19.6	17,000	85,000
South Africa	5,500,000	18.8	320,000	1,200,000
Swaziland	220,000	33.4	16,000	63,000
Tanzania	1,400,000	6.5	140,000	1,100,000
Zambia	1,100,000	17.0	98,000	710,000
Zimbabwe	1,700,000	20.1	180,000	1,100,000
Total/Average	14,799,000	15.4	1,152,900	6,388,000

Source: UNAIDS (2006) *Report on the Global AIDS Epidemic* (Geneva: World Health Organization).

war applied here), a number of effects can be achieved. These include the inculcation of a sense of imminent threat, the creation of an identifiable and common villain, and the rapid mobilization of the required state/governmental resources required to respond to that threat, as well as myth-making around who the saviours or victors might be.

Since AIDS first made headlines in the early 1980s this narrative or culture of securitization has come to be associated with the epidemic, and one purpose of this article is to analyse the implications of such securitization. In the context of the 'war against terror' after 11 September 2001 we are becoming increasingly familiar with the super-patriotic proclivities and nationalistic pathologies that securitization can enable, so a closer look at the powerful constructivist role of specific conceptualizations of the pandemic is in order, and timely. One analyst (Garrett, 2005, p. 64) observes that,

> [i]n the aftermath of September 11, 2001, the United States tends to define all national security concerns through the prism of terrorism. That framework is overly limited even for the United States, and an absurdly narrow template to apply to the security of most other countries. The HIV/AIDS pandemic is aggravating a laundry list of underlying tensions in developing, declining, and failed states. As the burden of death due to HIV/AIDS skyrockets around the world over the next five to ten years, the disease may well play a more profound role on the security stage of many nations, and present the wealthy world with a challenge the likes of which it has never experienced. How countries, rich and poor, frame HIV/AIDS within their national security debates today may well determine how well they respond to the massive grief, demographic destruction, and security threats that the pandemic will present tomorrow.

There has, of course, been significant academic interest in the construction of metaphors and myths (including the securitization) of disease and also the AIDS epidemic in recent years.[1] This is happening within the context of a mostly discreet yet exceedingly influential battle between individual state sovereignty and its concomitant epidemic response imperatives on the one hand, and the multilateralization (via the World Bank's Millennium AIDS Program (MAP) and the US President's Emergency Program for AIDS Relief (PEPFAR)) as well as Global Fund initiatives (not to mention UNAIDS) of the pandemic on the other.

The scene is set for great tension between autonomous, state-centred interventions on the one hand, and multilateral initiatives on the other. Discursively, one of the ways in which this tension has been manifesting has been through appeals to either a (hard) securitization agenda, which emphasizes the dangers that AIDS implies for state survival, or an agenda that appeals more directly to a softer, human security approach which underlines the nefarious implications of the epidemic for individual human rights to health. The latter approach has been most closely associated with a developmental agenda.

The polemic

As AIDS only appeared on the public agenda in the 1980s, this context of contestation regarding the securitization of AIDS is a fairly recent phenomenon. The result has been that various AIDS watchers have been making claims and counterclaims regarding the link between the pandemic and its impacts. This discourse is constantly revised – a process that takes place in an increasingly political global and particularly multilateral environment, which is understandable given the high stakes; billions of dollars have been made available to counter AIDS and other chronic diseases. This has given rise to a nascent AIDS industry (in both financial and ideological terms) as the battle for control over who can and should shape global efforts to combat AIDS has taken hold (Garrett, 2007). In the high political discursive environment regarding the purported link between AIDS and state security there have been significant developments:

- in 1990 the US Central Intelligence Agency (CIA) added HIV to its 'state failure watchlist' as a variable that contributes to state collapse (CIA, 1990);
- in 2002 the US National Security Strategy identified failing states as the US's main threat, arguing that failed or failing states provide a fertile breeding ground for terrorism, and also leading to regional spillover effects (Wolff, 2006), dragging more than only the failing states into a condition of anarchy – this conclusion was reiterated by the 2006 US National Security Strategy document (Carment, 2003, p. 407); but at the same time
- in 2005 the US National Intelligence Council (NIC) stated that 'it is not clear if AIDS can be directly tied to state collapse in the way that was feared and anticipated a few years ago' (NIC, 2005, p. 2).

Even in the US homeland security environment there thus appears to be no consensus regarding the link between AIDS and state fragility. This in itself is not problematic, given that Kuhnian scientific revolutions are based on the testing and revision of theses; however, what is problematic is that the discourse is shaped by a surprising lack of attention to conceptual clarity and, importantly, empirical enquiry. As discussed below, the result has been that the debate about the purported link between AIDS and state fragility has been informed by (mostly unsubstantiated) normative and ideological agendas.

The central polemic can thus be summarized as follows: firstly, loose and unsubstantiated statements are made about the covariance of mature AIDS epidemics on the one hand, and state fragility on the other. In other words, there is an assumption that state fragility in itself creates an enabling environment for the vectoring of HIV. Rising prevalence levels in turn are seen to be contributing to state fragility and ultimate state collapse. This first polemic is for the most part untested.

Integrated with this first polemic is an implied polemic which provides the ideological environment for a broader *problematique*: state fragility in itself is seen as contributing to global insecurity (particularly as it is seen to act as a vector for terrorism) (Krasner and Pascual, 2005). In turn it is argued that this global insecurity provides an enabling environment for further instances of state fragility and eventual collapse.

Given the obfuscation and contestation associated with these arguments and the general AIDS–state failure discourse thus far, it is worth exploring what states are, in fact, supposed to do, as well as what is meant by state fragility. Once this has been more firmly established one should be able to speak more confidently to the possible impact of AIDS on state stability.

States and fragility

It is challenging to find a balance between not getting mired in the minutiae or tangentialism of opposing ideological debates about state functions on the one hand, and the imperative to do justice to the essential characteristics of functioning, effective statehood on the other. Political economy can assist by succinctly introducing the core high political intellectual input of three *eminences grises*: according to Adam Smith it is the role of a benign, effective state to facilitate economic growth and the allocation of scarce resources in society by championing the 'invisible hand' of the market; Karl Marx would add that this should be done with a focus on human development: fairly and equitably, with minimal exploitation and social class stratification; Max Weber would say that the creation of effective governance or implementing institutions is essential in all of this, and that the state should ensure order by using its monopoly on the use of violence.

Essentially, then, the core functions of the state are to provide physical security to everyone living in its area of jurisdiction; to build and maintain legitimate political institutions to implement government programmes and sustain the whole; to provide sound and consistent economic management; and to provide mechanisms of social welfare to those who need them (Patrick, 2006, p. 29; Eizenstat et al., 2005, p. 136). In this logic those who argue that AIDS is weakening the state should be able to demonstrate that the pandemic is directly eroding and reversing the state functions as prescribed by Smith, Marx and Weber, as well as the application of those roles as described here.

In the literature on state fragility an important distinction is made between *capacity* and *will* as determinants of state weakness (DFID, 2005, p. 8; Patrick, 2006, p. 30). The key message is that states should manifest both of these aspects when judged as to their robustness. Some states may have the capacity to fulfil all of the functions of statehood, but may lack the will to provide all of them to certain sections of society; conversely, some states may be perfectly willing and even eager to provide these services and functions to their constituents, but may simply be unable to. What is the effect of AIDS on such governance modalities? As pointed out below, the pandemic may lead to stratification in societies and the strengthening of neo-patrimonial linkages between the state and certain sections of society, resulting in effective statehood for some and not for others – the result of will rather than of capacity. The distinction between capacity and will as determinants of state weakness has led to the development of a tacit typology of state resilience. This includes 'good performers', 'weak but willing', 'strong but unresponsive' and 'weak-weak' states (DFID, 2005, p. 8). Again, when addressing the link between the AIDS pandemic and state fragility, one should take into account this differentiation of determinants of state weakness; in a worst-case scenario AIDS would negatively affect both the capacity and the will of states to execute their core functions.

Analysts of state fragility stress a number of qualifications to be borne in mind. For instance, one should not assume that the weakest states are necessarily the poorest; weak states tend to have bouts of political instability in common; state weakness spillovers are not linear, but vary by threat (Patrick, 2006, pp. 31–2). In other words, any analysis of state fragility as an independent variable is contingent; except for the manifestation of political instability, state fragility manifests in exceedingly granular ways. It is thus easier to initially describe fragile states in terms of what they are not: stable or resilient states have effective institutions, the political will and capacity to fulfil the core functions of the state referred to above and to achieve and maintain a greater degree of social cohesion and social equality, and an ability to withstand exogenous and endogenous shocks. Fragile states, on the other hand, are broadly associated with social dissent, lack of border control, predation by the state on their own constituents, flawed institutions, deteriorating infrastructure, endemic corruption, a declining gross domestic product (GDP), food shortages, loss of legitimacy, an increase in infant mortality, a closed economic system and a general informalization of the economy towards localized subsistence rather than commercial surplus production (Patrick, 2006, pp. 45–9; Vallings and Moreno-Torres, 2005, p. 4).[2]

In his recent analysis of state-building, Francis Fukuyama (2004) re-emphasizes the Weberian imperative: the crafting and maintenance of state institutions are seen as central to the state project, and any threat to it is seen as exacerbating and hastening state failure. Here are a few quotations from Fukuyama's book to illustrate:

- 'State-building is the creation of new government institutions and the strengthening of existing ones';

- 'Weak or failed states are the sources of many of the world's most serious problems, from poverty to AIDS to drugs to terrorism';
- 'The essence of stateness is enforcement';
- 'Since the end of the Cold War, weak or failing states have arguably become the single most important problem for international order';
- 'Since September 11 ... they shelter international terrorists who can do significant damage to the United States and other developed countries';
- 'The failed state problem that was seen previously as largely a humanitarian or human rights issue suddenly took on a major security dimension'.

These quotations are significant in that they restate the state fragility–insecurity–terrorism nexus, and of course the link to AIDS is made explicit as well. However, amongst those states about which there is general consensus regarding their fragility or their danger of failing,[3] it is important to note that AIDS does not appear as a common feature. In fact, for the most part AIDS is not an issue in most of these states at all.[4] Given this reality, it is prudent to ask whether the link between AIDS and state fragility in general is not in fact a matter more of ideology than description:

> At bottom, the entire literature on fragile or failed states assumes a particular normative model of the state – a liberal democratic state that is market-friendly, transparent, and accountable, with very specific institutional requirements – without analysing that model at all. It is a given in identifying failure. (Woodward, 2004, p. 6)

Significantly, the metatheoretical or ideological prescriptions resulting from this normative model also form the basis of an evolving multilateral or 'Geneva Consensus' not only for good governance, but also for good AIDS governance (see below). This has exceedingly political implications for the purported links between HIV and democracy, democratic remedies/vaccines against HIV, the inferred links between HIV and fragile states, and (as mentioned above) the evolution of the discourse of securitization regarding both state failure and HIV post-9/11.

Given this context, let us move to interrogate the individual aspects of how HIV has been proffered as a variable that directly causes or exacerbates state fragility. These include discourses on HIV and increased manifestations of violence, HIV and curtailed governance capacity, and HIV and economic atrophy, as well as the covariance of the pandemic and liberal democracy.

AIDS and violence

The central argument regarding the relationship between mature AIDS pandemics and an increase in violence in high-prevalence states pertains to the implications of derivative demographic changes. These analyses emphasize the Weberian tenet that the state should have a monopoly on violence in society, the implied premise being that AIDS would dilute that monopoly, emasculate the state, and vest the ability for violence in different sectors and actors in society.

Figures 5.1, 5.2 and 5.3 and Table 5.2 illustrate the demographic impact that mature AIDS pandemics is having on populations.

These figures demonstrate fundamental features of mature AIDS epidemics, including:

- a spike in the mortality rates amongst younger, economically active population cohorts; this means that more people in their 20s to their 40s die than older people, with women affected more severely, and also earlier, than men (see the first two figures regarding South Africa above) (Statistics South Africa, 2005);
- radically reduced life expectancy at birth (LEB) and life expectancy at reaching adulthood (LEA) (the figure above demonstrating the impact in Swaziland is particularly powerful in this regard) (Whiteside et al., 2006a, p. 10), as well as
- the creation of a drastically altered population pyramid for entire populations – this leads to a demographic 'chimney effect', leaving a vast youth bulge, and the elderly (this is dramatically demonstrated by the last figure, which reflects the projected impact in Botswana by 2020) (Barnett and Prins, 2006, p. 62).[5]

Those who argue that AIDS will lead to more violent societies point to these three key demographic shifts and justifiably question whether social order is sustainable under such an extended catastrophe. It is clear that the pandemic is already changing societies in profound ways. However, the societies noted in these figures do not appear to be collapsing; until now state-level collapse simply has not occurred.

Crime is used as one possible proxy indicator of such collapse, or, rather, as an indication of the state's loss of the Weberian monopoly on violence (Schönteich, 1999). This proxy linked the so-called 'security demographic' of a youth bulge and a generation of AIDS orphans and vulnerable children (OVCs) in particular as a potential threat to social order – a 'Lord of the Flies' scenario has been presupposed, in which it is feared that youths will discount their much-abridged futures and thus will have fewer qualms about engaging in violent criminal behaviour. Again, the actual data that is available does not support this thesis, although one analyst in 2006 reported some evidence that property crime in particular may be linked to an increase in AIDS prevalence in South Africa (Naidoo, 2006).

However, there is no evidence to support a direct link between OVCs and violent crime. This finding should, of course, be qualified by pointing out the reality that (as noted above) in epidemiological terms these are early days yet;

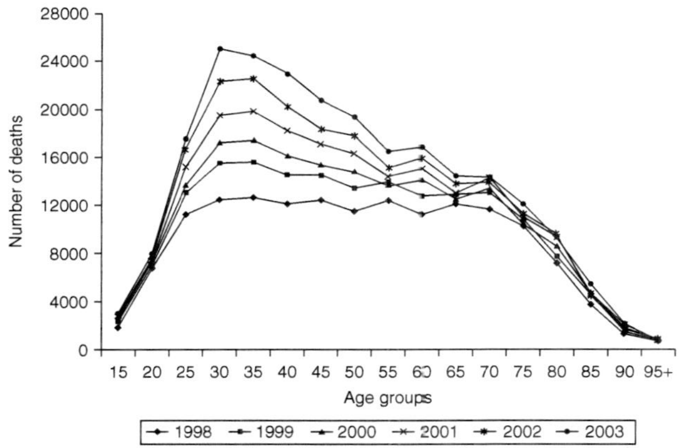

Figure 5.1 Male mortality in South Africa

Source: Statistics South Africa, Mortality and Causes of Death in South Africa, 1997–2003: Findings from Death Notification, P0309.3, 18 February 2005.

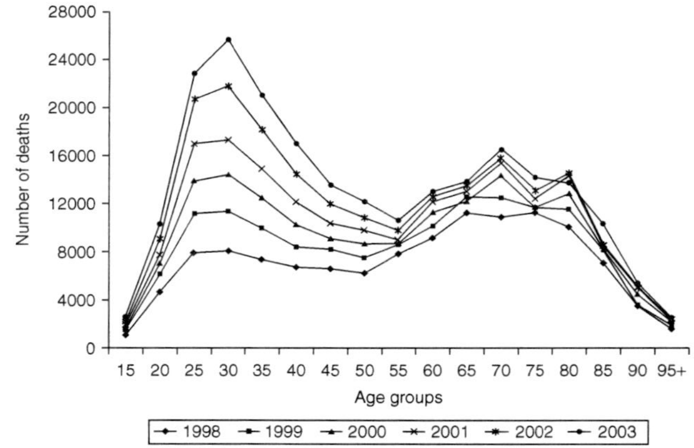

Figure 5.2 Female mortality in South Africa

Source: Statistics South Africa, Mortality and Causes of Death in South Africa, 1997–2003: Findings from Death Notification, P0309.3, 18 February 2005.

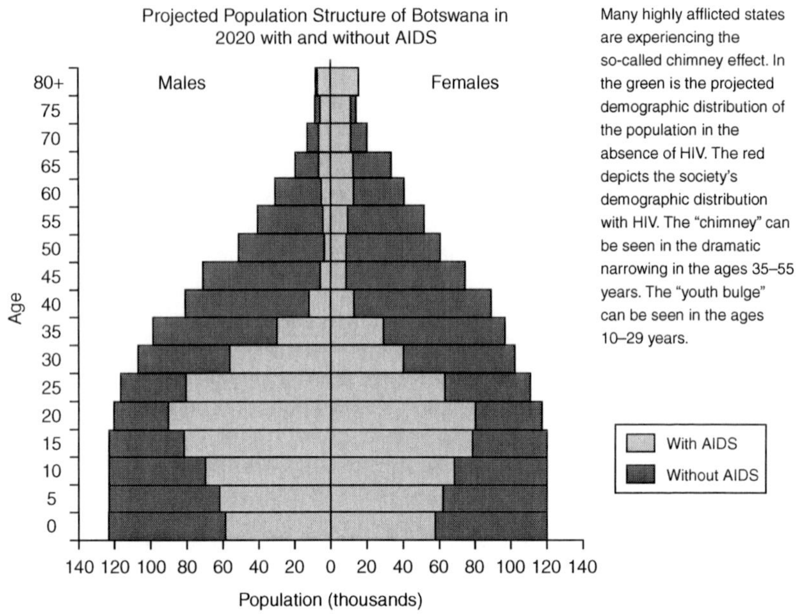

Figure 5.3 The 'Security Demographic'

Source: Tony Barnett and Gwyn Prins (2006) *HIV/AIDS and Security: Fact, Fiction and Evidence* (Geneva: UNAIDS), p. 62.

Table 5.2 Projected life expectancy (in years) in Swaziland

Year	Without AIDS	With AIDS	Difference (%)
2004	64.2	37.5	41.6
2005	64.5	37.4	42.0
2006	64.9	35.3	45.5
2007	65.2	33.7	48.3
2008	65.6	32.5	50.4
2009	65.9	31.7	51.9
2010	66.2	31.3	52.7
2011	66.5	31.2	53.0
2012	66.8	31.4	53.0
2013	67.1	31.6	52.9
2014	67.3	32.0	52.5
2015	67.6	32.5	51.9

Source: Alan Whiteside et al., The Socio-Economic Impact of HIV/AIDS in Swaziland, Report prepared by the National Emergency Response Council on HIV/AIDS (NERCHA), Mbabane, Swaziland, and the Health, Economics and HIV/AIDS Research Division (HEARD), Durban, South Africa (2006), p. 10.

we do not know what the indirect effect can be of increases in criminality due to AIDS-related breakdowns in national criminal justice systems and corruption. In terms of the current manifestation of the supposed impact of AIDS on social criminality and its link to OVCs and the security demographic, however, it seems as though analysts have thus far underestimated OVCs' ability to adapt to or absorb the impact of the pandemic.[6] Clearly AIDS-watchers should revisit notions regarding 'the family' and positive socialization; one should not assume that such socialization only takes place in nuclear families.

The impact of AIDS on uniformed forces in general and armies in particular is also mentioned as a factor that could not only contribute to the vectoring of HIV (particularly during armed conflicts), but also erode the state's monopoly on violence. Thus far these claims were based on anecdotal 'evidence' regarding HIV prevalence in armies of three or four times that found in the general population. The argument was that the epidemic adversely affects the combat-readiness and overall discipline of armed forces, and that soldiers, due to their age, income levels and culture of aggression, act as vectors of the epidemic – particularly during operational duty. In so doing, a discourse was created equating the virus with the uniformed individual, and thus with 'the enemy'.

Most seriously, the inevitable breakdown in the ranks was therefore seen as an eventual threat to the state itself. However, as is the case with OVCs, these grim anecdotes and predictions simply have not materialized; in the Democratic Republic of the Congo (DRC) and Angola (two states in Southern Africa recently emerging from long histories of violent armed conflict) AIDS prevalence rates are amongst the lowest in sub-Saharan Africa.[7] It may be that the disciplined ethos found in most militaries mitigates against the impact of the epidemic; also, armies have built-in redundancy, with lower ranks ready to fill vacancies where AIDS leads to structural attrition; it may be that the public health interventions that are less concerned with individual human rights and focus on excluding infected recruits have had positive consequences (UNAIDS, 2006d; Whiteside et al., 2006b, p. 211). Whatever the case may be, despite the scaremongering, about infected militaries contributing to state collapse, this simply has not happened.

A recent study for UNAIDS (Barnett and Prins, 2006; Berhe et al., 2005) has also clarified and debunked some of the myths associating AIDS with uniformed forces. The main finding is that military groups appear to have HIV prevalence levels no higher than their age cohorts amongst the general population. Again there is a disconcerting lack of data about prevalence levels amongst uniformed personnel everywhere, and therefore '[i]t is premature to generalize about the direction or the dynamic of the relationship between uniformed forces and the spread of HIV' (Barnett and Prins, 2006).

> Suggestions either that AIDS is a threat to 'national security' or that it necessarily leads to political and governance problems are facile and

> self-fulfilling. We can speculate but we just do not have the evidence on this, either way, for countries in sub-Saharan Africa or, for that matter, anywhere else. (Barnett, 2006, p. 313)

AIDS and governance

The available evidence regarding a direct link between AIDS and governance attrition for the most part supports this last conclusion, casting doubt on those who equate the pandemic with 'Weber or Fukuyama in reverse'. That said, the literature on the impact of AIDS on effective governance has produced some conclusions regarding procedural governance practices such as elections (Chirambo, 2006; Strand, 2005). The main conclusion of these studies is that AIDS is a long-term threat to the efficacy of electoral processes, eroding actual electioneering and also curtailing parliamentarians' ability to do their work. For instance, in Kenya 85 per cent of parliamentarians estimate that most of their fundraising engagement is devoted to the medical requirements of constituents (Kimotho, 2005, p. 3). Also, this is taking place in a context where there is an increase in absenteeism amongst members of parliament (MPs). Any conclusion regarding 'Africa' should, of course, be qualified: the continent consists of 53 countries with widely varied AIDS epidemics; generalizations are not useful.

The recent studies mentioned here provide a more nuanced analysis of the impact of AIDS in various mature epidemics, and some conclusions are possible. These include warnings that the impact of AIDS on LEA in particular does have an adverse effect on democratic consolidation: mortality levels amongst registered voters in the 30–49-year age range are increasing dramatically, and decreasing voting ratios may mean that political mandates are weakening (Strand and Matlosa, 2004). The pandemic is thus changing the voting demographics in some countries. This necessitates AIDS-related reforms of electoral processes for the longer term. For instance, the Westminster system of first-past-the-post (FPTP) elections may no longer be appropriate in many countries, given that there is increasing mortality amongst elected representatives, and by-elections are expensive; a proportional (list) system may thus be more appropriate in mature epidemics, as this will bypass the need for by-elections (Strand, 2005, p. 5). However, such an intervention needs to be balanced against the implications for the direct accountability of MPs.

Although no electoral crisis seems to be looming, the Institute for Democracy in South Africa (IDASA) and other studies on AIDS and electoral politics do indicate that the impact of the pandemic is most severe at the local government level: Africans tend to equate democracy with delivery, and thus any breakdown at this coalface of governance could be dangerous in the longer term; by-elections are more inevitable and have become more frequent at the local government level; any lack of formal representation is seen as denying constituents a sense of direct input into the system of governance; it becomes easy to politicize even trivial matters at the local government level; increasingly there are instances where AIDS has been used as a political football during local government elections, for instance to demonize political opponents (Bratton and Sibanyoni, 2006; Caesar-Katsenga and Myburg, 2006). IDASA's Afrobarometer project surveys the opinions of Africans in 18 countries in sub-Saharan Africa, and their findings over the last few years with regards to public perceptions about AIDS and governance are telling.

As delivery is deemed to be more important than abstract aspirations regarding democracy, elections *per se* are not viewed as that important for accountability. However, there does appear to be a gradual erosion of trust in democracy on the whole, and levels of satisfaction with democracy are declining sharply in Nigeria, Malawi, Zambia and Zimbabwe (however, in the latter case this is linked to hunger more than any other factor). Also, HIV lags behind employment, the state of the national economy, crime and security, health services, poverty and hunger as a political priority. As individual levels of poverty increase, people become less likely to cite HIV as an important problem; two-thirds of those interviewed approve of their governments' management of HIV. Also, mainly elites are interested in and mobilising around HIV, and there appears to be little pressure on governments regarding HIV (Bratton and Logan, 2006; Bratton and Cho, 2006; Logan et al., 2006; IDASA, 2004; 2005; 2006).

Importantly, then, state legitimacy in Africa – even in the context of mature AIDS epidemics – does not appear to face serious challenges. However, populations have increasing misgivings about the performance of local governments. This conclusion leads the authors of the Afrobarometer reports to speculate that '[p]erhaps...Africans see HIV/AIDS as a problem for families and communities, and not for governments' (Whiteside et al., 2002, p. 26).

Reviewing the relationship between AIDS and governance, the main conclusion has to be that '[t]he lack of a coherent theory has led some analysts to rely on statistical correlations between measures of state capacity and indications of disease, but, however impressive the statistics, these tell us little about causal relationships' (de Waal, 2003, p. 2).[8] This early into the pandemic there are few certainties: we do know that there is a massive and sustained reduction in LEB and LEA; we also know that existing models for democratization and good governance are premised on different and inappropriate assumptions about LEA. However, by varying the longevity factor, one can speculate as to some likely impacts:

- There is and will continue to be some measurable erosion of parliaments, some public sectors, members of civil society and electoral processes;
- However, there has been little empirical study of these impacts;

- Governments should be particularly concerned by reduced institutional efficacy, particularly at the local government level;
- The curtailed LEA of bureaucrats may lead to a strengthening of neo-patrimonialism;
- There are direct costs associated with the roll-out of health and other social services, and
- This necessitates some policy and programmatic triage.

AIDS and economic atrophy

Those who claim that AIDS is leading to state collapse seek to demonstrate that the pandemic is reversing national GDP growth and development to such an extent that the state becomes incapable of sustaining its population. In such analyses AIDS would nullify the ideological prescriptions of either Adam Smith or Karl Marx. Although it is not the purpose of this article to ridicule the 'dismal science' for its lack of accuracy, it is surprising that econometrics has not, apparently, been able to offer much that is either definite or supportable by quantifiable evidence – at least not at the macro (state) level. Most of the studies regarding the impact of AIDS on states' economies are sectoral and suggest qualitative inferences regarding 'AIDS' versus 'no-AIDS' scenarios. Little modelling is done at the macroeconomic level. I am not suggesting that economics is at fault: again one should note that AIDS has only been with us for 25 years; this is an unprecedented event; the worst is yet to come.

The conclusions that are appearing regarding macroeconomic impact are surprisingly counter-intuitive. Most economists are in agreement that AIDS may be causing a 0.3–1.5 per cent contraction in GDP in the worst-affected economies (Barnett and Whiteside, 2006, p. 305; Quattek, 2000). Given that even the worst epidemics are currently manifesting in developing economies that for the most part are expanding at rates in excess of 5 or even 10 per cent per annum, this impact does not in itself constitute a crisis – at least not in terms of threatening states' capacity to self-perpetuate. In fact, a perverse statistic is developing where AIDS mortality occurring in contexts of high economic growth may actually have the effect of an increased GDP per capita (de Waal, 2003, p. 7).[9] Macroeconomic models focus on the size of economies and tend to neglect changes in the overall long-term structure of economies – not because of a weakness inherent to the discipline; the reality is that economists (like all AIDS analysts) simply do not have any clear understanding of how AIDS is impacting on the systemic variables that drive patterns and events in various societies. Of course, this problem is not unique to the economic modelling of AIDS: there are weaknesses in macro-modelling in general,[10] suggesting that economists do not really understand processes that drive growth. Growth models tend to perform poorly at prediction, and problems with assessing HIV and AIDS provide a specific (albeit important) example of this general problem.

One welcome exception is a recent study which conceptualizes an 'overlapping generations framework' (Bell et al., 2006). The model attempts to measure the impact of AIDS in South Africa across several generations. This is done by quantifying the socio-economic impact of the pandemic, which results from the resultant loss of human capital. The assumption is that every generation teaches the next generation valuable skills in terms of sustaining and developing its production structure. The model logically assumes that, due to contracting LEB and LEA, this generational (memetic)[11] transfer will be eroded to such an extent that there will be concomitant attrition in society as a whole, resulting in an inability to adapt to the realities of AIDS. This will make socio-economic learning increasingly difficult, shorten the socio-generational time horizon, and systemically increase inequalities. The result will be socio-political collapse in South Africa a few generations hence.

The key lessons from attempts at macroeconomic modelling on the impact of the pandemic are twofold:

1. For the moment AIDS does not appear to be significantly contributing to state collapse at the macro level.
2. However, models that measure this impact need to be adjusted – with a much longer time horizon in mind.

Although it falls beyond the ambit of this article, the impact of AIDS at the household economic level is significantly easier to demonstrate – and here the pandemic has devastating consequences that are readily quantifiable. The following quotation suffices for our purposes:

> A man is taken ill. While nursing him, the wife can't weed the maize and cotton fields, mulch and pare the banana trees, dry the coffee or harvest the rice. This means less food crops and less income from cash crops. Trips to town for medical treatment, hospital fees and medicines consume savings. Traditional healers are paid in livestock. The man dies. Farm tools, sometimes cattle, are sold to pay burial expenses. Mourning practices forbid farming for several days. Precious time for farm chores is lost. In the next season, unable to hire casual labour, the family plants a smaller area. Without pesticides, weeds and bugs multiply. Children leave school to weed and harvest. Again yields are lower. With little home-grown food and without cash to buy fish or meat, family nutrition and health suffer. If the mother becomes ill with AIDS, the cycle of asset and labour loss is repeated. Families withdraw into subsistence farming. Overall production of cash crops drops. (quoted in Fourie, 2006, p. 39)

Tragic as this illustration is, there is no indication that the household impact of AIDS provides a threat to the state in terms of 'reversing' Adam Smith, Karl Marx or Max Weber. However, what this dynamic does contribute to is a 'new variant famine' (de Waal and Whiteside, 2003) – and famines are exceedingly frightening to governments, since they can provide a direct threat to socio-political stability. Simply put, the 'new variant famine' thesis states that '[t]he nature of food crises in Africa is changing on account of the co-occurrence of a generalized epidemic of HIV/AIDS and other concurrent shocks such as drought' (de Waal, 2006a). By weakening the productive and regenerative capacity of micro economies (households), AIDS may be creating a 'Swiss cheese' pattern of vulnerability: one household, unaffected by AIDS, lives in abundance (within a larger, national context of food sufficiency), whilst those households in which HIV is present suffer food shortages.

New variant famine thus describes a context in which HIV is not causing famine at the macro level, but it is exacerbating chronic food insecurity for some. The new variant famine thesis is only a few years old and justifies further study, but for the moment it does serve to emphasize the complexity of the impact of AIDS. The latter has severe consequences – but it is supremely significant where one looks, how one measures impact, and which level of analysis is under scrutiny. Generalizations regarding macroeconomics run the danger of ignoring the daily tragedies in individual households. However, on the whole hunger from AIDS is diffuse rather than concentrated, and thus does not pose a threat to governments (de Waal, 2006b, p. 92). Also, as noted elsewhere (Keen, 1994), governments' response to famine also depends on the political and economic power of those starving.

Conclusion

The manifestations of state fragility – broad reversals of economic growth and development, a loss of the state's monopoly on violence and a weakening of government institutions as well as the concomitant implications thereof for responses to the political management of the pandemic – can contribute to the vectoring of HIV as well as exacerbating the negative impacts of AIDS.

However, there is little reliable evidence to suggest that HIV by itself causes state fragility or collapse. 'Rather, like the effect of HIV on the human body, an "AIDS-related national crisis" will consist of a range of pre-existing social and political pathologies, rendered more common and more severe by the underlying vulnerability caused by human resource losses due to AIDS' (de Waal, 2003, p. 3).

Separating AIDS as an independent variable for study from its wider socio-political ecology is like trying to separate a dancer from the dance; this has particularly challenging implications for generating reliable data regarding the impact of this long-wave event. AIDS as a political construct is not in itself an objectively separable, visible, morally salient and tractable issue, which makes it particularly challenging for collective action (de Waal, 2005, p. 3).

However, we do know for certain that AIDS is creating demographic pressures (a youth bulge, decreasing LEB and LEA, and rapid urbanization into underdeveloped cities, as well as new variant famine), which are variables that should be taken very seriously as indices of possible future stresses on the state.

Given these realities, as well as the fact that AIDS is set to be a permanent presence in our lives, the moral imperative remains for states and individuals to maintain a sense of urgency and purpose – as Susan Sontag wrote, 'That even an apocalypse can be made to seem part of the ordinary horizon of expectation constitutes an unparalleled violence that is being done to our sense of reality, to our humanity' (quoted in de Waal, 2006b).

Notes

This article first appeared in the journal *Global Change, Peace & Security* 19(3). It has been amended and is reproduced here with permission.

1. For instance, see the following: Elbe (2006); Altman (2003); Sontag (2002); Altman (1999); Fourie and Schönteich (2001); Heinecken (2001).
2. Of course, these characteristics may not be agreed by all. For example, although a 'closed economic system' is associated with weak or failing states, 'openness' does not equate to economic robustness – see, for example, evidence on a number of poorly performing African states that have very open trade systems, many of which also appear in lists of failing states. For a general discussion on openness and growth, see Oscampo and Taylor (1998).
3. Prominent recent studies to develop more quantifiable methodologies regarding fragile states include the following: World Bank Independent Evaluation Group (2006); Fund for Peace (2006).
4. For a discussion on the relationship between wealth and HIV prevalence, see Gregson et al. (2001). Evidence for Africa suggests a complex relationship between wealth and prevalence; many African countries with relatively high per capita incomes have the highest HIV prevalence levels on the continent (although some with lower incomes also have high HIV prevalence). Interestingly, this complexity is also true at the micro level – see, for example, Bujra (2006).
5. Analysts know very little about the real demographics; there are data available (for example, for the Rakai project in Uganda) which could be analysed to demonstrate actual effects, but for the most part the analysis is not done.
6. This conclusion finds support from studies which show that the impact of orphanhood on education depends greatly on government policy and household wealth. That means that some OVCs are able to continue with their education, depending on what education policy is and how wealthy their households are. This supports the contention that different households will be able to bear the burden of AIDS differently, as well as that a rise in the number of OVCs will not always lead to the social/economic breakdown predicted. See Ainsworth and Filmer (2002).
7. The mentioned lack of empirical evidence regarding the link between AIDS and state fragility also extends to the evidence on HIV prevalence. Witness debates over HIV prevalence in Kenya, South Africa or Zambia, where population-based surveys have found prevalence levels quite different from those of UNAIDS. For example, see Bennell (2003). For this reason, it is likely that the margins of error are high.

8. The impressive statistics are based on historical relationships between prevalence and state capacity. However, full impacts of prevalence have only been felt in a few countries at most (for example, Uganda). In all others, impacts have yet to be fully played out, and so it is inappropriate to extrapolate past correlations of prevalence and state capacity. No African country has yet experienced the full impact of the likely demographic changes and so the current reality provides no basis for modelling these effects. See McPherson (2003).
9. Another study (Young, 2005) recently predicted that GDP per capita will rise in South Africa (that is, higher mortality will bring economic benefits).
10. For a good discussion of the lack of robustness of growth models in general, see Kenny and Williams (2001).
11. Although the Bell, Devarajan and Gersbach study does not refer to 'memes' *per se*, they are instructive constructs that at their simplest conceptual level refer to 'units of cultural inheritance' or replication essential for social evolution – see Dawkins (2006, pp. 191–201).

Part III

From International to Global Health Governance

6

Transnational Norm-Building in Global Health: The Important Role of Non-State Actors in Post-Westphalian Politics

Wolfgang Hein and Lars Kohlmorgen

Introduction

The International Compact on Economic, Social and Cultural (ESC) Human Rights constitutes codified international law, but many of its provisions are still far from being respected. This paper discusses the hypothesis that global civil society strengthens subsidiary norms (as the right to access to essential medicines) and that the successful fight for the implementation of the norm 'universal access to essential medicines' proves the discursive power of civil society organisations (CSOs) in the field of human rights.

We will explain that this role of CSOs in the norm-building process is related to the transformation of international relations dominated by nation states to a global system of politics including a variety of non-state actors and hybrid institutions challenging the dominant role of states. Whereas in the Westphalian system the nation-states and their governments were the main institutions as well as actors in setting and implementing norms (the *norm carriers*), this changed with the greater relevance of the global level of politics and of private actors at least in some policy fields. We will analyse the role of CSOs as norm carriers in the norm-building process for the field of access to medicines and use the Finnemore and Sikkink (1998) approach of the *norm-building cycle* as a starting-point. We suggest that – while international law continues to depend on the acceptance of legal norms by nation states – in post-Westphalian global politics multiple actor constellations are playing a growing role in substantiating the content of primary norms of international law by subsidiary norms, which are to a large degree implemented through non-state actors in an increasingly global society. We argue that ESC human rights constitute a field of international law, in which this interaction is of particular importance, referring to the field of health.

Then, the dynamics of post-Westphalian politics related to norm-building processes are explained and finally the norm-building process in the case of access to essential medicines is analysed in more detail.

Norms and the norm-building cycle

We understand a *norm* – following Martha Finnemore and Kathryn Sikkink (1998, p. 891) – as 'a standard of appropriate behaviour for actors with a given identity'. In contrast, *institutions* describe the way norms and behavioural rules are interrelated, combined and structured in a 'common surrounding' or – referring to a definition by March and Olsen (1989) – 'for specific groups of actors in specific situations' (Finnemore and Sikkink, 1998, p. 891). With *subsidiary norms* we refer to norms that are supplementing primary norms fixed in international law and that are not necessarily legally binding for nation states (or, at least, do not imply serious sanctions if they are not respected), but which might in fact constitute a necessary component for a substantial implementation of international legal norms.

Within a national legal system, these primary and subsidiary norms are mostly defined by law, backed by the state monopoly of legitimate use of force. In international politics, primary norms are agreed upon – in spite of the transformations of the international system – by nation states and therefore need the persuasion of a critical mass of nation states (Finnemore and Sikkink, 1998, p. 895). However, mostly rather general rules are defined, which lack a specification for effective implementation in legal form, as there is no consensus between the many states. With the transformation to a post-Westphalian system, frequently (see below for exceptions) implementation depends on the development of socio-political norms by transnational non-state actors which might increasingly be able to use their discursive power to implement norms. While subsidiary norms are developed as a means to guide the implementation of primary norms, they are much more contested if they 'only' take the form of legally non-binding socio-political norms. Thus, norms of this type often take a long time to reach the 'taken for granted quality' that Finnemore and Sikkink (1998, p. 904) assume for internalized norms in general. They describe these norms as not being controversial. In contrast, we argue that socio-political subsidiary norms are contested and controversial during and even after their implementation, but that they are still an important substitute for legally guaranteed secondary norms.

To better understand the dynamics of the norm-building process and the role of the different involved actors (CSOs in our case) we refer to policy analysis (Anderson, 1975; Hill, 1997; Sabatier, 1999) and to the approach to theorizing norms by Finnemore and Sikkink (1998). They conceptualize a norm 'life cycle', distinguishing 'norm emergence', 'norm cascade' and 'internalisation'. We modify their approach and differentiate – creating a heuristic model – between the following three stages of a *norm-building cycle*:

1. *Norm generation*: Norm entrepreneurs (Finnemore and Sikkink, 1998) – we prefer to call them *norm carriers* – such as CSOs, International Governmental Organizations (IGOs) and governments raise a certain issue and try to disseminate and generalize these in the general public and among decision-makers, aiming to make the underlying ideas and concept hegemonic by making claims and framing the discourse. As the acceptance and implementation of norms depend mainly on governments and nation states, it is most important to convince a critical mass of governments and decision-makers to agree to the norm and to support its dissemination. However, in this phase of agenda setting, civil society actors play a very important role, as it is an open and not formalized process of communication. At this stage, of course, the further diffusion of the norm can fail, if the norm carrier cannot convince a critical mass of the other actors and thus cannot put through and generalize his or her ideas.
2. *Norm diffusion and norm acceptance*: If a critical mass of states – but also of the general public – is convinced, the norm reaches the 'tipping point' and is accepted by more and more governments and other actors – Finnemore and Sikkink (1998, p. 895ff.) call this 'norm cascade'. The norm then diffuses and results in a broad acceptance. Whereas the general public – in both the national and global spheres – is important for a norm to gain recognition, the formal acceptance of norms normally occurs in state formal institutions such as governments and IGOs. Whereas Finnemore and Sikkink (1998, p. 899) include nongovernmental organizations as organizational platforms only in the phase of norm emergence, but see no role for them in the other two phases, we argue that not only states, but various types of global actors, play a crucial role in all phases. We will show this for the case of access to medicines in the following.
3. *Norm implementation*: After the norm is accepted by a majority of actors (including critical actors) it is implemented. We already differentiated between primary and subsidiary norms in the global realm and outlined that the latter can also be implemented by non-state actors, for example, if they run programmes to provide drugs in developing countries. Subsidiary norms are often accepted by almost all actors, including the governments of critical nation states (such as 'fighting poverty' or 'access to medicines'), but not implemented by all actors (in particular nation states); in some cases civil society actors are the main implementing force.

Of course in reality the generation of a norm is never as clear as suggested in this heuristic model. The different phases cannot be separated strictly and sometimes overlap. The question 'When does a norm become a norm?' is often difficult to answer. This also points to the fact that the 'identity of actors' who act according to a specific norm is increasingly determined in a transnational space. 'Access to essential medicines' might be guaranteed by national health systems, but where health systems are not in a position to implement this guarantee implementation depends on transnational networks like CSOs and Public–Private Partnerships, which are able to create islands of norm implementation already in early phases of norm development. Moreover, norms are not static and do not retain their original meaning throughout the norm-building cycle, but are modified – sometimes even significantly – in the conflictive process of norm-building (see, for example, van Kersbergen and Verbeek, 2007, p. 218ff.).

Economic, social and cultural human rights and the right to health

In the Western world in particular, civil and political rights have been treated for a long time as the core of human rights. In effect, the inclusion of ESC Rights in the Universal Declaration of Human Rights and the negotiation of an international covenant on ESC Rights have been largely pushed by developing and socialist countries. Though the World Conference on Human Rights in Vienna (1995) declares that both are 'universal, indivisible and interdependent', there is a fundamental difference between them. While civil and political rights refer to specific rights of citizens (and also foreigners) against the state and their protection against the illegitimate use of force (which is basically independent of the level of economic development), ESC rights refer to the duty of states to deliver specific goods. Frequently, one finds these distinguished as 'negative rights' and 'positive rights' respectively. In the case of ESC rights, a state may simply not dispose of the necessary resources to deliver these goods. Article 2(1) of the International Covenant on Economic, Social and Cultural Rights (ICESCR) recognizes this problem, stating that a state ought to implement these rights 'to the maximum of its available resources' and 'with a view to achieving (them) progressively'. In addition, Article 11 stresses the importance of international cooperation.

This leads to a significant difference with respect to extraterritorial obligations, which basically refer to the conditions under which military force might be used to force compliance. In the case of ESC rights, however, the situation is much more complex as it implies a transfer of resources without the existence of institutions to make binding decisions on the level and character of resource transfers. Furthermore, as has been argued in the human rights discourse (Windfuhr, 2005), it should oblige member states not to take over international obligations which might have adverse effects on the realization of ESC rights.

The ICESCR states that all 'States Parties recognize the right of everyone to the enjoyment of the highest attainable standard of physical and mental health' (Art. 12.1), which includes 'The prevention, treatment and control of epidemic, endemic, occupational and other diseases' as well as 'the creation of conditions which would assure to all medical service and medical attention in the event of sickness' (Art. 12.2) (http://www1.umn.edu/humanrts/instree/b2esc.htm). These documents, however, are rather inconclusive with respect to the 'standard of health' which is supposed to be 'attainable'. The Committee on Economic, Social and Cultural Rights (CESCR), which was established to carry out the monitoring functions assigned to ECOSOC in the Covenant, also publishes interpretations of its provisions in the form of General Comments.

In 2000, the ICESCR adopted a 20-page document on 'The right to the highest attainable standard of health',[1] confirming that state parties have an obligation '... to provide essential drugs, as from time to time defined under the WHO Action Programme on Essential Drugs' and 'to ensure equitable distribution of all health facilities, goods and services'. As drugs for an anti-retroviral therapy are on the WHO Essential Drugs List, states are formally obliged to provide this therapy to HIV/AIDS patients, but many sub-Saharan African states (with per capita public annual health expenditures of between US$20 and 80)[2] are certainly not in a position to fulfil such an obligation. States, however, also have the obligation to assist other states in fully realizing the right to health.

Moreover, the 'Right to Health' is codified in slightly different formulations in a number of other international agreements.[3] As such, it constitutes binding international law, but it is widely seen as a typical example of 'soft law', which corresponds to principles of basic human rights but is certainly also far from being an obligation enforceable by any institutionalized processes.

Transformation from a Westphalian international system to a post-Westphalian global system

We have argued that some weaker and poorer states, in sub-Saharan Africa in particular, are not able to fulfil the obligations deriving from international ESC human rights law. Additionally, due to internal power relations and the interests of national elites, some of these states are not even willing to direct available resources to fight infectious diseases and to guarantee a right to health for their citizens. Furthermore, with the transformations of the international political system we can observe a shift of political authority away from nation states. Capacities to regulate and conduct policies are transferred upwards and downwards from the nation state to international actors on the one hand (internationalization) and local actors on the other hand (regionalization, localization), as well as sidewards from state actors in general to a wide range of non-state actors (privatization, transnationalization) (Rosenau, 1997; Jessop, 2004). The following figure gives a schematic representation of this spatial shift of authority and of the transformation of a *Westphalian*[4] *international system of politics* to a *post-Westphalian global system of politics*.[5]

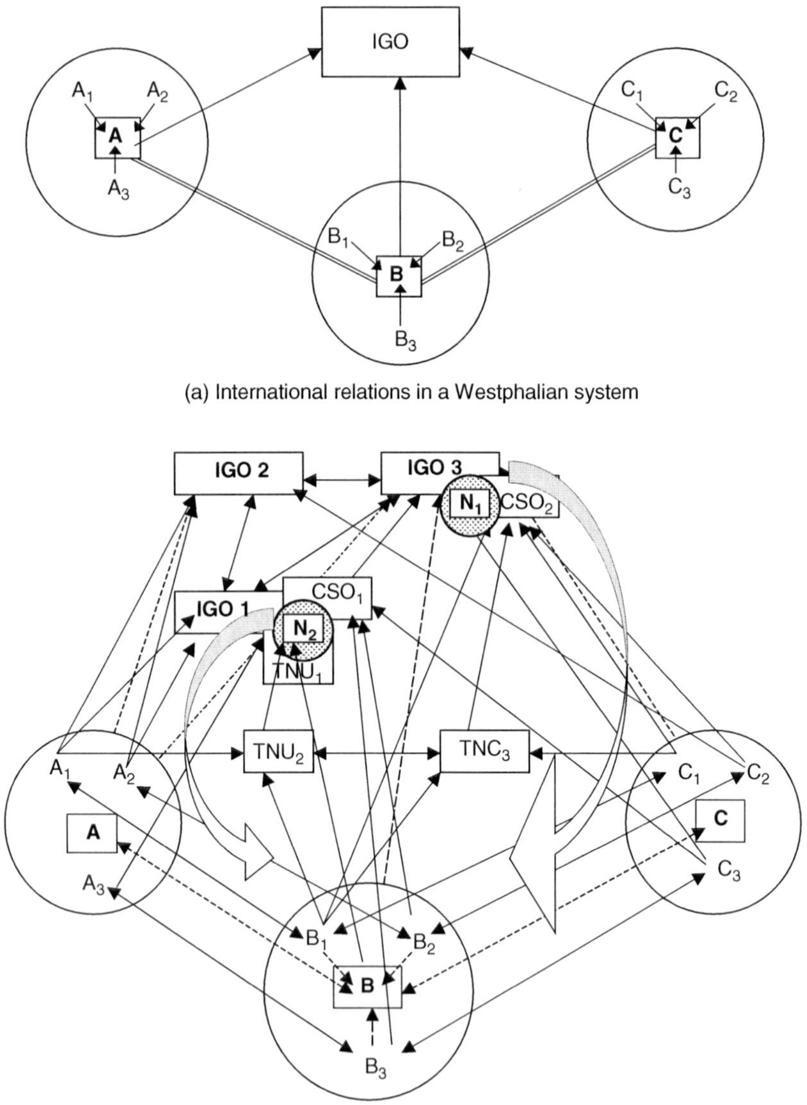

(a) International relations in a Westphalian system

(b) Global politics in a post-Westphalian system

Figure 6.1 Transformation of international relations into a system of global politics

The traditional system of international relations was based on *an aggregation of interests at the national level* (see Figure 6.1: A1, A2 and A3 represent the various interest groups – business, unions, CSO – in nation A, and so on). Thus, negotiations at the international level were led by governments on the basis of these nationally aggregated positions, which, in the first instance, reflected power relations within nation states. The outcome of these negotiations was a result of power relations between nation states, partially mediated by decision-making procedures within International Governmental Organizations (IGOs). Meanwhile, globalization, the liberalization of markets, and the increasing need to deal with transnational and global problems created opportunities for the direct interaction of non-state actors, thus establishing new transnational spaces of interests and power that prevent a full aggregation of interests on the national level but produce dynamics and opportunities through a transnational cooperation of non-state actors, which increasingly limit the political options of nation states.

We have arrived at quite a complex structure of interaction and relations between the different actors. Whereas in the ideal Westphalian system there are basically the two alternatives of cooperation in an IGO or a bilateral cooperation between states, in the post-Westphalian structure there are many possibilities for cooperation and conflicts among nation states, IGOs, CSOs, and transnational corporations. The 'old' actors of the Westphalian systems are included, but their roles are transformed by challenging their political monopoly through the emergence of new, genuinely transnational actors. New nodes appear in the transnational political space (N_1; N; see Hein et al., 2009, for the concept of nodal governance), which coordinate power resources and compete for shaping global governance processes. These nodes, which might be CSO networks linked to IGOs but also specific coordinating bodies within IGOs integrating other transnational actors, interfere with the aggregation of interests at the level of the nation state. As the nation state was the main institution for norm-setting in the Westphalian System, we can now observe new modes, spatial levels and institutions that are additionally important for norm-setting.

International law: mechanisms of norm-building and compliance when a unified state authority is missing

Compliance with respect to the adaptation of internal politics and national law to international rules

In a system of global politics the high density of transnational social relations and of systems of international law and transnational rules in many different policy fields have created a very high complexity of relations beyond the nation state: powerful non-state actors (in particular, transnational corporations) challenge the hegemonic position of powerful nation states and norms set in one policy field challenge norms in other fields (such as regarding the WTO and human rights).

These developments are closely linked to the question of extraterritorial obligations of international human rights laws. In a Westphalian system of sovereign states it might have been a moral issue (or an issue of 'national interest'), but there was a lack of power to support these obligations in an *international* human rights system, while at the same time contravening interests prevented compliance with human rights norms in national political systems. With the increasing power of a global civil society and a growing interest in solving problems which historically were treated as internal matters of foreign countries, the issue has changed its character: to accept extraterritorial obligations might become a matter of legitimacy in a global society.

International Organizations and non-state actors in the development of transnational norms

WHO is the formally legitimized UN organisation in the norm-building process in international health. The WHO sets internationally accepted norms and standards and gives technical guidance and advice to member countries in promoting health. But it is not only involved in building subsidiary norms; the WHO offers an institutional basis on which to propose and negotiate rules, conventions, and thus forms of international law (for example, the WHO Framework Convention on Tobacco Control, International Health Regulations). Thus, the WHO is (or should be) at the centre of the norm-building process in global health governance.

Although these described functions generally have not changed in the transformation of the international system, WHO plays a different role as a norm carrier. In the Westphalian System, WHO was both the 'organisational platform' (Finnemore and Sikkink, 1998) for nation states as norm carriers and an important norm carrier as actor itself. However, in spite of some relevance at the international level, the nation state constituted the main area of politics. In the post-Westphalian System, IGOs such as the WHO are supposed to become more important due to the increased international and transnational interconnectedness. At the same time, nation states (and IGOs) have to compete with CSOs and other non-state actors in the process of generating and disseminating claims and norms. Also within the WHO, non-state actors have – informally – more influence: first, as the WHO is influenced by the activities and discourses of global health governance and thus internalizes trends and claims form 'outside'; and second, as the WHO has opened itself at least to some extent for more participation of non-state actors, for example, of CSOs but also of private for-profit actors or by attending and creating global public–private partnerships (Bartsch and Kohlmorgen, 2007). As actor in the more important global realm of health politics, the WHO has to face competition in establishing norms by non-state actors, and at the same time is criticized very often for being ineffective or for being not forceful enough in striving for human rights by CSOs.

The case of health: from 'health for all' to 'access to medicines'

In the following, we analyse how the broad universal norm 'health for all' has been concretized – under the influence, besides other factors, of CSOs – to the norm 'access.to medicines'. The WHO constitution declares that 'the enjoyment of the highest attainable standard of health is one of the fundamental rights of every human being'. 'Health for All' is not only the aim of WHO as an organization but is also established as the central objective of international and national health activities by the nation states throughout the world. The International Conference on Primary Health Care in Alma Ata in 1978 proposed, and the World Health Assembly in 1979 endorsed, Primary Health Care as a strategy to achieve the objective of 'Health for All by the Year 2000', not just by giving the poor a minimum of health services (in a more liberal sense), but by providing health services for all as the foundation of a comprehensive health system (in a more universalistic sense). During the 1980s the concept of Selective Primary Health Care became dominant in discourses and in health activities. This strategy focused on specific diseases in developing countries and on the lack of immunization and defined so-called attainable goals. Some donors, international organizations and scholars favoured this concept, and its influence reaches to the current focus on fighting specific (mainly infectious) diseases.

As we know, by 2000 the objective of 'Health for All' was not attained, and the likelihood of attaining it in the near future remains rather slim. Nevertheless, in 1998, WHO (to be precise, the World Health Assembly) renewed this objective under the label of 'Health for All in the 21st century'. This statement also proclaims that the availability of essentials of Primary Health Care should be ensured. We can state that 'Health for all' has been established as a norm since the 1980s, even if it is contested and not implemented in all countries (Cueto, 2004; Thomas and Weber, 2004, p. 192 *et seq.*; Kohlmorgen, 2007).

Norm generation and diffusion: campaign for access to essential medicines

Since the 1990s, 'Health for all' has been in a sense substantiated by focusing on the fight against poverty-related diseases, other specific fields (for example vaccination campaigns) and the claim 'access to medicines'. Initially, the discussion focused on neglected diseases, but then the process gained momentum around access to antiretrovirals (ARVs) in the fight against HIV/AIDS. The new focus on infectious diseases and access to medicines is a differentiation of the general norm 'health for all'. While 'health for all' seems to be an overambitious target, 'universal access to essential medicines' appears as much more manageable and realistic – in particular, since it is widely known that the generic production of medicines can be comparatively cheap. Thus, it seems obvious that the denial of access to life-saving medicine constitutes a global scandal. Picking up this scandal for campaigns together with a rapidly growing global civil society with corresponding means of communication developed a high level of discursive power of CSOs. Since the late 1990s, a large network of CSOs, led by Médecins Sans Frontières (MSF)[6] and Health Action International, have been advocating and campaigning for access of poor AIDS victims to ARVs in the 'Campaign for Access to Essential Medicines' (Sell, 2002; Schultz and Walker, 2005). The campaign for low-cost medicine was carried out not only at the global level – by means of activities and lobbying within the WTO and other IGOs – but also in particular countries.[7]

The high prominence of the fight against infectious diseases, however, can only be partly explained by the influence of CSOs and perspectives on poverty reduction that became relevant in the 1990s. Its significance was also a result of the perception that ill health in developing countries and the global spread of infectious diseases like HIV/AIDS, SARS, or tuberculosis could pose a dual threat to global security: one that results from the global spread of these diseases, and one that is linked to political and economic instability resulting from ill health, poverty, and underdevelopment and that has an indirect effect on national and international security (Peterson, 2002; Fidler, 2004). In July 2000, the UN Security Council convened its first-ever session on health and acknowledged 'that the HIV/AIDS pandemic, if unchecked, may pose a risk to stability and security' (SC Resolution 1308, p. 2). The report of the UN 'High Level Panel on Threats, Challenges and Change' stresses that 'any event or process that leads to large-scale death or lessening of life chances and undermines States as the basic unit of the international system is a threat to international security', listing infectious diseases and other social threats like poverty as one of six clusters of threats (UN, 2004, p. 23).

Thus, we argue, the social and human rights interests of CSOs coincide with the self-interests of industrialized countries, such as containing the risks of a global spread of infectious diseases and of political instability. This political constellation of interests provided an environment that made it possible to run an at least partially successful campaign for access to medicines (Hein and Kohlmorgen, 2008). The claim 'access to essential medicines' was first and foremost raised and postulated by CSOs, so we can identify them as main norm carriers in the norm-building phase of *norm generation*. Besides CSOs also some Southern governments, particularly the Brazilian government, argued for increased treatment, for a strengthened involvement of treatment in the HIV/AIDS programmes of international governmental organizations (such as WHO and UNAIDS) and for greater commitments of G8 to enhance access to medicines.

At this stage of the norm-building process, in particular the TRIPS agreement within the World Trade Organization (WTO) became the centre of the CSO campaigns. CSOs argued that intellectual property rights were not only a trade but also a public health issue and thus managed to link these two aspects.

Thus, after the claim 'access to medicines' was established in the global health and development discourses, and many hesitant actors (such as some G8 countries and IGOs) were convinced and/or morally compelled not to reject these demands, the *diffusion of the norm* proceeded and led finally to a broad *acceptance* at least on the level of agreements, statements, commitments, and programmes. The Doha Declaration (which supplemented the TRIPS agreement) and the agreement on §6 of that Declaration on 30 August 2003 can be interpreted as a result of the activities of the main norm carriers, the CSOs, in cooperation with some governments of developing countries. CSOs not only lobbied representatives of IGOs and Northern governments, but also became increasingly important as advisors to developing country members of WTO and helped them coordinate their positions in the subsequent renegotiations of the TRIPS agreement (UNDP, 2002, p. 104ff.). Hence, during this process, CSOs were changing their character from basically mobilizing and advocatory actors towards cooperating experts and actors with a negotiating role in the global political process.

The influence of CSOs is also apparent in the initiative for a 'Global Framework on Essential Health Research' at WHO, which links up the question of prices of medicines with the problem of investments in research and development (R&D) and the organization of incentives for research (which patents are expected to provide). This initiative was influenced and kicked off by a proposal for a 'Medical Research and Development Treaty' made by the US-NGO Cp-Tech and supported by many CSOs in 2005. It was brought into the Executive Board in January 2006 by Kenya and Brazil and thereafter debated in the World Health Assembly in May 2006, which then decided to establish the Intergovernmental Working Group on Public Health, Innovation and Intellectual Property (IGWG), which worked until May 2008 and made some recommendations for an improvement of health research for neglected diseases and for the conflict between intellectual property rights (IPRs) and public health. These recommendations (concerning, for example, prices, patent pools and a research and development treaty) remain vague but will be further discussed within the WHO until the World Health Assembly in May 2009. Although it seems quite improbable that we can expect quick concrete measures and that this will result in the incorporation of the 'right of universal access to essential medicines' as an effective norm into international law, this initiative shows that the norm 'universal access to essential medicines' is widely accepted globally.

Norm implementation: many commitments but slow progress

Taking into account the complexity of international rules and global social and economic inequality impinging on the problem of access to medicines, it is obvious that this norm cannot be implemented as a simple legal norm (for example, based on the General Comment of the CESCR quoted above). As shown in Table 6.1 (see next section), compliance with this norm is based on its acceptance and creative adaptation by multiple actors in the post-Westphalian global polity, which has led to a considerable fall in prices of ARVs, making it basically affordable to the international community to pursue a strategy of universal access to treatment for HIV-infected people. Since the late 1990s the prices for AIDS treatments in developing countries fell from well over US$10,000 to about US$140 (for generics, per person and year, in some countries) in 2005 (MSF, 2005, p. 10). The main reason for this decline in prices was the competition by generic producers. But also the CSO campaigns – which, aside from TRIPS-focused activities, include campaigns against transnational pharmaceutical corporations (TNPCs) with the objective of reaching low prices – and the increased global consciousness concerning the need for AIDS treatment have led to a price reduction. However, even though it is to some extent an accepted global norm, its *implementation* lacks progress. Still most poor countries are dependent on financial transfers to pay for medicines and treatment institutions.

Indeed, the G8 countries, and Kofi Annan and the UN, supported the establishment of the Global Fund to Fight HIV/AIDS, Tuberculosis and Malaria in 2001. The Global Fund is a new form of hybrid regulation typical of current structures of global health governance (Bartsch, 2007). It can be characterized as a multilateral funding mechanism that works like a global public–private partnership (GPPP). It has a new and – compared with IGOs – unconventional governance structure as it includes nation states (eight from the North, seven from the South), CSOs (three), foundations (one) and companies (one) as voting members in its Executive Board. Recipient countries have to create a Country Coordinating Mechanism with the participation of all stakeholders (including civil society and private sector) to apply for funds to conduct programmes. The Global Fund has attracted pledges of US$9.7 billion until 2008 and has received US$6.7 billion to support programmes in 132 countries thus far (June 2007).[8] Although 95.5 per cent of the money donated is provided by governments (almost exclusively from OECD countries), the Global Fund can be interpreted as a governance mechanism that gives non-state actors a greater influence in the implementation of the global norm 'access to medicines'.

Furthermore, the role of private foundations shows that non-state actors have an important function for the implementation of the norm. In particular, the Bill and Melinda Gates Foundation is a very influential actor. After Warren Buffet's gift of more than US$30 billion and with annual spending grants for global health initiatives and programmes of approximately US$900,000 million[9] it is one of the greatest funders of global health promotion and the fight against infectious diseases. Also the activities and negotiations of the Clinton Foundation play an important role in the diffusion and implementation of the 'access to medicines' norm. For example, it initiated negotiations – with participation of the World Bank, UNICEF and the Global Fund – with Indian generic producers to reduce the prices of ARVs for developing countries.

Besides the Global Fund, state (or IGO)-run programmes such as the Multi-Country HIV/AIDS Program (MAP) and the President's Emergency Plan for AIDS Relief (PEPFAR)[10] contribute to an expansion of treatment in the field of HIV/AIDS. Although there are significant improvements – the number of people receiving antiretrovirals increased from 300,000 in 2002 to 2 million in 2006 (WHO/UNAIDS/UNICEF, 2007: 5) – it is obvious that there are great challenges for the international community. In 2006, 7.1 million people still were in need of ARV treatment (WHO/UNAIDS/UNICEF, 2007: 5). To some extent the commitments of the powerful Northern governments seem to be lip service only. For example, there are manifold conflicts between developing countries and industrialized countries, as the governments of industrialized countries are still not ready to lower the protection of intellectual property rights. There are a number of issues which need further analysis before the question whether 'universal access to essential medicines' can be considered to constitute a firm norm in global politics:

- The pharmaceutical industry successively accepted the need to improve access of the poor to medicines and, in effect, provided some mechanisms to support this goal (differential pricing, participation in global public–private partnerships to ease access). Nevertheless, they pursued their agenda of trying to secure strong international IPRs, now shifting the forum of their activities towards bilateral and multilateral trade agreements. Taking into account the possibility of a limited impact of the newly introduced patent right in India with the possible use of compulsory licenses for producing second-line ARVs and, for example, Tamiflu, the main drug against the virus-borne influenza , TNPCs did everything to include clauses which forced the trade partners to exclude the possibility of using flexibilities included in TRIPS, therefore called TRIPS+ clauses. If 'universal access' had been established as a true global norm, one would assume that these clauses in bilateral trade agreements could not become effective without mobilizing large resistance. This is an important question to pursue.
- *Universal access to essential medicines* has developed as a norm due to the conflicts around access to ARVs. Of course, there are many other essential medicines and the norm must be applicable to all of them. The question of the so-called neglected diseases has been the focus of the second great debate in this field; it refers to another aspect of the global medical R&D system that creates incentives only for research on medicines which promise to have a large monetary demand.[11] Another field similar to the situation of ARVs is developing with the increasing importance of the so-called 'diseases of the rich' in poor and middle-income countries: heart

diseases, cancer, and so on, where patent-protected medicines also play a significant role. More recent conflicts in the access field have to be scrutinized in order to exclude the possibility that access to ARVs only constitutes a special case due to the strong international attention paid to HIV/AIDS. In fact, recent conflicts on compulsory licences suggest that the issue will in fact increasingly spread to others. One of the two compulsory licences Thailand issued in early 2007 concerns Clopidogrel, a medicine against heart diseases.[12]

- Still, the problem of financing R&D of medicines cannot be solved by simply providing (or assuring) flexibilities in the use of intellectual property rights. The issue of the neglected diseases points to the fact that differential pricing (to provide cheaper medicines to poor countries) cannot be a successful way to 'save' the property rights system. In addition there also is a growing access problem in industrialized countries due to the scientific and technical potential to develop ever newer medicines and forms of medical treatment which put health systems in rich countries under pressure as well. It remains to be seen whether the discussion on R&D for neglected diseases, patents and innovation within the WHO will show some results and further the incorporation of the 'right of universal access to essential medicines' as an effective subsidiary norm into international law.

Conclusion: the important role of non-state actors in the development of subsidiary ESC norms

In this paper, we have described the transformation of a Westphalian system of international politics to post-Westphalian global politics, which implies a shift of authority from the national to the international and transnational levels of governance and politics. In addition to the 'old' actors – the nation states and IGOs, which retain power – civil society and private-for-profit actors are important players in the global realm. This creates a complex governance structure with manifold interactions and relations between different actors and institutions spanning different levels of action. Thus, whereas in the Westphalian system the nation states and their governments were the main norm carriers setting and implementing norms, this has changed at least in some policy fields. Notwithstanding the greater relevance of IGOs, we can identify a lack of governance at the global level. There is no global state, and IGOs are far from developing global statehood. Social policy-oriented IGOs are sometimes overstrained as they do not have enough resources and formal power to conduct sustainable social and health policies. At the same time, nation states keep their formal power and cannot be forced by existing law to guarantee social rights and implement norm health for all. Thus, there is a kind of vacuum in the global realm, which is filled partially by civil society organizations and foundations. They take over functions to establish and also implement norms (transnational subsidiary norms) and therefore are important norm carriers in the current system of global governance.

In global health, the norm 'health for all' has been widely accepted since the establishment of the WHO in 1948. However, its implementation lacks progress and many countries do not have the ability to guarantee even a minimum of health care. Since the mid- 1990s, the global health community has focused more and more on specific facets of this general norm, such as neglected diseases, infectious diseases and the issue of access to medicines. The claim 'access to essential medicines' was raised by CSOs, which started a successful campaign focusing on affordable prices and IPR and trade policy inside the WTO and TRIPS against the background of the HIV/AIDS pandemic. Thus, CSOs are the main norm carriers in the phase of *norm generation*. They framed this conflict by addressing the scandal of the disaccord between high prices of drugs and the suffering and dying of millions of AIDS victims. Furthermore, this campaign fell on fertile ground as the governments of industrialized countries were more and more anxious about the transborder spread of infectious diseases and the consequences for international security.

The norm 'access to essential medicines' has been diffused through many organizations and institutions and has been widely accepted in the course of time. There is both formal (or at least implicit) *acceptance* of the norm in state institutions (for example, WHO, World Bank, WTO), programmes (UNAIDS) and agreements (TRIPS) and also acceptance amongst non-state actors such as foundations and other civil society organizations. These non-state actors play an important role in the *implementation* of the access norm. Although state actors (G8 countries, US government (PEPFAR), some Southern countries) increased their efforts and spending to fight HIV/AIDS, foundations such as the Gates Foundation and the Clinton Foundation and many bigger and smaller CSOs are involved in the endeavours to provide access to medicines in poor countries.

Non-state actors are crucial at all stages in the process of building subsidiary norms. However, finally we have to ask whether we can generalize this case to other fields of social policy. Certainly, the case of HIV has a specific character, as the disaccord between the availability of drugs and the suffering of millions of AIDS victims is so obvious. However, this could be also said for the fight against hunger, as globally there are enough resources to end all starvation. We have to ask why scandalizing other dimensions of poverty like the lack of access to clean water and sanitation, chronic hunger and starvation, and so on, does not lead to such a great global awareness as in the case of access to medicines. One reason may be that the fight against one single disease such as HIV/AIDS and/or the focus on the medicines issue is much more concrete and tangible than fighting against poverty in general or against hunger in all poor countries. However, these are just preliminary

Table 6.1 Access to medicines: norm-building process and main norm carriers

Main type of norm carrier/stage of norm-building	Civil society	Private for profit	Hybrid	State
Norm generation	• Campaign for Access to essential medicines • Public debate			• Brazilian government conducts HIV and AIDS programme and argues for increased access
Norm diffusion and norm acceptance	• Campaign for access to essential medicines • Public debate		• Conflicts on TRIPS and IPRs: e.g. USA vs. Brazil inside WTO; debates within WTO, WIPO and WHO • WTO: TRIPS and Doha Declaration • WHO: IGWG	• Governments of Southern countries arguing for increased access • WHO, UNAIDS, World Bank and UNICEF arguing for increased access • Conflicts on TRIPS and IPRs; debates within WTO, WIPO and WHO WTO: TRIPS and Doha Declaration WHO: IGWG
Norm implementation	• Codices and guidelines for CSOs Distribution programmes • Continued attention and pressure of CSOs for norm implementation	• Codices and guidelines for companies • Accelerating access initiative • Donation programmes • Activities of Gates Foundation	• Global Fund to Fight HIV and AIDS, TB and Malaria GPPPs (R&D, funding) • 3 by 5 (initiated by WHO) Codices and guidelines for nation states, companies and CSOs • Clinton Foundation negotiates lower prices for ARVs	• Southern governments • Northern governments (funding and treatment programmes, bilateral ODA) • PEPFAR • Commitments of G8 • Activities of IGOs

Source: Compilation by the authors.

explanations. A comparative study of civil society activities and the constellations of interests in different fields of global social policy could be helpful to answer the question of different conditions and outcomes of ESCR norm-building. For the case of health, we can conclude that the densification of global social relations and the strengthening of global civil society, linked to a situation where instability in poor regions is perceived as an increasing threat to the security of 'the rich', have led to the establishment of a norm of helping the poor. This norm is still contested in its implementation, but it is widely accepted and cannot be denied.

Notes

1. This document is part of a series of comments by the CESCR called 'Substantive issues arising in the implementation of the International Covenant on Economic, Social and Cultural Rights' adopted since 1989, here 'General Comment No. 14' (document E/C.12/2000/4) (http://www.unhchr.ch/tbs/doc.nsf/(symbol)/E.C.12.2000.4.En).
2. See, for instance, the WHO website at http://www.who.int/countries/en.
3. In addition to the International Covenant on Economic, Social and Cultural Rights, see the Convention on the Elimination of All Forms of Discrimination against Women (Articles 10, 12 and 14), the Convention on the Elimination of All Forms of Racial Discrimination (Art. 5) and the Convention on the Rights of the Child (Art. 24). In addition, Art. 35 of the Charter of Fundamental Rights of the European Union refers to the rights established by 'national laws and practices'. Furthermore, we find commitments by governments to improve human health in a number of declarations and Programmes of Action (Agenda 21, chapter 6, §§ 1 and 12, Cairo Programme of Action, Principle 8 and § 8.6; Copenhagen Declaration, Commitment 6; Beijing Declaration, §§ 17 and 30, Habitat Agenda §§ 36 and 128) and, of course, in the Millennium Declaration.
4. This refers to the role of the Westphalian Peace in 1648 in the development of a system of international relations between sovereign nation states.
5. David Fidler (2004; 2005) has thoroughly analysed 'Post-Westphalian Public Health' with respect to the global reaction to SARS and the revision of the International Health Regulations (IHR), he concludes that the new IHR constitute a shift towards 'an expanded governance strategy that integrates multiple threats, actors and objectives in a flexible, forward-looking and universal manner' (Fidler, 2005, p. 68).
6. MSF invested the money they received for winning the Nobel Price in 1999 for greater parts in this campaign.
7. Prominent examples are the conflicts concerning patents and drug prices in South Africa and Brazil (von Soest and Weinel, 2007; Calcagnotto, 2007; see also Hein, 2007).
8. Fifty-six per cent of these funds are provided for HIV/AIDS measures like prevention and treatment.
9. See http://www.gatesfoundation.org/nr/public/media/annualreports/annualreport06/R2006GrantsPaid.html.
10. The bilateral programme PEPFAR will provide US$15 billion to fight HIV/AIDS until 2009 (US$9 billion for new bilateral programmes in 14 African and Caribbean countries, US$5 billion for existing programmes in 75 countries

and US$1 billion for the Global Fund). In 2008 it was announced that another US$50 billion will be provided until 2013.

11. For a concise report on the links between intellectual property rights and access to medicines see the final report of the WHO Commission on Intellectual Property Rights, Innovation and Public Health (CIPIH and WHO, 2006).
12. See various entries of the e-mail list ip-health; for example http://lists.essential.org/pipermail/ip-health/2007-January/010471.html.

7

Global Public Health and Innovation in Governance: The Emergence of Public–Private Partnerships

*Carmen Huckel Schneider**

Introduction

The global health landscape is changing, not only in terms of the ways in which globalization affects the spread of diseases (and vice versa) but also in terms of how global health is being governed. The roles of, and relationships between, global organizations (such as the World Health Organization (WHO) and the World Bank), states in the South and the North, and other key actors (for example, NGOs and businesses) are being reconstructed. One key feature of the global health landscape today is the apparent proliferation of hybrid forms of governance, where actors of various organizational types (states, intergovernmental organizations, non-governmental organizations, academia and business) work together. There is a wide range of institutionalized settings in which such cooperation takes place, from small meeting groups to formally organized inclusive institutions (Rittberger et al., 2008, pp. 17–18). These governance forms embody principles of, and use a language of, 'partnering', and are often referred to as 'public–private partnerships' (PPPs).[1] They can be seen as symbolic of innovation in governance in global health.

Although public–private partnerships are also found in a wide range of other issue-areas, notably environmental protection, education, and development, it seems that they have become particularly abundant, influential and sure-footed within the field of global health. Furthermore, within global health, 'partnering' is taking place on fundamental levels, not just in terms of policy implementation, but in policy development as well.

For many health policy practitioners and observers alike, the apparent growth and normalization of public–private partnerships have become the subject of both interest and, in some cases, concern. Over the past few years, several key studies have examined what public–private partnerships actually do, what their different forms, compositions and aims are, and the normative–ethical issues that arise when there is a redistribution of power, and responsibility, towards private actors (Buse and Walt, 2000a; Nishtar, 2004; Buse and Harmer, 2007).

Key to understanding the challenges, potential and risks of public–private partnerships within the global health architecture is the question of why they have emerged and appear to have become such a dominant mode of policy practice. Why has this phenomenon eventuated now? Are PPPs a genuinely new mode of health policymaking? And why is health an issue-area that is apparently so receptive to PPPs?

This chapter begins with a description of the rise in prominence of PPPs within the health sector, followed by an elaboration of three possible explanations of their rise in health. In the concluding section of the chapter, specific aspects of global health that make it a unique issue-area requiring and supporting innovative forms of cooperation and governance, such as PPPs, are discussed.

Public–private partnerships for health

Although there are excellent typologies systematizing the different roles and organizational structures of PPPs for health (Buse and Walt, 2000a; Widdus, 2003), confusion still exists over the exact definition of public–private partnerships and the extent to which they really are new in public health practice (Malena, 2004, pp. 2–4). Regardless of any vagueness in definition, however, it is observable that increasingly actors from both public and private sectors do work together in organized environments that externally present themselves as embodying a certain working principle, namely that of 'partnering'. In presenting themselves in this way, PPPs can be seen as portraying themselves as following a certain policy paradigm in which it is implied that it is both possible and desirable that public and private actors jointly contribute to the production of public goods (Richter, 2004, p. 45). In this chapter, the term PPP is used to mean organized cooperative action involving both public and private actors that follow this policy paradigm.

There are generally four dimensions by which we can observe a proliferation of public–private partnerships in global health: first, the sheer number of partnerships that have been established; second, the scope of these partnerships in terms of geographic reach, their types of activities, and acquired resources; third, the level of organizational sophistication of PPPs; and fourth, the level of acceptance that they now appear to enjoy (see Table 7.1).

In terms of *quantity* a rapid increase in the number of PPPs over the past 10–15 years can be asserted. In 2003 Roy Widdus reported on over 50 PPPs operating internationally (Widdus, 2003), and by 2005 the International

Table 7.1 Monitoring the growth of PPPs for health

Dimension	Manifestation	Current trends
Quantity	Number of active PPPs	Significant increase in number of PPPs over past 15 years
Scope	Geographical reach	PPPs present in increasing number of countries; PPPs active in the field in increasing number of countries
	Range of activities	PPPs addressing a broader range of health challenges
	Resources	Increasing funds and numbers of staff
Sophistication	Level of formalization in decision-making and bureaucratic organization	Increasing organizational complexity
Acceptance	Reactions of actors in the health policy field towards PPPs	Increasing funds and policy compliance

Source: Compiled by author.

Public–Private Partnerships for Health database listed over 80 PPPs for health with a global focus, with most formed later than 1995. There are many more PPPs which operate on local and national levels. While the formation of prominent large-scale PPPs for health seems to have reached a peak around the turn of the century, the number of smaller-scale, region-specific partnerships appears to be still increasing.

In terms of *scope*, PPPs now have an astounding range of activities and goals, and the types of health challenges they address appear to be evolving. A large number of product donation and development PPPs which emerged in the late 1980s to mid-1990s (examples include the Mectizan Donation Program, founded in 1987, and the International AIDS Vaccine Initiative, established in 1996). Around the turn of the century, several disease-focused PPPs were founded (for example Roll Back Malaria and the Stop TB Partnership). More recently, PPPs have emerged focusing on issues such as education resources (such as the Health Communication Partnership, founded in 2004) and health worker shortages (for example The Global Health Workforce Alliance, founded in 2006). PPPs have also widened their geographical scope. Whereas partnerships in the 1980s and early 1990s involved mainly service provision in developed countries, or global coordination, today PPPs, both global and local, are active in almost every country on the globe. The increase in the scope of PPPs is also reflected in the increasing levels of resources at their disposal, allowing them to employ more staff and follow through with more field projects. For example, the Global Fund to Fight AIDS, Tuberculosis and Malaria

(GFATM) has disbursed over US$7.6 billion in funds to date and the Global Alliance for Vaccines and Immunization (GAVI Alliance) has increased its budget significantly from US$93 million in 2001 to US$960 million in 2006 (GFATM, 2008a; GAVI Alliance, 2008).

In terms of *sophistication* many PPPs within the health sector have undergone, and are undergoing, changes in terms of their organizational structure, indicating a shift to greater organizational robustness. The level of institutionalization increases as modes of cooperation are regulated and the roles of partners are clarified (Huckel et al., 2007). Several PPPs now have multilevel structures with executive boards, technical advisory committees and stakeholder forums.

Finally, PPPs seem to be gaining increasing levels of *acceptance* as vital, stable and even taken-for-granted organizations within the global health policy field. The United Nations explicitly promotes closer ties with the business sector to increase effectiveness and efficiency, and in 1993 the World Health Assembly called on the WHO to 'mobilize and encourage the support of all partners in health development, including nongovernmental organizations and institutions in the private sector, in the implementation of national strategies for health for all' (World Health Organization, 2003b). At national levels development agencies and finance ministries have officially promoted the use of public–private partnerships as a strategy for global health in white papers.

Together, these four elements – quantity, scope, sophistication and acceptance – indicate that PPPs have become a prominent, if not dominant, strategy for addressing deficiencies and problems in global health. They appear to have 'become the method of choice to address a large component of international public health efforts' (Reid and Pearse, 2003). However, the desirability of this trend, in particular the effectiveness and legitimacy of PPPs, is still debated. A lot of disagreement in this debate can be traced back to differences in opinion on whether the growth of PPPs can be seen as a logical, even natural, progression towards more advanced global governance, or whether certain ideological shifts, structural changes or historic events have in fact spurred an artificial phenomenon which is neither sustainable nor desirable. Whereas for some observers powerful actors have steered global governance in a direction where the private sector has gained bargaining power, for others PPPs can be seen as a variation of an already long-standing dispersion of roles between public and private actors throughout history.

The emergence of PPPs in health

There are several possible explanations for the emergence and proliferation of PPPs in health. A historical view serves to highlight some of the new and not-so-new aspects of PPPs; critical views seek explanations on the macro level, and see the growth of PPPs as part of, and as a consequence of, a worldwide ideological shift towards neoliberalism. Others see PPPs as a consequence of increasing resource interdependence and changing motivations of actors to cooperate in the field of health.

Public–private cooperation in health as a historical legacy

Although often breaking with governance conventions of the past in terms of substantial participation of non-state actors in high-level decision-making, PPPs have arisen on the back of a long history of non-state actor participation in health. For some, any explanation for the growth of PPPs in health should therefore keep this legacy in mind. Although historians have noted that 'the sheer scale and complexity of developments (in global public health) preclude any easy synthesis' (Loughlin and Berridge, 2002, p. 21), there are at least four key historical legacies that have particular relevance for how we might view the growth of PPPs in the health policy field.

First, non-state actors have played a significant role in health care provision throughout history. For example, in many countries, privately operated hospital services run by churches and other charitable groups pre-date those run by the state. Even now non-state actors, both non-profit and for-profit, play a large role in the provision of health services. It can therefore be misleading to think that within the health sector provision has always been, and should therefore continue to be, provided primarily by the public sector. Non-state actors have also played vital roles in global health interventions. Immunization campaigns in the developing world were conducted with support from high-profile NGOs such as Rotary International, the International Red Cross and volunteer groups of teachers, religious leaders, journalists and police (Cueto, 2004, p. 1868). Against this historical backdrop, PPPs may be seen as a method through which expectations for the state to ensure the provision of adequate health care can be met by incorporating private activities into a publicly controlled arena.

Second, public health concerns have long struggled to carry weight against issues such as trade and commerce. For example, trade interests dominated talks at the International Sanitary Conferences of the nineteenth century (Loughlin and Berridge, 2002, p. 7).[2] In recent history, several clashes between trade and health regimes can be interpreted as part of the ongoing conflict between trade and health regimes, including controversies over the World Trade Organization TRIPS agreement to promote investment into research of new technologies, including medicines, and structural adjustment programmes from the World Bank. Against this historical backdrop, PPPs can be seen as a strategy to overcome long conflicting policy regimes and to negotiate exceptions to dominant trade rules.

Third, there is a near-century-old tradition of private foundation contributing to global-scale health projects. From the 1920s onwards private donors such as the Rockefeller and Ford Foundations have been especially active. For example, a large proportion of the budget of the League of Nations

Health Organization (LNHO) came from the Rockefeller Foundation. Today, several large-scale PPPs have been founded and supported by initial pledges from foundations such as the Bill and Melinda Gates Foundation and the Ted Turner Foundation. Against this historic backdrop, PPPs today can be seen as a reinvigoration of private donor involvement that has actually been around for a long time, but was less visible during the 1970s and 1980s.

Fourth, civil society has played a low-profile yet steadily advancing role in global health policy over the last 50 years. Non-governmental organizations (NGOs) have long been recognized as a supplier of public services and involved with agenda setting and policy implementation, but they have also been active in steering the direction of health policy. It can be observed that non-for-profit entities have played a variety of roles in global public health, such as contributing technical expertise to policy development, making global policy processes more accessible to individuals through information dissemination, and promoting public accountability. Although the acceptance of NGO activities has varied in different cultural regions, the high level of involvement of NGOs in UN projects such as the Framework Convention for Tobacco Control and United Nations Joint Programme on HIV/AIDS (UNAIDS) can be seen as an extension of the existing formal ties already awarded to NGOs under WHO and ECOSOC consultation arrangements.

The above examples highlight just four aspects that demonstrate how important it is to question common assumptions about global health governance today. The historical viewpoint does not necessarily always view PPPs as a natural progression of developments in time. Rather, it points out that PPPs sometimes represent newly modelled variations of cooperative arrangements that have existed in the past or can be seen as possible solutions to long-standing conflicts between different regimes. To the extent to which they *are* new, PPPs can be seen as a reaction to demands on state actors to control more aspects of public health than they have done in the past, while NGOs and other expert communities may be seeking formal recognition of the roles that they have long been playing.

A neo-liberal turn: system level changes

Public–private partnerships have become the subject of considerable scrutiny amongst researchers and practitioners alike (Fort et al., 2004; Richter, 2004). This is because they seem to indicate an entrenchment of a power shift towards business and other resource-rich actors (Thomas and Weber, 2004, p. 192). For some, the emergence and increase in influence of the public–private partnership paradigm have arisen as part of, and as a consequence of, a global ideological shift towards neoliberalism, which led to a failure to address key social determinants of health, increased the power of industry to demand a greater role in determining health policy and steered global health governance towards narrow, 'popular' or profitable programmes, such as PPPs.

Many observers suggest that processes of globalization have led to a widening in the gap between wealthy and poor and unequal access to the resources required to maintain good health, and that this has been exacerbated by certain elements of global politics. Porter et al. (2002, p. 185) refer to 'evidence that adjustment to fundamental social changes... has been worsened by the introduction of particular policies by the aid community, such as structural adjustment and other forms of liberalisation, without sufficient consideration of the social impacts'.

In the 1980s and 1990s policies of the WTO and the World Bank emphasized the need for economic development in order to achieve health aims, stressing correlations between increasing per capita incomes and a range of other health determinants (Bloche and Jungman, 2007, p. 252). In 1993, the World Bank published the report 'Investing in Health', which is seen as the point at which neoliberal approaches came to dominate global health policy. The state was meant to withdraw its influence on markets and reduce spending. Certain policies such as 'Structural Adjustment Programmes' and measures to protect intellectual property and encourage product research and development through the trade-related intellectual property rights (TRIPS) agreement emerged and were heavily criticized as restricting access to vital products and services. At the same time the work budget of the WHO stagnated and global economic institutions became increasingly influential in global health.

Although both the World Health Organization and the World Bank later adjusted their policies, recognizing interventions for health as exceptional cases, the shift away from the broad-based Primary Health Care (PHC) approach, which was advocated in the Declaration of Alma Ata from 1979, persisted. Policies of donor states and the global economic institutions were steered towards advocating market 'modification' through increased cooperation with the wide range of stakeholders, including those from the private sector, for the effective provision of essential services. For some the historical consequence was that 'the PHC strategy was modified/derailed before it got going' (Thomas and Weber, 2004, p. 193). Business actors became wealthier and more influential, while the intergovernmental WHO needed to seek innovative ways to ensure adequate resources.

Public–private partnerships can therefore be seen as a policy preference based on the presumption that, given the current roles and distribution of resources amongst various actors, such as states, development agencies, NGOs and industry, it is necessary to enter into cooperative arrangements based on mutual benefits. Critical perspectives crucially question the driving forces which have led to such a distribution of resources and power in the first place (HAI Europe, 2001, p. 12). The dominant neoliberal policies of the 1980s and 1990s led to certain actors acquiring an overproportion of financial and knowledge wealth which has awarded them advantages in bargaining power. The promotion of PPPs amongst powerful states and transnational corporations both accepts and compounds these advantages.

Actor motivations and interdependence: unit-level changes

The most commonly examined explanations for the growth of PPPs in health are concentrated on the unit level – in other words, examining actor motivations. In short, an increasing awareness that achieving solutions to global health challenges is beyond the capacity of any one actor alone led to the realization that it is necessary to pool resources (financial, technical, social) in order to achieve common goals. In addition, advances in communication technologies allowed for more intense interaction and sharing of ideas, allowing for broader participation and reducing the logistical barriers to multi-actor cooperation (Buse and Walt, 2000a, p. 550; Rittberger et al., 2008, p. 27).

Several observers take actor-motivation explanations as the most obvious reason behind the proliferation of PPPs and multi-stakeholder initiatives in the health policy field. They cite dissatisfaction with intergovernmental institutions and negotiating processes, as well as optimism that new public–private arrangements will allow for broader representation of neglected citizens' groups and more efficient problem-solving as motivating elements. For example, Martens writes that: 'The root causes of this general tendency are manifold and include a...general dissatisfaction on the part of governments, international organisations and NGOs with the agonizingly slow pace of the cumbersome global negotiation process...' (Martens, 2007, p. 4). Buse and Walt (2000a, p. 552) suggest that partnerships housed outside the UN bureaucracy were viewed as 'a way of getting things done, and where industry is involved, getting things done efficiently' following negative perceptions of UN effectiveness.

Some level of common goals is said to be a prerequisite for the establishment of partnerships. If relevant actors are convinced that placing their resources at the disposal of other partners offers the most promising approach towards achieving global health aims, then PPPs will be seen as a viable and legitimate option (Rittberger et al., 2008, pp. 27–30). Still, the motivations of actors can differ considerably. Several of the larger PPPs for health have a founding history that points towards specific actor initiatives as the reason behind their formation. The GAVI Alliance, for example, has been cited as having been founded as a revived version of the Children's Vaccine Initiative following a financial commitment from the Bill and Melinda Gates Foundation (Muraskin, 2004, p. 1923).

The reasons why business actors become involved in PPPs are the most extensively analysed of all stakeholder groups. Transnational corporations and other large private donors involved in global health set out to gain from the opening or securing of market opportunities, reputation and image enhancement. Buse and Walt (2002, p. 49) document a 'multi-pronged strategy' on behalf of business to gain access to and influence health policy-making on the global level during the 1990s. But increasing industry participation in partnerships has also come as a result of increased pressure, articulated through advocacy groups, to engage in corporate social responsibility. The desire to gain a better reputation through social engagement therefore also provided a motivating factor. At the same time, public actors and advocacy groups might see public–private partnerships as a mechanism through which pressure can be placed on business actors to conform to certain standards and keep a check on their activities (Huckel et al., 2007).

The motivations of large donor states and transnational corporations that advocate disease-specific 'vertical' approaches appear most obvious in the context of PPPs, which are inherently narrow in focus. Reasons for acceptance or engagement on behalf of recipient states and NGOs are more ambivalent. While for some the decision to enter into partnerships can be traced to rational calculations of the benefits of pooling of resources, others might be traced back to logics of appropriateness, lack of alternatives or simply 'going with the times'. The leadership role played by large states and prominent private donors has not only spurred the formation of large-scale global PPPs but contributed to a pool of 'gold standards' for the ways in which developing states could and should engage with non-state actors. These standards have been replicated on regional as well as local levels.

Unique features of health as an issue-area open to innovative governance

There are several peculiarities about health as an issue-area that have contributed to a high level of engagement in new and innovative forms of governance in this policy field, whether in the form of PPPs, inter-agency and intergovernmental cooperation or public sector programmes with private sector participation. This concluding section briefly introduces five unique features of health as an issue-area that serve to influence actor motivations to engage in PPPs and create background conditions that have led to the promotion of PPPs as a particularly viable strategy for achieving health aims.

Goal-oriented governance

Health is a policy area with a strong biomedical basis, and health challenges are often presented to the public through the use of scientific data, the dissemination of statistics and images of individual cases of ill health within wider acute health crises. Policy solutions therefore also tend to be presented in terms of achieving disease eradication or increasing vital health indicators along the lines of health as the absence of disease. This is coupled with a strong reliance on technological solutions (Bonita et al., 2007, p. 267). Throughout history health has therefore been an issue-area that tended towards a narrow goal orientation seeking clear, measurable results; and PPPs embody these principles.

Several historical examples demonstrate how narrow goal orientation has shaped global health governance, such as the International Sanitary Conferences of the late 1800s, which were convened following specific concerns over how to control the spread of cholera, and the WHO's Smallpox Eradication Programme is considered one of its greatest successes (Beigbeder, 1998, p. 132). Goal-oriented governance in health has provided a fertile ground for the formation of public–private partnerships that by nature are specific in focus. This is for two main reasons. First, clear goal orientation lends itself to approaches that emphasize cost-effectiveness and efficiency.[3] Second, the promise of observable and measurable results through statistics on mortality and morbidity and the publication of 'intermediate indicators of success' makes results-oriented action attractive for stakeholders that seek to advance their reputation through partnering or demonstrate to constituencies the efficacy of aid programmes. It is therefore not surprising that PPPs concentrate heavily on measuring and displaying their levels of performance.

The epidemiological transition

One of the most devastating features of the global health landscape over the past 30 years has been the widening health gap between the world's most privileged peoples (mostly in the North) and underprivileged peoples (mostly in the least developed countries) (Bonita et al., 2007, p. 268). This has been exacerbated by the so-called 'epidemiological transition' experienced by developed countries in the second half of the twentieth century, 'where infectious diseases stopped being the most important causes of death, and cardiovascular diseases and cancer became the main concerns' (Foladori, 2003, p. 84). Accompanying this process, investment in health research within developed countries came to concentrate on cancer, circulatory diseases, skin problems, and other diseases associated with high living standards (Foladori, 2003, p. 85). This transition has led to the need to artificially encourage research and development into non-profitable medicines.

Many public–private partnerships for health are aimed at the development, supply and distribution of medical services for non-profitable diseases. The epidemiological transition has been one-sided, leading to often radically different national priorities in wealthy countries compared with developing countries. The inability of state-based governance or market-driven development alone to achieve universal improving health and living standards can be seen as a driving force behind the proliferation of PPPs for health.

The role of the World Health Organization

The WHO represents a special institution even amongst the group of specialized agencies incorporated into the UN system. Founded by the bringing together of several already strongly established regional organizations and given a strong mandate based on technical expertise, it has been situated at the centre of global health policy since its inception. It is therefore not surprising that changes in the internal organization and leadership of the WHO have a profound effect on the general direction of global health policy.

In the 1970s the WHO went through a major transition following a significant increase in membership of developing countries in the World Health Assembly (as was the case with the United Nations in general). The balance of power shifted away from previously dominant members and an increased concern with social determinants of health led to a change in strategy direction towards strengthening health systems and in-country projects. During several years from the 1970s onwards, the WHO faced frozen budgets in real terms and increasingly wealthy donors moved towards supporting extra-budgetary goal-oriented programmes which were intended to 'boost the organisation's routine activities, using international and regional expertise and a project based approach to attack specific diseases or health issues' (Godlee, 1995, p. 179). These special programmes, and the way they were funded and organized, are an important precursor to public–private partnerships.

The WHO is so large in terms of the number of activities and affiliated projects and staff that regular criticisms and calls for reform are probably unavoidable, as coordination between departments and regions is difficult. Each election of a new leader is usually accompanied by calls for new directions and new hopes for a more effective and just approach to global health, often resulting in attempts at new and innovative governance.

Strong epistemic communities

Today, many PPPs have decision-making structures that not only rely on the input from representatives of the relevant 'partners' or stakeholders, but include executive or advisory boards occupied by 'experts'. In this sense PPPs can be seen as a mode through which experts that make up epistemic communities in health have been institutionalized into decision-making roles. Within public health, such epistemic communities are particularly active and influential, due to the highly scientific nature of the issue-area and the reliance on a background understanding of modes of disease transmission, aetiology and epidemiology. Experts with strong medical, public health and health economy backgrounds can therefore present themselves as being 'an authority' in global health, and technological approaches have thus dominated international and global health research and policy-making. Several authors even hint at forms of elitism and exclusivity being created through the formation of closely networked epistemic communities in global health.

Epistemic communities can be seen as providing the basis for the initial contacts and cross-sector trust relationships required for the establishment of public–private forms of cooperation. They can also be seen as a particularly powerful group of actors that promote biomedical approaches to global health and belief in technical solutions that are manifested in goal-oriented public–private partnerships.

The influence of acute and chronic pandemics: HIV/AIDS and SARS

Health crises often occur at unpredictable times, and when they occur on a large enough scale they pose a highly visible and direct acute threat to individuals, and economic and political systems. Acute health crises have therefore provided an impetus to change political strategies and have influenced the motivations of states and other actors for entering into innovative governance forms, including PPPs. Two pandemics from relatively recent history have had a significant impact on global health governance – HIV/AIDS and SARS.

David Fidler has suggested that the SARS outbreak in 2002/2003 triggered significant changes in global health governance trends and represents a 'coming-of-age' in global health governance (Fidler, 2004b, p. 799). SARS highlighted the vulnerability of communities all around the world to newly emerging infectious diseases, and as a consequence the involvement of non-state actors in roles of epidemiological tracking and the provision of global public goods for health was encouraged.

The HIV/AIDS epidemic has had an even more visible and long-standing influence on political strategies towards global health. It is a unique epidemic, which has been described as a long-wave event, because its effects compound over generations, slowly undermining social structures and economies (Barnett, 2006, p. 931). The AIDS pandemic has spurred an increase in financial resources flowing from development agencies into health projects in recent years, and advocacy groups have demanded action from states and for-profit actors alike to address a massive long-term threat and seek innovative solutions to achieve results (Kickbusch, 2007, p. xi).

PPPs for health: much more to know

With their massive presence, it is not surprising that public–private partnerships have been the focus of much attention amongst observers of public health and global governance alike. They have been welcomed for the opportunities they bring, as well as criticized for the power they 'lend' to private actors (Bartsch, 2002; Sridhar, 2003; Richter, 2004). It is important to critically question the extent to which public–private partnerships really represent something new in global health, so that the ways in which power relationships have changed can be identified precisely. On the one hand, certain key political events and the spread of certain diseases have had a profound impact on the motivations of actors to accept existing power constellations for the purpose of goal achievement. On the other hand, public–private partnering has formed out of pressure placed on those who preside over valuable resources to contribute more to alleviate poor health in the most vulnerable communities. Currently, we are still in a period of waiting to see whether PPPs will be able to deliver more effective global health governance, and whether they will become further established as a key part of the global health architecture.

Notes

The author thanks Wolfgang Hein, Sherri Brown, Sandra MacLean and other participants at the Sixth Pan-European Conference on International Relations, Turin, 12–15 September 2007 for comments on an earlier draft.

1. Throughout this chapter, the term public–private partnership will be used; however, there is a lack of consensus on the term. Some consider the alternative 'public–private interactions' to be more suitable. Variations include: hybrid governance networks and public policy networks.
2. Eleven International Sanitary Conferences took place between 1851 and 1903 in several European countries as well as Washington, USA. The final conference in 1903 covered, amongst other aspects, the obligatory notification of epidemic diseases and the recommendation to establish a permanent international office for public health.
3. For example, the Bill and Melinda Gates foundation has repeatedly named immunization as a cost-effective investment in health. Bill Gates has named GAVI as: 'the best investment we've ever made' (Bill and Melinda Gates Foundation, 2005).

8

Philanthropic Foundations and Global Health Partnership Formation: The Rockefeller Foundation and IAVI

Michael Moran

Large-scale philanthropic foundations based in the United States and elsewhere in the developed world have long had an interest in the area of health. This interest has extended to the institutional arrangements established to deliver essential medicines and also to promote sexual and reproductive health as a means to curb population growth and reduce infant mortality rates. However in recent years we have seen a significant scaling-up of foundation funding for seemingly intractable transnational health problems, notably in the area of infectious diseases such as HIV/AIDS, malaria and tuberculosis, which disproportionately affect communities in low and lower-middle income countries (LMICs). While this can largely be attributed to the emergence of the Bill and Melinda Gates Foundation (Renz and Atienza, 2006), it is also broadly indicative of trends toward greater private sector intervention in global health policy, and, by implication, governance of global health (Bull and McNeill, 2007). This can be seen as a continuation of earlier programmatic work of private foundations, notably the Rockefeller and Ford Foundations, who pioneered research and development (R&D) and established policy networks in health, paving the way for the present wave of philanthropists from Clinton through to Soros.

Nonetheless, while we have seen much media commentary on this phenomenon – particularly surrounding investor Warren Buffett's announcement that he would be handing over the bulk of his assets to the Gates Foundation – there has been limited scholarly analysis of the implications of this scaling-up for health policy-making and financing. Scholars and practitioners have focused their energy on examining the implications of public–private partnerships (PPPs) on health outcomes in LMICs and the normative desirability of multi-actor collaboration, but have (largely) seen foundations as benign agents rather than actors with considerable ability to leverage outcomes. This chapter seeks to address this vacuum by undertaking a case study analysis of the Rockefeller Foundation's (RF) support for Product Development Partnerships (PDPs), in particular the International AIDS Vaccine Initiative (IAVI), throughout the 1990s and early 2000s in an attempt to offer some conclusions as to its influence in global health governance. In doing so it argues that *private* foundations have not only played a central role in the emergence of partnerships – arguably the dominant policy paradigm in global health governance – they have also further normalized private sector involvement, sometimes, but not always, at the expense of proactive state and intergovernmental interventions, while acting as interlocutors between the public, private and third sectors.

The chapter begins by examining the reasons why partnerships have emerged as a common policy response to development problems, particularly in health. It then goes on to define and critique the partnership model in an effort to remove some of the ambiguities associated with the term, before situating philanthropic foundations in the formation of these arrangements. Finally it provides a case analysis of the RF's support for the budding PPP model in the 1990s, examining why this institution sought to attach itself to a series of PDPs which led to the formation of structured transnational policy networks and ultimately promoted resource mobilization.

Partnerships and the emerging global health landscape

The rise of partnerships as an instrument in health can be attributed to a number of changes that have occurred in the global political economy since the 1970s. Firstly, the ascendance of neoliberalism as a policy philosophy in the 1980s – particularly within multilateral development institutions – led not only to structural adjustment but also to greater use of not-for-profit and for-profit actors in service provision due to the (perceived) inefficiencies associated with official aid programmes and monopolistic bureaucracies (Scholte, 2000). Secondly, as states restructured and adopted the tools of 'new public management' they not only began to rely on non-state actors but also became more open, integrated, and thus constrained in their ability to address global problems unilaterally, leading to the search for partners to help combat health problems. Thirdly, while the decline of statism and Keynesianism created a space for greater involvement of non-state agents in governance, this also coincided with a belief, particularly toward the end of the 1990s, that crude market-led development strategies, as espoused by key agencies in the form of 'Washington consensus' policies (Stiglitz, 2002), not only failed to act as an engine of sustainable growth in LMICs, but had a detrimental impact on health outcomes.

The gradual erosion of the state as the sole arbiter of protection has therefore rendered it unable to act 'alone or in cooperation with other states, to deal with global health challenges' (Dodgson et al., 2002, p. 8). Instead states must navigate an increasingly complex array of issues in concert with other important players including private sector entities, NGOs, philanthropic foundations, affected communities and IOs. This has led to a rise in the literature (see, for instance, Lee et al., 2002) of the use of the phrase *global health governance* to describe the myriad of ways in which state and non-state actors now interact in the health sphere to set rules, define agendas and deliver products and services, which contrasts with the *international* character of health for much of the twentieth century.

The partnership, in its various forms, has emerged as the *de rigueur* (Martens, 2007), and some argue natural, policy response to health challenges. Health problems, which are comparatively fluid and have to a certain degree always been a concern of non-state actors, necessitate cooperation that is not only multisectoral but innovative, transnational and open to flexibility – traits oft cited as characteristic of these arrangements (see, for instance, World Economic Forum, 2005) – due to the intractable nature of the threats posed to human security. This is compounded by the stymieing effect that disease, particularly communicable disease, has on development, which has not been adequately addressed by conventional government-to-government or IO-to-government aid programmes. As a consequence we have seen actors from across the political spectrum support partnerships that harness the expertise and capabilities of various agents and break down the sectoral divides and 'division of labour' that have historically characterized multilateral responses to health (Buse and Walt, 2000).

Health partnership typologies

Despite widespread usage of the term, confusion still remains on what actually constitutes a 'health' PPP. Many authors (see, for instance, Lewis, 2005) argue that the term is often ill-defined and employed loosely and, according to Utting and Zammit (2006, p. iv), is thus rendered an 'infinitely elastic concept'. Critics note that what is often labelled a PPP is actually more of a loose alliance that lacks effective coordinating structures and mechanisms and may merely be ad hoc coalitions. The comparatively large volume of literature on global health PPPs that has arisen in the past few years makes such definitional ambiguity less of an issue, mainly because the PPP model is more well-established in this sector. Perhaps the most comprehensive typology of global PPPs is forwarded by Kaul (2006), and proves particularly useful when discussing philanthropic foundations. After surveying a sample of 100 global PPPs, Kaul (2006, p. 223) has constructed a typology based on 'three venture classes and seven functional types'. These classes – *business ventures, double-bottom line ventures* and *social ventures* – are designed to provide a working analytical model through which partnerships can be examined. Within the social venture class – broadly defined as those 'oriented toward public service' (Kaul, 2006, p. 235) – two functional types are applicable to partnerships financed (and often initiated) by philanthropic foundations. Among these is 'Type 5' – *brokering affordable price deals.* In these partnerships a key mediator 'with political clout and persuasiveness' brokers a 'market transaction' between a purchaser (for example, a developing country state) and supplier (for example, a pharmaceutical company) to facilitate pro-poor access to essential medicines (Kaul, 2006, p. 235). Kaul (2006) uses the example of the Clinton Foundation's negotiation of a favourable contract with pharmaceutical companies, in tandem with the Global Fund, the World Bank and UNICEF, under which developing countries commit to 'longer term purchase' agreements in exchange for lower-cost access to HIV drugs.

'Type 6' partnerships – *leveraging research and development* – seek to mobilize the resources, expertise and knowledge of the private sector by setting the appropriate incentives to stimulate investments in 'products for which there is no readily available market' (Kaul, 2006, p. 237). This is achieved by establishing 'push policies' (Grace, 2006, p. 1) – direct research funding, tax incentives, R&D expenditure etc – that reduce industry costs and offset risks, while incentivizing R&D input into diseases which commonly, although far from exclusively, affect those in the LMICs. Ultimately these financing instruments aim to bring these products to market 'acting as a sort of virtual non-profit pharmaceutical company' that promotes drug R&D activity in neglected diseases, while ensuring that there are sufficient incentives to invest in poor-country diseases such as HIV/AIDS, malaria, dengue and tuberculosis (Grace, 2006, p. 1).

As a consequence these instruments mirror those in operation in the private sector, but function as *quasi-markets* with outwardly public goals and objectives (Carlson, 2004). They are therefore sometimes portrayed in the literature (see, for instance, World Economic Forum, 2005) as situations in which all actors accrue a mutually beneficial gain. This claim is not without merit. First, as Caines et al. (2004) note, PPPs add intangible benefits such as an enhanced profile for neglected diseases outside IOs and the traditional health community, while garnering significant tangible resources. Second, as Buse and Harmer (2007, p. 261) have argued, such resource mobilization has produced concrete results, generating 'efforts to combat communicable diseases and to stimulate the development of new products'. Third, they have 'improved access to cost-effective healthcare interventions', and, in some cases, an improved policy-making environment, facilitated by country-level coordinating mechanisms (Buse and Harmer, 2007, p. 261). It must be noted, however, that health PPPs are not without their critics.

Critical perspectives on health PPPs

Critics can be broadly placed in two, sometimes overlapping, camps. The first camp, whose primary concern is the narrow and technical nature of these interventions, can be labelled the *systems* critics. From this perspective most PPPs are seen as top-down, vertical interventions that do not adequately tackle problems associated with capacity. In particular, many PPPs do not adopt sector-wide approaches, popularized in other development spheres, which are designed to improve country-level systems, while harmonizing aid policy programmes (and relations between actors). It is argued that this reduces duplication and waste and ultimately improves aid effectiveness (Buse and Harmer, 2007). This is seen as a broader symptom of the malaise that has beset aid financing and service delivery in health for decades and which, ironically, PPPs and other horizontal approaches have been established to curtail.

The second camp, while also wary of the impact of PPPs on fragile health systems, is more concerned with the broader *structural* (and *ideational*) implications of multi-actor collaboration, and in particular the involvement (limited as it often is) of the corporate sector and emulation of its practices. This grouping, which includes critical political economy and post-development theorists, frames partnerships in a combination of Gramscian (see, for instance, Utting, 2005), neo-Marxist (see, for instance, Zammit, 2003) and on occasion Foucauldian (Abrahamsen, 2004) terms. The primary argument of those in the critical school is that partnerships are part of a broader hegemonic shift, primarily discursive, which acts as a continuation of the neoliberal dominance of development theory and practice. The depoliticized language evident in much of the policy research and official documentation on partnerships, these critics attest, falsely suggests that power relations within partnerships are equitable and benign – a kind of 'win–win–win' scenario in which all agents are party to an absolute gain (Richter, 2004, p. 45).

Indeed, commentators in this school assert that the partnership model has been uncritically adopted by the UN and its agencies, including the World Health Organization, which played a central role in promoting take-up, particularly under the stewardship of former Director-General Gro Harlem Brundtland. These commentators (see, for instance, Martens, 2007; Richter, 2004) have argued that, contrary to the conventional wisdom, these arrangements pose a number of dangers not just during implementation – where issues have arisen – but also to the wider multilateral system. From this perspective partnerships represent a kind of 'privatisation' (Bull et al., 2004, p. 481) of governance by stealth, which enhances the power of business at the expense of critical voices (Martens, 2007). This can be evidenced by the lack of representation of affected communities and NGOs on partnership governing boards (Buse and Harmer, 2007) and what some see as a privileged position of multilateral agencies, the private sector (and foundation) representatives in decision-making. However, such change, that is, the apparent shift toward greater private sector involvement in governance, has always, to a degree at least, been a feature of international development and also has historical parallels to the programmatic work of foundations.

Philanthropic foundations and health partnership formation

The emergence of philanthropic foundations as actors in health is not a new phenomenon. Some commentators (see, for instance, Levy and Chernyak, 2006) cite the Rockefeller and Ford Foundations as pioneers in multisectoral collaboration in international development. Indeed, as early as the 1970s observers (see, for instance, Thompson, 1972) looking at the role of foundations in facilitating the green revolution in agriculture in Mexico and India noted that these agents played a central role in uniting actors from across sectors in novel institutional arrangements which in hindsight closely resemble contemporary strategic partnerships. This approach, however, was not confined to agriculture but was also employed in the health arena, which had been a core concern of the 'big' foundations from their emergence in the late nineteenth and early twentieth centuries. Widely known programmes such the RF's search for a vaccine for yellow fever and its efforts to eradicate hookworm in the southern US – as well as its central role in financing the failed League of Nations Health Organization (Weindling, 1997) – to some degree acted as an antecedent to the modern global health partnership (Rodin, 2007).

It is not surprising then that philanthropic foundations have found the PPP model attractive. These organizations have always had a strong interest in promoting intersectoral cooperation while their relationship with both the private sector, as a source of seed funds, and civil society, as financers of non-governmental activity, has meant that the partnership model would seem a natural fit. The early foundations, such as Carnegie and Rockefeller, also emerged at a time when state intervention in society (not to mention multilateral cooperation) was comparatively limited. This meant that these foundations assumed a role of almost governmental importance in American public life (Bulmer, 1999) – and aspired to do so – while their interwar and post-war activity in the development field was pioneering in both scale and scope. Parallels can therefore be seen with the contemporary era, in which developed states have largely been lagging in their commitment to allocate 0.7 per cent of GDP to official development assistance, not to mention the floundering Millennium Development Goals. This has meant that private philanthropy (and of course development NGOs) retain significance as funders, partners, implementers, and, by default, policymakers, as states appear unwilling or unable to make the fiscal commitments required to improve development outcomes.

Nonetheless, there are a number of important distinctions between early US philanthropy, which was often domestically or nationally concentrated, and contemporary philanthropy, which is often more diffuse, issue-specific, delivered horizontally in collaboration with diverse agents from the public, private and non-government sectors, and increasingly oriented to programmes outside the US. Indeed, according to Renz and Atienza (2006, p. 3) of the Council on Foundations, we have seen 'international grants as a share of overall grant giving' increase from 4 per cent in 1982 to over 18 per cent in 2004, health programmes experiencing the largest rise. While the most recent data indicates that this can be attributed to the Gates Foundation's shift from a domestic to an international orientation – in particular its 10-year grant of US$1.5 billion to the GAVI Alliance skewing sample results – health 'far surpassed all fields by share of international giving in 2004' (Renz and Atienza, 2006, p. 5).

This trend is set to continue for a number of reasons. Firstly, the tech boom of the 1990s led to the creation of a number of new foundations – for example the Gates Foundation, the Skoll Foundation and more recently Google.org – which have adopted an 'internationalist' outlook in the tradition of Carnegie, Ford and Rockefeller, while bringing a 'business-like' approach to giving. Importantly these 'philanthrocapitalists', as *The Economist* (2006, p. 9) has labelled them, are generally less risk-averse, more 'entrepreneurial' and therefore more likely to favour interventions which mirror 'for-profit capital markets', while possessing a natural affinity with the private sector which places them at ease with cooperative arrangements with these actors. Secondly, the growth of corporate social responsibility as a mainstream function of many transnational pharmaceutical corporations, in rhetoric if not always in practice, has deepened engagement between foundations, the private sector and multilateral institutions in the health sphere, culminating in an increasing propensity for strategically geared partnerships.

Indeed, key scholars of global health partnerships (see, for instance, Buse and Lee, 2005; Kaul, 2006) have recognized that philanthropic foundations remain important drivers of collaboration. Foundations, notably the Gates Foundation, remain a key source of funds for many of the major health PPPs (Buse and Harmer, 2007), while others, such as Rockefeller, have been instrumental in their adoption by the international community by acting as key advocates of collective action. Some, such as Bull and McNeill (2007), go further, arguing that increasing foundation funding for partnerships, coupled with an emphasis on the application of private sector tools to public problems, sometimes referred to as 'venture philanthropy' or 'social entrepreneurship', is a factor in the ascendance of this model in international public policy, as the new philanthropists are not only more materially influential, but are also inclined to take an active interest in both the procedural and the operational aspects of partnerships. This raises a number of important issues regarding the legitimacy, accountability and sustainability of these organs – and indeed networked governance arrangements – given that foundation funding sometimes has a limited life and does not always extend far beyond initial capital outlays. Nonetheless, this suggests that these actors have gained deeper influence in the multilateral system via partnership brokerage, and can be identified as part of a growing trend toward private sector intervention in global governance (see, for instance, Bull et al., 2004;

Hall and Biersteker, 2002). To investigate this proposition further, and examine one of the key sources of this trend, particularly as it pertains to collaboration, I undertake a case study analysis of the RF and IAVI.

New models, new approaches: the Rockefeller Foundation and the IAVI

In the early 1990s the RF began to review its approach to health programmes. Partially inspired by internal organizational changes and by external shifts in the strategic direction of pharmaceutical product development – which experienced a move away from investment in communicable diseases associated with LMICs – the RF instituted a shift from scientific research-based advocacy, mainly through research papers, toward PDPs (Evans, 2002). This shift has been seen as instrumental in the ascendance of this model, and, as Evans (2002, p. 2), a former researcher with the Rockefeller health programme, has argued elsewhere, the RF's 'niche has been a catalyst or incubator of public-private partnerships for specific global product development priorities'. Although other actors clearly played an integral role, such statements are not unwarranted, as evidenced by the RF's position at the launch of many successful and prominent PDPs. This has enabled the RF to punch above its weight – the former behemoth's endowment is now ranked 13th in the US (Foundation Center, 2007) – through effective networking strategies that have built on the organization's historical position as a partnership broker in international development.

Towards a vaccine initiative: the RF as network facilitator

In March 1994 the RF convened a meeting 'of 24 AIDS authorities from around the world' at its Bellagio Centre in Northern Italy (IAVI, 2006, p. 2). The chief purpose of the meeting was to 'investigate the state of progress toward the development of preventative HIV vaccines appropriate in developed and developing countries, and to explore possible routes for accelerating the development of HIV vaccines' (RF, 1994a, p. 2). The meeting found that, while there was a (limited) research programme currently in progress, this was highly concentrated in candidates for subtype 'B', which was dominant in communities in industrialized countries where the bulk of the research funding was at the time allocated. This meant that subtypes circulating in Asia and Africa – where the vast majority of new infections were occurring and the disease was likely to have a severe impact on social and economic development – would be excluded, should any trial prove successful (IAVI, 2006).

The group, initially known as the International Ad Hoc Scientific Committee (hereafter the Committee), determined that there were a number of barriers inhibiting progress toward a safe, viable and cost-effective programme. These barriers ranged from the vast scientific difficulties associated with viral vaccine development through to a host of economic, political, cultural and regulatory obstacles. Of paramount importance was the need to address the profound lack of investment in vaccine research, which comprised less than 7 per cent of total public and private spend (RF, 1994b). It became clear that this was the product of 'serious market failures' in the vaccine sector (RF, 1994a), namely a combination of prohibitively high-cost and logistically complicated trials and the limited size of markets in developed countries, where the virus affected a small 'at-risk' population, and low per capita health spending and low purchasing power in developing countries (RF, 1995). Consequently there was a fundamental disconnect between the purchasing power of those most in need (that is, those in LMICs, including governments) and the market requirement that products yield a sufficient return on investment.

The overall consensus, then, was that in order to overcome these market failures institutional design would need to move beyond an *ad hoc* approach toward a *globally networked* series of trials conducted across a range of regions and test sites. This approach would attempt to exploit, rather than challenge, existing market barriers as a medium to boost public and private investment.

The (public–private) PDP: the RF as partnership broker

The type of arrangement that eventually emerged was not necessarily born as a conscious decision to emulate the R&D practices of for-profit pharmaceutical companies or to create a hybrid governance structure, at least to begin with. As one interviewee explained when the key figures in the meetings that led to the establishment of the IAVI initially met, there were few instruments that could act as precedent. Furthermore, while there was recognition that the 501(c)(3) legal structure – which grants tax-exempt status in the US Internal Revenue Code to non-profit entities – was the most appropriate vehicle to establish future modalities, there was less certainty about the actual characteristics of this venture. Nonetheless, by 1995, after the Committee met to discuss financial arrangements in New York, something resembling the public–private health PDP, akin to Kaul's (2006) *leveraging research and development* functional type, had emerged as the consensus response among a range of experts in 'public and private finance, law, the pharmaceutical sector and public health' (RF, 1995, p. 1). This initiative, it was determined, should have a two-pronged focus: 'supporting targeted research and development activities' and 'creating a more enabling environment for vaccine development' (RF, 1995, p. 6). This would be achieved by using a range of push and pull incentives which supported promising vaccine product developments, through grants, contracts or collaborative research, while at the same time sending the signal to pharmaceutical companies that there would be a market for future products in LMICs.

As the modality mirrored private sector operations, it was at the time considered controversial within the RF, where concerns were raised regarding the appropriateness of such instruments. Context is important here. While we now generally see support for PDPs, such programmes were at the time a radical departure from traditional financing models and to a certain degree ran counter to the RF's conventional approach. Certainly these arrangements, with their emphasis on funding disease-specific programmes, resembled earlier RF work on hookworm and yellow fever, but the use of quasi-market mechanisms and incorporation of private sector entities into the policy network was controversial, not least because of the poor reputation of the pharmaceutical industry among sections of the public health community. There were also more immediate internal organizational concerns about whether this move would constitute a shift from a *grant-making* foundation, the dominant model for large-scale US foundations, toward an *operating* foundation, which had not been in the RF's remit since prior to the 1950s, when the organization actively conducted in-house research and programmes (Community Wealth Ventures, 2004).

At one level the RF's shift can be attributed to wider structural changes in the global political economy, which gave rise to multisectoral approaches, as well as the broader external debates regarding the need to find novel solutions to intractable health problems. From this perspective the RF and other supporters of PDPs were responding to external drivers such as those mentioned earlier in this chapter, and in particular, the new 'geo-political climate' which facilitated cooperation while diminishing 'the polarisation between public and private that was characteristic of the Cold War era' (interviewee). However, while it is evident that wider macro changes in part engendered the shift, as they clearly did with other concurrent and subsequent hybrid governance models, it is also clear from published interviews (see, for instance, Berkley, 2004) and a discursive examination of available documentation that, like much policy change in complex social and health domains, there were also key agents who acted as 'champions'. The RF's shift, and in particular the decision to move forward with the IAVI, was therefore also embedded in internal debates which occurred from Board level down to practitioners in the health programme where employees such as Seth Berkley spearheaded the push. In an interview with Community Wealth Ventures (2004, p. 81) for example, Kenneth Prewitt, a former senior vice president at the RF, indicated that that there 'was the question of whether this was the moment when private philanthropy should form partnerships with the for-profit sector'. He argued further that without the presence of venture capitalist Paul Klingenstein and the favourably disposed Rockefeller president Peter Goldmark on the Board, and in particular Berkley's sustained lobbying, IAVI would not have moved forward due to resistance from sceptical staff.

The concept of the *policy entrepreneur* – a term originally coined by Kingdon (1995) to explain agenda-setting processes in domestic public policymaking – proves useful here. It is clear that Berkley played a decisive role in convincing senior members of the RF Board to break with past practice and trial this collaborative instrument (Community Wealth Ventures, 2004). His insistence that a lack of financial (and political) will was the main impediment to a substantive HIV vaccine programme was pivotal in the Board's ultimate decision to run with the partnership, and planted the seed for the RF's support for other similar modalities. Nonetheless, importantly the participants – in what was essentially an embryonic transnational policy community – had a plan for action that could be readily adopted at an opportune time. Kingdon (1995) argues that in domestic public policymaking certain actors operate across three process streams – *problems, solutions and politics*. When these streams converge, or are coupled, 'the greatest policy changes occur' (Lewis, 2005, p. 8). It can be observed that Berkley and others identified the problem (a lack of investment in an AIDS vaccine), attached a solution (a multisectoral PDP) and brought this to the attention of organizational decision-makers. This occurred at time when there was a changing political climate that would make such programmes not only possible but politically feasible, enabling these actors to utilize a policy 'window' to engender policy change.

The IAVI was initially operated as an 'in-house' programme within the RF, but was 'spun-off' in 1997 (RF, 2007, p. 1) and adopted its own institutional form, with a scientific advisory board, a governing board and a small team of staff helping to establish an organizational structure framework for future PDPs (IAVI, 2006). After the experience with the IAVI, the RF, urged on by other champions of public–private cooperation such as Ariel Pablos-Mendez, Tim Evans and Lincoln Chen (Widdus, 2004, p. 8), backed the PDP model and subsequently 'provided management advice and seed funding to establish five such organisations' to 'foster an enabling environment for product development and access more broadly' (RF, 2007, p. 1). As these entities have matured, and the RF entered a period of restructure, it has reduced or ceased funding for these partnerships (which has concerned some, such as Berkley (2004), who argue that foundations still have an important role beyond seed funding, as Gates continues to do so).

It therefore appears that a confluence of forces, both internal and external, drove the RF's shift. However, while organizational change must be viewed within its structural context – in this case the ascendance of neoliberalism, increased interdependence, etc – it can also be argued that the RF's shift had broader implications beyond the confines of the policy communities which formed in and around the issue-specific PDPs it resourced. In this respect, while the PDP model would no have doubt have materialized independently of the RF's involvement, the RF, as organization, and agents within this organization, also arguably informed the wider discursive context. In addition, while moderated forms of neoliberalism were already gaining traction, it is reasonable to infer that the RF contributed to the further dissemination of quasi-market norms in global health governance, while solidifying its own reputation as a key agent in public health.

Conclusion

This chapter has attempted to illustrate how one of the world's most prominent private philanthropic foundations, the Rockefeller Foundation, played a significant role in establishing the PPP model as a norm in international public policy. It was suggested that the RF managed to influence the trajectory of global health policy through partnership brokerage. It did this in three ways. First, it utilized its financial assets to garner *material support* from other actors by providing seed funding for health PDPs, which acted to reassure other contributors that projects were both financially viable and likely to achieve measurable outcomes, a core of objective of public and private donors. Second, its position at the intersection of the public and private enabled it to capitalize on its *intersectoral relationships* to nurture dialogue between (antagonistic) actors (for example, pharmaceutical companies, non-governmental organizations). This served to promote what Bull and McNeill (2007, p. 86) have tentatively termed elsewhere *'new norms of collaboration'*. Finally, it was suggested that private foundations, such as the RF, have been able to attract networked employees and management who have acted as *policy entrepreneurs*, alerting decision-makers and other influential agents to policy problems and offering solutions that enable these to be quickly absorbed and acted on. This placed the RF in a central position within health policy networks, in PDPs at least, as evidenced by the presence of former RF employees on the governing boards of key partnerships and its privileged access to decision-makers in governmental and intergovernmental bodies, which ultimately enabled the RF to advance its interests, its preferences, and, importantly, its ideas within the international system despite a decline in assets relative to other players.

9
Southern Actors in Global Public–Private Partnerships: The Case of the Global Fund

Sonja Bartsch

Introduction

Hybrid forms of regulation between state and non-state actors have been an essential part of global health governance since the beginning of the 1990s. Today we find about 80 GPPPs in the health sector (Carlson, 2004; Caines et al., 2004), ranging from small initiatives for single issues to large institutions for multiple diseases, and differing in terms of disease focus and area of activity and legal status.

Among the most prominent of the partnerships in the health sector is the Global Fund to Fight AIDS, Tuberculosis and Malaria (GFATM). It was established in 2002 as a financing mechanism in order to 'attract, manage and disburse additional resources' for the fight against the three major poverty-related diseases. Until April 2008 it approved, in seven funding rounds, US$10.8 billion to support programs in 136 countries and received pledges of more than US$19.6 billion until 2010 (Matlin et al., 2008). It has become the leading financing mechanism in the case of tuberculosis and malaria, where it contributes to roughly two-thirds of all international funding. In the case of HIV/AIDS, the GFATM interacting with other financing institutions like the World Bank or the bilaterals makes up 21 per cent of all international funding (GFATM, 2007d).

But the GFATM is not only an important actor of global health governance; it is also a major organizational interface, linking different kinds of stakeholder groups – donors, recipients, private sector, civil society, bilateral and multilateral institutions – in its governance bodies. It is often considered a new mechanism in development cooperation, as it does not design or implement its own programs or projects, but finances proposals that are developed by recipient countries, following the principle of country ownership.

Although Southern actors play a role in various GPPPs, their involvement is not well recorded in the literature, perhaps because most of the material on

GPPPs has been written from a Northern perspective (Reinicke et al., 2000; Buse and Walt, 2000b; Richardson and Allegrante, 2001; Reich, 2002). This chapter addresses this limitation by focusing on the GFATM as an example for Southern participation in Global Public–Private Partnerships. It argues that, although Southern participation helps to enhance the GFATM's legitimacy as an actor of global health, the partnership approach is connected with some problems in terms of effectiveness. The example of GFATM suggests that GPPPs, in general, offer a new institutional option to mediate between interests and to negotiate conflicts between different types of actors. They may under certain circumstances contribute to a better integration of actors of the South and an empowerment of weak actors, but can also be used by powerful actors of the North to pursue their interests and contribute to a weakening of established organizations in global health governance.

The GFATM is often seen as a model for partnerships in the health sector (for example, Summers, 2003; Radelet, 2004), as it tried to build on lessons learned from other GPPPs, and it corrects some imbalances, especially in terms of Southern participation and country ownership. In the following these issues will be addressed more in detail with regard to four core issues[1]: (1) the role of Southern actors in the establishment of the GFATM; (2) the representation of Southern state and non-state actors in the governing bodies at global and national level; (3) Southern influence on the decisions and policies of the GFATM; (4) the connection between Southern participation and the GFATM's legitimacy and effectiveness.

The role of Southern actors in the establishment of the Global Fund

The establishment of the GFATM was due to both demand and supply factors. The global governance discourse tends to focus on the former and highlights aspects like interdependencies between different types of actors and difficulties of state regulation in an era of globalization to account for an increasing demand for new forms of regulation (Kaul et al., 1999; Reinicke et al., 2000). In the case of the GFATM, the inability of the existing (bilateral and multilateral) structures to mobilize enough resources to effectively fight HIV/AIDS, tuberculosis and malaria – estimated to be approximately US$15 billion annually (CMH, 2001) – was the most important argument on the demand side.

Southern needs and discourses played an important role in that context. More than 45 million people worldwide are infected with HIV, 95 per cent of them living in developing countries. Malaria is prevalent in a total of 105 countries; approximately 1 million people die of malaria each year, 90 per cent of them in sub-Saharan Africa. Tuberculosis is one of the world's leading infectious causes of death among young people and adults and kills about 2 million people annually, with low- and lower-middle-income countries accounting for more than 90 per cent of TB cases and deaths (Matlin et al., 2008).

High disease rates have devastating effects not only for individuals directly affected, but also for their families and for entire societies that are threatened in terms of social cohesion, stability and economic development. The 2001 report of the Commission on Macroeconomics and Health (CMH, 2001) analyzes in detail the impact of health on development in low- and middle-income countries. It points out that 'each 10 percent improvement in life expectancy at birth is associated with a rise in economic growth of at least 0.3 to 0.4 percentage points per year' (CMH, 2001, p. 24) while high prevalence of diseases such as malaria, tuberculosis and HIV/AIDS are associated with persistent and large reductions of economic growth rates.

Developing countries, Southern NGOs and the World Health Organization (WHO) argued in both bilateral and multilateral contexts that there were ethical obligations to provide stronger financial support, especially since effective interventions are available to prevent and treat these diseases. For tuberculosis, DOTS (Directly Observed Therapy Short-course) had proved successful, and, for malaria prevention, methods like insecticide-treated bed nets and various methods of treatment exist. Even HIV/AIDS can be treated (although not cured) at reasonable costs, as prices for antiretrovirals – due to competition from generics – have declined continuously, from originally over US$11000 a year per patient for an ARV triple combination in 2000 to US$400 in 2001 and US$99 by 2007 (MSF, 2007). These interventions, however, were not sufficiently applied, as health systems in the Southern countries are not adequately resourced. So a number of strong arguments, especially from a Southern perspective, called for a new financing mechanism like the GFATM.

But the existence of a demand for additional financing to fight the three diseases is a necessary but not sufficient condition to explain the establishment of the GFATM. Only if we add the supply side – the power resources, interests and activities of different types of actors – do we get the full picture. While the literature on regime formation is quite extensive with regard to this issue (for example, see Hasenclever et al., 1997), the literature on public–private partnerships for a long time tended to ignore the supply side and followed a functional logic of demand in explaining the emergence of new forms of regulations like networks or partnerships. In the process of establishing the GFATM in 2000/2001, however, a number of factors were crucial on the supply side.

The first factor was the existence of political commitment among the donor community to tackle the most important poverty-related diseases. International attention to health issues in developing countries was propelled by the renewed focus on poverty reduction that came with the Post-Washington Consensus (WDR, 2000/2001; HDR, 1997, 2003), studies on the relationship between health and macroeconomic development (CMH, 2001) and an increasing notion of health as a global public good (Kaul et al., 1999; Smith et al., 2003). These three approaches deal with health at different societal and political levels, but all contributed to a stronger commitment of political leaders towards the fight of poverty-related diseases and inequalities. Without these developments the G8 meeting in Okinawa in July 2000, where the idea of establishing a new financing mechanism was discussed for the first time, and the further processes until the start of the GFATM in January 2002, probably would not have created such a momentum among the donor countries as they eventually did.

A second important factor on the supply side was the perception that ill-health in developing countries and the global spread of infectious diseases represented a threat to security at national and international level (Ostergard, 2002; Peterson, 2002; Youde, 2005). This is related to a broadening of the security concept that can be observed since the end of the Cold War. While security was traditionally perceived as military protection against external threats to national territory and population, the concept has been expanded since the 1990s towards non-military threats emanating from economic risks (for example, oil dependency, financial volatility), illegal activities (drug trafficking, organized crime), environmental changes (global warming, conflicts over water) and social problems (migration, infectious diseases). Health issues in this concept pose a dual threat to the security of states: one that results from the global spread of infectious diseases and affects the domestic population directly, and one that is linked to political instability resulting from ill-health, poverty and underdevelopment and that affects national and international security indirectly. Especially in the case of the United States, the perception of health-related insecurities was decisive for its stronger orientation towards health issues and its leadership role in establishing the GFATM as a new financing mechanism (US National Intelligence Council, 2000).

The third important factor that supported the establishment of the GFATM was the desire of some G8 countries – especially the US and Japan – to circumvent the UN system, which had experienced serious difficulties and was considered inefficient and bureaucratic. The idea of installing a new institution outside that system – and thus more directly under control of the donor countries – seemed appealing to these actors, as it converged with their own interests in bypassing to some extent the established UN organizations in the field of health, like WHO or UNAIDS, and shifting their activities to a new forum.

Representation of Southern actors in the governing bodies of the Global Fund

While Southern actors had only indirect influence during the establishment of the GFATM, they play a major role in the GFATM's current governance structure. This is due to a participatory preparation process that started in

June 2001 with the first informal meeting in Geneva, then gained momentum with the establishment of the Transitional Working Group (TWG) in August 2001 and the subsequent consultations of the various stakeholder groups in Fall 2001.

That the GFATM was established as a public–private partnership with considerable representation of non-state actors can be largely attributed to the corresponding activities of a strong coalition of NGOs, mainly from the field of HIV/AIDS. Many developing countries – most decisively, South Africa – preferred a fund with a strong representation of recipient and donor countries and only marginal influence from non-state actors. However, NGOs, from both the North and the South, successfully claimed that they represent and advocate the interests of those people who are at the centre of the activities of the GFATM: the people affected by diseases, ill-health and poverty in developing countries. This was a claim of legitimacy on the part of NGOs that convinced the donor countries to fully include them in the governance structures of the GFATM and provide them not only with consultative rights but with actual decision-making power. That Southern governments would be included in the governing bodies was not controversial, but that they managed to claim as many Board seats as the Northern governments can be attributed to the strong influence that Kofi Annan and WHO representatives were able to exert on the TWG.[2]

The governance structure of the GFATM, as it was set up by the TWG, consists of four governing and administrative bodies at the global level:

- Executive Board (responsible for strategies, policies, operational guidelines and funding decisions of the GFATM);
- Secretariat (day-to-day operations, management of the grants);
- Technical Review Panel (review of applications);
- Partnership Forum (biennial gathering of stakeholder groups); and three entities at the national level;
- Country Coordinating Mechanism (responsible for proposal process and application to the GFATM);
- Principal Recipient (PR) (responsible for the management of the grant after the proposal is approved);
- Local Fund Agent (monitoring function; in most cases a private accounting firm).

In the following, the two central elements of the GFATM governance structure – the Executive Board and the CCMs, which are both multi-stakeholder entities – will be discussed more in detail in terms of participation of Southern state and non-state actors.

The Executive Board

The Executive Board today consists of five types of constituencies that are grouped into two voting groups of the same size and one non-voting group.

The donor group is composed of eight representatives of industrialized countries and two representatives of the private sector (one company, one foundation); the recipient group consists of seven representatives of developing countries and three representatives of the NGO sector (one Northern, one Southern, one from affected communities). In the non-voting group are representatives of international organizations (one from each of WHO, UNAIDS and the World Bank, and a Swiss member, as the headquarters of the GFATM is in Geneva). While seats for governments in the donor group depend on allocations of funds or initial pledges to the GFATM (minimum: US$100 million), the selection of the other Board members is the responsibility of the respective constituencies.

NGOs representing the people living with the diseases (so-called 'affected communities') were initially part of the non-voting group. These NGOs continued advocating for a third voting seat, however, and received strong support at the first Partnership Forum of the GFATM in 2004. They finally managed to convince the Board that it would be positive for the GFATM's reputation to change their status, as this would demonstrate that the interests of the people living with HIV/AIDS, tuberculosis and malaria in the developing world really are taken into account by the GFATM.

The role of NGOs in the governance structure of the GFATM increased over time (this was also reflected by the selection of a NGO member as Vice-Chair of the GFATM in 2004 and 2007). NGOs now play important functions in terms of advocacy, mobilization of support and implementation of programs, as well as enhancing the legitimacy of the GFATM as a whole (see section below on Southern participation). The NGO constituency in itself, however, shows a considerable bias in terms of disease focus. Board members tend to represent NGOs from the area of HIV/AIDS, and organizations from the areas of tuberculosis and malaria are often absent from the wider NGO Board delegations. The relative weight of governments from the developing countries decreased when 'affected communities' were added to the Board composition, as their number of Board seats remained the same, while the third NGO seat was compensated for with an additional seat for the donor countries in order to restore the balance between the two voting groups. This led to considerable tensions between Southern governments and the NGO constituency, as could be observed, *inter alia*, with regard to the composition of the Country Coordinating Mechanisms.

The Country Coordinating Mechanisms

At the national level the GFATM requires a multi-stakeholder institution in order to apply for funding and handling of the grants: the so-called 'Country Coordinating Mechanism' (CCM). Country ownership is one of the central principles of the GFATM – that is, the Board and the Secretariat do not design or implement any programs or projects, but the CCMs themselves elaborate proposals based on national strategies and priorities and are responsible for their realization. Therefore, this body is crucial to the governance structure of the GFATM. The functioning of CCMs, of course, varies from country to country, but a number of typical problems can be identified that are relevant for the overall question of Southern participation in the GFATM (GNP+, 2003; LSHTM, 2003; UNAIDS, 2003; DFID, 2003; GFATM, 2004; ICASO, 2004).

One of the most critical issues is the fact that many CCMs are dominated by the respective governments. Many governments in the recipient countries were either not prepared or not willing to work with non-state actors, and NGOs thus were originally not represented sufficiently in the CCMs or were handpicked by the governments. CCMs in many cases were built because the GFATM required them in the proposals process, but not because cooperation with civil society was a goal in itself. Most CCMs had no clear rules on the selection of members or the composition of the CCMs. Especially people living with the diseases, women's organizations and rural NGOs often have not been represented in the CCMs at all.

A second problem involves participation. Even where formal representation of non-state actors is given, practical constraints often inhibit weaker actors from truly participating in the CCM processes and articulating their interests. While this to a limited degree is also the case at global level (where preparation for Board meetings is more difficult for Southern NGOs than for better-resourced Northern delegations), it is especially crucial at the national level. Travel costs, language barriers, lack of organization, scarce resources, information deficits, limited transparency or short-term planning in many cases are obstacles for participation of non-state actors, especially from outside the national capitals.

The third important issue is the unclear role of CCMs after the proposal has been submitted to the GFATM secretariat. Although CCMs are expected to oversee implementation, during the first funding rounds little support was given to CCMs to fulfil this role. The CCMs had to rely on the GFATM's bilateral and multilateral partners to support proposal development and the overview of implementation and were in a relatively weak position compared with the PR, the Local Fund Agent (LFA) and the GFATM Secretariat and Board. Since Round 5, technical assistance and capacity-building for CCMs can be included in the grant proposal up to a certain degree in order to better equip CCMs for their oversight function and to strengthen their position in the overall governance structure of the GFATM.

The GFATM also reacted to two other critical points – representation and participation – by changing its respective guidelines. These oblige CCMs, *inter alia*, to 'show evidence of membership of people living with and/or affected by the diseases', and to ensure that 'CCM members representing the non-government sectors must be selected by their own sector' (GFATM Board Meeting 9, GFATM/B10/2). The Global Fund Secretariat also set up a Screening Review Panel (SRP) to check whether or not CCMs submitting proposals were complying with these requirements. The SRP reports that in Round 7 more than two-thirds of the 84 CCMs proposals were recommended as fully compliant with the guidelines.

Influence of Southern actors on decisions and policies of the Global Fund

The question is how Southern representation in the governance structures of the GFATM translates into influence on the Fund's policies. At the national level the principle of country ownership is crucial in this context, and at the global level important issues include resource mobilization and in-kind contributions. Each of these issues has been a subject of intense discussions from the beginning of the GFATM.

The principle of country ownership

The most obvious influence of Southern actors, of course, emanates from the principle of country ownership. It encourages bottom-up processes and Southern participation and represents a shift away from conventional top-down approaches, as followed by other financing institutions in health such as the World Bank or PEPFAR. It also allows the GFATM to leave politically delicate decisions, such as the use of generics or the question of adequate prevention strategies, to the recipient countries instead of defining the respective policies at the global level.

The question is, however, how thoroughly this principle is applied in practice. In order to successfully apply to the GFATM, the vast majority of countries require technical assistance from bilateral and multilateral institutions (mostly from WHO, UNAIDS, GTZ). This is an important channel of influence, as priorities, norms or strategies of the respective actors are likely to find their way into the national proposal. In some cases a relabeling of existing programs of other donors has been reported, so that national priorities may not be represented as clearly as the principle of country ownership suggests. And also the GFATM itself limits the leeway countries have, as they must follow a number of procedures when applying for funding. The 'Guidelines for Proposals', which are renewed for each round, specify eligibility criteria (which countries can apply, the types of proposals (who can submit a proposal)) and – since Round 5 – requirements regarding the composition of CCMs. They also list criteria for the possible scope of the proposal and give advice for proposal development (program design, nomination of the PR, implementation processes, and technical assistance). So the proposal process in practice is often influenced by strategies and policies of actors outside the countries themselves, which leads to a restriction of Southern ownership.

Resource mobilization strategy

As the GFATM was created as a funding mechanism to support the fight against HIV/AIDS, tuberculosis and malaria, the mobilization of resources is of crucial importance. For 2010 the resource needs of the GFATM will be approximately US$6 billion (Matlin et al., 2008).

The general agreed formula for GFATM financing is that one-third each of the funds should come from the US, the EU countries and the rest of the world. A review of the total pledges until 2010, however, shows that only 21 per cent comes from the US and 10 per cent from Japan and other countries, while Europe accounts for 65 per cent of all pledges. The private sector – with the exception of the Bill & Melinda Gates Foundation, which pledged US$650 million – does not as yet play an important role in funding the GFATM. Only 4 per cent of all contributions come from non-state actors (Matlin et al., 2008). So in that sense the GFATM can be considered more a multilateral financing institution than a true public–private partnership (although contributions from the private sector and the NGO sector are not limited to funding alone).

Resource mobilization always was a controversial issue for the GFATM, and two options were discussed frequently, the first mainly raised by the Southern governments and the second put on the agenda by Northern and Southern NGOs: (1) Should the GFATM be demand-based or supply-based; that is, should donors be expected to fund the demand expressed in each proposal round or should the number of possible proposals be limited by the respective state of funding? and (2) Should contributions to the GFATM be voluntarily or mandatory, that is, should donors be free to give whatever they wish or should they be obliged to contribute in relationship to their share in world GNP?[3] With regard to the first issue the Southern actors were partly able to reach their goals, as the Board decided on the demand-based approach (although it developed a prioritization system if not enough funding is available). The second option, however, was blocked by the main donor countries on the Board (especially the US and Japan), which did not want to bind themselves in their funding decisions. Instead, the GFATM in 2005 introduced a so-called 'replenishment mechanism' by which donors declare their pledges for the next 2 to 3 years at fixed replenishment meetings, thus giving the GFATM some planning reliability. So far three replenishment meetings for the period of 2006–8 and two meetings for 2008–10 have taken place, with US$4.4 billion pledged for the first period, and US$6.3 billion for the period until 2010.

In sum, Southern actors have been relatively weak in influencing GFATM policies with regard to resource mobilization compared with donor countries that account for most of the GFATM's contributions and thus are reluctant to let other actors determine their funding policies.

In-kind contributions

A different picture can be observed in terms of the second contested issue: the question of in-kind contributions. A study commissioned by the private sector delegation in 2004 suggested that up to one-fifth of all GFATM cash commitments could be replaced by in-kind donations (of drugs, commodities and products, human resources and training, infrastructure, monitoring and evaluation (M&E) assistance, administration), with drug donations amounting to 30–35 per cent of all expenditures (Accenture, 2004, p. 18). This idea, however, was then rejected by the recipient group at the GFATM Board, who feared undue influence of commercial interests, conflicts of interest and limited sustainability.

The issue was brought up again by the private sector delegation at the first replenishment meetings and a Board meeting in 2006. It was decided that a Steering Group on Product and Service Donations should be established (with representatives of both the private and the NGO sector). Based on the recommendations of this group, the Board decided in November 2008 that only service donations to the Secretariat are possible; in-kind donations of health products, however, are still not an option for the GFATM.

So, in the debates on in-kind contribution, Southern governments and NGOs have managed to exert considerable influence on the policies of the GFATM. They have been able to convince the Board members (against the resistance of the private sector delegation and the US) that the potential benefits of such a strategy in terms of resources would be outweighed by their disadvantages and an undue influence of private interests and motivations on the GFATM activities.

Southern participation: enhancing legitimacy and effectiveness?

The literature on GPPPs often stresses that participation, especially of non-state actors, increases the legitimacy and effectiveness of the respective governance processes (Reinicke et al., 2000; Benner et al., 2004; for a critical review, see Börzel and Risse, 2005). On the input side,[4] the participation of those groups of actors that are the beneficiaries of governance decisions is expected to establish some kind of congruence between 'the rulers and the ruled' – a basic normative feature of legitimate governance. On the output side it is argued that the ability to participate in decision-making processes positively influences the 'belief in legitimacy' and thus contributes to a better compliance of the respective actors and – via the voluntary pooling of resources – enhances the effectiveness of the GPPP.

As far as input legitimacy is concerned, however, it must be seen that the GFATM – an entity that is positioned outside the UN system and not hosted by any organization – cannot derive it from any other institution but depends on the legitimacy of those who represent the different constituencies. While the participating governments are elected by the people in their respective countries and thus can claim to be legitimized by democratic voting processes (although in reality in some Southern countries this is not always the case), the case is different for civil society and private actors which are not democratically elected and which are not representative of larger groups of people, but are advocates for special interests. Also, as was shown above, most NGO Board members and the vast majority of the NGO delegations come from the HIV/AIDS field, so that representation at global level to a certain degree is selective and biased (although the GFATM is better than many other GPPPs in balancing between Northern and Southern NGOs).

In order to address the legitimacy problems of non-state actors in global governance, the concept of accountability was introduced by a variety of authors (for example, Keohane and Nye, 2001; Risse, 2004; Grant and Keohane, 2005). Broadly defined, accountability refers to a relationship 'in which an individual, group or other entity makes demands on an agent to report on his or her activities, and has the ability to impose costs on the agent' (Keohane, 2002, p. 12). Risse (2004) further differentiates between internal and external accountability. While the former refers to 'authorization and support by principals to agents who are institutionally linked to one another', the latter encompasses 'accountability to people outside the acting entity, whose lives are affected by it' (Risse, 2004, p. 7; see also Keohane, 2002, p. 14f). Thus, non-state actors become legitimate participants in global decision-making processes when they establish mechanisms to ensure both internal and external accountability (see, for instance, Wolf, 2001; Grant and Keohane, 2005; Benner et al., 2004; Zuern, 2004; Held and Koenig-Archibugi, 2005; Kovach et al., 2003; Buse, 2004).

Accountability is an especially complicated issue in PPPs, as their multi-actor constellation complicates both the identification of the agent and the control through the principals. In order to make partnership activities transparent, information on a number of issues (for example, sources and use of funding, governance structures, performance) is essential. This information needs to be accompanied by mechanisms that ensure responsiveness towards the stakeholders, for which participation is key. Finally, principals need to be able to sanction undesired behaviour of the partnership (for example, through non-compliance, withdrawal of support, reputational damage) (Bartsch, 2008).

While the external accountability of NGOs in the GFATM generally can be considered high – as they advocate for groups whose lives are directly affected by its activities: the people living with HIV/AIDS, tuberculosis and malaria in the developing world – their internal accountability is often limited. Although the GFATM, for example, has clear rules on membership selection, a limited transparency can be observed in the selection process itself. The responsible organizations – the International Council of AIDS Service Organizations (ICASO) in the case of the NGO sector and the Global Business Coalition on HIV/AIDS in the case of the private sector – do not publish any information apart from the nominations for vacant positions and do not document the selection process publicly.

The GFATM itself has clearly defined accountability mechanisms, including rules for composition and operation of its governing and administrative bodies, policies on conflicts of interest, an early-warning system, focal points for communication purposes and a high degree of transparency (with most documents made available on its website). Because of this, the GFATM is able to compensate for the deficits of its individual member groups in terms of internal accountability and to benefit from their high external accountability. The participation of Southern state and non-state actors thus contributes to the input legitimacy of the GFATM and enhances its 'moral authority' (Wolf, 2001).

The picture is mixed regarding effectiveness (output legitimacy). Although actors that are integrated in decision-making procedures tend to comply better with the rules set by the respective organization, it depends on the respective governance structure and network management how the potential of participation is used, and factors such as mutual trust, learning processes and relative cooperation gains play an important role in the way GPPPs function.

The more partners a GPPP has, the more important are clearly defined roles and responsibilities (McKinsey, 2003; Caines et al., 2004; Buse, 2004; Buse and Harmer, 2007). As the GFATM was established in a relatively short time there was not enough time to discuss divergent expectations and interests of the participating actors. Conflicts over certain issues, such as resource mobilization or in kind donations, tended to erupt frequently and are not entirely solved to this day. Also, the division of labour between the GFATM and its partners was not precisely defined. The GFATM was structured as a public–private partnership, but it was not clear what roles the different types of partners would play. Also, it was not considered sufficiently that competing interests, different organizational cultures, a lack of trust and/or resource constraints could hamper effective cooperation.

Effectiveness of the GFATM at the global level has been hampered mainly by the unclear relationship between the GFATM and its multilateral partners. This is observed in tensions especially between the GFATM and WHO and UNAIDS, who had to invest additional resources for technical assistance in proposal development without compensation. The GFATM in the beginning was not very sensitive towards these issues as it took for granted that WHO and UNAIDS, as partners of the GFATM, would carry out these tasks in the context of their overall mandates. Over time, however, a learning process took place and the GFATM is now more aware of the fact that it cannot expect its partners to support the GFATM for altruistic reasons, but has to offer them something in exchange.[5]

At national levels, however, substantial challenges remain in the areas of donor harmonization and CCM processes. Especially in the field of HIV/AIDS (where the GFATM is only one funder among others) a stronger coordination of activities is necessary to avoid duplication of activities and fragmentation of policies. Although donors committed themselves to better practices with the 'Rome Declaration on Harmonization' in 2003 and the 'Paris Declaration on Aid Effectiveness' in 2005, rhetoric and practice tend to differ considerably. GFATM programs are not sufficiently integrated into broader horizontal strategies like Sector Wide Approaches or budget financing, as they focus on vertical, disease-specific interventions. Although the GFATM states that it strives for integration into existing structures wherever possible (Global Task Team, 2005), the relationship between the CCMs and other coordinating institutions at the national level (for example, National AIDS Councils, UN Theme groups) often is not thoroughly defined. This often leads to substantial bureaucratic burdens for the recipient countries and stresses scarce country capacities. Finally, poor functioning of CCMs can contribute to a reduced effectiveness in terms of grant performance. Studies by the GFATM (2005, 2007e) found that grants with well-functioning CCMs and NGOs as Principal Recipients (PR) were performing better than those with government PRs. Ensuing discussions on the appropriateness of the CCM model resulted in a system of 'dual track financing' that was established in Round 8. The GFATM now recommends that CCMs nominate at least two PRs, one from the government sector and one from the non-government sector, which shows an increasing influence of non-state actors in the GFATM also at national level.

Conclusions

This chapter looked at the influence of Southern actors on establishment, governance, and policies of the Global Fund and discussed the connection between Southern participation and the GFATM's legitimacy and effectiveness. It argued that the establishment of the GFATM was dominated by the G8 countries, especially the US and Japan. Although Southern countries' needs and discourses influenced that process, they were objects rather than subjects in that early phase. In the architecture of the GFATM we find multi-stakeholder bodies with a broad representation of Southern state and non-state actors at both global and national level. However, the underlying assumption of that structure – that the interests of NGOs and Southern governments tend to converge – is not true. Instead, these two constituencies frequently have competing interests, as was shown in the case of Board composition and CCM requirements, and, over time, a shift has occurred that has strengthened non-state actors at the expense of Southern governments.

If we look at the influence of Southern actors on the policies of the GFATM, the principle of country ownership has proved most important and constitutes a central element for increasing bottom-up processes. With regard to resource mobilization the influence of Southern actors has been relatively weak, but they have had considerable influence in successfully opposing initiatives of the private sector to allow for in-kind donations of health products. Overall, Southern actors are relatively influential in comparison with the private sector, but they are not able to influence the decision-making of the GFATM as much as the donor countries who are responsible for the lion's share of the GFATM funding.

Considering the effect of Southern participation on the legitimacy and effectiveness of the GFATM, the question arises: Should participation of a large number of actors – especially from the South – be a goal in itself or should the issues be viewed from a more functional perspective? On the one hand, it can be argued that broad participatory models create input legitimacy in global governance processes as they allow a congruence between policymakers and those who are affected by a policy; on the other hand, broad participation can hamper effective policymaking if competing interests, lack of cooperation, high transaction costs or inefficient mechanism for partnership management prevail. As Börzel and Risse (2005, p. 215) put it: '"All-inclusive" governance arrangements might lead to a serious lack of efficiency and reduced effectiveness. In other words, a trade-off between legitimacy and effectiveness might arise.'

But, even if partnerships like the GFATM could successfully claim to be both legitimate and effective organizations, they will not necessarily contribute to a more legitimate and effective overall structure of global health governance. First, the goals of single GPPPs do not necessarily harmonize with the goals of other actors at global and national levels. Most of the partnerships in the health sector aim at producing goal-oriented policy outputs in a clearly defined issue area. The sum of these activities, however, need not lead to a coherent health policy but can contribute to a further fragmentation at both global and national levels. GPPPs, secondly, compete with each other and with other actors in global health for scarce resources and influence. As funding sources are limited and additionality is more a normative concept than an empirical reality, the proliferation of GPPPs might lead to a distortion of funding and a further verticalization of health policies instead of a strengthening of horizontal approaches to health system development. Thirdly, GPPPs can be used by powerful actors of global health to circumvent established organizations such as WHO and pursue their interests in other fora and institutional contexts, thus leading to a weakening of these organizations as actors of global health. Although new forms of governance such as GPPPs by no means substitute for traditional modes of regulation, they offer the actors another institutional option to mediate between interests and to negotiate conflicts. They may, under certain circumstances, contribute to a better integration of actors of the South and an empowerment of weak actors, but can also be used by powerful actors of the North to pursue their interests, so we should be careful not to overestimate their potential.

Notes

1. The section on the GFATM is based on qualitative interviews of the author with representatives of the GFATM secretariat and the major stakeholder groups, analysis of GFATM original documents and the first results of the GFATM's 5-year evaluation, as well as a review of existing studies on the GFATM by other authors. See, for instance, Summers (2003), Gootnick (2003, 2005, 2007), Radelet (2004), Radelet and Caines (2005) and Sidibe et al. (2006b); for a comprehensive list see the evaluation library of the GFATM at: www.theglobalfund.org/en/links_resources/library/ and the paper archive of Aidspan at: http://www.aidspan.org/index.php?page=publications
2. The source for this material is interviews with representatives of NGOs, WHO, UNAIDS and the GFATM.
3. NGOs have been advocating since 2002 for such an 'equitable contributions framework'; see France et al. (2002), Oxfam (2002), Aidspan (2004).
4. The differentiation between input and output legitimacy was introduced by Scharpf (1999): input legitimacy refers to the question of who should be involved in rule making; output legitimacy refers to problem-solving capacity of the rule-making institution.
5. Resources for technical assistance can now be included in the grant proposal, which was not the case before. Also, the support of the Three Ones and the 3x5 Initiative, as well as the engagement of the GFATM in global initiatives such as the Global Task Team, the High-Level Meetings on the health MDGs or the Global Joint M&E Facility, shows that the GFATM is trying to improve its cooperation with other actors in global health.

10

'Making the Money Work'*: Challenges towards Coordination of HIV/AIDS Programmes in Africa

Siri Bjerkreim Hellevik

Introduction

Several new actors are now funding global health. In HIV/AIDS funding, these actors range from multilateral organizations to private foundations and large-scale bilateral programmes, such as the President's Emergency Plan for AIDS Relief (PEPFAR). HIV/AIDS funding globally has seen 'a six-fold increase' from 2001 to 2007 (UNAIDS, 2008a, p. 3).[1] This rapid increase in funding has resulted in 'a crisis of implementation' due to 'national capacity gaps in areas such as programme management and service delivery' (UNAIDS, 2005b, p. 14). The crisis is exacerbated by insufficient donor coordination, which creates redundancies in programming. It is exacerbated also by divergent aims and distinctive programming of the different actors (McKinsey, 2005; Bernstein and Sessions, 2007).

The main global actors funding HIV/AIDS programmes, such as the Global Fund to Fight AIDS Tuberculosis and Malaria (GFATM), the World Bank and various UN organizations, have identified coordination and harmonization of their efforts as important in 'making the money work' within HIV/AIDS (UNAIDS, 2005b; Sidibe et al., 2006a; PEPFAR et al., 2006). One effort to enhance coordination and harmonization was the Paris Declaration on Aid Effectiveness, which was signed on 2 March 2005 by more than 100 countries as well as several international organizations (DCD-DAC). The Declaration is a general commitment to 'ownership, harmonization, alignment, results, and mutual accountability' of all development aid and it has made coordination a top priority (OECD, 2005).

Another policy response, this one specific to increased coordination around HIV/AIDS, was the joint agreement in 2004 of most bilateral and multilateral donors and recipients of HIV/AIDS funding on the 'Three Ones' principles. These principles state that each recipient country should institutionalize its response by establishing one National AIDS Coordinating Authority (NAC)[2] with a multisectoral mandate, one strategic HIV/AIDS framework for all actors at the country level, and one national monitoring and evaluation system (UNAIDS/WHO, 2004a). In the years following the adoption of the Three Ones principles, several efforts towards coordination have been made at global and national levels (see GTT, 2005; Attawell and Dickinson, 2007; Sepulveda et al., 2007; UNAIDS, 2006a).

In this chapter, I evaluate the progress made in coordination among the three global actors that are the major funders of HIV/AIDS programs, according to the World Bank (World Bank, 2007c). These are: the GFATM, a public–private partnership (PPP); the World Bank Multi-Country HIV/AIDS Program for Africa (MAP), a multilateral organization; and the PEPFAR, a bilateral program of the US government. One dimension of the coordination project is horizontal. While coordination may be defined as 'the attempt to optimize the coherence and consistency of political decisions as well as policy implementation' (Wollman, 2006, p. 594), *horizontal coordination* implies coordination taking place between actors situated at the same organizational (and territorial) level. Such horizontal coordination may be termed a governance network,[3] as defined by Sørensen and Torfing (2007). According to these authors, a governance network is: '1. a relatively stable horizontal articulation of interdependent but operationally autonomous actors; 2. who interact through negotiations; 3. which take place through regulative, normative, cognitive and imaginary frameworks; 4. that is self-regulating within limits set by external agencies; and 5. which contributes to the production of public purpose' (Sørensen and Torfing, 2007, p. 9). To analyze the progress on horizontal coordination of the three programs, I draw on the theoretical framework of Guy Peters (1998). Peters (1998, p. 303) identifies three main problems with horizontal coordination: (1) two or more organizations 'perform the same task (redundancy)'; (2) 'no organization performs a necessary task'; and (3) there is 'incoherence' in aims and 'requirements'.

In addition to horizontal coordination, these three organizations also coordinate with African governments. In considering this level of coordination, I will focus mainly on the National AIDS Coordinating Authority (NAC), since this entity was developed to coordinate HIV/AIDS responses in African countries. Overall, coordination for delivering AIDS programming involves coordination at the *international* and the *national* level, as well as at the intersection of these levels. Given that the global actors and the governments that are studied in this chapter operate at different levels, the global and the national, one may argue that they form what Anthony McGrew (2002, p. 279) calls a 'transnational policy network'. McGrew (2002, p. 279) states that: 'A proliferation of transnational policy networks and multilateral institutions give form and substance to global governance and are central to the formulation and implementation of effective and legitimate global public policy.' My analysis, therefore, is an attempt to look in detail at the problems and possibilities involved in developing more effective global governance in HIV/AIDS.

On the three global actors

Global HIV/AIDS funding is not easily mapped, due to the rapid increase in funding and actors in recent years. Also, there is a gap between *commitments* and *disbursement* of funds, although this gap has been closing since about 2006 (Bernstein and Sessions, 2007). The challenges of coordination are evidently great. Indeed, 'according to Peter Piot, the Executive Director of UNAIDS, the global aid architecture for HIV/AIDS is a "mess"' (World Bank, 2007c, p. 11). Nevertheless, a mess or not, according to Swidler (2006) global HIV/AIDS funding has a hierarchical structure, with the UNAIDS at the top, followed by a number of multilateral organizations, foundations and bilateral donors, and, after these, numerous international NGOs. At the country level, the national and local governments and country-based civil society organizations, including community-based organizations and faith-based organizations, add to this picture. MAP, the Global Fund and PEPFAR are three of the main actors among the diverse group of actors mentioned in this section, and they are described briefly below.

The World Bank Multi-Country HIV/AIDS Program for Africa (MAP)

MAP Africa was established in 2000 and it represents one part of the total HIV/AIDS assistance that the World Bank provides globally. 'The overall development objective of the MAP is to dramatically increase access to HIV/AIDS prevention, care, and treatment programs, with emphasis on vulnerable groups' (World Bank, 2007d).

The four eligibility criteria that had to be met in order for countries to gain access to these funds were: 'having a strategic approach to HIV/AIDS'; having established a NAC; 'government commitment to quick implementation arrangements'; and 'agreement by the government to use multiple implementation agencies, especially NGOs/Community Based Organizations' (World Bank, 2007d). In 2007, MAP Africa entered its third phase, and the funds were substantially reduced (World Bank, 2007c). In line with the reduced funding, the role of MAP is envisaged to change from providing substantial financial contributions to facilitating technical expertise at the country level (World Bank, 2007c). It is too early to say whether, or to what extent, the decrease in funds available will reduce MAP's role as one of the three major global actors in African countries.

The Global Fund (GFATM)

The Global Fund is an independent public–private partnership established in 2002 as a mechanism for providing more rapid disbursement of funds towards HIV/AIDS than the UN organizations and the World Bank had been able to channel (GFATM, 2007b; Poku, 2002). The Fund receives donations from many sources, including the Gates Foundation and several countries, with the US as 'the largest contributor nation' (PEPFAR et al., 2006, p. 4).

In order for countries to apply for funding from the Global Fund, Country Coordinating Mechanisms (CCMs) had to be established (GFATM, 2008b). These CCMs are 'public–private partnerships' responsible for administering and assisting in the development of grant proposals from different actors, such as NGOs and national governments (GFATM, 2007c). In most cases, the CCM has representatives from the government, civil society and businesses in the country, as well as 'people living with and/or affected by the diseases' (GFATM 2007c, p. 4). After grant approval, the CCMs 'oversee progress during implementation' (GFATM, 2007a). In addition to the CCM, all countries receiving funds have a Local Funding Agent that completes an annual performance review of each Principal Recipient of funds (for example, national government ministries or consortiums of NGOs).

The PEPFAR program

PEPFAR was launched by the US government in 2003 to provide a unified response to AIDS and thus to coordinate all US AIDS funding (OGAC, 2005). The US Government, through various amendments and laws passed in Congress, has set the operating principles and priorities of PEPFAR. The Office of the Global AIDS Coordinator (OGAC) manages the PEPFAR program (Sepulveda et al., 2007, p. 66). PEPFAR employs a partnership approach and channels money to international NGOs, national governments and American organizations and universities that engage with partners in the recipient countries. In the recipient countries, country teams have been established, coordinated by the US Embassy (OGAC, 2005). PEPFAR supports HIV/AIDS programs in 123 countries, but two-thirds of the funds are channelled to 15 focus countries (Sepulveda et al., 2007, pp. 58, 64, 66).[4] Following an original US$15 billion[5] expenditure, the Reauthorization Act signed on 30 July 2008 provided for another US$39 billion of funding to be spent from 2009 to 2013 (OGAC, 2008).

Coordination policies among the three global actors

Coordination is not a new phenomenon within bilateral or multilateral aid, but has been 'a key form for organizing development practice for a long time' (Robinson et al., 2000, p. 7). With the acceptance of the Three Ones principles as the overall global framework of coordination within HIV/AIDS, the NAC was embraced as the leading coordinating unit by African governments, multilateral and bilateral partners (PEPFAR et al., 2006, p. 3). By 2008, 92 per cent of all reporting countries had established NACs (UNAIDS, 2008a, p. 206). But 'none of the "ones" has been easy to implement, even in the few countries where governments have taken charge of their national strategies' (Lele et al., 2005, p. 154), and, therefore, in 2005 The Global Task Team on Improving AIDS Coordination among Multilateral Institutions and International Donors (GTT) was formed to improve coordination (Attawell et al., 2007; GTT, 2005). Later that year, this Task Team came up with a number of recommendations, focusing on four areas: (1) 'empowering inclusive national leadership and ownership'; (2) 'alignment and harmonization'; (3) 'reform for a more effective multilateral response'; and (4) 'accountability and oversight' (GTT, 2005). These recommendations were endorsed by the United Nations General Assembly in 2005 (UN General Assembly, 2005).

Perspectives on horizontal coordination

In this section, I will discuss the efforts towards horizontal coordination among the three HIV/AIDS programs with regards to the general theoretical problems that may occur in such efforts according to Guy Peters (1998). The three problems introduced and discussed below are: (1) redundancy; (2) lacunae; (3) incoherence in aims and requirements. The three problems are dealt with in separate sections, but they are all discussed with reference to the four areas of improvement of coordination as identified by the Global Task Team recommendations (see section above). The UN system (including the World Bank) made a follow-up plan based upon the recommendations from the GTT, the UNAIDS Technical Division of Labour plan. In this plan, each of the relevant UN organizations involved ('lead organizations') has been assigned particular responsibility for one of the 17 areas identified as being necessary to focus on. Although the US government, along with several other governments, was involved in the GTT work, the division of labour involves only UN organizations, including the World Bank (UNAIDS, 2005b, p. 34). Being a financing entity and not an implementing agency, The Global Fund is left out of this detailed plan of division of work, except for being represented in the Global Joint Problem-Solving and Implementation Support Team (GIST) (see UNAIDS, 2005b, p. 34). Still, the Global Fund is involved in other measures of coordination with the PEPFAR and the World Bank, as well as the UNAIDS, which may compensate for its minor role assigned in the UN Division of Labour. In this chapter I deal only with the efforts that concern the three actors, but in most of them the UNAIDS also plays a part.

Problem 1: Redundancy

The first problem that may appear in efforts towards horizontal coordination is that two or more organizations 'perform the same task (redundancy)' (Peters, 1998, p. 303). The PEPFAR, MAP and the Global Fund clearly have similar tasks or issues that they deal with, and thus horizontal coordination among these actors can be expected to be difficult. On the other hand, the fact that these actors all focus on halting and reversing the spread of HIV/AIDS in accordance with the Millennium Development Goals (MDGs) makes the potential challenges in coordination seem likely to be solvable. According to Peters (1998, p. 303), 'redundancy should be the easiest co-ordination problem to solve'. This problem goes into the discussion of efforts towards harmonization and alignment of the HIV/AIDS programs, one of the four themes of the GTT recommendations. At the international level, 'the UNAIDS Programme Coordinating Board, UNAIDS Secretariat and Cosponsors have taken steps to support implementation of the GTT recommendations on harmonisation and alignment within the UN system' (Attawell and Dickinson, 2007, p. 34). Several measures have been put in place, such as Joint UNAIDS Teams and Joint UN Programmes,[6] and some of the measures include the three global actors discussed in the chapter. However, according to the GTT report and the Paris Declaration as well as several observers (Sepulveda et al., 2007; Attawell and Dickinson, 2007; Shakow, 2006), one form of redundancy, in particular, hinders both horizontal coordination among the three global actors and vertical coordination with African governments. This is the existence of parallel structures for implementation and coordination of programs in recipient countries.

The existence of parallel structures and duplication of assistance at the national level was one of the reasons for the establishment of the GTT (GTT, 2005, p. 9). The GTT report mentions 'the Global Fund CCM in addition to the NAC as an example of duplication' (ibid., p. 10), that is, redundancy, to use Peters's term. On a general level of development aid, the Paris Declaration deals with the problem of what it calls 'parallel implementation units' and a specific goal is set for reducing the number of such units by 2010 (OECD, 2005, p. 1). On the problem within the area of HIV/AIDS, Shakow (2006, p. 25) states that, in many countries, the CCM has become 'a new and separate channel which competes with and confuses the role of other bodies'. For instance, the CCM and the NAC represent duplicating structures in many countries, having 'competing roles' (Shakow 2006, p. 7; see also UNAIDS, 2006b, p. 4).

Moreover, '[w]hile providing much needed funding for the AIDS response, parallel mechanisms like the Global Fund Country Coordinating Mechanism (CCM) can lead to a confusion of roles when it comes to policymaking' (UNAIDS, 2006b, p. 4). As a consequence, the country structure of the Global Fund has 'led to considerable duplication in requirements, procedures, and institutional arrangements at the country level' (Lele et al., 2005, p. 160). According to a recent Global Fund report (GFATM, 2008a, p. 55), 'an examination into the reasons why most countries chose to form separate CCMs as opposed to building upon pre-existing structures could prove to be instructive'. Nevertheless, until such an examination is completed, 'anecdotal evidence suggests that many countries created CCMs as distinct entities, because this is what they thought the new donor required' (ibid.). Another reason given by some countries was that the NACs were not operational when Global Fund funding was granted (ibid.).

The problems of parallel institutions have been complained about in Tanzania, Swaziland, Mozambique and Malawi (UNAIDS, 2005a, c). However, the complaint from Tanzania that 'GFATM proposals have been developed in parallel to existing strategies and ongoing activities' (Lake, 2004, p. ix) has motivated some action. Since 2005, the Global Fund has attempted to move towards more horizontal coordination through the merger of CCM and other coordination mechanisms for the three diseases of HIV/AIDS, Tuberculosis and Malaria with the Tanzanian National AIDS Coordinating Authority (TNCM) (TACAIDS, 2006; GFATM, 2005, p. 16). However, there are still two coordinating mechanisms in the country, one for national government coordination and one for coordinating external funding (TNCM). In Mozambique, there has been some progress in that the 'CCM has been restructured so it is aligned with government mechanisms for AIDS coordination' (Attawell and Dickinson, 2007, p. 41). There has also been progress in 'joint reporting' in Mozambique and Swaziland (ibid., p. 36). Further, in Swaziland, Malawi and Mozambique, the Global Fund now 'participates in pooled funding arrangements' (ibid., p. 36).

Nevertheless, 'there is consensus that more needs to be done to harmonise NACs and CCMs' (ibid., p. 41), and in several African countries various types of coordination measures have been put in place – between the CCM and the NAC in countries and between the Global Fund and the World Bank on the global level – through joint missions and reviews (Shakow, 2006; Attawell and Dickinson, 2007; Dickinson et al., 2008). The Global Fund has attempted to harmonize its procurement policy with receiving countries (Ryan et al., 2008. p. 114) through efforts in joint planning, reporting procedures and reviews. Despite this, institutional coordination under the umbrella of the NAC remains underdeveloped (see Attawell and Dickinson, 2007; Shakow, 2006). Only 38 per cent of the Global Fund and MAP funding is managed by the same unit of coordination (World Bank, 2007b, p. 6). In addition, in only one-third of the African countries do NACs have representatives in the CCM (Attawell and Dickinson, 2007, p. 41).

Due to these problems of parallel institutions and duplication, Shakow (2006, p. 49) suggested the merging of the NAC and CCM 'wherever possible'. He added that the two actors should consider having 'a common procurement system as well as a common monitoring and evaluation system' (ibid.). According to Attawell and Dickinson (2007, p. 36), 'the recommendations of this review have not been fully accepted or taken forward'. Still, the Global Fund has recently opened up for the use of 'existing coordination structures', but these have to 'meet CCM requirements' (GFATM, 2006, p. 35). MAP Africa, on the other hand, being the program that funds the running of the NACs, actively supports the latter structure for horizontal coordination.

There have been several efforts to harmonize and align the CCM with the NAC and other donors, including the forming of joint management units between the World Bank and the Global Fund in Rwanda and Chad, as well as joint procurement planning of these and the PEPFAR in Mozambique and Rwanda (Attawell and Dickinson, 2007, pp. 8, 36).

To conclude, it seems as if the existence of parallel institutions, that is, the CCMs and NACs, has created redundancy in some African countries. However, several efforts have been launched in recent years to improve this situation. The Fund seems to move towards more horizontal coordination with the two other actors both at country level and at the global level. Nevertheless, the continuing existence of the CCM seems to be hindering horizontal coordination, given that issues concerning the Global Fund grants are handled by CCMs in most cases and not by NACs (Lele et al., 2005, p. 156).

Problem 2: Lacunae

The second possible problem of horizontal coordination is that 'no organization performs a necessary task (lacunae)' (Peters, 1998, p. 303). According to Peters (1998, p. 303), lacunae in policies, for instance, may take place in organizations because policymakers believe that it is more costly to deal with the task than not.

Although most African countries and the three global actors have attempted to reduce lacunae by establishing and supporting the National AIDS Coordinating Authority (NAC) as the body for horizontal coordination, it is questionable whether NACs live up to expectations as national AIDS coordinating authorities.

While most countries have established a NAC and have a national plan/strategic framework, the 2008 UNAIDS report states (UNAIDS, 2008a, p. 209) that 'these achievements are more evident on paper than in practice'. It is important to remember that NACs are 'relatively new organisations' (Dickinson et al., 2008, p. 9). In general, there are great differences in the efficiency of the work of NACs around the world, and NACs thus seem to work as *the* national coordinating bodies in some cases, while not in others (UNAIDS, 2006c; Ainsworth et al., 2005; Dickinson et al., 2008). Lacunae are thus more of a problem in some countries than others. The specific lacuna discussed here is the lack of capacity in the NACs, which makes it difficult for a NAC to act as the horizontal coordinating unit (UNAIDS, 2006c; Dickinson et al., 2008; Ainsworth et al., 2005). Lacunae in capacity are present in several African countries; 'capacity constraints undermine the functioning of the AIDS coordinating entities and inhibit their effectiveness' (UNAIDS, 2006b, p. 7).

NACs have a difficult job because the framework for coordination is, in several cases, poorly defined and the staff of the NACs may thus be unclear about what are the goals of their commissions (Mackay and Laurence,

2005, p. 2). The functioning of the NAC as a coordinating entity is touched upon in all of the GTT recommendations, such as through the focus on the need for national strategic AIDS plans, the alignment of donors to national plans, and ensuring technical assistance to the NAC and other country institutions to make such plans and build up capacity to handle 'implementation bottlenecks' (GTT, 2005, p. 23). For instance, planning is the major issue in the GTT recommendations on 'empowering inclusive national leadership and ownership'. Improving planning is important, given that, of the 41 reporting African countries to the UNGASS in 2008, only about 50 per cent had 'a quality national strategy'[7] (UNAIDS, 2008a, p. 28).[8] Furthermore, turning to the GTT recommendations on alignment and harmonization, Attawell and Dickinson (2007) observe that donors have improved their alignments with national plans. However, while the Global Fund and the World Bank have made some improvements on alignment to national plans, the PEPFAR 'remains largely external to harmonisation and alignment processes and this undoubtedly presents coordination challenges for the NACs' (Dickinson et al., 2008, pp. 10–11). PEPFAR is weak on alignment with country structures, because it 'manages its funding outside of government frameworks through cooperating partners and contractors' (ibid., p. 11).

In addition to the focus on planning, the GTT (2005) recommendations on 'reform for a more effective multilateral response' also deal specifically with lack of capacity in the NACs in suggesting the strengthening of technical support. Improving technical capacity in recipient countries to plan, implement and coordinate programs seems to be high on the agenda for bilateral and multilateral actors within HIV/AIDS, identified as a major hindrance to implementation of the Three Ones and addressed in a number of initiatives in recent years (World Bank, 2007c; McKinsey and Company, 2005; Attawell and Dickinson, 2007, p. 29). An important reason for the lack of capacity is that 'the availability of technical assistance has not kept pace with the increase in resources for AIDS programmes' (UNAIDS, 2005b, p. 13). Thus, several African NACs have served as implementing agencies rather than as horizontal coordination units of all HIV/AIDS programs in the respective countries (Ainsworth et al., 2005). Consequently, more attempts towards horizontal coordination could have been made, and the ones that exist could probably have been improved, if the NACs had not had such problems with lack of capacity and thus fulfilling their mandates.

Major institutions and initiatives set up to strengthen technical capacity by means of funds and/or human resources include the Global Joint Problem-Solving and Implementation Support Team (GIST),[9] the Technical Support Facilities (TSFs) by UNAIDS, the Country Harmonization and Alignment Tool (CHAT), WHO 'regional knowledge hubs', AIDS Strategy and Action Plan Service (ASAP), Joint UNDP, World Bank, UNAIDS Poverty Reduction Strategy Mainstreaming Programme, and the Coordinating AIDS Technical

Support database[10] (CoATS) (Attawell and Dickinson, 2007, p. 29; UNAIDS, 2008a, pp. 29–30; UNAIDS, 2008d; World Bank, 2008a).

The GIST is a committee at the international level, with representatives from UN organizations and major bilateral and multilateral actors funding HIV/AIDS, which is to 'help diagnose national technical support needs, address urgent implementation issues, and ensure that the deployment of UN support is well-coordinated within the framework of the UNAIDS Division of Labour and Consolidated Plan for Technical Support' (UNAIDS, 2005b, p. 5). The Technical Support Facilities assist the Global Fund in 'grant implementation' (UNAIDS, 2007; UNAIDS, 2008a; UNAIDS, 2008b, p. 30). The Aids Strategy and Action Plan (ASAP) 'helps clients develop well-prioritized, evidence-based, results-focused and costed AIDS strategies and action plans', and since its inception in 2006 it has assisted 21 African countries (World Bank, 2008a; World Bank, 2008b, p. 2).

The GIST has to some extent been successful in terms of giving joint technical support to a number of countries since 2005 (Attawell and Dickinson, 2007, p. 28). There have, however, been 'differing perceptions about its technical support role' among the organizations participating in the unit, for example, whether it is to be a mechanism for assisting with 'implementation problems at country level' or 'systemic issues at global level that impact on country implementation' (ibid., p. 28). In addition, there has been lack of commitment on the part of some of the GIST partners (ibid., p. 29).

Both UNAIDS through the TSFs and PEPFAR are to assist the Global Fund in developing technical capacity at the country level (OGAC, 2007, p. 192; UNAIDS, 2008c). The TSFs, the GIST, and PEPFAR assistance all base their support on 'demand-drivenness', that is, the demand for assistance must come from the recipients of funding (OGAC, 2007, p. 191; UNAIDS, 2006c; UNAIDS, 2008c). Attawell and Dickinson (2007, pp. 27, 29, 33) list several challenges to date that confront this approach at the country level: little knowledge of the existence of these mechanisms in several countries; where knowledge does exist, 'national governments and agency field offices do not always alert the GIST to problems'; and/or there is in some cases 'unwillingness to acknowledge the need for technical support'.

Turning to the international level, UNAIDS is to be the coordinating body. However, UNAIDS cannot adequately address the problem of lacunae, because it is dependent on the willingness of the three major global HIV/AIDS actors to coordinate their work. This willingness is seen in the global actors' initiatives to coordinate their work better in response to the GTT recommendations on harmonization and alignment, as well as the many efforts on facilitating joint technical assistance as already described. Additional measures include joint meetings, country visits, joint procurement planning and joint procurement (Global Fund and World Bank). Also, focusing on giving more technical assistance seems to be an efficient strategy for 'making the money work', and hence reducing lacunae at the national level as well, because in the cases where this has been done already (outside the GIST) access to grants has improved and implementation has speeded up considerably (see examples, UNAIDS, 2005b, pp. 15, 16). Finally, the Coordinating AIDS Technical Support (CoATS) database, launched in 2008, is to provide information on all technical support activities so that duplication is hindered (UNAIDS, 2008d). However, it remains to be seen how CoATS will work in practice. Also, as Attawell and Dickinson (2007, p. 27) demonstrate, the many recent efforts towards enhancing technical capacity also create challenges in coordination and ensuring that the initiatives are smoothly run and do not create duplicating mechanisms.

Problem 3: Incoherence in aims and requirements

According to Peters (1998, p. 303), horizontal coordination is difficult to achieve when there is 'incoherence' in aims and 'requirements' (ibid., p. 303). In his words, 'Incoherence may be the most difficult co-ordination problem to address effectively', due to, among other things, that 'each organization has a rationale for its action and is linked to a clientele' (ibid., p. 303). In this section I argue that incoherence in aims and requirements is a problem for the three actors examined in this chapter, in terms of their relations with national governments (that is, vertical coordination) as well as with each other (that is, horizontal coordination). All three actors work for halting and reversing the spread of HIV/AIDS, but there are differences among the three actors in aims when broken down to specific policies. Also, there is a tendency among the individual actors to focus on the results of their own specific programmes within countries rather than the joint results of the three actors and their programmes.

PEPFAR, in particular, focuses on its own initiatives as much as or more than on joint ones and its aims have often appeared to be at odds with the other HIV actors (Patterson, 2006; Dickinson et al., 2008). While the MAP and the Global Fund support a wide variety of treatment, prevention and care initiatives, the Congress Leadership Act of 2003 required PEPFAR to earmark its spending by using '55% of its global funding on treatment, 20% on prevention, 15% on care, and 10% for orphans and vulnerable children'[11] (US Congress, 2003, p. 746). Further, out of the 20 per cent on prevention, the Leadership Act stated that 33 per cent was to be spent on abstinence and fidelity (AB) programmes (ibid.).[12] Other policies that have made PEPFAR different from the other actors include the prostitution pledge, which is the requirement for organizations to certify that they have a 'policy explicitly opposing prostitution and sex trafficking' in order to receive funding (US Congress, 2003, p. 734), and the policy on injecting drug users, which states that 'Emergency Plan funding may not be used to support needle or syringe exchange programs (NSEP)' (OGAC, 2006, p. 2; Sepulveda et al., 2007, pp. 124–25). PEPFAR's policy priorities have been out of alignment with recipient countries' priorities and have impeded coordination with recipient governments (Patterson, 2006; Oomman et al., 2007, p. 6; Sepulveda et al., 2007, p. 82; Dickinson et al., 2008, pp. 10–12; GAO, 2008). Funding allocations based on these policy priorities have 'limited PEPFAR's ability to tailor its activities in each country to the local epidemic and to coordinate with the level of activities in the countries' national plans' (Sepulveda et al., 2007, p. 82). Also, as Sepulveda et al. (ibid., p. 101) assert, PEPFAR's focus on specific results 'creates disincentives for international coordination among donors and harmonization at the country level'. 'By far the most often-cited obstacle to harmonization, however, is the requirement that US funds be used only for medications that have received approval from the US Food and Drug Administration' (ibid., p. 88). To some extent, this requirement has been superseded by 'work-around arrangements' at the country level, but the latter have been 'difficult to administer, reducing the ability of PEPFAR and the host countries to use funds in the most cost-effective manner possible' (ibid., p. 88).

Concern has been voiced by both global health experts and activists[13] regarding the effect of PEPFAR earmarking on 'country ownership' of the anti-HIV/AIDS strategies. In response, the United States Government Accountability Office recommended in 2008[14] that PEPFAR lift the spending directives in favour of 'a more country-based and evidence-based approach' (GAO, 2008, p. 37). The Office of the Global AIDS Coordinator (OGAC) responded that country ownership and an evidence-based approach have been practised from the very start of the PEPFAR programme in 2003 (GAO, 2008, pp. 53–60). Nevertheless, the reauthorization of the PEPFAR from 2008[15] has changed the AB policy somewhat; now, countries with a generalized epidemic spending less than 50 per cent of the funding allocated towards 'prevention activities' on AB programmes have to notify the Global AIDS Coordinator, who then has to report to Congress on this matter (US Congress, 2008, p. 49; Brown, 2008, p. 1).

PEPFAR's earmarking has created challenges to coordination among the three global actors and with national governments and thus has impeded fulfilment of the GTT (2005) recommendations on 'harmonization and alignment' and 'reform for a more effective multilateral response'. Yet, PEPFAR has made several efforts at coordination both with recipient governments and with the Global Fund and the MAP. In Nigeria, for instance, a PEPFAR coordinator position was created to facilitate harmonization of implementation of funds among PEPFAR-funded partners and the government (Attawell and Dickinson, 2007, p. 38). Also PEPFAR has coordinated with the two global actors through joint meetings in 2006, 2007 and 2008,[16] in the GIST committee and in planning (HIV Implementers, 2007, 2008; Sepulveda et al., 2007, p. 88). Finally, the recent changes in PEPFAR's mandate (US Congress, 2008), although minimal, do herald a move towards greater coordination and greater coherence in the deepening global governance network on HIV/AIDS.

Governance networks and accountability

The difficulties that the three major HIV/AIDS donors have in establishing effective coordination among themselves (horizontal coordination) and with African governments (vertical coordination) indicate some of the problems inherent in creating effective global governance networks on HIV/AIDS. The definition of governance networks by Sørensen and Torfing (2007) that was introduced at the beginning of the chapter suggests that such arrangements exist where there is 'a relatively stable horizontal articulation of interdependent but operationally autonomous actors', working in a particular area, who interact through negotiations that take place through 'regulative, normative, cognitive, and imaginary frameworks' and 'contribute to the production of public purpose' (Sørensen and Torfing, 2007, p. 9). Having assessed the efforts towards coordination among the three international actors, they seem to be in the process of forming such a governance network. They are autonomous yet interdependent organizations contributing to 'the production of public purpose' (ibid., p. 9) by working to combat the societal problem of HIV/AIDS. All of the actors have acknowledged that, in order to solve the crisis of implementation and '[make] the money work', they need to coordinate their actions, thus deepening the network structure of global health governance.

As concerns negotiations and frameworks, I argue that the work on HIV/AIDS coordination has moved forward through negotiations and these have taken place through previously established frameworks, starting with the Abuja and UNGASS Declarations of 2001 (Patterson, 2005, p. 182). The Three Ones Principles followed in 2004, established through negotiations in the UN. While the Abuja Declaration may be seen as a normative framework, the UNGASS Declaration and the Three Ones have to some extent been regulative and institutional frameworks. The UNGASS is regulative through its system for reporting on progress adhered to by an increasing number of countries: from 126 countries in 2006 to 146 in 2008 (UNAIDS, 2008a). The Three Ones is a regulative and most of all an institutional framework, but has only been partly implemented.

Further, the many efforts resulting from the GTT negotiations and final report may be seen to be an institutional framework, which again has spurred the establishment of several institutional frameworks/mechanisms/tools for work in particular areas, especially on scaling up technical capacity in recipient countries, through, for instance, the GIST, the TSFs, and the CHAT. Given that donors engage in these structures and agreements, I argue that they represent limits for self-regulation. But, as the efforts towards coordination assessed in the chapter reveal, the frameworks do not yet set sufficiently *effective* limits to self-regulation, because coordination efforts are being challenged by the three actors, through, among other things, the presence of parallel structures and the special goals and interests by the PEPFAR programme. Nevertheless, the many efforts taking place to improve harmonization and alignment among the three actors as well as to strengthen NACs' capacity to coordinate seem to indicate a developing global governance network on HIV/AIDS coordination. However, it is far from being effective yet. What still needs to be developed in order to make such a developing network effective? In line with Patterson's (2006) more general argument that African politics has to institutionalize the fight against AIDS in order to make an effective response to it, I argue that the African states and donors must make sure that the Three Ones Principles are put into practice. Given recent 'focus on providing technical assistance to scale up NACs' capacity, one may expect that their capacity to fulfil their mandate will improve in years to come. However, there are more general impediments to the efforts launched towards coordination, in terms of a general 'lack of state capacity' in African countries (Patterson, 2006, pp. 21–5), as well as patron–client relationships dominating politics in several states (ibid.; Chabal and Daloz, 1999), and relationships between members of the NAC Board and the Prime Minister or President seem in some cases to be imperative for a NAC to have 'power, authority and legitimacy' (Dickinson et al., 2008, p. 6).

Further, when dealing with governance networks, an important question is: to whom are these actors accountable? The GTT recommendations addresses the issue of accountability by suggesting that the global actors, among other things, improve information regarding financial commitments to national governments, as well as assist NACs in making assessments of the 'performance of multilateral institutions, international partners, and national stakeholders' (GTT, 2005, p. 24). The CHAT is an instrument for NACs to hold donors to account, assessing their efforts on harmonization and alignment at the country level. Early results from pilots show that it can 'strengthen engagement from partners', but that it 'will only be effective if…multilateral and bilateral development partners respond to their findings' (Attawell and Dickinson, 2007, p. 42). The question of accountability is complex in the context of development aid, because the relationships of accountability are to some extent diffuse and indirect. For instance, while the national governments that receive HIV/AIDS funding clearly have to be accountable to their populations, The Global Fund and the World Bank MAP are exempted from this accountability relationship, because relations of accountability are indirect, given that governments in the North channel money to be spent on programmes in African countries. The PEPFAR has a more direct relation of accountability, considering that it has to report to the US Congress. However, such a direct relation of accountability, it seems, has also created problems in recipient countries, as seen by the earmarking of funds.

The wider issue of accountability brings forward the question of power distribution among the donors and the recipient countries. As Patterson

(2006, p. 143) states, the focus on numerical results by PEPFAR in particular 'reinforces the understanding of AIDS as an emergency, instead of viewing AIDS as a reflection of uneven global development, gender inequalities, or human right inequities'. HIV/AIDS is a disease that exacerbates the already existing inequality between the North and the South, since its losses are mainly in the South.

Conclusions

In this chapter I have identified and discussed some of the hindrances towards horizontal coordination that the three major global actors and their HIV/AIDS programmes meet in relating to each others' programmes and recipient countries by using three general problems of horizontal coordination described by Peters (1998) to structure and guide the analysis. These general problems were strikingly descriptive of the challenges that the three global actors face. The problem of redundancy (in the existence of parallel institutions and duplication of assistance) might be solvable in the near future, as reforms of the CCM are occurring or have already taken place. Moreover, there is reason to believe that lacunae in capacity in recipient countries and incoherence in the aims and requirements of donors may also in years to come become less prevalent. Overall, the situation of coordination is improving within the HIV/AIDS network, given the cooperative efforts taking place, for instance, in technical assistance, joint meetings, procurement planning, and reporting.

Of all the efforts towards coordination, increasing technical capacity in countries receiving aid seems to be key to 'making the money work'. However, governance capacity is also critical. Given that the political situation differs among African countries, coordination efforts such as the initiatives described in this chapter are likely to result in different outcomes at the country level. Moreover, horizontal as well as vertical coordination is inherently about attempts towards collectively governing a sector or issue area. Such coordination is challenging given the unequal power distribution among different actors engaged in the evolving global HIV/AIDS governance network. Addressing coordination given these different sets of inequalities is a difficult but critical challenge in constructing an effective global governance network for fighting HIV/AIDS.

Notes

'Making the Money Work' was the theme of a follow-up meeting called 'The Global Response to AIDS: "Making the Money Work," The Three Ones in Action', in London on 9 March 2005, in which 'leaders of government, civil society, UN agencies, and other multinational institutions met' and decided to set up 'The Global Task Team on Improving AIDS Coordination Among Multilateral Institutions and International Donors' (see GTT, 2005, p. 9). The phrase is also the subtitle of the 2006 UNAIDS

Annual Report as well as being part of the title of the 2006–2007 Consolidated UN Technical Support Plan for AIDS outlining the UN organizations' response towards the acknowledged 'crisis of implementation' within HIV/AIDS programmes, including the UN Division of Labour. The phrase has since been used in several documents as a proxy indicating what coordination is to contribute.

1. Funding increased from US$1.67 billion in 2001 to US$10 billion in 2007 (UNAIDS, 2008a, p. 188).
2. These are sometimes referred to as National AIDS Councils or National AIDS Commissions.
3. Three 'ideal types' of coordination have been described: market, hierarchy and networks (Wollman, 2006, p. 595; Robinson et al., 2000).
4. These African focus countries are Botswana, Côte d'Ivoire, Ethiopia, Kenya, Mozambique, Namibia, Nigeria, Rwanda, South Africa, Tanzania, Uganda, and Zambia.
5. In reality, according to Africa Action, 'Of the total, only $9 billion was new money, to be added to $5 billion in old bilateral assistance programs. In addition, only a portion of that money was to be dedicated to fighting HIV/AIDS in Africa, despite the President's original promise that the initiative would focus on the HIV/AIDS crisis in Africa and the Caribbean' (Africa Action, 2006).
6. A Joint UN Programme 'is a set of activities contained in a common work plan and related budget, involving two or more UN organization and (sub-) national partners. The work plan and budget will form part of a joint programme document, which will also detail roles and responsibilities of partners in coordinating and managing the joint activities. The joint programme document is signed by all participating organizations and (sub-) national partners' (UNDG, 2006, p. 7, quoting UNDG, 2003, p. 5). The formation of Joint UN Teams and Programmes was suggested in the GTT recommendations as well as the Paris Declaration (see UNDG 2006). According to UNDG (2006, p. 3), 'The purpose of the Joint UN Team on AIDS is to promote coherent and effective UN action in support of an expanded national response to HIV'.
7. 'A quality national strategy' is defined as having 'one national multisectoral strategy and operational plan with goals, targets, costing, and identified funding per programmatic area, and a monitoring and evaluation framework' (UNAIDS, 2008a, p. 28).
8. Ninety-seven per cent of all reporting countries to the UNAIDS in 2008 had national AIDS plans/strategic frameworks, but only 69 per cent had had these strategies 'translated into costed operational plans with programme goals, detailed programme costing, and identified funding sources' (UNAIDS, 2008a, p. 206).
9. The members of the GIST are the following: The Global Fund, UNAIDS, UNFPA, UNICEF, WHO, the World Bank, UNDP, GTZ, the US Government, the AIDS Alliance, ICASO, ICAD, and ICTC of Brazil (UNAIDS, 2008a, p. 199).
10. This measure was established on 3 October 2008, so it is too early to assess its impact on strengthening technical capacity at the country level.
11. The degree to which the earmarking has been seen as mandatory has changed over the years : 'the earmarks for prevention and care are "soft" earmarks, meaning that they are suggested. The earmarks for treatment and orphans and vulnerable children became mandatory in fiscal 2006' (Oomman et al., 2008, p. 6).
12. According to the United States Government Accountability Office, 'since January 2004, the OGAC has defined abstinence-until-marriage spending programs as

comprising both activities promoting abstinence (A) and activities promoting fidelity (B)' (GAO, 2008, p. 2).

13. See, for instance, the Africa Action's Campaign Against HIV/AIDS in Africa, in which one of the goals is 'Pressuring the next president to work with congress to pass legislation to address the deficiencies in the Reauthorization Act' (Africa Action, 2008, p. 2).
14. Increased PEPFAR funding from 2008 (OGAC, 2008) has been announced to meet the '2-7-10 goals', that is, 'treating two million people, preventing seven million new infections and caring for ten million people' throughout the programme period (PEPFAR, 2006).
15. The new goals for PEPFAR until 2013 are to support 'treatment for at least 3 million people, prevention of 12 million new infections, and care for 12 million people, including 5 million orphans and vulnerable children' (PEPFAR, 2008).
16. The Joint Meetings of 2007 and 2008 referred to here are 'The Implementers Meeting' in Kigali, Rwanda on 16–19 June 2007 and in Kampala, Uganda in 3–7 June 2008. In these meetings, however, many other stakeholders also participated. See http://www.hivimplementers.org/.

Part IV

The Governance of Global Health Research and Product Access

11
The Political Economy of Global Health Research

Sandra J. MacLean and David R. MacLean

> ...only about 10 percent of potential [health] improvements in developed countries will come from advances in health technology and management. Almost half will come from preventive personal health practices. And half will come from improvements in the environment we provide for human life.
>
> (Naidoo, cited in Cleveland, 2005, p. 56)

Introduction

A recent article on the front page of our local newspaper carried the arresting title, '"Landmark Breakthrough" in Breast Cancer Research' (*Vancouver Sun*, 2007, p. 1). The article, which described research findings regarding gene mutations that lead to breast cancer, proclaimed that the discovery could, in the future, have major positive implications for the prevention and treatment of breast cancer. The following day, the *Globe and Mail* (2007, p. L.4), a national daily newspaper, carried an article entitled, 'New Cancer Genes are Low-risk'. This article emphasized that these gene mutations were actually 'common' and 'relatively low-hazard', meaning that 'women who have them run a comparatively small risk of developing cancer'. Because the genes are so common and low-risk, the article concluded, there may not be any benefits achieved by screening individuals. This article was published on the fourth page of the 'Life' section of the newspaper.

The difference in the way the research findings were framed by the two articles is illustrative of a broader, important debate in the health field. On one hand, we see each new scientific discovery in health being heralded as a triumph of technology and a probable advancement in the human condition. On the other, we see – albeit less often and usually on inside pages – caution expressed regarding scientific discovery. The latter perspective recognizes that, while health is obviously conditioned by biology, it is not necessarily determined by it (that is, the expression of health will depend on environment as well as genetic make-up). Moreover, while science may assist in preserving or restoring health, its abilities to do so are limited, and sometimes its solutions are more costly than socially based alternatives. This perspective takes the social determinants of disease to be as significant as biological predisposition (more significant at a population level), and it promotes prevention of disease through the improvement of social conditions as preferable to relying primarily on technological treatment of disease already established.

There is good evidence, based on research conducted over the past two to three decades, to support the assumptions and prescriptions of the second perspective. However, the scientific/technological discourse has continued to dominate, to the extent that the vast majority of health research has been carried out within this paradigm and most of the funding for health research has been designated to the support of technological innovation and intervention. The explosion of interest in global health would appear to be an opportunity for changing these inequities in health research, given that globalization – a distinctly social process[1] – is at the core of the health changes that make the concept of 'global health' meaningful. Yet, although the social changes behind the emergence of global health problems are frequently acknowledged, the preponderance of research on issues defined as global health concerns the biology of specific diseases and/or the need for developing or distributing technological treatments.

In this chapter we explore why, given the strong evidence supporting a social determinants approach to population health (and the knowledge that social inequities are among the strongest determinants), the biomedical model continues to direct the research and policy agendas. We argue that the biomedical model dominates, not because it necessarily produces optimum health outcomes, but because business interests benefit from the prevailing structure of health research and policy, which is based upon a historically entrenched conceptualization of health as freedom from disease rather than a state of human well-being.[2] Although the emergence of global health as a new disciplinary focus offers a unique opportunity for changing this inequity, current trends suggest that traditional thinking about health, including global health, creates artificial barriers: between academic disciplines; between state, business and civil society; between government departments; and between scientific and social theory – thus perpetuating silos of knowledge which undermine the interdisciplinary approaches required to advance prospects for reducing the inequities that now characterize global health.

Social determinants and the political economy of global health

The introductory chapter of this volume outlines a range of diseases and conditions described as 'global health' issues that have gained the attention of scholars of international relations (IR) and international political economy (IPE) as well as of public health. The growing awareness of health as a relevant research topic among IR and IPE scholars and practitioners is particularly interesting because it reflects growing awareness that political and economic dimensions of globalization are affecting human health, and also that health trends are markers for contemporary global changes, and particularly profound recent transformations in political economy. To define global health adequately[3] and to treat problems of global health appropriately, therefore, requires an awareness of these transformations. At the same time, understanding the mechanisms by which health is achieved and maintained, and exploring contemporary trends in health, helps to illuminate the nature and extent of these transformations. Impacts on health of social change tend to be manifested with immediacy and clarity; therefore research on (global) health helps to facilitate the timely exposure of the local, people-centred impacts of globalization.

Extensive research, conducted over the past two and a half decades, underscores that health, at least at a population level, is largely determined by social condition and status. A comprehensive analysis of population data published as the Black Report (UK Department of Health and Social Security, 1980) was a watershed in thinking about health; it provided evidence of a strong, inverse association between mortality and social class, thus challenging the assumption that health was a function only or mainly of biological predisposition and/or technical responses to disease. The Black Report stimulated research that confirmed the initial findings (Kawachi and Kennedy, 2002; Marmot, 2003; Marmot and Wilkinson, 1999) and ascertained that, after fundamental basic needs are met, socioeconomic gradient is an even greater determinant of health than is poverty. This association was found consistently for virtually every cause of ill health that was studied in the early research that emerged from these findings (Evans et al., 1994).

The realization that health conditions are socially induced as much as (perhaps more than) they are biologically/genetically preordained has been gaining acceptance in the global health discourse (see, for instance, CSDH, 2008, as well as MacLean and MacLean, 2008, and Schrecker, in this volume). This realization has significant theoretical and policy implications. It suggests, first, that health needs to be understood within social context, which is determined largely by political economy. Or, to put this another way, the political economy of health should be central to health research. Second, regarding policy, it suggests that strategies aimed at a population level can be at least as effective at reducing overall rates of disease as treatments directed at individuals who have already acquired a disease or who have biological/genetic predispositions for acquiring it (CSDH, 2008; MacLean and MacLean, 2008). More specifically, this means that among the most effective strategies for improving health outcomes of populations are policies directed toward reducing poverty and reducing inequality.

There is considerable debate about the extent to which globalization has contributed to inequalities in the world.[4] However, according to some authoritative sources, inequalities have been increasing. The World Bank (2006, p. 7), for instance, has noted that, 'if China and India are excluded, global inequalities have continued to rise [since the beginning of the twenty-first century], owing to the continuing divergence between most other low-income countries and rich countries'. Also, while China and India have narrowed the equity/equality gaps according to such macro-level national comparisons, increasing inequalities within these countries have been identified (see, for instance, Chaudhuri and Ravallion, 2006). Finally, ultimately, inequality is expressed at the human level, where the impacts of inequalities are most apparent. Dallmayer (2006, p. 67) observes that '...between 1995 and 1999 the world's two hundred richest people doubled their wealth to more than $1 trillion, while the number of people living on less than $1 a day...remained steady at 1.3 billion'. Now, in 2008, as affirmed in the recently released report by the WHO Commission on the Social Determinants of Health, inequalities continue to be a major impediment to improving health outcomes in the world (CSDH, 2008).

While it has been known for some time that inequalities have significant impacts upon the health of people, it is only recently that the impacts of health inequalities on national and global security have been identified. But, reflecting a move over the past decade towards the 'securitization of health' (MacLean, 2008), health issues have begun to figure prominently in contemporary debates on justice/order and security/development (Chen et al., 2003; Annan, 2005; McInnes and Lee, 2006; Owen and Roberts, 2005). It is argued that '...poor health undermines the economic and social structures of the state' and '[p]oor health may contribute to economic decline, fueling discontent' (McInnes and Lee, 2006, p. 16). Alternatively, good health is portrayed as a necessary precondition for economic development (and by extension, stability) (Sachs, 2005). A political economy of health framework that takes seriously the social determinants of health is necessary for establishing the relevant connections within this justice/order/security/development nexus.

Some progress is being made in assessing these connections, and also in institutionalizing the ideas. For instance, several countries, including Sweden, Norway and Canada, have indicated their intentions to include consideration of social determinants in policy calculations. Meanwhile, at the international level, one of the most important developments was the establishment of the WHO Commission on Social Determinants of Health,[5] mentioned earlier. However, despite such initiatives, as well as the considerable attention to global health by an expanding array of state, interstate and non-state actors, underlying social problems – especially inequity and inequality – are not being adequately addressed in terms of their impacts on health. Or, as Lawrence Gostin (2007b, p. 225) asserts, '[i]nternational health assistance is provided in an ineffective way that does not enhance the capability for human functioning'. As Gostin (2007b) argues, in poor countries, health policy is heavily influenced and shaped by the immediate self-interests of powerful external actors or by fleeting efforts to 'do good' following highly publicized, disastrous events. Meager funds are devoted to public health through initiatives that would have long-term, sustainable effects in preventing and controlling disease.

Inadequate policy reflects inadequacy either in the research that informs the policy or in the translation of the research findings. In an attempt to expose the nature and extent of the problem in the research–policy nexus, in the next section we explore the state of global health research. Drawing on Robert Cox's (1981) observation that 'theory is always for someone and for some purpose,' we ask who is funding what areas of global health research and who is benefiting from that research.

Funding global health research

Health agencies

Several national and international initiatives have been introduced recently to respond to what are described as 'global health' problems.[6] Correspondingly, several government-led or government-supported national funding agencies have begun to institute research funding programs designated to address concerns under the rubric of 'global health'. For example, in 2001, the Canadian Institute for Health Research (CIHR) launched the Global Health Research Initiative in conjunction with the Canadian International Development Agency (CIDA), the International Development Research Council (IDRC) and Health Canada. Several other countries are similarly engaged: Norway has established the Norwegian Forum for Global Health Research; the German National Commission on Global Change Research includes health as one of four research foci; and the US National Institute for Health Research (NIHR) doubled the amount it spent on research defined as 'global health' between 1999 and 2004 (Fleck, 2004, p. 1220).[7]

Major funding agencies in the Social Sciences are also beginning to devote more attention and resources to research designated as 'global health' research. In the UK, although most of the health research supported by the state-based Economic and Social Research Council is traditionally focused, some initiatives are now specifically directed at 'global health'. In Canada, the Social Science and Humanities Research Council (SSHRC) does not fund 'global health' as a specific thrust, but it does support Tri-Council (SSHRC, CIHR and the Natural Sciences and Engineering Research Council (NSERC)) programs on health, including a 'global health' component. The US Social Science Research Council does not specify global health as a thrust, but it does now fund projects that many working in health areas would consider to be not only within a 'global health' framework, but also within a framework that addresses social determinants: for example, social impacts on (and of) HIV/AIDS or the health impacts of China's rapid industrialization.[8]

While the majority of research dollars for research labelled 'global health' comes from such national agencies that fund health and social science research, pharmaceutical companies are now also major contributors. Pharmaceutical funds devoted to research in all health, overall, are significant. For instance, the US-based Pharmaceutical Research and Manufacturers of America (PhRMA), which 'represents the country's leading pharmaceutical research and biotechnology companies', reports that '[i]ndustry-wide research and investment reached a record $[US]55.2 billion in 2006' and that 'PhRMA members alone invested an estimated $43 billion in 2006 in discovering and developing new medicines' (see PhRMA website). PhRMA does not segregate 'global health' as a separate research category, but it professes a commitment to health on a global scale, and to research on Southern diseases, as the following assertion indicates:

> PhRMA member R&D investment is global, including supporting biopharmaceutical research efforts in Africa, Asia, Australia, Europe, and the Middle East. While the North American market for medicines is the world's largest, American-funded research targets many diseases that do not affect North American patients. (PhRMA, 'Industry Profile')[9]

One researcher who has investigated this sector's research investment in 'global health' reports that it contributes nearly as much as governments do (42 per cent contributed by pharmaceuticals compared with 50 per cent by governments) (Fleck, 2004).

The third group of funding agencies that contribute to areas designated as 'global health' research includes private trusts and philanthropic agencies. By Fleck's (2004) estimation, these actors contribute 8 per cent of the total spent. Many of these 'private' contributors are established trusts that have only recently become engaged in what they consider to be 'global health' issues. These include such organizations as the Wellcome Trust in the UK, which now 'covers a broad range of activities that support *global health* research' (emphasis added), and the US-based Kaiser Foundation, which describes itself as having 'a growing role in *global health*' (emphasis added). This category also includes the Bill and Melinda Gates Foundation, which was established expressly for funding 'global health' research and currently is, without doubt, one of the most significant contributors to health research being conducted in developing countries. Often the Gates Foundation and other philanthropic agencies operate within public–private partnerships. For example, the European Partnership for Global Health seeks to create 'a bridge between governments, civil society and the private sector' for promoting global health research; the Global Health

Council is 'comprised of health-care professionals and organizations that include NGOs, foundations, corporations, government agencies and academic institutions who work to ensure *global health* for all' (emphasis added); and 'the 2008 [Bamako] Global Ministerial Forum on Research for Health aims to bring together 1000 stakeholders including ministers of health, science & technology, and social development; researchers; civil society organizations; national research councils; donor agencies; philanthropic foundations; and representatives of the private sector' (Bamako, 2008).[10]

The above examples indicate a notable growth in commitments to funding global health research. However, the expressions of interest may not be as impressive as they seem on the surface. For one thing, despite rhetorical pledges, the percentage of research dollars devoted to areas designated as 'global health' tends to be rather small compared to amounts being spent on health research overall. Secondly, there is no clear or consistent definition of 'global health' within the research funding community; in some cases, it is difficult to discern what is actually 'global' about the research, and how 'global health' is distinguished from *any* health research conducted abroad. A third, related issue is that the majority of research funded in areas designated as 'global health', however defined, is concentrated on biotechnical advancements. Much less is spent on the social determinants of disease and the political economy factors that influence social conditions that affect health. As the introductory chapter in this volume argues, 'global health' makes sense as a distinct and unique concept only when it is understood within the context of change within the contemporary global political economy. The next section, therefore, explores the limitations in current global health research with regard to the discrepancy between funding resources and rhetoric, inattention to careful definition of the term and relative indifference to the salience of social determinants and political economy.

Who gets how much to do what?

Insufficient funding

Clearly, the *idea* of global health has taken root in the funding community. However, it is difficult to discern exactly what is being spent on so-called global health. The Global Forum for Health Research, which was founded in 1998 to reduce North–South inequalities in health research,[11] has discovered that there are serious impediments to acquiring the information needed to evaluate the situation. In particular, there are problems with estimation methodology as well as with inadequate accounting measures; as the Forum notes, '[r]outine, comprehensive statistics on expenditures on research for health simply do not exist for any country in the world' (Burke and de Francisco, 2006, pp. 9–10). Overall, given incomplete information and blunt methodological instruments, estimates on spending on specific health areas are markedly imprecise at present.

Despite the inchoate nature of data on funding, however, there is information available to provide a broad sense of funding trends in health, including in areas that have been designated as 'global health'. For instance, the Global Forum has discovered that there has been a substantial increase in funds for overall health research and development in recent years – from US$30 billion in 1986 (ibid., p. vii) to US$84.8 billion in 1998, US$105.9 billion in 2001 (ibid., p. 9) and US$160.3 billion in 2005 (Burke and Matlin, 2008, p. xiii). However, of this total amount on health, only a portion is expressly devoted to 'global health'. To put the amount spent on 'global health' in some perspective, Wooley et al. (2005, p. 092) observe that the US$49.5 million spent on what was defined as global health research in 2003 by the US, as the world's largest contributor, is 'less than 1 cent of each dollar spent on health in the US each year'. Moreover, while only a small proportion of health research dollars go to global health, only about 10 per cent goes to research in the South, which has 90 per cent of the disease burden. Since the Global Health Forum's mandate was founded a decade ago with the mandate to reduce this 10–90 gap, improvement has been slight, as the following from its recent report indicates: 'Together the G7 countries invested more than 88% of publicly funded health R&D in high-income countries (down from 92% in 2003)' (Burke and Matlin, 2008, p. xvi).

Defining global health

Available figures, while helpful in providing a general indication of how research dollars are being spent, should be treated with some caution, not only because of the imprecision in assessing amounts spent, as noted above, but also because it is not clear what is being included as 'global health' research.

The Global Forum's reports on health research calculate all expenditures – from multilateral, bilateral, and national sources (state and non-state) – on health research around the world. This suggests a possible definition of 'global health' as the total of the world's health issues, rather than as a distinct and separate set of conditions or issues, distinguishable from, say, 'international' or 'national' health. However, the main concern of the Global Forum is North–South health inequities, which is closer to the way global health appears to be conceptualized by most research funding agencies. For example, the founding document of the Canadian Coalition for Global Health Research states that: '"Global Health" in this document refers to the health of individuals and societies within less developed, less resourced, poorer nations and regions of the world' (CCGHR, 2001). The NIHR (UK) defines global health similarly 'as areas where the health need is identified in developing countries (that is, including diseases of developing countries)'.[12] The Bill and Melinda Gates Foundation does not specifically define 'global health' in its instructions for researchers seeking funds. However, its stated 'global health' funding priorities[13] suggest that the Foundation defines global health as a set of conditions – mainly infectious diseases – that disproportionately impact the South.

The common theme that runs through most definitions of global health is a focus on health conditions of the South. Clearly, researchers' relative neglect of health problems in the South is a significant global health problem; indeed, one might argue that this neglect is, in itself, a social determinant of the world's present health conditions. However, health problems of the South have been understood as 'international health' for several decades.[14] And, just as 'globalisation', to be meaningful, must be distinguished from 'internationalization' (Scholte, 2000, pp. 46–50), 'global health' is understandable as a new and unique concept only when it is differentiated from international health. Lee et al. (2002, p. 5) make the point that there is a need to distinguish between the two, and they differentiate global from international health '...when the causes or consequences of a health issue circumvent, undermine or are oblivious to the territorial boundaries of states and, thus, beyond the capacity of states to address effectively through state institutions alone'. This definition is an improvement in that it ties global health to features of globalization; however, it does not make explicit that the new context is the result of unprecedented changes of political economy in this global era. In other words, while it is an adequate description of global health, it does not suggest explanation. In Chapter 1 of this volume, global health is defined as 'health conditions and outcomes that are determined by changes due to globalization in relations among state, business, labour and civil society'; that is, changes in governance as a result of global political economy processes. What distinguishes a certain set of contemporary diseases in the South as global health, then, is that they are determined or affected by global economic, political and social forces. The South bears a significantly disproportionate burden of disease, and, given that inequality is a major determinant of health status, global health conditions as a function of North–South inequality are a critically important focus for research. However, to define global health either as all the health issues of the world or only as a set of predominately Southern health issues misrepresents what is most significant about the concept of 'global health' as distinct from the long-standing concept of 'international health': that is, global health issues can only be fully understood within the framework of the social (especially political economy) determinants of disease.

Low priority of social determinants research

It is difficult to determine exactly what is 'global' about many of the funding agencies' claims about commitments to global health research. Also, it is difficult to separate out those that investigate social determinants of global health. The Global Forum (Burke and de Francisco, 2006, p. 11) points out that there may actually be more research on social determinants than is accredited, given that data used to compile figures on research funds tend to refer to biomedical research. This is relevant in the sense that research on social conditions such as inequities and inequalities may be informative with respect to health even if health is not expressly designated as an area for investigation in the project. However, currently, it appears that research which consciously and unambiguously investigates health as a socially determined condition is conspicuously underfunded both in the health field and in the social sciences. It is true that some countries have begun to respond to calls to support international health research that addresses social determinants of health (for example, see DH, 2008).[15] However, while such commitments are promising, the total amount designated for social determinants remains small relative to overall spending on health. For instance, the UK's Medical Research Council's only reference to social determinants in its call for proposals in 2005/6 was in the area of 'Population-based studies...with particular emphasis on lifestyle and psychosocial factors'. This item was but one of several in the budget for 'Health Services and Public Health Research', which received only 11 per cent of the £224 million spent on research that year (Medical Research Council website). Similarly, in the US, social determinants research is a low priority, comprising fewer than 5 per cent of the areas funded by the US NIH.[16]

A recent review of health funding in the UK reveals one reason why social determinants receive significantly less attention. The author of the report (Cooksey, 2006) indicates that, in gathering the information, it was discovered that there was '...a body of opinion which argued that prioritization of spend [sic] on research should be proportional to monies spent by the NHS, to the socio-economic burden of disease'.[17] Nevertheless, despite this body of opinion, and despite the author's acknowledgment that 'two-thirds of public and charity funding of health research is invested in basic science projects', the report recommended *'future increases in funding should be weighted towards translational and applied research until a more balanced portfolio is achieved'* (ibid., emphasis in original). The interest in translational and applied research could be construed as an effort to investigate how and why information gained from research is or is not taken up by policy/decision-makers. In other words, this type of research could be very useful in understanding why policymakers, who are obviously well informed about the social determinants of health, are unwilling or unable to devote sufficient and appropriate resources to make significant improvements. It could also be useful in devising projects that show the socioeconomic impediments to and/or impacts of application. This seems not to be the intent of promoting translational and applied research, however. Instead, the report emphasizes that the main objective is to gain information on how research findings can be translated and applied for economic gain. In particular, it stresses the importance of maintaining the UK's edge in health research in order to continue to entice the pharmaceutical industry to locate research and development (R&D) operations in the UK:

> The quality of the health research base, combined with a national health service, creates a unique selling point that attracts R&D investment from the pharmaceutical, devices and biotechnology industries. These industries form a major part of our knowledge economy. They are prime investors in R&D. The pharmaceutical industry alone accounts for 25 per cent of UK business investment in R&D and it is a significant employer of highly-skilled staff. Given the sector's contribution to the UK economy, the healthcare industries are a key driver of wider productivity and make a significant contribution to the UK Government's vision, as set out in the Science & Innovation Investment Framework 2004–2014, of increasing aggregate investment in R&D to 2.5 per cent of GDP by 2014. (Cooksey, 2006, p. 3)

Sir Cooksey did not overlook the South in his report; he notes that '…emerging economies also provide new markets and opportunities which the UK is well placed to exploit…' (ibid., p. 9).

The top priority among agencies that support health research, whether global or otherwise, is evidently biotechnology. Genomics, in particular, have captured the interest of the major funding agencies (see Topol et al., 2007). The World Survey of Funding for Genomics Research, located at Stanford University, estimates that the government and nonprofit sectors spent US$1,805 million on genomics research in 2000; genomics firms spent US$2,061 million; and the pharmaceutical and biotechnology sector spent US$900 million (Stanford in Washington, 2002).[18] Yet, while enthusiasts speculate about the vast therapeutic potential of genomic research, the translational prospects have not yet been clearly established. For instance, recent findings suggest that RNA fractions, rather than genes, determine physical expressions, and, because these fractions exist in vast numbers and in exponentially numerous combinations, it will likely take considerable time, and certainly immeasurable resources, to sort out the therapeutic possibilities. The relatively new field of epigenetics is also complicating the picture with information on apparent epigene changes in response to environmental factors. That these changes appear to be transmissible to future generations contravenes the prevailing assumption that physical characteristics result from immutable gene codes (Gosden and Feinberg, 2007, p. 371). To put it another way, epigenetics research indicates that the long-established debate over the nature-versus-nurture dichotomy has been rather pointless; that in fact, both are in play in determining health and disease (Hoover, 2000).

National ambitions to attract R&D industries or individual aspirations to develop lucrative patents are strong incentives to disregard the nurture part of the equation; and the result is a highly skewed research agenda that grossly favours genomes (nature) over social determinants (nurture). This impacts the North–South research imbalance in two ways. First, almost all of this research is being conducted in the North, thus adding to the gap in respective Northern and Southern contributions to 'cutting-edge' research. Moreover, even if genome research eventually proves to have significant therapeutic value, the translational costs are likely to make advances prohibitive for treating disease in the South.

Still, not all the news regarding research being conducted under the title of 'global health' is bad. Increased levels of research with more practical benefit, at least in the short term and probably also in the long term for the majority of the world's people, is being undertaken in diseases that primarily affect the South. Historically, such diseases have been largely neglected in the development of pharmaceuticals. However, recently, pressures from global civil society, multilateral engagement (as with the Millennium Development Goals) and economic opportunities accruing from Southern diseases have created new research interest in several diseases. Among several initiatives evidencing this is the Global Fund to combat HIV/AIDS, malaria and TB, which several other contributors to this volume examine. The Fund and various other PPPs are generating significant interest both in developing pharmaceutical products to combat these diseases and in translational research into areas such as country capacity to uptake the products. They have also spawned new research interest in the emergence of global governance of health, an area that leads logically and necessarily into research on the political economy of global health.

Private donors are now major actors in several of these initiatives. The Bill and Melinda Gates Foundation is the most visible and probably the main private contributor to 'global health' issues; that is, global health defined as diseases of the South. The Foundation is concerned with conditions of poverty as well as the high-profile diseases like HIV/AIDS and malaria. Yet, while there is a clear acknowledgement of causal conditions of poverty and inequality, and a recent turn to a broader agenda that moves into social determinants territory (for example, tobacco and governance), the main emphasis has been and continues to be on technological solutions (for example, vaccine development and technologically enhanced food products to treat malnourishment). Researchers seeking funds in the 'global health' division of this organization are provided with the following comment on the Foundation's philosophical position: 'Our grantmaking is driven by the unprecedented opportunities in science and technology to transform health throughout the world' (Gates Foundation). Further, in a speech to the World Economic Forum in January 2008, Bill Gates (2008) stated that:

> The challenge is to design a system where market incentives, including profits and recognition, drive the change. I like to call this new system creative capitalism – an approach where governments, businesses, and

> nonprofits work together to stretch the reach of market forces so that more people can make a profit, or gain recognition, doing work that eases the world's inequities. I believed that breakthroughs in technology could solve the key problems. And they do, increasingly, for billions of people.

Seeking health solutions in science and technology is practical and important, and there is no reason to assume that the motivation behind the philanthropic gesture is anything but noble. However, the quotation suggests an unquestioning assumption that health problems are solved best or only through science and technology. It reinforces the emphasis on biotechnical solutions to the detriment of exploring solutions in the social environment. By leveraging their funds through partnerships with governments and research funding, foundations like Gates have been able to influence research priorities around the world and, in doing so, skew research agendas in directions which favour the development of new health technologies and support for biomedical research (Okie, 2008). This kind of leverage can act as an opportunity cost to research funding agencies that might otherwise have supported research projects in broader areas such as the determinants of health.[19]

Moreover, as corporate actors become more heavily involved in the governance arrangements by which health issues are addressed, a business rationale is creeping into the arguments for supporting a biomedical model. Raymond V. Gilmartin (2005, p. 11), Chief Executive Officer (CEO) of the pharmaceutical company Merck and Co., Inc., argues that '...improving global health is not merely a charitable goal; it is a business imperative'. The assumption is that greater access to medicine in poor countries will improve individuals' health, thus creating healthier, more productive populations that will contribute to economic growth and the expansion of markets.

Not only is the notion of health as a human right being denigrated by this bias towards a biomedical/business approach to health (Barr, 2007; Scott-Samuel and O'Keefe, 2007), but the assumption that the biotechnical approach will solve all health problems, and most effectively, goes largely unquestioned. It is generally assumed that the main problem of social inequalities as they affect global health is poor people's lack of access to medicines and health care. The point is not that these are issues are unimportant; in fact, access to treatment is a critical component of restoring health. But what tends to be ignored or overlooked is that poor social conditions increase the need for treatment. Poor people whose human needs are not adequately met are more likely to develop health problems. Therefore, before putting all reliance on addressing diseases already established, more emphasis is needed on achieving and maintaining health through preventative measures. These include good public health infrastructures, but much more – good-quality education, gender equality, safe housing conditions, relief from psychosocial tensions, etc. It is crucial, given the impact of globalization on social environments and relations, that considerably more funding be devoted to these items within the global health research framework.

IR/IPE contributions to global health research

International relations and international political economy can offer useful insights in these areas. However, to date, the contributions in these fields have been limited, in part because scholars in the field have been interested in only a narrow range of health issues. More importantly, they tend to accept the preeminence of the biomedical health paradigm without question and thus lack a critical analysis of the politics and political economy of health.

Regarding a narrow focus on health, IR and IPE scholars are mostly interested in the impact of certain global health problems on national security or wealth (the effects of HIV/AIDS on economies or militaries; the economic costs of SARS; the threat of bioterrorism) (MacLean, 2007, 2008) or emerging governance structures, especially public–private partnerships (Brown, 2006). Referring specifically to IR, McInnes and Lee (2006, p. 9) argue that the focus on foreign and security policy analysis obscures important issues of public health generally, and, because of the preoccupation with infectious epidemics and bioterrorism, other specific health concerns that are relevant to IR are neglected. McInnes and Lee contend that the agenda needs to be broadened to include health-destroying illegal activities such as trafficking in drugs and in people. This is a useful corrective to the present state of research, but, in our opinion, the list of topics to be explored should be extended even further. For example, although the rapid, worldwide growth of chronic diseases such as cardiovascular disease and cancer is largely triggered by economic, political and social processes associated with globalization, little interest has been generated in IR/IPE fields (MacLean and MacLean, 2008). However, simply extending the list of health items that IR/IPE should address is insufficient, if meaningful strategies are to be devised in the analysis (and enhancement) of global health.

Most IR/IPE scholars appear to conceive of 'global health' as a set of certain diseases. Moreover, although it is acknowledged that these diseases are being spread, or have a greater threat potential, because of globalization processes, there is little evident awareness of the role that the economics and politics of globalization play in creating the global disease burden – including the types and rates of diseases as well as the inequitable impacts – of the contemporary world. To achieve both public health improvements and the human and national security benefits of improved health, much greater attention, in IR, IPE and other social science research, as well as in public health, needs to be paid to the power dynamics in society that determine the state of global health, and particularly the health inequalities that currently characterize global health. Moreover, IR and IPE are well situated to investigate who global health research is for, and for what purpose.[20] What are the power dynamics that determine what is taken as a relevant topic for research and what topics receive the majority of research funding? As argued above, there is clear and convincing evidence to show that health is largely determined, especially at a population level, by social factors. This means that susceptibility to disease is established by the conditions in which humans live and the relations by which those conditions come into being. To address health only after disease is established is to miss, arguably, the most important factors that contribute to health outcomes.

Conclusions

Global health, characterized by new or altered diseases and illnesses and by significant inequalities (especially North–South), is a function of changing political economy. To put this another way, the emergence of global health as a separate area of investigation demonstrates clearly that health, at population levels, is largely socially determined. Yet, as the Global Health Forum (Burke and de Francisco, 2006, pp. 11–12) notes, there continue to be major gaps in knowledge regarding social determinants. The Global Health Forum has indicated that the figures it uses to assess the level of research funding in global health are biased in favour of biomedical research funding (see above). It also recognizes that its own modelling of research funding may contribute to a misrepresentation of the type of research that is required:

> a single global aggregate figure might 'obscure or distract attention not only from the real health needs of many populations (given the diversity of health problems in different populations and sub-groups in countries and regions) but from the more complex determinants of health such as poverty, inequities, gender, violence and abuse, access to education, and opportunities to participate and be part of decision-making processes'. (ibid., p. 11)

Investigations conducted for this chapter suggest that, even if social determinants research is underestimated in the Forum's calculations, the amounts missed are not likely to be significant, relative to those spent on biomedical research. The reason for the lack of emphasis on social determinants is not so much that the connections are not being drawn between research on social issues and their health impacts, but rather that well-established evidence showing that health is strongly determined by social conditions does not facilitate lucrative research agendas. The recent surge of interest in the translational quality of research is similarly motivated. While such research could be directed to determine where social interventions are more appropriate than technological interventions, or where combinations of social and technological approaches could enhance positive outcomes, the main objective in this research area has been to investigate how research on drugs or other products can be translated most profitably.

Social sciences, and particularly international relations and international political economy, are well situated to contribute to investigations in these areas. However, to date, these fields have focused too narrowly on a small set of health problems, and, most importantly, the fields have accepted without question that health can be understood largely as biomedical problems amenable to technical solution. Similarly, if not quite with the same degree of parochialism and narrow-mindedness, many public health scholars have tended merely to rename international health as global health without acknowledging the extent to which global health is actually a feature of profound contemporary political and political economy changes. Combining insights from the respective disciplines is critical in addressing these limitations in current research. Rich and productive global health research calls for partnerships and teams of public health and IR/IPE scholars who seriously engage with the ideas of global health as socially determined. But to create such teams requires a conducive environment, one that is not currently supported by the prevailing biomedical model that dominates in setting current research structures, values and norms.

Notes

1. The term 'social' here is being used in a broad sense, encompassing economic and political processes, which have been implicated in proliferation of globalization.
2. The World Health Organization (WHO, 2006) recognizes the negative implication for health of this situation and has attempted to promote a definition of health as 'a state of complete physical, mental and social well-being and not merely the absence of disease or infirmity'.
3. See the definition of 'global health' in Chapter 1 as the 'health conditions and outcomes that are determined by changes due to globalization in relations among state, business, labour and civil society'.
4. See, for instance, Dreher and Gaston (2008) on income inequalities due to globalization.
5. The Commission was launched in Santiago, Chile, in March 2005. See http://www.who.int/social_determinants/en/.
6. See, for instance, US Institute of Medicine (1997); Ministers of Foreign Affairs (2007); Donaldson and Banatvala (2007).
7. See the following websites for more on these organizations and/or initiatives: Global Health Research Initiative (http://www.idrc.ca/en/ev-114548-201-1-DO_TOPIC.html/); Norwegian Forum for Global Health Research (http://www.globalhealth.no/); German National Commission on Global Change Research (http://www.nkgfc.org/uni-muenchen.de/nkgcf/english/frameset.htm); (US) National Institutes of Health, http://www.nih.gov/
8. For the funding priorities of these agencies, see websites: UK Economic and Social Research Council (http://www.esrcsocietytoday.ac.uk/ESRCInfoCentre/research/index.aspx); the Social Science and Humanities Research Council (SSHRC)

(http://www.sshrc.ca/site/home-accueil-eng.aspx); and the US Social Science Research Council (http://programs.ssrc.org/), respectively.

9. PhRMA specifically notes attention to the diseases malaria, trachoma, dengue fever and tuberculosis.
10. For detail of the research funding guidelines of the organizations listed here, see websites: Wellcome Trust (http://www.wellcome.ac.uk/); Kaiser Family Foundation (http://www.kff.org/about/index2.cfm); Bill and Melinda Gates Foundation (http://www.gatesfoundation.org/global-health/Pages/overview.aspx); European Partnership for Global Health (http://www.efc.be/projects/health/default.htm); Global Health Council (http://www.globalhealth.org/view_top.php3?id=25); and 'the 2008 [Bamako] Global Ministerial Forum on Research for Health' (http://www.bamako2008.org/).
11. The objective of the Global Forum for Health Research is to reduce the so-called 10–90 gap, where 'less than 10% of the world's resources for health research ... were being applied to the health problems of developing countries, where 90% of the avoidable burden of ill-health was to be found' (Global Forum for Health Research, 2006, p. vii).
12. This definition is provided on the NIHR website with regards to the Efficacy and Mechanism Evaluation (EME) programme, which does not fund 'global health'. See http://www.eme.ac.uk/
13. The Foundation's website states that: 'We target diseases and health conditions that cause the greatest illness and death in developing countries, yet receive little attention and resources.' Its 'global health funding priorities' are listed as: 'diarrhea, HIV/AIDS, malaria, maternal, newborn & child health, neglected diseases, nutrition, pneumonia & flu, polio, tobacco, tuberculosis, vaccines'.
14. Note, for example, the following program description at the Johns Hopkins Bloomberg School of Public Health. 'The Department of International Health seeks to understand health problems and develop means of disease reduction and health protection in underserved populations around the world. International Health draws on all public health disciplines for application in global settings and emphasizes master's and doctoral training programs for students with international and cross-cultural interests.' Available at http://www.jhsph.edu/dept/IH/index.html.
15. Also, several countries have introduced projects within their national constituencies that have a social determinants focus or component. Sweden and Norway are probably the most advanced in this (Ågren, 2003; Norwegian Ministry of Health and Care Services, 2007), but others are beginning to commit resources. Note, for instance, the increasing references to the social determinants of health by the UK Department of Health at http://www.dh.gov.uk/en/Publicationsandstatistics/index.htm.
16. The figure is probably much less than 5 per cent; that percentage was arrived at by counting all the projects constructed to have a social determinants focus that were funded by the NIH in 2006 (as listed at the time on the organisation's website: http://grants.nih.gov/grants/oer.htm).
17. The report also acknowledges '...calls for increased funding in specific areas such as: epidemiology; public health; health promotion; disease prevention; service delivery; diseases which burden society/chronic diseases; aging; maternal health; orthopedics; musculoskeletal disease; lung disease; kidney research and midwifery/maternity care'. Several of these areas reflect health issues that relate directly to socioeconomic conditions.

18. See PowerPoint slide entitled 'Funding: Public>Private (Year 2000)' (Stanford in Washington, 2002).
19. To illustrate how agendas are presently skewed, at a meeting of the CIHR (Canadian Institutes for Health Research) HIV/AIDS Research Advisory Committee in June 2007, a 'question was put forward as to why a large investment was being made in a [clinical trials] facility when there are no effective vaccines currently' (CIHR, 2007).
20. This paraphrases Robert Cox's (1981, p. 128) well-known aphorism that 'theory is always for someone and for some purpose'.

12

Dealing with Public Health and Intellectual Property for Pharmaceuticals at the World Trade Organization

Valbona Muzaka

Introduction

Amongst other World Trade Organization (WTO) agreements, the Trade-Related Aspects on Intellectual Property Rights (TRIPs) Agreement has perhaps been the most contested since its coming into force in 1995, both within the global trade regime and in other regimes and issue-areas, such as those dealing with human rights, biodiversity, genetic resources and public health. Of these contests, those over public health issues within the trade regime came centre stage in the late 1990s and resulted in the amendment of certain TRIPs provisions that dealt with pharmaceutical patent protection and compulsory licensing in 2005. Dealing with public health issues and pharmaceutical patent protection at the WTO may appear surprising at first sight, given that global trade is an issue-area not generally understood to be concerned with private intellectual property rights (IPRs) or public health issues. However, as will become clearer, the linkage established between IP protection and trade rules in the WTO TRIPs agreement has had the effect of limiting the space available to governments in dealing with certain public health responsibilities. This has certainly been the case for the majority of developing and least developed (WTO) members, who, already struggling to deliver on the public health front, are required to make substantial changes to their IP laws, especially with regard to pharmaceutical IPRs, in order to comply with TRIPs provisions.

Indeed, perceiving some of the difficulties in dealing with public health concerns associated with implementing the TRIPs-mandated IP protection for pharmaceuticals, certain state and non-state actors were instrumental in problematizing the impact of TRIPs on public health at the WTO in the late 1990s and in securing certain (qualified) flexibilities through the TRIPs amendment process initiated at the WTO Doha Ministerial in 2001 and concluded in 2005 at the Hong Kong Ministerial. Far from being an exercise in legal technicalities, the amendment process represents a set of complex contests between state and non-state actors (such as industry representatives, health NGOs and IP experts) over both rules of IP protection pertaining to pharmaceuticals and norms guiding public health and IP protection more broadly.

The aim of this chapter is firstly to explain why and how the public health issue became important within the trade regime in the late 1990s and, secondly, how the issue was dealt with and resolved therein. In order to better understand the contests over trade rules, IP protection for pharmaceuticals and public health, the first section focuses briefly on how the link established between IP protection and trade in TRIPs limits governments' policy space necessary to deal with certain public health responsibilities. The second section focuses on the emergence of the IP-public health contests at the WTO during the late 1990s. Two clear outcomes of these contests were the 2001 WTO Doha Declaration on the TRIPs Agreement and Public Health (the Doha Declaration) and the subsequent TRIPs amendment in 2005, which is covered in the third section.

Linking IP protection to trade: implications for public health

Prior to the TRIPs agreement, the international IP regime consisted of principles, norms and rules regarding IP protection as developed through centuries in response to continuous technological, economic, political and ideological developments. These had resulted in an international regime that dealt with IP protection issues in an atomized fashion, with a variety of IP protection forms contained in separate treaties with varying membership and managed largely through the World Intellectual Property Organisation (WIPO). One main characteristic of this regime was that its members retained enormous sovereign discretion over IP standard-setting, procedures and enforcement. As a result, the standards of IP protection varied widely in different countries. This changed with the coming into force of the WTO TRIPs agreement; TRIPs legislated strong and binding substantive and procedural norms, made such legislation universal through the trade linkage which ensures that most countries are on board (or soon will be), and provided an institutional structure (the WTO) to ensure compliance with these norms (Murumba, 1998).

Although at face value TRIPs is an agreement only on the trade-related *aspects* of IPRs, in reality it mandates WTO members to take positive legislative action to establish, protect and enforce almost all IPR forms in use in key developed countries in the early 1990s, such as patents, copyrights, trademarks, geographical indicators, industrial designs, integrated circuits and trade secrets. Essentially, TRIPs is primarily an agreement concerned with the global protection and enforcement of these private monopoly rights and is the result, to a large degree, of the political agency of certain global IP-reliant industries (high-technology, luxury goods and entertainment sectors) during the 1980s (Ryan, 1998). It was these actors that first linked IP protection to trade outside the trade regime by framing the lack of uniform IP protection worldwide as 'theft' and a non-tariff barrier to free trade and (legitimate) competition. Such formulation resonated well with certain (broader) material and ideological changes during the late 1970s and 1980s which saw key WTO members (the US and EU) increasingly concerned with their competitive positioning in the global markets and the subsequent shift of the trade regime towards detailed legalism and inside-the-border policies (Ostry, 1997; Dunoff, 1996–97).

It was during these changes within and without the trade regime that the TRIPs agreement emerged, concerned, in essence, with protecting the competitive advantage of certain key global industries and their home countries (primarily the US, EU, Switzerland and Japan) in intellectual property goods and services (May and Sell, 2006). But, by linking IP protection to competitiveness and trade, it paid insufficient attention to other crucial links that exist between IP protection and certain public goods, such as education, scientific research, agriculture, the environment and public health. The relationship between IP protection and the provision of these other complementary goods is hard enough to balance at the national level; by projecting a narrow and distorted IP-trade and competitiveness link to the global level, TRIPs has made it even harder to balance IP protection with other competing concerns at the global level. It is partly for this reason that IPRs as mandated by TRIPs have become increasingly contested in several fora, such as the WTO, WIPO, World Health Organization (WHO), the UN human rights bodies and the UN Food and Agriculture Organization (FAO).

Because it links IP to competitiveness and trade, TRIPs is not concerned with public health issues *per se*, or how the IP protection it mandates might affect them. It must be noted, however, that it does recognize *in principle* the need to protect public interest in the area of IP protection (Article 8). But, importantly, although measures can be taken to promote and protect public interest, including public health, they cannot be inconsistent with TRIPs provisions, which, broadly speaking, extend, expand and strengthen private IPRs (May, 2000). Some of the most important provisions in the agreement which may impact on public health are those related to pharmaceutical products, such as patent protection (Articles 27, 28 and 33), compulsory licensing (Article 31), protection of (pharmaceutical) data (Article 39.3),[1] and parallel importation. These issues are part of the TRIPs agreement due to the insistence of research-based pharmaceutical industry in the US, EU and Japan and were largely dealt with satisfactorily to their interests, a few exceptions aside (Sell, 2003; Drahos and Braithwaite, 2002).[2]

The protection granted to patents has been particularly controversial, as patent protection term was extended to 20 years and its subject matter was expanded to include any invention (whether products or process) in any field of technology. This controversy is more obvious in the case of pharmaceuticals because, prior to TRIPs, many (developing) countries did not provide patent protection for pharmaceutical products, with a view to allowing either the production of cheaper generic versions when production facilities existed, or the importation of cheap generic drugs from elsewhere, as a means of ensuring a secure supply of affordable pharmaceuticals. These options are almost eliminated once developing and least developed countries provide product patents for pharmaceuticals (2005 and 2016 respectively), although some flexibilities exist insofar as the practice of compulsory licensing[3] and parallel trade has been retained in TRIPs. Nevertheless, Article 31 of TRIPs, dealing with compulsory licensing, also subjected the practice to further procedural requirements in line with the general aim of TRIPs to protect the 'legitimate' interest of IPRs-holders. It must be noted, however, that this article does not limit the grounds on which a compulsory licensing can be issued, although it does limit its use, among other things, to the supply of the domestic market (Article 31.f). As we shall see, some of these flexibilities, particularly those related to compulsory licensing, became the key issues over which the IP-public health contests were fought within the trade regime.

In sum, then, it becomes clear that the main public health-related aspects of TRIPs provisions, particularly for developing countries, actually relate to pharmaceuticals, and, more precisely, affordable pharmaceuticals. TRIPs restricts access to the latter insofar as, by obligating all members to provide pharmaceutical patents, it allows IP-holders to charge (nearly) monopolistic prices for patented pharmaceuticals and delay the entry of cheap generic versions. This is especially true of newly patented medicines, amongst which the expensive second and third-generation medicines used to combat HIV/AIDS epitomize well the nature of the problem. Some scholars and pharmaceutical industry representatives have argued that pharmaceutical patent protection is vital to ensure the continuous and increasingly expensive development of new pharmaceuticals,[4] and that such protection is not a main barrier to access to health care and treatment (particularly in developing countries), listing the lack of public health infrastructure, international aid and poverty as more important barriers (Attaran and Gillespie-White, 2001; Attaran, 2004; IFPMA, 2006). Obviously, public health responsibilities go well beyond simply ensuring a steady supply of affordable pharmaceuticals, and the lack of a developed public health care infrastructure and widespread poverty affect patients' access to needed treatment. Nevertheless, it is precisely because of these other tenacious barriers that access to cheap and effective pharmaceuticals becomes a more (rather than less) urgent and important issue. Indeed, it was on these lines that the IP-public health contests unfolded within the trade regime in the late 1990s.

The emergence of IP-public health contests at the WTO

Compared with the WTO TRIPs negotiations, and despite focusing only on one area affected by TRIPs rules, contests over IP and public health were much more complex, in that they engaged many more state and non-state actors and unfolded in various fora simultaneously. Just as the origins of TRIPs hark back to non-state actors outside the trade regime, the origins of these contests can also be traced outside the WTO, to a network of international NGOs that linked global IP protection to high prices and inaccessibility of (initially HIV/AIDS) medicines in the developing countries in the latter part of the 1990s. Concerns about restricted access to medicines and unnecessary loss of human health and life resonated well with growing concerns about the unfolding HIV/AIDS crisis, which reached appalling proportions by the mid-1990s. Indeed, such was the appeal and strength of the IP-public health debate that it superseded all other IP-related issues being debated at the WTO as late as the 1999 Seattle Ministerial and culminated with the 2001 Doha Declaration on TRIPs and Public Health a mere 2 years later.

NGOs such as the Consumer Project on Technology (CPTech) and Health Action International (HAI) were the first to raise concerns over the impact of IP protection on access to affordable medicines in the developing world in the mid-1990s, and were soon joined by an array of other NGOs including, most importantly, two heavyweight, non-partisan international NGOs, Médicins sans Frontières (MSF) and Oxfam (Matthews and Munoz-Tellez, 2006). Once the IP-access to medicines linkage was made, the NGO network focused its attention on raising awareness on this issue in international organizations and national governments through mobilizing the media and organizing various campaigning initiatives with a view to achieving an eventual solution that would place 'patients before patents'. Two early steps towards this end were the participation in the crafting of a revised strategy for pharmaceuticals at the WHO in 1998 and in requesting the WTO at the Seattle Ministerial meeting in 1999 to establish a working group on access to medicines (MSF, HAI and CPTech, 1999a; 1999b). The former step was important not only because it raised the profile of the IP-public health issue among state actors, but also because it opened up another (perhaps the legitimate) intergovernmental forum to deal with such issues, one which continued to do so thereafter. On the other hand, efforts directed at initiating work at the WTO on access to medicines foundered momentarily as the Seattle Ministerial collapsed, only to resurface again in 2001.

The organizational and discursive strategies of the NGO network were successful in raising awareness on the IP-public health issue not least because certain developing countries themselves were slowly coming to a better understanding of the full extent of TRIPs obligations, costs and implications by the late 1990s. In addition to this realization, developed and developing countries alike were paying increasing attention to global public health concerns by the late 1990s, as the UN Millennium Goals, a series of World Health Assembly resolutions[5] and efforts to create the Global Fund against AIDS, Malaria and TB demonstrate. Apart from increased awareness of global public health needs and growing criticism on the part of developing countries towards TRIPs at the WTO by the late 1990s, certain post-TRIPs strategies followed by some pharmaceutical business and state actors were crucial in inadvertently raising the profile of the IP-public health debate within and without the WTO.

Having secured a legally binding agreement that locked in their competitive advantage in IP goods, and continuing with the discourse of strong IP protection as a prerequisite for free and fair trade, pharmaceutical business actors (particularly the PhRMA, IFPMA and EFPIA)[6] and their home countries (mainly the US, EU, Switzerland and Japan) entered the post-TRIPs period with a mission to both ensure a 'proper' and timely implementation of TRIPs and to further expand IP protection in areas not covered by or dealt with ambiguously by TRIPs (such as parallel imports and pharmaceutical data protection). Their efforts found expression simultaneously at the multilateral, bilateral, and unilateral levels; namely, at the WTO through its surveillance and dispute settlement mechanism, bilaterally through free trade agreements (FTAs), and through unilateral pressure, particularly from the US Trade Representative (USTR) Office. Together, these efforts resulted in narrowing down flexibilities afforded in TRIPs, broadly construing private IP rights contained in TRIPs and expanding IP protection levels to other IP forms.

At the WTO, early surveillance work at the TRIPs Council with a view to achieving effective implementation and enforcement of TRIPs was crucial in propagating a restrictive interpretation of TRIPs provisions which limited the flexibilities afforded to governments therein. This was particularly the case for developing and least developed countries which, although yet to implement TRIPs, found themselves during the late 1990s on the receiving end of pressure by the USTR, which had taken upon itself, largely at the behest of business actors, to 'educate' them in these TRIPs meetings as to how TRIPs must be implemented (Sell, 2003). Likewise, technical support to these countries, mandated by TRIPs Article 67 and offered mainly by the WTO and WIPO, has been forthcoming primarily in the shape of ready-made draft IPRs laws, some of which were 'TRIPs plus',[7] designed not with a view to promoting developing countries' best interests and use of TRIPs flexibilities, but to avoid them becoming involved in dispute resolutions related to IPRs enforcement (Drahos, 2002; Musungu and Dutfield, 2003).

WTO dispute settlement mechanism was also used strategically by pharmaceutical business and key state actors to bring cases that had good chances of success and represented issues that would set powerful examples and eventually develop the necessary body of precedent on pharmaceutical

IPRs. Among such cases, five cases were particularly important in the IP-public health debate: the case against India and Pakistan in 1996, the case against Canada in 1997, the case against Argentina in 1999, and that against Brazil in 2000, all filed by either the US or the EC (or both) on behalf of complaints raised by their pharmaceutical business actors. Some of these cases were settled bilaterally, with the Canadian and Indian cases being the only ones to go through the WTO dispute settlement procedures, including the Appellate Body in the Indian case. In both these latter cases, the Panel decision arguably adopted a relatively strict interpretation of the disputed TRIPs provisions (Articles 30, 70.8 and 70.9), while together they clearly demonstrated the determination of pharmaceutical business and key state actors to ensure a 'proper' and effective enforcement of TRIPs across the world.

In addition to this relentless multilateral pressure to 'improve' IP protection for pharmaceuticals post-TRIPs, some developing countries have also seen their margins of TRIPs-afforded flexibility narrow through bilateral free trade agreements (FTAs), involving the US or the EU, in which the IP-trade linkage has been pursued further via inserting certain 'TRIPs plus' provisions of interest to the pharmaceutical industry (amongst others), in exchange for access to the lucrative markets of these countries (Drahos, 2002). Since the late 1990s, the bilateral route has proven to be an effective way to drive IP protection standards upwards and ensure the developing countries' swift integration into the global IP regime. This route has been used most aggressively by the US, which, from 1995 until 2000, signed no less than four FTAs with developing countries, most of which have demanded from the latter the implementation of 'TRIPs plus' standards in exchange for the seemingly more immediate interest of access to the lucrative US market (Okediji, 2004). This trend has accelerated even further after the 2001 Doha Declaration. Similarly, the USTR also continued to keep the unilateral pressure up under the US Section 301 mechanism; indeed, only 1 year after TRIPs entered into force in the developed countries, the number of trading partners that came under pressure from Section 301 increased by 25 per cent (USTR, 1998). A review of the USTR categorization of countries under Special 301 into the 'priority watch list' and 'watch list' from 1996 until 2000 indicates that countries such as Canada, Brazil, Chile, Colombia, Costa Rica, Pakistan, the Philippines and Thailand made regular entries in the 'watch list' each year without fail, while countries such as Argentina, India, Turkey and Israel saw their IP laws secure them entries into the higher-profile 'priority watch list' for each year during the same period. Although trade sanctions under Section 301 have not been used routinely by the USTR, the effectiveness of the Special 301 process rests on it keeping the 'heat up' in the IP protection and enforcement front abroad, by pressurizing weaker partners to adopt US-like or 'TRIPs plus' IP laws so as to avoid further action under the 301 process.

Overall, then, whether within the WTO or outside it, these post-TRIPs strategies adopted by certain IP-reliant business actors, featuring most prominently the pharmaceutical industry, and the US and EC demonstrate their collective determination both to ensure an implementation of TRIPs that concurred with their interests and the achievement of concrete results in areas dealt with ambiguously or not covered by TRIPs at all. This generally meant narrowing down TRIPs flexibilities and construing IP rights broadly. But, as these post-TRIPs strategies intensified, so did the NGO network's scope and membership, as did awareness about and resistance against further encroaching upon TRIPs flexibilities. In particular, the unfolding of one event helped perhaps more than any other both to strengthen the network's cause and to raise internationally the profile of the IP-access to medicines debate. This was the infamous court case brought against the South African government by 41 research-based pharmaceutical companies in February 1998, which challenged some of the provisions of the 1997 Amendment Act related to parallel importing of pharmaceuticals and compulsory licensing as unconstitutional and non-TRIPs-compliant. The South African court case also attracted considerable attention and proved controversial, not least because of the considerable pressure from pharmaceutical companies, the USTR office and, at some point, from the US Presidential office, the EC Trade Commissioner and even US Congress (t'Hoen, 2005) for provisions, probably consistent with TRIPs, designed to deal with its raging AIDS/HIV crisis. By 2001 the chorus of criticism, often cast in terms of 'medical apartheid', coming from the NGO network and other civil society groups, international organizations and governments, eventually had its effect and the companies decided to withdraw their case in April 2001. This signalled the end of perhaps their biggest public relations disaster to date, as well as the moment in time when the IP-public health debate officially entered the trade regime; prompted by such developments, the WTO African Group requested the TRIPs Council to consider the effects of patents on prices, accessibility and affordability of pharmaceuticals in June 2001.

The WTO TRIPs Council discussions resulted in the Doha Declaration on the TRIPs Agreement and Public Health in November 2001. The Doha Declaration, while not introducing new obligations or rights, recognized the flexibilities provided in the TRIPS Agreement and the right of WTO Members to use them, stating that these flexibilities should be interpreted in a way supportive of public health. Importantly, it reinforced the right of the Members to grant compulsory licences, the freedom to determine the grounds upon which licences were granted and the freedom to determine the regime of exhaustion of IPRs (closely linked to parallel importing). Such reaffirmations of flexibilities available to governments to undertake measures to promote public health ran directly against the restrictive interpretation given to the respective provisions until then. Indeed, the language adopted was opposed by some developed countries, particularly the US, for fear that such language would weaken the commitment to patent protection and TRIPs obligations in general. The Declaration countered these concerns well, as it also reiterated members' commitment to TRIPs and recognized that the latter was not in conflict with members' right to protect public health.

In other words, the Declaration managed in one stroke to vindicate simultaneously the position of pharmaceutical business actors and NGOs, formulated as 'IPRs = research = cures' and 'copying = cheap medicines = life' respectively. By explicitly recognizing the significance of IP protection to the development of new medicines and establishing that TRIPs provisions did not prevent public health measures, the Declaration legitimized the role of pharmaceutical IPRs and other TRIPs provisions, rather than problematizing them. The Declaration, then, challenged neither IPRs standards mandated by TRIPs nor the IP-trade linkage established by it, although it did highlight the newly established IP-public health dimension. It must be noted, however, that the main proposition of the IP-public health debate had not been so much that IP protection *per se* ran counter to ensuring access to medicines and public health in general, but rather that the *restrictive* interpretation and implementation of certain TRIPs provisions significantly reduced governments' options to ensure such access in affordable terms, particularly in developing countries. Hence, the aim both of the NGO network and of developing countries was not so much to overhaul TRIPs, but mainly to protect and use the flexibilities contained therein. It is in this sense that the Declaration was a victory for these latter actors, in that it succeeded precisely in claiming back such flexibilities, without adding or subtracting anything to TRIPs provisions as such.

Amending the TRIPs Agreement, 2001–5

As we argued in the previous section, while a veritable achievement, the Declaration did not seriously threaten the IP-trade link established by TRIPs. Indeed, IP protection has continued to be closely linked to trade imperatives; in fact, as the Doha Declaration was being negotiated, both the US and the EU gave a boost to their trade–IP protection strategy at home and abroad. After deliberations during 2001, the US Congress enacted in 2002 the Trade Promotion Authority Act, which called for accelerated compliance with TRIPs agreement provisions as well as for any multilateral or bilateral trade agreements to reflect standards of IP protection similar to those found in US laws (Trade Act, 2002, S.2102). Similarly, the Lisbon Agenda for Europe of 2000, establishing the strategic goal for the EU of becoming the most competitive and dynamic knowledge-based economy, recognized innovation, opening of international markets and IP protection as the key to success. In addition, frustrated with the lack of concrete results in recent multilateral trade negotiations, both the US and the EU have been eager to liberalize further and faster through the regional and bilateral trade agreements route. One implication of this route has been that, given the established IP-trade linkage as a competitiveness issue in these two major trading countries, many regional or bilateral trade agreements contain an IP chapter designed with a view to protecting and promoting their respective IP-reliant industries' competitive advantage.

Some of the IP provisions in these FTAs go beyond those mandated by TRIPs. This is more the case with US than the EU FTAs. Despite the EU having achieved a great degree of internal IP harmonization, it has not demanded similar legislative sophistication of its trading partners (except for EU accession countries), although this has been shifting towards more elaborate and comprehensive IP provisions recently (Santa Cruz, 2007). Nonetheless, it is in the US FTAs, which often incorporate provisions mirroring provisions of its IP law, that 'TRIPs plus' provisions such as stronger protection for pharmaceutical test data, extended patent protection, narrow exception to patent rights and addition conditions on the use of compulsory licences, are more obvious. All these provisions have a direct impact in strengthening the position of patent-holders and limiting or delaying access to affordable pharmaceuticals. In addition, these provisions run counter to the spirit of the Doha Declaration. With regard to compulsory licensing, for instance, the US FTAs with Jordan (2000), Singapore (2003), Australia (2004) and those initiated in 2003 with the South African Custom Union limit the grounds upon which a licence can be granted (Morin, 2006), although TRIPs does not specify any such grounds and the Doha Declaration clearly stated that governments are free to determine the grounds for granting such licences.

The issue of limiting the grounds for compulsory licensing through bilateral or regional trade agreements is important, because after the Doha Declaration the IP-public health debate at the WTO had started to focus precisely on compulsory licensing. While the Declaration was being debated, the issue arose with regard to compulsory licensing for countries with insufficient or no pharmaceutical manufacturing capacities, whose options to address public health concerns through compulsory licensing were further reduced by stipulations found in TRIPs Article 31(f). They were limited not only by their inability to work a compulsory licence, but also because other countries that could were not permitted to issue a compulsory licence for export. Thus, with the Doha Declaration commissioning work on finding a practical solution to this issue (paragraph 6), another set of contestations was set in motion within the trade regime on compulsory licensing as it related to the IP-public health linkage, one which engaged state and non-state actors until TRIPs was amended in 2005.

For over four strenuous years, these contests were fought over issues related to the legal form of the solution, which diseases and countries would be eligible to use a possible paragraph 6 solution and what safeguards there would be in place to avoid the 'misuse' of such a solution. In the end, an exception was carved out of Article 31(f), which originally limited compulsory licences to the domestic market. The amended article allows the issuing of compulsory licences for import and export in case of public health crisis in the importing country, but it does so through establishing a mechanism burdened with procedural requirements, designed with a view to protecting the interests of patent-holders. These safeguards included requirements that the TRIPs Council be informed of the intention to use the mechanism and given a detailed justification for such a decision, the patent-holder be approached for a voluntary licence beforehand, production under licence be limited to the quantity required by the importing country, and measures be taken to prevent trade diversion and compensation paid to the patent-holder. Because of these requirements, many developing countries and health NGOs have considered the 2005 amendment as a step backwards from the Doha Declaration.

The amendment will formally be part of TRIPs once two-thirds of its membership has accepted it, but so far only 11 countries and the EU have done so at the time of writing. Interestingly, despite the urgency to deal with the matter, no country notified the TRIPs Council of its intention to use compulsory licences for import or export, with the exception of Rwanda in July 2007. Rwanda's experience with the mechanism, if successful, would serve to counter concerns that the mechanism is too complicated and unworkable. Currently, its feasibility remains questionable, thus making it difficult to evaluate whether it really provides a flexible solution to the public health concerns of developing and least developed countries. Nevertheless, the threat of compulsory licensing (although not for import) has been used with some success by some developing countries, most notably Brazil, which has recently been able to negotiate considerable price reductions for some HIV/AIDS pharmaceuticals from patent-holders under such threats.

Despite the 2005 amendment being greeted by the US and the EU as a means of enhancing access to pharmaceuticals in developing and least developed countries, efforts by the latter to deal with their public health concerns through overriding patent rights for pharmaceuticals have not received a sympathetic response. For instance, considerable pressure was placed on Thailand and Brazil by pharmaceutical companies, the USTR and the EU Trade Commissioner for issuing compulsory licences on antiretroviral medicines in 2006 and 2007. In addition to such pressure, the USTR has continued to list several developing countries in its Special 301 'priority watch list' and 'watch list' for lack of 'effective' patent and data protection for pharmaceuticals while negotiations at the WTO on compulsory licensing and access to medicines were ongoing. Further to such pressure, as we noted, several US FTAs signed with developing countries have included 'TRIPs plus' provisions for pharmaceutical IP protection, which, although not generally proscribing compulsory licensing for health purposes, are expected to limit the availability of affordable generic pharmaceuticals. The combined effect of these developments within and without the WTO on the ability of developing countries' governments to deal with public health concerns is yet to unfold.

Conclusions

With the establishment of the WTO TRIPs agreement, the discourse of strong, harmonized global IP protection as a prerequisite for free trade has superseded all other concerns, including those related to public health. The post-TRIPs period has seen this discourse being contested at various levels, but in this paper we have focused specifically on contests amongst state and non-state actors taking place within the trade regime on IP protection and public health issues. We have noted that the Doha Declaration in 2001 was a victory in terms of at least raising public health concerns at the same level as protecting private IPRs, but this linkage has not truly replaced that originally established by TRIPs. This is so because, as we have also noted, the major trade regime members have continued to give primacy to IP protection as an international trade and competitiveness issue, a formulation which has continued to inform both their multilateral and bilateral trade strategies. Indeed, it may well be that what was 'given away' in terms of verbiage in the Doha Declaration will be claimed back by the trade–IP protection linkage being pursued further by these members on behalf of their industries within the trade regime and outside it.

Meanwhile, in the contests over compulsory licensing at the WTO, all efforts were made by these members and the pharmaceutical business actors to ensure that the 'legitimate' property protected by TRIPs was not appropriated 'arbitrarily', even for public health purposes, by other members of the regime. The 2005 amendment represents a solution which is laden with safeguards aimed at preserving the rights of patent-holders, rather than at providing flexibilities to deal with public health concerns. With international IP protection for pharmaceuticals being defined as a competitiveness issue by the key regime members, it is not surprising that the IP-public health debate was dealt with in a manner which primarily safeguards the interest of the IP-holders. Some qualified policy space to deal with public health concerns by developing and least developed members was also ensured in the TRIPs amendment, but, like the TRIPs agreement itself, its effective implementation will depend on the interpretation given to the amendment provisions and governments' political will to make use of it, or allow other governments to do so. While the issue of compulsory licensing, access to pharmaceuticals and public health in general may appear to have been settled at the WTO, at least for the moment, we have noted that other developments at the bilateral level have continued to further increase IP protection standards worldwide, including those pertaining to pharmaceuticals. In addition, these recent developments have also set in motion another set of contests between state and non-state actors unfolding currently, whose outcomes in terms of improving governments' abilities to deal with public health concerns remain to be seen.

Notes

1. In addition to the above, another layer of protection is afforded to pharmaceuticals through Article 39(3), which mandates the protection of pharmaceutical test data. Pharmaceutical test data refer to data related to clinical trials submitted to health authorities in order to obtain market authorization for a pharmaceutical product.
2. One such exception relates to the parallel importation of pharmaceuticals; TRIPs stipulates in Article 6 that it takes no stand on the related issue of exhaustion of IPRs, thus allowing *in principle* the practice of parallel trade. However, it does so only for WTO dispute settlement purposes (Article 6); in light of Article 28, which includes in the bundle of rights granted to patent-holders the right to prevent other parties from importing, for our purposes, pharmaceutical products, legal opinion remains divided as to whether TRIPs eliminates parallel importing.
3. Compulsory licensing essentially involves the authorization (by a public authority) of other parties to use the invention, in our case the pharmaceutical product, without the consent of the patent holder.
4. This argument is based on the long period of time (8–12 years) and considerable costs to develop a new pharmaceutical product, around US$802 million in 2000 US$, and the unique vulnerability of pharmaceuticals to reverse engineering
5. World Health Assembly 'Revised Drug Strategy' Resolution (WHA 52.19) of 24 May 1999; World Health Assembly 'Scaling Up the Response to HIV/AIDS' Resolution (WHA 54.10) and 'WHO Medicines Strategy' Resolution (54.11) of 21 May 2001.
6. IFPMA (the International Federation of Pharmaceutical Manufacturers and Associations), EFPIA (the European Federation of Pharmaceutical Industries and Associations) and PhRMA (the Pharmaceutical Research and Manufacturers of America).
7. TRIPs plus provisions may refer to both obligations that are of a higher standard than those specified in TRIPs and introduction of other obligations which are missing or ambiguous in the TRIPs text. Some of these are extending patents and copyright to new kinds of subject matter; eliminating or narrowing permitted exceptions including those still provided in US and European IPR laws; extending protection terms, and so on.

13

Patents, Policies and Pricing: Access to Medicines for Vulnerable Populations in a Global Economy*

Shree Mulay, Eowynne Feeney and Daya R. Varma

Introduction

Many factors contribute to ensuring affordability of medicines for vulnerable populations, for whom cost of medicines constitutes a significant proportion of a family's budget. Suffice it to say that social determinants of health, such as household income, gender, race and class, determine who will have access to medicines, and at what price. Our underlying premise, in keeping with the theme of the book, is that we consider health to be a fundamental human right, where health is defined in broad terms to include health infrastructure, human resources, preventive and curative aspects of health and affordable medicines. We are also convinced that the state has a pivotal role, directly through the provision of drug plans or universal medical plans or indirectly through price controls and patent policies, in ensuring quality, affordable and accessible health services and medicines for its entire population. Moreover, capacity to develop and market new drugs for the benefit of the vast majority of vulnerable populations in developing countries requires investments by the state in the development of drugs for neglected diseases. In short, a comprehensive approach to public health instead of a piecemeal, disease-based approach is needed.

In this chapter, we examine patents, policies and pricing, all of which contribute to making drugs unaffordable. We also examine the factors that promote or hinder research and development (R&D) in neglected diseases, which disproportionately affect the poor. Finally, our premise is based on a social justice lens for 'health in an unequal world' and the need to influence policies at the local, regional and international levels so that good health is available for the vast majority of people.

In analyzing how patents, policies and pricing affect access and affordability of medicines for marginalized families, we have chosen Canada and

India as representative of a developed and a developing country, respectively, for the following reasons:

1. Both Canada and India have strong generic drug manufacturing sectors. Although the experience in Canada has been mixed, policies that promote rapid production of generic drugs would benefit both countries.
2. Canada has experience with up to 20-year product patent protections, the same rules that have been imposed on developing countries as a precondition to joining the World Trade Organization (WTO). Therefore, Canada's experience for the past 18 years can serve as a benchmark for developing countries like India.
3. The Indian pharmaceutical industry is seeking ways of mitigating the anticipated decline in profits by developing partnerships with Multi-National Corporations (MNCs) for new drug development. The Indian government is also encouraging such partnerships. Therefore, looking at Canada's experience with incentives to MNCs to relocate R&D initiatives in Canada to build a stronger knowledge-based economy would be useful for India and other developing countries as well.
4. Concessions sought by India, Brazil and South Africa during the Doha Round of WTO negotiations in 2002 have not resulted in better access to medicines under the WTO rules. Whatever the final outcome of the WTO agreements, a direct dialogue amongst researchers who shape public policies is needed to develop strategies to enable access to medicines by vulnerable populations.
5. Finally, despite obvious differences between Canada and India in the health status of their populations, disease profiles, and health care systems, a comparison of factors involved in access to affordable medicines would be useful in developing alliances and strategies at the international level.

Patents, policies, pricing and drugs in Canada

The Government of Canada first regulated the pharmaceutical industry to provide affordable generics in 1922 when the Canadian Commissioner of Patents 'allowed any Canadian manufacturer to imitate and produce drugs of another manufacturer, even if there was an existing patent' (Anis, 2000). In 1969, the government further facilitated production of affordable generics by implementing a policy that allowed import and/or manufacture of patented products subject to a 4 per cent royalty payment under section 41(4) of the Canadian Patent Act through compulsory licensing (ibid.). However, the pharmaceutical industry lobbied to reverse some of these provisions and the Conservative government of Brian Mulroney conceded to their demand in 1987 by approving Bill C-22, which provided patent protection for 10 years. Further amendments to the Canadian Patents Act (S-17 and Bill

C-91) – compliant with the TRIPS and WTO rules – granted a minimum of 20 years of protection for applications filed in Canada after October 1 1989 (Rx&D, 2001). These bills weakened and then abolished compulsory licensing provisions (Lexchin, 1993).

In return for the increased patent protection, the Canadian Government asked the brand-name manufacturers to invest 10 per cent of their profits into research and development (R&D) in Canada. At the same time, the Patented Medicine Price Review Board (PMPRB), an independent semi-judicial body responsible for drug price control, was set up to ensure that:

1. the price of an existing patented medicine does not increase by more than the Consumer Price Index;
2. the cost of a new patented drug therapy remains in the cost range of existing drugs in the same class; and
3. the price of a breakthrough drug is limited to the median of its prices in France, Germany, Italy, Sweden, Switzerland, Britain, and the US; and no patented drug can be priced above the highest price in this group of countries.

Despite these provisions, instituted in the 1990s to control the price of individual drugs, spending on medicines has risen steadily (Lexchin, 1997; Henry and Lexchin, 2002) because of physician preference for newer drugs, an increase in the aging population that needs many more medicines, the variation in reimbursement policies for drugs across the provinces and territories (Morgan, 2004; Lexchin, 2007) and finally active lobbying by the brand-name manufacturers to make it difficult for generic companies to produce generic versions of medicines when the patents expire. The Pharmaceutical Patents Act was intended to allow rapid regulatory approval of generic versions of patented medicines while the patent was still in effect so that the generic version could enter the market as soon as the patent expired (Rx&D, 2001). However, the provision was revoked when Canada lost a WTO case (Raghavan, 2000; Howse, 2000), which was followed by further limitations on generic manufacturers. For example, under the Notice of Compliance 'Linkage' Regulation, an automatic 24-month stay-order prevents Health Canada from approving a generic drug until any claim of alleged patent infringement is decided in court (CNW, 2003; Valiquet, 2006). This has meant that the brand-name drug companies are able to resort to 'ever-greening' of their patents, which involves listing and litigating additional patents after the main patent on the active ingredient has expired, thus prolonging the brand's monopoly (Lexchin, 2004). This is estimated to have cost Canadians over $1–2.1 billion between 1993 and 2007 (CNW, 2003; CGPA, 2007).

However, the early stimulus provided to generic pharmaceutical companies, by what was essentially a process patents act, has meant that Canada continues to have a very robust generic pharmaceutical industry. It also has had the benefit of several provisions not available to generic manufacturing companies in many other developed nations. These provisions include substitution of generic products by pharmacists (this is mandatory in 9 out of 10 provincial benefit plans) (Anis et al., 2001) and the ability to rely on the innovator's data on health and safety for regulatory approval of their products (Menon, 2001).

The majority of generic products sold in Canada are produced in Canada; the exception is Novopharm, which is owned by Teva, an Israeli company, the second largest (by net revenue) generic producer in the world. The generic industry in Canada has been successful because two generic companies, Apotex and Novopharm, have made it into the top 10 pharmaceutical companies in the world (IMS Health Canada, 2007). Other foreign-owned generic manufacturers, such as Ranbaxy Canada, are relatively small at this time.

Large foreign-owned MNC companies, mainly concerned with brand-name products, have dominated the Canadian pharmaceutical market. In 2007, their total sales were $12.3 billion, up by 3 per cent from 2006 (PMPRB, 2007, p. 24) and a whopping increase of 723.5 per cent from 1990. Not surprisingly, patented drugs as a percentage of total drug sales increased from 43.2 per cent in 1990 to 66.0 per cent in 2007; this increase was not necessarily all due to rising drug prices but a result of increase in volume, prescribing habits of physicians and demographic shifts (PMPRB, 2007). However, according to the Canadian Generic Pharmaceutical Association (CGPA), 48.1 per cent of prescriptions filled, used generic drugs but only accounted for 20.1 per cent of the drug sales (CGPA, 2007). Moreover, Canada continues to have the second highest drug prices amongst its peers, with the USA being at the top (PMPRB, 2007, p. 33). Another disparity that is of concern is the decline in R&D expenditures as a percent of sales by brand-name manufacturers from 11.7 per cent in 1995 to 8.3 per cent in 2007; the expectation of the Canadian Government was that at least 10 per cent of sales would be invested in R&D (PMPRB, 2007, p. 42).

Canada has a mix of private and public coverage for prescription drugs. The relative share of private spending (60 per cent) versus public spending (40 per cent) has changed little since 1985 (CIHI, 2007). However, actual coverage has declined with increased use of patented medicines; more money is being spent on a smaller volume of patented medicines. Those who do not have access to employer-sponsored private group insurance rely on the publicly funded drug plans; a much larger proportion has to be paid as an out-of-pocket expense, which can be a big burden for people on low fixed incomes (Kapur and Basu, 2005).

Patents, policies, pricing and drugs in India

When the allopathic system of medicine was introduced in India during British colonial rule, most drugs were imported from Britain. The first indigenous company, the Bengal Chemical and Pharmaceutical Works, was set up in 1892 and incorporated in 1905. Initially, it manufactured commonly used medicines that were being imported from Britain, but later introduced therapeutically effective Ayurvedic formulations. Other indigenous companies were started by individuals, trained in Germany and Britain, who, influenced by anticolonialism, wanted to establish national self-sufficiency in medicines (Chaudhuri, 2005, p. 21).

Several companies were started between the two World Wars, including the Chemical Industrial and Pharmaceutical Works, now Cipla, the largest manufacturer of pharmaceuticals for the domestic market (Chaudhuri, 2005, p. 22). By 1950, 62 per cent of pharmaceuticals needed by the Indian population were manufactured by Indian companies (Chaudhuri, 2005, p. 23).

In the early 1950s MNCs started major R&D programs, and introduced many new drugs (Chaudhuri, 2005, p. 25). Under the existing patent laws in India at the time, these newly introduced medicines enjoyed patent protection. In fact, policies granting the MNCs 'national treatment' allowed them to diversify and increase production by 25 per cent without expending additional foreign exchange; this meant that these MNCs were able to expand rapidly by importing bulk drugs and formulating them in India. Indigenous manufacturers were not able to take advantage of the liberal licensing policy because they could not ramp up the production of bulk drugs. As a result, the market share for the indigenous companies declined from 62 per cent in 1950 to 32 per cent by 1970 (Agarwal and Saibaba, 2001; Chaudhuri, 2005).

In response to concerns that India was not self-sufficient in the manufacture of drugs, the Patent Act of 1911 was amended in 1970; it came into effect in 1972, two decades after the reform was first proposed at the time of independence in 1947. The 1970 Patent Act allowed for the process used for the manufacture of the active ingredient to be patented rather than the chemical entity. Moreover, a company could not register numerous processes, but could register only the one procedure that it used most frequently. The time period for patent protection was reduced from 16 years to 5 years from the date of sealing, and 7 years from the date of filing of the patent (Hamied, 1988, p. 2). Since process patents allowed indigenous companies to develop new methods for the manufacture of drugs produced elsewhere, the Indian Government implicitly provided rewards to local manufacturers to develop drugs using alternate production methods. Important contributions were made by the two state-owned institutions: the Council for Scientific and Industrial Research (CSIR), which supported initiatives to innovate in alternate processes, and the Indian Drug and Pharmaceutical Laboratories (IDPL), which developed new methods for drug synthesis. These institutions collaborated with private pharmaceutical companies and could be considered to be forerunners of the much-lauded private–public partnerships (Chaudhuri, 2005, p. 20).

Dr Yusuf K. Hamied, Chief Executive Officer of Cipla Company, summed up the impact of the 1970 Patents Act on the pharmaceutical industry in the following words: 'The India Patents Act of 1970 has served one of its main purposes. It has enabled the national sector to make an increasingly significant contribution towards self-reliance and self-sufficiency, utilizing innovative and appropriate technology, based essentially on indigenous raw materials and resources.' He further added: 'It is significant to note that only those drugs which are of proven efficacy and safety are approved by the (Indian) Ministry of Health. Thanks to this cautious policy, our country has been spared several drugs such as Thalidomide, Benoxaprofen, Zomipirac, Isoxicam, etc. which were introduced abroad, later found harmful and subsequently withdrawn' (Hamied, 1988, p. 3).

Generic versions of newly developed drugs were often available in India within 4 or 5 years after they appeared in the world market (Lanjouw and Cockburn, 2001). This change in the patent structure initiated a renaissance in the pharmaceutical industry of India: the number of pharmaceutical manufacturers increased from a mere 200 in 1950–51 to more than 6,000 during the 1980s, reaching 23,790 in 1998–99[1]; the market share of MNCs gradually declined to 40 per cent by 1999 (Agarwal and Saibaba, 2001). These changes have enabled India to achieve self-sufficiency in the production of bulk drugs (Agarwal and Saibaba, 2001; Consumer Protection Network, 2006; Babar, 2007).

At present, India is one of the top 15 pharmaceutical manufacturing countries in the world, with a pharmaceutical market of $4.9 billion and exports of over US$1.5 billion (that is, 4.1 per cent of India's total exports) (Agarwal and Saibaba, 2001). Eight per cent of global pharmaceutical production occurs in India and it is the fifth largest manufacturer after the US, Japan, Europe and China (Pradhan, 2006; Löfgren, 2007). India has the largest number of US Federal Drug Administration-approved manufacturing facilities outside the US (Pradhan, 2006). Thus, the Indian pharmaceutical industry, like the information technology industry, is among important knowledge-based industries in which India has a comparative advantage (Dyer, 2004).

Nearly 95 per cent of the domestic demand for pharmaceuticals in India is met through indigenous production. Imports have been limited to a few life-saving drugs like anticancer, cardiovascular, antihypertensive and other newer patented drugs (Agarwal and Saibaba, 2001). Also, the competition among indigenous firms has kept drug prices among the lowest in the world. Nevertheless, they are still too high for impoverished people and medicines are still out of reach for a majority of people living in rural areas and in urban slums (Ranson et al., 2006; Chaudhury et al., 2005; Phadke, 1998). As well, irrational use of medicines is quite rampant, resulting in wasteful expenditure (Phadke, 1998).

Liberalization of the Indian economy, globalization and new obligations enforced in 2005 under the WTO agreements have posed new challenges for the Indian pharmaceutical industry. Our case study of Ranbaxy Pharmaceuticals, discussed later in the chapter, illustrates that the larger pharmaceutical companies have chosen to challenge and litigate specific patents, as well as exploring opportunities for partnerships with MNCs. However, in reality, TRIPS-compliant mechanisms, including compulsory licensing, differential pricing, national drug price controls, parallel importations and Bolar provisions, have been difficult to implement despite the Doha Declaration on the TRIPS Agreement and Public Health (WTO, 2001), which was intended to address the problem of inaccessibility of medicines by the poor nations with no manufacturing capacity using compulsory licensing (WTO, 2001). Canada was the first country to adopt an amendment to its patent laws that would permit export of medicines to developing countries in May 2004; however, it is only now, 4 years after the adoption of the amendment, that the first shipment of medicines has been made to Rwanda by Apotex Canada in September 2008 (Apotex, 2008) because of the road blocks posed by MNCs (Oxfam, 2001).

R&D in neglected diseases

Negotiators for TRIPS contended that product patents would lead to an increase in R&D by pharmaceutical companies for the development of new drugs for diseases in developing countries, including those that have come to be known as diseases of the poor, such as tuberculosis, malaria and HIV/AIDS, and neglected diseases such as Chagas, trypanosomiasis, leishmaniasis and dengue fever (Satyanarayana and Srivastava, 2007). According to some experts, India would be in a good position to take advantage of production needs, since it has a well-developed pharmaceutical industry. However, an examination of what has occurred in India reveals a very different picture.

The Indian pharmaceutical industry had traditionally been involved in R&D for developing new processes for the manufacture of drugs developed and tested elsewhere. Since the mid-1990s, however, about 14 Indian companies have started investing in R&D for new drugs (Chaudhuri, 2005, p. 155) and, thus far, have formulated approximately 29 new chemical entities (NCEs) (Chaudhuri, 2005, p. 161). However, due to the huge operating costs, particularly at the clinical trials stage, none of these companies are engaged in the entire process of drug development; instead, they develop new molecules and license them out to MNCs (Chaudhuri, 2005, p. 159). As a result, Indian companies are not targeting diseases of the South, such as HIV/AIDS, tuberculosis and malaria, except when there is an interest stimulated by philanthropic efforts like the Gates, Clinton and Packard Foundations (Indo-Asian News Service, 2008).

Although the Government of India has initiated some collaborative research to synergize the strengths of publicly funded R&D institutions and the Indian pharmaceutical industry (Chaudhuri, 2005, p. 176), there are no special funds allocated or activities commissioned for the development of novel drugs for neglected diseases. Although several indigenous pharmaceutical companies like Dr. Reddy's or Ranbaxy (Dyer, 2004; Löfgren, 2007) have formed alliances with MNCs to conduct R&D, they have not invested in developing medicines for 'neglected diseases' because the possibilities of making a profit are limited (Lanjouw and Cockburn, 2001; Chaudhuri, 2005, p. 175). It is worth looking at the track record of Ranbaxy Pharmaceutical Company to better understand the strategies used by some of the larger pharmaceutical companies in India and why research on diseases of the poor has such low priority.

Ranbaxy case study

Ranbaxy Laboratories Limited, with headquarters in Haryana, India, was sold in 2008 to the Japanese multinational pharmaceutical giant, Daiichi Sankyo Company. Ranbaxy had actively striven to position itself as an international player and the merger with Daiichi allows it to do just that. Ranbaxy was started in 1937 to distribute products of Shionogi Company of Japan. But, according to Malvinder Singh (2005), the Managing Director (MD) of Ranbaxy, it was under the stewardship of his father and grandfather that the company expanded and began manufacturing medicines. When the patent regime changed in the 1970s, Ranbaxy began to focus on assuming leadership in domestic business. In the late 1970s the company began its first joint venture in Nigeria and in the 1980s started to introduce its products to the Southeast Asian markets (Singh, 2005).

While senior Ranbaxy executives may not identify the liberalization programs of the 1990s as a catalyst for their expansion, undoubtedly their global expansion was facilitated by these programs. Ranbaxy has presence in most major pharmaceutical markets in the world, receiving 50 per cent of its total revenue from the US market (Abboud, 2005), 23 per cent from Europe (Singh, 2005) and the rest from Latin America, Africa and Southeast Asia. In total, 80 per cent of revenues are derived from international operations and only 20 per cent from India (ibid.).

Ranbaxy has been able to catapult onto the global market by using Indian science and technology to manufacture drugs while at the same time challenging proprietary rights through patent litigations. It would appear that the company feels patent challenges are necessary risks because the payoff is enormous. Market analysts have critiqued this strategy of Ranbaxy and attributed the company's downward trend in 2006 to their patent litigations (*Economic Times*, 2006). For example, Ranbaxy was taken to court by Pfizer for patent infringement for Lipitor and Accupril, drugs used in the treatment of cardiovascular disease. Ranbaxy was willing to take the risk because, although patent challenges combined with research on new chemical entities may be high-risk strategies, they eventually pay off, and

50 per cent of their Para IV filings (the filing required for entering a generic on the market in the US) go unchallenged. Although Ranbaxy's patent challenges are very specific, they are mainly for large blockbuster money-making drugs such as Lipitor and Accupril. Expanding into other markets, along with partnerships, patent litigations, acquisitions and mergers, characterizes Ranbaxy's *modus operandi*.

Ranbaxy was the first Indian company to commercialize a new drug in Western markets (ibid.). It has actively engaged in Intellectual Property (IP) partnerships, co-marketing alliances and patent litigations in order to try and minimize the risks of their R&D ventures (ibid.). For example, Ranbaxy entered into partnership with Bayer for a once-a-day version of Cipro. First, Ranbaxy acquired 30 per cent of Vorin Lab, the manufacturers of ciproflaxin (Kutty, 2000), then developed a new dosage formula which was licensed out to Bayer, who conducted the clinical trials following which Bayer collaborated with Ranbaxy to commercialize the drug in different markets. Ranbaxy also entered into co-marketing alliances with Glaxo-Wellcome and Elli Lilly. As Sudip Chaudhuri has noted, 'earlier these partnerships used to be drug specific but Ranbaxy is now entering cross-therapeutic areas' (Chaudhuri, 2005, p. 164). Ranbaxy MD Singh (2005) is much more explicit about TRIPS:

> Ranbaxy has always promoted a pro-patent regime in terms of intellectual property protection. At the same time we are saying we don't need to be TRIPS plus, we need to be TRIPS compliant. You got a lobby from the big pharmaceutical companies that want excessive protection, which I would call ever-greening, and then there are domestic companies who want little protection so they can keep copying products. And then you have Ranbaxy that has a balanced view that says, 'look India needs to integrate itself into the global economy, we need to have an environment that encourages innovation and creation of intellectual property and protection of the same'. But also there comes a time when patents expire and generics must come in.

Ranbaxy has pursued private–private and private–public partnerships vigorously in order to expand its share of the market. Ranbaxy entered into very complex negotiations with the Government of India as well as Roche, Hetero and other pharmaceutical companies, for instance, on Tamiflu, one of two drugs effective against avian flu. The case of Tamiflu shows three things: first, the Indian generic companies and the government are hesitant to use the flexibilities provided in the TRIPS agreement; second, the Indian government is ceding greater control over provision of medicines to the corporations; and, third, companies are more willing to enter licensing arrangements instead of applying for compulsory licenses in order to obtain additional markets. This means that, while they may obtain a smaller proportion of the global market, thus having to sell their medicines for a higher price, they will not have to enter into legal battles with brand-name manufacturers. Ranbaxy's Malvinder Singh (2005) was forthright: 'from our perspective we are a generic company and we supply products to everybody, but we also respect patents, we have to find ways to deal with these issues when they arise'. He continued, 'I think that in today's society more and more companies, the industry as a whole, and the governments create a collaborative effort to create a solution.'

Ranbaxy's R&D initiatives, research partnerships, co-marketing alliances and patent litigations seem to have allowed them to respond quite adequately to a product patent regime. The question is whether or not these initiatives deprive the Indian population of affordable generic medicines at low cost by shifting the company's focus to drugs for the export market for the more developed countries. The case of Tamiflu sheds light on the possibility for public–private and private–private partnerships to ensure access to a medicine, but unfortunately these types of collaborative efforts to ensure the supply of Tamiflu for the 'potential' epidemic have never been used to ensure access to essential medicines. Chagas, trypanosomiasis, leishmaniasis, dengue fever, HIV/AIDS, TB, malaria and a long list of other neglected diseases continue to have inadequate treatment regimes due to inadequate research, and, while there is adequate treatment for many strains of HIV, TB, and malaria, many Southern populations cannot access these drugs. For example, leprosy is a major problem in India,[2] yet the government does not have an appropriate treatment regimen for its population, but relies heavily on the NGO sector to help in the treatment and rehabilitation of people with the disease. Developing nations, companies and governments have failed to respond adequately to epidemics of such diseases as *P. falciparum* malaria, Chikungunya fever, dengue fever and Japanese encephalitis (Bhargava and Chatterjee, 2007). While effective control requires public health measures to prevent the spread of vectors, new therapies are also needed to replace those that have become ineffective due to drug resistance. In this context, the MD of Ranbaxy has said: 'our objective is clear; we want to bring world class service, in terms of delivery, product and services at prices that are competitive and affordable'. When asked whether or not this meant that they would be affordable for the poor, the response was 'prices are competitive and affordable for people; these same products and services we provide here, I think, would be priced very differently anywhere elsewhere in the world' (Singh, 2005). The fact is that generic companies want to remain competitive, but not sell below profit level; 'it must be a commercial venture' (Abboud, 2005). In summary, Ranbaxy seems to be faring well under a product patent regime, but its research initiatives with Bayer, Glaxo-Wellcome and Roche are directed towards drugs for the more profitable Western markets.

While Ranbaxy wants to ensure that generics enter the market at the time of patent expiry, they seem to have no intention of using the compulsory licensing provision at any time to ensure affordable access to medicines. With the implementation of TRIPS, the patents are awarded 20 years protection, allowing high prices and thus denying the poor access to these medicines. Ranbaxy would be willing to provide affordable generic versions of essential medicines in countries where product patents have not been filed (Singh, 2005). However, it would have to be in the company's interest to do so. This means that there would have to be large enough market or state subsidies to justify production. The fact is that companies are driven by profit; therefore an unprofitable venture, no matter how necessary, will not be taken on by a for-profit private corporation.

When there are incentives, Ranbaxy is willing to work with private–public partnerships such as Medicines for Malaria Venture (MMV), the Bill and Melinda Gates Foundation and the Clinton Foundation to provide affordable treatment to people in developing countries. Ranbaxy hopes that their work with MMV, which is currently in advanced stages of clinical trials, will lead to a cure for malaria by 2009 (Singh, 2005). This MMV project is partially funded by the Bill and Melinda Gates Foundation. Ranbaxy had previously signed an agreement with the Clinton Foundation in 2006 to offer the antiretroviral therapy Efavirenz for US$240 per patient per year to poor people in 50 developing countries (PTI, 2006). While these are both encouraging initiatives, the question is whether or not they are the best and the most sustainable solutions. In the deal between the Clinton Foundation and Ranbaxy to supply Efavirenz, licensing arrangements are conditional on volume; if the order is too small, a surcharge may apply (Singh, 2005).

The current trend for charitable ventures to address the inadequacies of health care, including medicines, while laudable, fails to use India's research resources to their fullest extent, and may not be the most adequate or sustainable way to address health needs of developing nations. Most charitable organizations focus on tuberculosis, malaria, and HIV/AIDS; while these represent a large proportion of the disease burden, research into diseases like leprosy are often neglected. Although charitable organizations assist with research on some neglected diseases, they do not ensure that efforts are made to develop drugs to treat every disease, and, more importantly, they do not guarantee that treatment will be available for all. The sustainability of this type of research funding has also been questioned, keeping in mind the whimsical nature of charitable donations. Furthermore, charitable organizations are sometimes influenced by popular interest, which may affect investment decisions. This concern was recently voiced by Tim Weber (2006) in his piece entitled 'Should celebrities decide what a good cause is?' While celebrities like Bono may draw attention to the plight of people in poor countries, they often are not well informed about the diseases that require the most research, like Chagas disease (ibid.).

Governments, not charities and philanthropic organizations, should be developing and guiding the research agenda. Public–private partnerships could be one way to balance and maximize research skills and at the same time bring revenue to Indian companies, while ensuring affordable medicines for vulnerable populations.

Indian companies like Ranbaxy, Dr. Reddy's and Cipla are prime candidates to provide affordable essential medicines. Ranbaxy is the top investor in R&D in pharmaceuticals in India. It has the ability to do the research, as well as to produce drugs at low cost. However, India and the entire continent of Africa together represent roughly only 2.3 per cent of the global pharmaceutical market (Satyanarayana and Srivastava, 2007); there is not much incentive to develop products specifically for these markets.

If more effective treatments for malaria and leprosy are found, will they be registered in developing countries? India has been identified as a future site for vaccine development. It is currently the site of clinical trials for vaccines against malaria, HPV and diabetes (PTI, 2006). These trials are run by international and local companies. If the trials are held in a developing country but the benefits go to the developed world then justice will not have been served; at least this is the opinion expressed by organizations like Médicins Sans Frontières (MSF), Oxfam and others, who led the campaign for cheap antiretroviral drugs in developing countries and challenged MNCs to provide drugs at a reasonable price. For example, Viread (Tenofovir), an effective new antiretroviral produced by Gilead and tested in developing countries, was not registered for use in 91 developing countries (Elias, 2006). When Cipla made a generic version available, the patent-holder filed a patent claim in India; this was opposed by many Indian groups, such as the Third World Network (Shashikant, 2006), and fortunately the drug was made available at a lower price in many countries (Ford et al., 2008).

Ranbaxy officials see a limited role for the company as a provider of medicines to poor people; they consider this as the job of the government. The MD of Ranbaxy has stated that as a company '...there is a certain role for the government and a certain role for the private sector. And if you start doing one another's job you are going to be most ineffective' (Singh, 2005). Therefore, while Ranbaxy is doing some research on neglected disease in antimalarials and anthelmintics (PTI, 2006), they believe that it is the government's role to ensure that medicines get to the poor.

The 10 June 2008 announcement of the sale of Ranbaxy Company to the Japanese pharmaceutical giant, Daiichi Sankyo Company, will be the start of a new era among the Indian pharmaceutical companies and perhaps the start of the end of family-owned companies (*Hindustan Times*, 2008). Whatever the repercussions of the sale on the indigenous pharmaceutical industry, consolidation and expansion of MNCs in India may not necessarily mean more R&D in neglected diseases or better access to medicines by the marginalized.

Experiences of many countries suggest, on both medical and economic grounds, that it is beneficial to adopt a limited drug list comprising safe and effective drugs and to ensure their supply at reasonable cost (WHO, 2004). The important question is – do patents prevent access to essential medicines?

Conclusions

Undeniably, patents and TRIPS impact on the cost of medicines, and we have illustrated that patents, policies and pricing affect access to medicines. Our comparison of Canada and India shows that the growth of the generic pharmaceutical industry was stimulated by changes to the patent law that allowed duplication of patented medicines within a short period of time. Both countries have undergone major restructuring of their pharmaceutical industries with the introduction of the WTO-compliant patents laws; this change occurred much earlier in Canada than in India, where the WTO rules came into effect in full in 2005. In the case of Canada, the market share of brand-name medicines has increased significantly, whereas in India indigenous generic companies are the main providers of medicines even though the market share of patented medicines is on the rise and expected to increase further as the full effects of WTO rules are felt. Access to medicines for Canadians has been financed through provincial drug plans and private funding either through insurance companies or as out-of-pocket expenses borne by the individual; therefore, people have access to medicines, but their capacity to pay depends on their socioeconomic status. Although R&D investment by patented medicine manufacturers is significant, it has declined and has not yielded the full benefits of a knowledge-intensive industry on employment in Canada. In the case of India, R&D by indigenous pharmaceutical companies in new chemical entities has mostly been through private partnerships with MNCs and has focused on chronic diseases of Western countries.

The Ranbaxy case study demonstrates that some Indian generic companies have responded to implementation of TRIPS by challenging patents on one hand and forming partnerships with MNCs on the other hand. They have not made any special commitment to invest in developing neglected diseases or diseases that affect the poor unless profitability can be assured.

The task of providing affordable, accessible essential medicines very much depends on the actions of the state. In our estimation, it is the obligation of governments to ensure health services and medicines for their citizens. Therefore, governments must develop policies and devote resources to provide affordable medicines and initiate R&D by providing incentives to, and regulating the functioning of, private pharmaceutical companies to ensure a healthy pharmaceutical sector that meets the needs of vulnerable populations (WHO and WTO, 2001; Love, 2001; Watal, 2001). They should not rely on charitable foundations to fulfil their own obligations. In this respect, the performance of both the Canadian and Indian governments falls short of ideal. Social pressure is therefore the only recourse to change governmental policies so that the dream of health for all becomes a reality.

Notes

We are grateful to Shastri Indo-Canadian Institute for a research grant under the SHARP program to one of us (SM) which made this work possible.

1. However, of the more than 20,000 manufacturers, only 6,000 received drug manufacturing licenses and only about 100 are considered to have full production capabilities, including R&D (Greene, 2007). Also, spurious or poor quality medicines – more than likely manufactured in unlicensed factories – pose a serious problem, especially in rural India.
2. The WHO reported 260,063 new cases of leprosy in India in 2005.

14

The Partnership Prescription: Access to HIV/AIDS-related Medicines and Public–Private Partnerships*

Sherri A. Brown

Introduction

Globalizing forces, including increasing interconnectivity in trade, finance, technology, communications, and population mobility, have created impacts and challenges for public health that transcend national boundaries. Neither communicable nor noncommunicable diseases can be contained or addressed solely within individual states. Furthermore, poverty-related diseases (HIV/AIDS, tuberculosis, malaria, etc.), have reached epidemic proportions, and have cross-cutting and complex economic, social, and political determinants and impacts. There is a growing awareness that 'institutions matter' in devising responses to complex global health issues (Dodgson et al., 2002; Kickbusch, 1997). One of these, enthusiastically recommended as a model for overcoming existing institutional deficiencies, is the creation of global public–private partnerships in health (GPPPs) (Reinecke et al., 2000). A GPPP is a collaborative relationship formed between at least three parties: (1) a corporation or industry association; (2) intergovernmental organizations; and (3) national authorities (Buse and Walt, 2000). Global public–private partnerships are created to develop new products (that is, drugs and vaccines), improve access to products, assist with global coordination mechanisms, strengthen health care services, provide public advocacy and education and for regulatory and quality assurance purposes (Nishtar, 2004). GPPPs are seen as a response to both market and government failure to provide health care goods and services, particularly in developing countries. Operating under the premise of 'mutual benefit', these partnerships are seen to provide needed resources and expertise to developing countries and international institutions in exchange for certain tax, marketing, regulatory and other benefits to commercial partners. Despite the enthusiasm surrounding GPPPs in health in the UN system, at this stage no global norms or frameworks have been established to help guide the development, implementation and regulation of GPPPs. Often, in fact, they operate in a highly unregulated and/or ad hoc fashion. The 'blind faith' accompanying the rising popularity of GPPPs has obscured the development of such frameworks, and there is a need for critical literature and evaluations of GPPPs, both for their normative and operational issues and impacts and for how GPPPs may, as a mechanism of global health governance, impact global health outcomes and cooperation.

This chapter provides an overview of the emerging architecture in global health governance and situates GPPPs within this architecture. The paper discusses the features and models of global public–private partnerships in health and discusses their real and potential normative and operational implications for national and global health governance. The paper examines two public–private partnerships for pharmaceuticals provision: the Accelerating Access Initiative (AAI) and the Diflucan partnership. The AAI is an initiative hosted by the Joint United Nations Programme for HIV/AIDS (UNAIDS) to facilitate differential pricing negotiations on antiretroviral therapies for the treatment of HIV/AIDS. The second partnership, the Diflucan Partnership Program, is a partnership between Pfizer and developing states which provides drug treatments for HIV/AIDS-related opportunistic infections. After analyzing the issues and implications associated with GPPPs and the specific cases, this paper considers the prospects and challenges of GPPPs in advancing health as a global public good. An analysis of GPPPs within the framework of the global public goods (GPG) concept provides insight into how these evolving mechanisms of global health governance contribute to global health outcomes and cooperation. Global public–private partnerships in health have real and potential normative and practical implications for national and global health governance, and, in their current state, yield little potential for advancing health as a global public good.

A changing global order in health and health governance

Globalization has ushered in new challenges for health and is the driving force behind emerging forms of global health governance. Zacher (1999) argues that globalization is reducing the capacity of states to provide for the health of their domestic populations. Increasing transborder flows of people, information, products (such as tobacco, alcohol) and externalities (such as pollution) create increases in health risks for domestic populations, and thus new challenges for national health governance. It has also been argued that globalization is sustaining or exacerbating economic inequalities and poverty in and among states (Dodgson et al., 2002) and is thus driving health and disease epidemics such as HIV/AIDS, malaria, tuberculosis, and so forth.

Lee (1999) argues that globalization is contributing to greater inequities in health, where poor and marginalized countries and populations share an expanding proportion of the global disease and poor health burden.

These trends have exposed the limitations of domestic health governance in a globalizing world. Governments are increasingly looking toward new forms of cooperation such as treaties,[1] global public policy networks, public–private partnerships (PPPs) and other arrangements to provide health research, services, products and policy development and coordination. Health care promotion and provision is increasingly characterized by a shift from government to *governance* modalities. Governance can be 'disentangled' from government (Reinicke, 1997; Rosenau and Czempiel, 1992) to describe formal or informal activities and mechanisms in the pursuit of social goals and objectives. Ultimately, we are witnessing considerable growth in the number and influence of non-state actors in health governance (Dodgson et al., 2002) at both the domestic and the international level, in developed and developing countries.

Global public–private partnerships in health: normative and operational challenges

Global public–private partnerships are voluntary and collaborative relationships (see Dodgson et al., 2002; Nelson, 2002) that bring together state and non-state actors to undertake specific functions in health governance. Nelson (2002, p. 47) suggests that partners agree to 'share risks, responsibilities, resources, competencies and benefits'. The proliferation of global public–private partnerships in health reached an apex in 2000, with the addition of 17 new partnerships. Fifty of the partnerships were established between the years 1998 and 2003.[2] Most of the 92 existing partnerships in health address infectious diseases and 19 identify HIV/AIDS as the health condition addressed by the partnership. Evans and Chen (2005) describe two broad groupings of GPPPs. The first type, partnerships operated by International Agencies, invites participation of private sector actors. These partnerships are under the administrative and financial control of the United Nations or World Bank staff and systems. The Roll Back Malaria Initiative, Stop TB Initiative and the Accelerating Access Initiative (AAI) are examples of this type of partnership. The other grouping includes partnerships that are independently structured non-profit entities with private governance, operations and financing (see Evans and Chen, 2005), such as the Diflucan Partnership, which will be discussed later in the chapter.

Much of the criticism launched against public–private partnerships pertains to their governing arrangements. There are concerns over GPPPs in terms of real and potential conflict of interest situations, accountability, transparency, decision-making structures and participation, sustainability and outcome orientations. In terms of membership, there are substantial problems with the selection and representation of partners. Richter (2004) contends that corporate partners are not adequately scrutinized by international agency partners for potential conflicts of interest. Buse's (2004) study supports Richter's claim, noting that only four out of the 19 partnerships in his study undertook formal assessments of the background of their commercial partners. Furthermore, as Buse (2004, p. 240) notes, there is a 'gross under representation of southern stakeholders' in the governing arrangements of GPPPs. Out of the 92 global public–private partnerships in health listed in the Initiative for Public Private Partnerships in Health (IPPPH) database, all but four have Secretariats in Northern countries (North America and Western Europe).

Kickbusch (1997) argues that one of the critical processes associated with the globalization of health is that decision-making processes are increasingly inaccessible to the public. GPPPs have the potential for exacerbating the problems of transparency and representation in decision-making. While partnerships make basic information (profile, programs, partners, contacts, public relations material)[3] available on their websites, few partnerships post annual budgets or program evaluation/impact documentation. Buse (2004) concludes that, regardless of whether the partnership is a publicly or privately hosted partnership, very little information is made publicly available on the partnership's governing arrangements.

There is considerable discussion on the issue of accountability of GPPPs in the literature (Buse, 2004; Buse and Walt, 2000b; Evans and Chen, 2005; Nishtar, 2004). Questions are raised such as to whom the partners are actually accountable, as well as the availability and employment of reporting mechanisms (Buse, 2004). Are they purely fiscal or are there other evaluations of performance? How and to whom are these reported? To whom are the partnering countries/agencies accountable? These and other questions have yet to be resolved and will continue to call into question the legitimacy and feasibility of GPPPs as a mechanism of global health governance.

There are also challenges and controversies with the outcome orientations of GPPPs. Partnerships in general report effectiveness in terms of value-added contributions (see Holm, 2001). Partnerships often report on the number of drug units distributed, the number of personnel trained, the total funds distributed and other quantitative impacts. For example, the AAI and Diflucan Partnership make this type of information available, but offer very little publicly available information on partnership governing arrangements and other operational aspects. There is little information on whether the partnerships actually contribute to improvements in the quality and efficiency of drug donations, health services, research, public information and advocacy and product development. Further complicating these issues, as Holm (2001) notes, there is very little baseline data upon which to conduct research on the effectiveness of partnerships in their specific contributions to health or health outcomes.

There are serious concerns surrounding the sustainability of the partnerships. Some of the partnerships do not have stated timelines, some have guaranteed drug donation until there is evidence of disease eradication (that is, Merck & Co. Mectizan® donation), while others have between 3 and 6-year life spans, after which the partnership is either terminated or extended by agreement of the parties involved. Furthermore, there is the question of whether drug donations are sustainable models for the provision of essential medicines (Gardiner, 2003). These partnerships, despite providing needed resources for the treatment of diseases and health conditions, are nonetheless a charity model of health, rather than a model of global collective action and responsibility for health. Policy levers or instruments compelling the donors to continue their programs are non-existent, and, short of moral suasion and tax breaks, leave the recipient countries and agencies largely at the mercy of the donors. GPPPs have responded (see Holm, 2001) to criticisms of sustainability, noting that many public sector organizations often do not make program commitments for longer than 5 years. While public sector organizations could potentially be charged with many of the same governance deficiencies and controversies as the partnerships, there are, at minimum, accountability expectations and mechanisms in public sector organizations that do not necessarily exist in the partnerships, particularly those that are independent non-profit entities.

At this time, there is very little empirical data available with which to test and assess these claims. This chapter forms part of a larger research program that will examine the normative and operational issues and challenges of partnerships through an investigation of two selected public–private partnerships in pharmaceuticals provision: the Accelerating Access Initiative and the Diflucan Partnership. The next section of the chapter overviews these two partnerships, including their real and potential normative and operational implications for national and global health governance.

Public–private partnerships in health and access to pharmaceuticals

It is now widely acknowledged that over one-third of the world's population lacks access to essential medicines, including HIV/AIDS-related medicines (Sterckx, 2004). Of this group, over 50 per cent live in the least developed countries in Africa and Asia (ibid.). Drug access, particularly for those living in countries with endemic infectious diseases, including HIV/AIDS, malaria, and tuberculosis, has become a matter of life and death. Fifteen years following the first case of AIDS in 1981, new hope emerged with the advent of highly active antiretroviral therapies. These ARV therapies were successful in providing life-sustaining support for people living with HIV/AIDS. While these therapies have been available since 1996, high prices of these drugs have put them out of reach for the majority of people living with HIV/AIDS. In the Western developed world, ARV treatments can cost between $10,000 and $15,000 per person per year (Joseph, 2003). Currently, 823,000 people in low and middle-income countries have access to anti-retroviral treatment (ARV); however, this means that eight out of 10 people who need ARV currently do not have access (UNAIDS/WHO, 2004b).

Pharmaceutical companies initially advanced an economic/property narrative on the issue of drug access. They argued that there was no relationship between the drug prices and access; rather, they claimed that social, political and infrastructural barriers impeded the broad rollout of complicated HIV/AIDS medications (Gellman, 2000; Joseph, 2003). Eventually, pharmaceutical companies conceded that prices charged for their drugs in developing countries made them largely prohibitive. However, they also argued that patent protection was necessary to stimulate drug research and development. International and domestic civil society organizations, including the Treatment Action Campaign (TAC) in South Africa, Oxfam, and Médecins Sans Frontières had conceptualized the issue differently and drew attention to the issue of patent protection, patent abuses and the lack of generic competition in constraining access to HIV/AIDS-related pharmaceuticals. Furthermore, groups such as the Harvard Consensus group refuted claims that it was not possible to administer widespread HIV treatment in poor countries.[4] The claim by pharmaceutical companies that patent protection is necessary to stimulate research and development has also been challenged.[5] Ultimately, however, the problem became defined as one of affordability for developing countries. The natural solution was, therefore, to provide deep price discounts or donations to developing countries to enhance access to these drugs. The Accelerating Access Initiative and Diflucan Partnerships emerged in these contexts to provide deeply discounted or donated HIV/AIDS-related pharmaceuticals.

The Accelerating Access Initiative

The Accelerating Access Initiative and the Diflucan Partnership were intended to 'problem-solve' the 'accessibility' issue of HIV/AIDS-related pharmaceutical products. AAI was intended to increase access to anti-retroviral therapies which provide life-sustaining support to people living with HIV/AIDS. The Diflucan Partnership provides fluconazole (brand name 'Diflucan'), an antifungal drug for the treatment of HIV/AIDS-related opportunistic infections. The Accelerating Access Initiative was announced in May 2000 and consists of a partnership between five UN organizations[6] and six pharmaceutical companies.[7] The partnership, according to the Initiative for Public–Private Partnerships, was intended to address issues of drug access and affordability in the 'hardest hit regions of the world'.[8] Currently, 17 countries are participating in the AAI (see Table 14:1). The AAI does not have separate legal status, and is coordinated by the Secretariat of the Joint United Nations Programme on HIV/AIDS (UNAIDS) in Geneva, Switzerland. The AAI works with governments, international organizations and the private sector to negotiate differential drug prices. Thus, all funding for HIV/AIDS pharmaceuticals comes from the countries themselves. Although the international public sector partners are involved in negotiating drug discounts, these negotiations occur primarily on a bilateral basis. AAI indicates that these negotiations are available to countries that can provide proof that they have the health services to handle the complicated HIV/AIDS medicines. This is an important equity consideration of the AAI. Partnerships that select countries on the basis of existing health infrastructure inherently exclude countries that may desperately need discounted drugs, but are unable to access them because of 'inadequate' health systems, and thus could exacerbate global health inequities. It is important to note that, of the 17 countries participating in the AAI, only six[9] are considered 'high HIV/AIDS burden' countries by the World Health Organization (WHO, 2005b).

The WHO lauds the success of the Initiative, claiming that a total of 823,000 people living with HIV/AIDS in developing countries receive ARV

Table 14.1 Accelerating Access Initiative country participants

AAI participants	**2004 GNI[10] Atlas Method (US dollars)**	**2004 GDP (US dollars)**	**2004 GNI per capita (US Dollars)**
Benin	3.7 billion	4.1 billion	530.0
Burkina Faso (hbc)	4.4 billion	4.8 billion	360.0
Burundi (hbc)	669.4 million	657.2 million	90.0
Cameroon (hbc)	13.1 billion	14.7 billion	800.0
Chad	2.3 billion	4.3 billion	260.0
Chile	78.4 billion	94.1 billion	4,910.0
Republic of Congo	3.0 billion	4.4 billion	770.0
Democratic Republic of Congo	6.4 billion	6.6 billion	120.0
Cote d'Ivoire (hbc)	13.3 billion	15.3 billion	770.0
Gabon	5.4 billion	7.2 billion	3,940.0
Mali	4.3 billion	4.9 billion	360.0
Morocco	46.5 billion	50.1 billion	1,520.0
Romania	63.9 billion	73.2 billion	2,920.0
Rwanda (hbc)	1.9 billion	1.8 billion	220.0
Senegal	7.0 billion	7.7 billion	670.0
Trinidad & Tobago	11.4 billion	12.5 billion	8,580.0
Uganda (hbc)	6.9 billion	6.8 billion	270.0

Source: Prepared by author from material at www.ippph.org and World Bank country data at http://web.worldbank.org/WBSITE/EXTERNAL/COUNTRIES/0,,pagePK:180619~theSitePK:136917,00.html.

treatment provided by AAI companies.[11] It is not clear how many of these people were recipients of treatment as a direct result of AAI-facilitated negotiations. However, the Initiative emphasizes the value-added benefits of the partnerships and claims that since its establishment there has been a 23-fold increase in the number of people receiving treatment from AAI companies.[12] The Initiative also claims that it has achieved significant price reductions on HIV/AIDS-related pharmaceutical products.[13] The AAI, from a functional or problem-solving perspective, has been quite effective. By negotiating lower drug prices, the Initiative has facilitated greater access to HIV/AIDS-related medicines. However, as discussed, there are normative and operational issues and challenges associated with the AAI. In terms of its governing arrangements, Buse (2004) notes that the executive of the AAI is not accountable to the governing body of the partnership (the Secretariat) but to the host organization. Buse (2004) argues that this limits the extent to which the partners can hold the Secretariat accountable for the workings of the partnership. The AAI also does not make available information on the management of its governing bodies or decision-making processes, nor does it publish (on Internet sites) its sources of funding or negotiated drug prices.

Thomas (2002) identifies real concerns with bargaining procedures and implications of the AAI and criticizes the AAI as an institution which reinforces and perpetuates structural inequality. Thomas (2002) argues that requiring countries to negotiate with individual pharmaceutical companies compromises their negotiating position. Table 14.2 presents total revenues and net incomes of AAI-participating pharmaceutical companies from 2004 and 2005.[14] When contrasting these figures with countries' GNI and GDP, it can be seen that only six of the 17 countries had a GNI in 2004 equal to or greater than that of the pharmaceutical company with lowest total revenues in 2004 (Boehringer Ingelheim at $10.3 billion). Furthermore, seven of the 17 countries are classified as severely indebted by the World Bank, four are moderately indebted, and five are less indebted (World Bank List of Economies, July 2005). This rather crude comparison nonetheless demonstrates the unequal bargaining positions of developing countries and pharmaceutical companies.

While Buse (2004) notes that the AAI was one of four partnerships in his study to undertake a formal assessment of the commercial partners in the partnership, he also refers to the limited pool of partner choices given the monopoly positions and patent protection afforded to pharmaceutical companies. At this point, there are several normative and operational challenges, including governing arrangements, transparency, sustainability, accountability, Southern representation and bargaining procedures, outcome orientations and equity considerations. Continuing research on the AAI will examine the normative and operational interfaces and impacts of the partnership on national health governance, including health systems, policy and decision-making and local pharmaceutical markets and distribution systems.

Table 14.2 Pharmaceutical companies' total revenues and net incomes from 2004 and 2005

Pharmaceutical company[15]	Total revenues 2005 (US Dollars in billion)[16]	Net income 2005 (in billion)	Total revenues 2004 (US Dollars in billion)	Net income 2004 (in billion)
Abbott Laboratories	$22.3	$3.3[17]	$19.6	$3.1
Boehringer Ingelheim[18]	$12.1	$2.1	$10.3	$1.5
Bristol-Myers Squibb	$19.2	$3.0[19]	$19.3	$2.3
F. Hoffman-La Roche[20]	$26.9	$5.1	$22.4	$5.3
GlaxoSmithKline[21]	$37.1	$11.5	$34.1	$9.7
Merck and Co., Inc.	$22.0	$4.6	$22.9	$5.8
Pfizer Inc.	$51.3	$8.0	$52.5	$11.3

Source: prepared by author from material available from the companies' 2005 annual reports.

The Diflucan Partnership

The Diflucan Partnership is actually more appropriately conceptualized as a donation program. It was launched in December 2000 by Pfizer Inc. in South Africa and has since expanded to over 29 developing countries. Diflucan, also known as fluconazole, is an antifungal medicine for the treatment of fungal opportunistic infections such as cryptococcal meningitis and esophageal candidiasis. These infections regularly present in people living with HIV/AIDS. Although the partnership does not have dollar or time estimates, Pfizer has estimated the total cost of its partnership commitments to be US$103 million (as of 2004), which represents 0.19 per cent of total revenues for Pfizer in 2004.[22] Of what little information is available on the partnership, Pfizer claims that it has distributed 7 million free doses of Diflucan to 1,100 sites in 42 developing countries across Africa, Asia, Latin America and the Caribbean. The program also trains health personnel in the treatment of opportunistic infections and appropriate dosing protocols. Pfizer, Inc. estimates the initial cost of training at US$2 million. Wertheimer et al. (2004) note that the program has since expanded and trained an additional 9,000 health care workers. The Diflucan Partnership makes available this type of 'value-added' information on its website, yet, like the AAI, offers no information on its negotiating and governing arrangements. Furthermore, there is no empirical data available to assess equity considerations in partnership development (that is, how are these drugs being made available within the country? and to whom?), or in terms of the impact of partnerships on health governance structures, including policy and decision-making structures, local pharmaceutical markets, and health care systems.

Pfizer makes their drugs available only to public sector and NGO partners, and thus there are likely effects on local pharmaceutical markets. Furthermore, there is also the question of the long-term sustainability of drug donation models (Gardiner, 2003).

In addition to some of the issues identified with public–private partnerships in an earlier section, an analysis of this partnership reveals how social relations figured significantly in its genesis. In South Africa, where the partnership was first launched, initially high prices of fluconazole constrained widespread access. The Treatment Action Campaign launched a major campaign against the high price of fluconazole on 13 March 2000. Initially, TAC demanded that Pfizer, Inc. reduce its drug prices,[23] citing significantly lower prices in the public sector in South Africa and internationally. The campaign resulted in mass protests to demand that the Medicines Control Council of South Africa grant a 'Section 21' exemption to the generic importation of fluconazole ('biozole') from Thailand. Within weeks of the filing, Pfizer announced that it would donate fluconazole to the public sector for people with cryptococcal meningitis and systemic thrush.[24] However, when Pfizer, Inc. failed to roll out its donation program in a timely manner, TAC began importing generic fluconazole for distribution. Pfizer eventually responded by accelerating its donation distribution. Because Pfizer's patent on fluconazole expired in 2004, it has been eager to gain a market threshold in many other developing countries, and continues to expand its donation program.

The Diflucan Partnership is therefore not merely a 'functional' or 'problem-solving' response to high drug prices. The Diflucan partnership is, in some senses, an institutional compromise midwifed by conflict between public and private interests. If the South African government were to exercise its options under TRIPS,[25] this could substantially drive down the prices of the drugs through generic competition. Until such time as Pfizer withdraws from the partnership, the South African government and its peoples are ultimately dependent upon Pfizer's generosity. Pfizer's private interests in the market are secured and enhanced by the partnership; they are insulated from compulsory licensing and parallel importation and generic competition; the partnership provides much-needed favourable publicity, and offers lucrative tax deductions on their donations in the United States, all at very little cost to their bottom line. The normative and operational impacts of these partnerships for national and global health governance require further investigation, although it can be argued at this point that there are important normative and operational issues which necessitate scrutiny and possibly reform.

Concepts of health and cooperation in global health

Global public goods are goods whose benefits transcend borders and benefit all countries, population groups and generations (Türmen, 1999, p. 9). Global public goods include clean air, peace and security and can be supplied through transnational agreements and protocols and other forms of collective action (Barrett, 2004). At the global level, there is no equivalent institution with the power to levy taxes to provide public goods. Thus, the global public goods (GPG) concept is intended to provide a rationale and framework for collective action on global health issues. By demonstrating that health risks, particularly in the context of globalization (Türmen, 1999), transcend national borders, the GPG concept encourages the global community to support efforts for disease eradication, health promotion and health protection. The GPG concept is part of the agenda promoted by the United Nations Development Programme (UNDP) (Woodward et al., 2001) and serves as a framework for action, as well as a normative premise and a 'paradigmatic shift in the conceptualization of public health' (Brando, 2004, p. 11). Under the UNDP agenda, the GPG concept is intended to improve outcomes in global health as well as to provide intermediate products and services through collective action.

Intermediate public goods are public goods that are nonexcludable, but rivalrous (Brando, 2004). Intermediate public goods are seen to 'bring us partially to the goal of global public health' (Brando, 2004, p. 3), by providing health services and products that contribute to global health. Global public–private partnerships provide intermediate public goods, including disease surveillance, disease control, disease eradication or elimination, disease treatment and resistance avoidance (Barrett, 2004, p. 1). Ultimately, however, the pursuit of intermediate public goods through global public–private partnerships has several negative externalities for the attainment of global health outcomes and global cooperation in health.

Global public–private partnerships are not *global* in design or implementation. The design and governance of GPPPs is highly asymmetrical, with governance of the GPPPs primarily residing in North American and Western European countries. While some GPPPs can claim that they have incorporated national health governance priorities and voices (for example, ACHAP) in the design and implementation of their programs, GPPPs continue to be criticized for the lack of representation and participation of Southern stakeholders in both the design and the governance of programs. GPPPs are intended to serve as a pathway to global health outcomes, yet ultimately may reinforce existing power and decision-making imbalances rather than advancing true global cooperation in health.

Instead of contributing to greater global health cooperation, drug donation programs reinforce the charity model of health, and potentially intensify dependency relations. Few partnerships address state capacity-building and health infrastructure development, which would support developing states in providing for the health of their populations, and enhance their role in both national and global health governance. While some GPPPs train healthcare personnel and work with national and subnational health governance authorities and institutions to provide a broader array of services, a large contingent of GPPPs provide vertical programs, which do not, in and of themselves, strengthen health systems. Indeed, these programs often entail significant costs, by requiring states to integrate programs into often overextended health systems. Thus, as an intermediate step towards global health cooperation, GPPPs offer much of the same in the way of existing power and social relations, and thus do not truly advance *global* health cooperation, but rather Northern dominance and economic privilege in health governance.

The intermediate goods and services that are provided by GPPPs are largely palliative; they do not address the underlying social determinants of health that render populations, particularly the poor, vulnerable to ill health. The World Health Organization defines health as 'a state of complete physical, mental and social well-being and not merely the absence of disease or infirmity'.[26] In policy and practice, health interventions have largely been focused on the latter aspects of the definition. Disease and morbidity eradication have achieved primacy in our notions and evaluations of health, as evidenced by the proliferation and increasing reliance on pharmaceutical and therapeutic interventions (drugs, chemical treatments, surgery, etc.). The provision of intermediate public goods via global public–private partnerships contains a strong biomedical and technological bias; health interventions are overwhelmingly focused on providing remedies (drugs, health services, vaccines), but very little attention is devoted to health promotion via the social determinants of health. At best, they provide gender or population-sensitive solutions (for vulnerable or marginalized populations), but do not access the root causes of vulnerability to ill health which drive the expression of epidemics and infectious diseases. GPPPs, as a pathway towards global health outcomes, are conceivably matching epidemiological, but not necessarily social, priorities of health. If the WHO's definition is employed as a measure of the effectiveness of GPPPs in advancing global health outcomes, it is clear that they advance a narrow conceptualization of health, and, in the case of pharmaceutical companies, advance their own interests for the continued reliance on drug interventions to support health. GPPPs might respond that it is not within their mandate to focus on the social determinants of health, given their core competencies, and that they are only in a position to offer biomedical and technological solutions. Global and national health governance institutions are thus left with the task of addressing the most complex aspects of health. Without the attendant national and global health architecture to support and provide interventions to address the social determinants of health, GPPPs' role as an intermediate institutional pathway to health leads global health governance largely into the management of illness rather than the promotion and protection of health. The obvious observation arising out of this analysis is that pharmaceuticals *cannot* address the underlying social determinants of health. Thus, for partnerships to be effective in health promotion there must be domestic and international institutions which possess the capacity to provide public health promotion and prevention services which, *inter alia,* access and respond to the social determinants of health, including socioeconomic status and income equality, environmental factors, health care services, social inclusion, employment, early childhood care, education and food security.

Finally, GPPPs do not necessarily include equity considerations in their program design and evaluation. Like the AAI, partnerships often choose countries that already have existing health infrastructure to administer and deliver their programs and products, and thus the poorest countries may be excluded (see Yamey, 2001, for a discussion of GAVI). Moreover, it is difficult to measure how equitably products and services are distributed within the country under partnership arrangements. Equity evaluations have been a critical oversight in the outcome and evaluation orientations of GPPPs. The global public goods concept has an inherent equity component, in that the goods must be *nonexcludable*. Intermediate goods are *nonexcludable* but rivalrous; however, GPPPs provide goods and services that are excludable. Global public–private partnerships have the potential to exacerbate health inequities, and thus, as a 'pathway' to global health outcomes, may undermine global health equity.

Conclusions and recommendations

Given the operational and normative implications of global public–private partnerships for national and global health governance, what is the way forward? Richter (2003) argues that UN agencies should abandon the public–private partnership paradigm altogether, while Buse and Waxman (2001) argue that a moratorium on GPPPs should be imposed while further research is conducted. Reforming GPPPs through transforming their research and outcome orientations would require the full cooperation of partners.

There are significant gaps in our knowledge about global public–private partnerships. Considerably more research needs to be conducted on the partnerships, particularly research about partnerships on the ground (Widdus, 2003). We need to develop criteria and measures of effectiveness for GPPPs to evaluate the specific contributions of GPPPs to their stated objectives as well as their contributions to global health goals and cooperation. Furthermore, it is important to challenge the functional narrative of partnerships by investigating and revealing the ethical, social, and normative underpinnings of partnerships.

Growing interconnectedness between states and non-state actors in health has the potential to yield improvements in global health outcomes and cooperation. However, *dependency* on private sector corporations and actors in global health governance may also result in a weakening of efforts to hold them accountable for their practices and actions. While it could be argued that these partnerships reflect the inclination of corporations to become 'good corporate citizens', they are not in and of themselves a proxy for good corporate citizenship in the global polity. Accordingly, there must be sufficient research and oversight to evaluate and monitor their normative and operational contributions to the emerging global health governance architecture.

Notes

This chapter is part of my dissertation research, which is supported by a Trudeau Foundation Doctoral Scholarship and a Social Sciences and Humanities Research Council (SSHRC) Canada Graduate Scholarship (Doctoral).

1. For example, the Framework Convention on Tobacco Control specifies principles for global tobacco supply and demand reduction. The Framework entered into force in February 2005 and currently consists of 126 parties (as of 16 May 2006).
2. www.ippph.org/index.cfm?page=/ippph/partnerships/date_established
3. See www.achap.org (African Comprehensive HIV/AIDS Partnership); www.securethefuture.com (Secure the Future); www.diflucanpartnership.org (Diflucan Partnership); www.lillymdr-tb.com/ Eli Lilly Multi-Drug Resistant Tuberculosis Partnership; www.iavi.org (International AIDS Vaccine Initiative), for a small cross-section of partnership websites. Note that not all partnerships have websites.
4. Consensus Statement on Antiretroviral Treatment for AIDS in Poor Countries By Individual Members of the Faculty of Harvard University, 2001. See www.hsph.harvard.edu/bioethics/pdf/consensus_aids_therapy.pdf.
5. For example, Bettcher et al. (2000) argue that the premises of patent protection (to stimulate innovation and generate money for research and development) fail to recognize that considerable research and development is conducted using government monies, that patents and intellectual property rights are relatively recent phenomena, that innovation and research and development have occurred in the absence of patent protection, and that intellectual property rights are afforded only when a country has achieved a certain level of economic development.
6. The World Health Organization, the United Nations Children's Fund, the United Nations Population Fund, the World Bank, and the Secretariat of the Joint United Nations Programme for HIV/AIDS (UNAIDS).
7. Abbott Laboratories, Boehringer Ingelheim, Bristol-Myers Squibb, F. Hoffman-La Roche, GlaxoSmithKline and Merck and Co., Inc.
8. See www.ippph.org/index.cfm?page=/ippph/partnerships/name&thechoice=show&id=2& typobj=0&id_chapter= abstract.
9. See Table 1.0. High burden countries are identified by 'hbc' in the AAI participants' column.

10. All economic data obtained from the World Bank website on country data: http://web.worldbank.org/WBSITE/EXTERNAL/COUNTRIES/0,,pagePK:180619~theSitePK:136917,00.html.
11. See AAI fact sheet for more information: www.who.int/entity/hiv/AAI_fs_4Q2005.pdf.
12. Ibid.
13. www.ippph.org/index.cfm?page=/ippph/partnerships/name&thechoice=show&id=2&typobj=0&id_chapter=impact
14. Pfizer, Inc. is not a participating company in the AAI. Data from Pfizer, Inc. is presented in this Table in reference to the Diflucan Partnership.
15. Financial data from pharmaceutical companies has been obtained from 2005 Annual Reports. All reports are publicly available on company websites.
16. All figures in the table have been rounded down to the nearest million.
17. Net income amounts from 2005 and 2004 are reported as 'after tax' income.
18. Amounts in Annual Report presented in Euros. Table reflects conversion to US$ based on nominal exchange rate of 1.1841 (rate from 30 December 2005). Conversion tables obtained from Bank of Canada Rates and Statistics: www.bankofcanada.ca/en/rates/exchform.html.
19. Net income amounts from 2005 and 2004 are reported as 'after tax' income.
20. Amounts in Annual Report presented in Swiss Francs. Table reflects conversion to US$ based on nominal exchange rate of 0.7598 (rate from 30 December 2005). Conversion tables obtained from Bank of Canada Rates and Statistics: www.bankofcanada.ca/en/rates/exchform.html.
21. Amounts in Annual Report presented in UK pounds. Table reflects conversion to US$ based on nominal exchange rate of 0.7598 (rate from 30 December 2005). Conversion tables obtained from Bank of Canada Rates and Statistics: www.bankofcanada.ca/en/rates/exchform.html.
22. Based on data obtained from Pfizer Annual Report (2005).
23. TAC launched a major campaign on 13 March 2000 to reduce the price of fluconazole.
24. Press Release, dated 28 November 2000, www.tac.org.za.
25. The Agreement on Trade-Related Aspects of Intellectual Property contains provisions to allow countries to issue compulsory licenses or parallel import patented products in situations of a national emergency.
26. World Health Organization (WHO) Constitution (www.who.int/about/definition/en/), accessed 19 November 2005.

Part V

Conclusion

15
Conclusion: Towards Equitable Global Health Governance

Sherri A. Brown and Sandra J. MacLean

Introduction: the state of global health

The Millennium Declaration, adopted by 189 heads of state at the United Nations Millennium Summit in 2000, committed governments and intergovernmental institutions to international cooperation on the achievement of eight Millennium Development Goals (MDGs) by 2015. Health figures prominently in these goals, three of which focus on health directly, and four on social determinants of health. Indicators surrounding these goals, therefore, provide a useful metric for assessing the current global health situation, particularly in the global South. As discussed in Chapter 1, there have also been significant transformations in health in the global North, including acute disease outbreaks (SARS, avian flu, influenza, etc.) as well as increases in chronic diseases such as lung disease and neoplasms. In early 2007, a midterm report[1] was released by the United Nations, which tracked each goal's progress and predicted the likelihood of its success. The report indicated mixed results; while considerable progress had been achieved on several goals, it was deemed extremely unlikely that others would be realized by the target deadline of 2015, especially in sub-Saharan Africa.

Regarding Goal 1 (to eradicate extreme poverty and hunger worldwide), the 2007 report acknowledged that the number of people in developing countries living on less than $1 a day had dropped from 1.25 billion in 1990 to 980 million in 2004. However, most of the gains had been made in Asia – Eastern and South-Eastern Asia, in particular – while poverty and hunger in Western Asia, Southern Asia and sub-Saharan Africa remain endemic. Thus, it is highly unlikely that targets will be reached in these regions by 2015. And, although small gains were made in sub-Saharan Africa between 1990 and 2005, the proportion of people living in extreme poverty in this region stands at a staggering 41.4 per cent (UN, 2007). Furthermore, rather than offering the promise of being the 'tide to lift all boats', globalization has ushered in a new era of widening income inequality (Birdsall et al., 2005). We therefore continue to witness not only unacceptably high levels of poverty and hunger, but also huge disparities between the poor and the wealthy. Income inequality is particularly acute in Latin America, the Caribbean and sub-Saharan Africa (World Bank, 2000).

Goal 4 aims to reduce the mortality rate of children under five by two-thirds. Every year 11 million children die before they reach the age of five, in most cases from treatable diseases. The UN interim report revealed that child survival rates show only slow improvement and are worse in sub-Saharan Africa. For example, rates have fallen by only 12 per cent since 1990. This poor result is partly a result of low levels of childhood vaccinations; 30 million children worldwide do not receive vaccinations for easily preventable diseases and only 78 per cent of children in the developing world are immunized against tuberculosis and 69 per cent against measles. Ultimately, this means that if this situation is not immediately changed, we will not see Goal 4 realized in sub-Saharan Africa until the year 2165 (UN, 2007). The fifth Millennium Development Goal is to reduce the maternal mortality rate by three-quarters. Approximately half a million women die each year during pregnancy or childbirth; 99 per cent of them come from the developing world and almost all from sub-Saharan Africa and Asia. In fact, women in sub-Saharan Africa are 175 times more likely to die during childbirth than women in industrialized countries (UN, 2007). For the most part, these are entirely preventable deaths. If these women had access to appropriate reproductive health services before, during and post-pregnancy the majority of these deaths would not occur. Furthermore, every year more than 2.2 million women who are infected with HIV give birth to HIV-positive children, when a drug called nevirapine substantially reduces the likelihood of passing HIV from mother to child (UN, 2007). Sadly, this drug is not universally accessible to women in the developing world and thus, year after year, far too many children are born HIV-positive.

MDG Goal 6 is to reduce the HIV/AIDS epidemic as well as tuberculosis and other diseases. In 2006, 37 million adults and 2.5 million children were living with HIV/AIDS, over 95 per cent of them in developing countries (70 per cent in sub-Saharan Africa). In 2006 alone, 3 million people died from AIDS; and over 20 million people have died since 1996. So far, over 14 million children have lost one or both parents to AIDS; and by 2010 the number is expected to reach 25 million (UN, 2007). The UN report (2007) revealed that HIV prevalence has levelled off in the developing world (see also WHO, 2008), but deaths from AIDS continue to escalate, particularly in sub-Saharan Africa. Signs of hope are that we are witnessing considerably expanded initiatives to provide treatment for people living with HIV/AIDS. Access to antiretroviral therapy continues to expand in developing countries. As of December 2006, approximately 2 million people were receiving drugs; however, this represents only one-third of the estimated 7.1 million people who need treatment (UN, 2007). Health systems lack capacity not only to deliver antiretrovirals but also to coordinate the various actors involved in supplying the drugs. Meanwhile, developing country governments face the extraordinary challenge of developing public and social systems of support and care for millions of children who have lost one or both parents to AIDS. We need immediately to imagine and plan for societies with millions of children who lack adequate access to water, food, shelter, clothing, education, health care, and, perhaps most importantly, the love and emotional support of parents.

Effective global health governance is critical if these problems are to be solved. The issues of global health governance include traditional ones such as efficiency and accountability of local and national governments, but they also include the emerging, novel structures of governance that have been termed 'global health governance'. The new global health governance architecture is multi-actor (state, inter-state and non-state) as well as multilevel (local, national, international). While this architecture involves multiple nodes of authority, several major players wield a disproportionate amount of authority. The way authority is being wielded, by whom and with what implications for improvements in global health, and reduction in inequities that contribute to poor health, are the issues that the authors in this book have sought to address. Each has attempted to uncover political economic factors that drive and influence the types of governance structures that have emerged. As well, the chapters expose who is winning and who is losing in the current political economy of global health.

New modalities of global health governance

As MacLean and Brown discussed in the first chapter of this book, the nation state has experienced significant transformations in the contemporary era of globalization. These changes, as they relate to both national and global health governance, have included states' increasing participation in multilateral, regional, and/or bilateral health, trade and investment agreements. For example, the Framework Convention on Tobacco Control, the world's first international health treaty under the auspices of the World Health Organization, signified that the globalization of the tobacco industry required international cooperation to contain and mitigate the effects of the global tobacco epidemic. However, contemporary globalization has also entailed changes in domestic policy environments which have had impacts on global health governance. Especially since the 1980s, the competitive environment of neoliberal globalization, increased mobility of labour and capital, and the increased fiscal authority and capacity of private sector actors (particularly corporations), coupled with ideological shifts evidenced in the Washington Consensus, have had important implications for the character and quality of social rights, economic security and governance, and ultimately for health and health outcomes. In many cases, domestic compensation policies were retrenched or abolished as the ideological climate under contemporary globalization favoured shifting responsibility for welfare from the state to the individual and the private sector. Thus, the state in the era of globalization faced substantial changes.

Richard Falk (1999) coined the term 'predatory globalization' to describe the effects of global capital on the sovereign state. The competitive environment of globalization and the neoliberal ideological climate that dominated for the past several decades created significant pressures and impacts for states in the global North and South. Notable among these are burdens and crises in global health, including acute and chronic disease epidemics that necessitate urgent and immediate action within state and multilateral institutions. This book presented multiple cases of new and emerging governance modalities under neoliberal globalization, describing some of the complex decision-making, service delivery, and governance arrangements that have arisen out of these configurations. Moreover, the chapters explored the interactions, tensions, challenges and opportunities arising out of these arrangements and discussed their impacts on global health. However, as the chapters within the first section reveal, powerful organizations such as the OECD (Schrecker) and countries – especially the US (Loeppky) – have exerted inordinate power in influencing global health governance. Individual states in the North (see O'Manique regarding Canada) and the South (see Fourie regarding South Africa) have been forced to adapt and seek new means for navigating the global health environment dominated by more powerful actors. In this governance framework, it has been clear, as several of the contributors indicated, that social determinants have not been adequately addressed.

Although powerful actors have the ability to influence the agenda disproportionately, the situation is much more complex than one governed by a few central actors. New governance modalities include expanded non-governmental, civil society and private sector participation as well as mixed actor coalitions. Growing interconnectedness between states and non-state actors in health has the potential to yield improvements in global health outcomes and cooperation. However, as several chapters within this book have demonstrated, there are challenges as well as opportunities inherent in these configurations. Under globalization, private authorities have amassed more power and influence due to the delegation of power by governments to private authorities and/or the retreat of government from certain policy areas such as health care. The rise of private authority under globalization – particularly *moral* authority or authority bestowed upon nongovernmental actors in civil society, such as religious and community-based organizations, as well as *market* authority or the growing power of the private sector, particularly transnational corporations – has received considerable scrutiny in international relations literature (Cutler, 1999; Cutler et al., 2003). Transformations in configurations of power and influence in moral and market authority were instrumental in the transition from international to global health governance – a transition characterized in part by an increase in the number and type of actors participating in health decision and policymaking as well as in service delivery.

Beginning in the 1980s, we began to witness an upsurge in international health collaboration. Collaboration emerged largely as a result of specific interventions for disease outbreaks (that is, Ebola, SARS, HIV/AIDS) and was predominately coordinated by the World Health Organization (Loughlin and Berridge, 2002). Both governments and nongovernmental organizations have participated in these efforts, and, increasingly, the latter have been called upon to contribute to national and international responses and initiatives. Accordingly, new mixed-actor coalitions and networks emerged, often around specific diseases and/or disease treatment. These organizations formed both to share information and resources on a health condition and/or to advocate for changes in funding, research and/or treatment. For example, activist networks[2] around HIV treatment proved instrumental in securing price reductions around antiretroviral drugs, as observed in chapters by Hein and Kohlmorgan and by Brown. Thus, global health governance has increasingly been characterized by a mix of actors in governance arrangements as well as the redirection of service delivery and decision-making functions from intrastate *and* interstate mechanisms to non-state actors.

Hein and Kohlmorgan's chapter demonstrated that non-state actors have played a central role in building subsidiary norms around key global health issues, and, in so doing, have contributed to the expanded access to essential medicines, such as HIV treatments. However, along with the positive outcomes of collaboration, there have also been complications. In her chapter, Siri Bjerkreim Hellevik explored the challenges imposed by growing proliferation of state and non-state actors within global health governance and found that the challenge of coordinating efforts so as to avoid redundancies, fill gaps, and manage decision-making and programming is so great that there is actually a 'crisis of implementation'. While greater numbers of actors have entered the global health governance arena, there are ongoing challenges as well as large gaps to be filled in scaling up health promotion, treatment and support responses. As Hellevik notes, however, there are massive initiatives by state and multilateral institutions that are underway.

Ways forward

In moving forward, there is a clear need for more research and oversight to evaluate and monitor practical and normative contributions to the emerging global health architecture. Hein and Kohlmorgan's chapter demonstrated that, indeed, non-state actors have played a central role in building subsidiary norms around key global health issues, such as access to essential medicines. Hein and Kohlmorgan suggested that it has been the coalescing of state and non-state actors which has been instrumental in norm generation, diffusion and implementation. Thus, not only have non-state actors played a key role in global health governance and service delivery, but they have also contributed to the development of norms around global health which have effectively expanded access to life-saving HIV treatment. Siri Bjerkreim Hellevik explored many of the challenges of this expanded arena of global health governance, including the often underexplored issue of coordination. With a growing proliferation of state and non-state actors within global health governance, the challenge of coordinating their efforts so as to avoid redundancies, fill gaps, and manage decision-making and programming becomes increasingly overwhelming. Hellevik argued that the challenge of coordination is linked to one of the recurring central themes of this book: that of the 'crisis of implementation'.

The phrase 'crisis of implementation' is perhaps not overstating the situation regarding global health governance overall. Several of the book's contributors, many of whom address PPPs as the most prominent example of the new global governance modalities, echo concerns about serious impediments and bottlenecks that exist in trying to effectively address the global HIV/AIDS crisis. This is only one disease (albeit one in critical need of solution), but there is a serious crisis of implementation surrounding myriad global health issues involving both infectious and chronic diseases. Despite considerable effort, and massive infusions of resources to address several of these health issues, it appears that we have only just scratched the surface on what needs to be done. Moreover, it appears that there is no consensus on where is the most effective place to begin, despite a well-developed, compelling argument that the health of populations is determined more by social conditions than by biotechnological intervention. Indeed, there has been more rhetoric than action to date on addressing the social determinants of health.

Recommendations for research

There are significant gaps in our knowledge about many of the new and emerging governance modalities in global health governance. For example, considerably more research needs to be conducted on public–private partnerships, particularly research about the operations of partnerships on the ground (Widdus, 2003). In particular, since funding and programmatic interventions by philanthropic foundations have been sizeable, and because these organizations now play a greater role at policy and decision-making tables, their roles in global health governance deserves more scrutiny and evaluation. For instance, we need to develop criteria and measures of effectiveness for governance arrangements to evaluate their success in meeting their stated objectives, as well as their contributions to cooperation with other actors in achieving overall global health goals. Indeed, the issue of coordination applies to the entire range of institutions and actors of global health governance; while the literature contains an extensive array of studies examining discrete actors and institutions in global health governance, very few examine the interfaces, conflicts, and methods of cooperation and coordination (as discussed by Hellevik in her chapter) among and between these actors and institutions. Even fewer assess how these contradictions, conflicts, and cooperation affect national health governance, or the normative basis of global health governance. Research into normative frameworks is critical to understanding: why social determinants of health continue to be underresearched (see the chapter by MacLean and MacLean); when research is necessary to investigate the sources and solutions of global inequality and inequity; and to question whether global health governance is becoming a euphemism for Western/Northern privilege in health and dominance in governance. While the global North has an important and necessary role to play in global health research, funding, and intervention, many of the chapters of this book also suggest that greater inclusion by actors from the global South will be critical to improving global health.

Recommendations for practice

The WHO Commission on the Social Determinants of Health (CSDH), launched in 2000,[3] completed its final report this year (CSDH, 2008). The report advances a new normative framework for health that would place the social determinants of health at the centre of research and policy on global health. Such a framework does not replace the currently dominant biomedical model that privileges curative care and technological intervention, rather, it underscores that a disproportionate emphasis on the biomedical model is inimical to producing optimum health outcomes. Instead, there must be simultaneous, adequate attention paid to societal conditions such as social gradient, poverty, education levels, housing conditions, gender inequalities, etc., that shape individual and population health risks and outcomes. The CSDH report includes recommendations that target three main areas to move the global health agenda forward. They include: seeking more accurate information (better monitoring and surveillance); improvements in health systems (developing capacity, competence and infrastructure at local and national levels); greater efficiency in multilevel governance (better coordination of state, interstate and non-state actors). With recommendations such as these, we can see the gradual advancement of the new normative framework noted above, but also a gradual advancement in strategizing about practical ways to approach health governance under such a framework. In doing this, the CSDH perhaps takes us a step closer to realizing the ambitious Millennium Development Goals.

This book has provided an overview of contemporary governance and political economic arrangements, limitations, and impacts on global health research and outcomes. We conclude this book by arguing that existing arrangements, while offering some improvements in global health, still have a long way to go in order to deliver on the weighty and critical promises offered to the world in the Millennium Declaration, which contains eight goals that each relate to a social determinants approach to human development and health.

The eighth MDG goal reflects the international community's commitment to joining together to provide the necessary energy and resources to support the realization of these critical human development goals. Official development assistance, or aid from developed countries to developing countries, continues to fall well short of the 0.7 per cent of gross national income target which former Canadian Prime Minister Pearson envisioned many years ago. The only donor countries to reach or exceed the 0.7 per cent target were Denmark, Luxembourg, the Netherlands, Norway and Sweden (UN, 2007).

In addition to failing to deliver on financial commitments, too many developed countries have turned a blind eye to the corporate practices of their private sector companies, which charge exorbitantly high prices for life-saving drugs, dump hazardous wastes and products in developing countries, contribute to civil and/or political conflict in their overseas branches and market carcinogenic products to children in developing countries. Furthermore, trade negotiations between the developed and developing countries in the World Trade Organization continue to reflect substantial inequities in terms of agricultural subsidies (namely in the United States and European Union Countries) that impede the ability of developing countries to sell their agricultural products on world markets.

The global patent system (discussed in several chapters of this book), otherwise known as 'TRIPs', which provides 20-year patent protections for newly developed drugs, has meant that pharmaceutical companies have enjoyed monopoly patent protection for many life-saving medications, particularly HIV/AIDS-related medicines. This global rule system has driven up the prices of drugs, making them largely out of reach for developing countries and their populations. Considerable and sustained social activism from groups like Medécins Sans Frontieres, Oxfam, Treatment Action Campaign and other international and domestic groups has pressured drug companies to substantially reduce their prices, which has expanded access. However, in sub-Saharan Africa alone, eight out of 10 people, including many children, requiring access to antiretroviral treatment currently have none and will ultimately die from a virus that can be suppressed for long periods of time with treatment.

The MDGs represent an important achievement by the international community; that is, the commitment of countries to come together with the United Nations to transform the human condition essentially and fundamentally. There is no more serious commitment than the promises and hopes that these goals represent; indeed, billions of people in the world are relying on states, institutions and private donors to put forth the requisite energy and resources necessary for their realization. In addition to the renewed energy and commitment required by all global health actors, this book has put forward the argument that there needs to be significantly greater emphasis on a social determinants of health approach to global health. Over 20 years ago the Ottawa Charter for Health Promotion (www.who.int/hpr/NPH/docs/ottawa_charter_hp.pdf) fundamentally transformed traditional notions of health that saw health as both the absence of disease and a product of individual decision-making and lifestyle choices. The Charter affirmed that the determinants of health were social, economic, political and environmental in nature, and, accordingly, that responsibility for health was not solely in the purview of individuals and the health sector. The Charter also stipulated that health equity must be built into the strategies for health promotion, and that men and women must be able to equally avail themselves of opportunities to protect and promote their health – opportunities which extend beyond, but include, access to health care. The Charter acknowledged the important role of healthy public policy in creating favourable conditions for health. While there have been indications of renewed commitment to the principles contained in the Ottawa Charter (for example, CDSH, 2008), fundamental changes to state, multilateral, and nongovernmental research, policy and funding priorities and interventions will be critical to shifting focus to a social determinants of health approach.

Prospects for such a shift are uncertain, at best, especially given the current financial and economic collapse. Certainly, there are strong pressures to rethink the ideology that has dominated for the past several decades and ultimately to dismantle neoliberal policies and structures. For instance, US President-elect Obama has indicated his intention to push for a 'big-spending, FDR-type solution' (Krugman, 2008, p. 7) to the crisis, and this strategy is supported by several economists, including recent Nobel Prize recipient, Paul Krugman, who is calling for a new economic order based on Keynesian prescriptions of 'large-scale deficit spending by the government' (ibid.). Meanwhile, other leaders of industrialized countries are calling for similar reforms. Germany's Chancellor, Angela Merkel, recently argued publicly 'that the world ought to be looking for its example in Germany's "social market economy" – a model involving heavy state intervention and tacitly bridled competition to find new rules for capitalism' (Vinocur, 2008, p. 2).

However, it is too soon yet to predict whether government support will extend beyond 'bail-outs' to the financial and business sectors to increased social spending, and hence greater health equity. Rather than moving toward a new Keynesian moment, governments may instead scale back on both domestic and foreign health commitments. The financial crisis is now reaching all corners of the world; oil and gas prices are plummeting, consumer spending is down, unemployment is on the rise, and there are major fluctuations in world financial markets generating insecurity in pensions, investments and employment. In this climate, not only governments, but also the private investors that have become significant players in global health governance, may significantly reduce their commitments to causes in developing countries and to initiatives such as the Global Fund. Presumably, it is fears about the likelihood of this scenario that prompted Margaret Chan, current Secretary-General of WHO, to observe in a recent speech that 'impoverishing health care expenditures – that in "good" times push more than 100 million people annually into poverty – are likely to increase dramatically.... [And, therefore] stronger social safety nets are urgently needed to protect the most vulnerable in rich and poor countries' (Chan, 2008).

In the same speech, Dr Chan makes the point that support for the social sector will not only protect the most vulnerable, but will also generate efficiency; such support, she argues, is one of the most cost-effective strategies to stimulate economic recovery and equitable distribution of resources (as through policies designed to achieve heath equity) and to encourage social stability and security. Obviously, navigating the financial crisis will require some careful management by the governmental, intergovernmental and nongovernmental actors that make up the global governance system; now, however, perhaps more than ever, it is critical that the central actors take note of overwhelming evidence that healthier populations make for wealthier populations. Thus, planning and investments for health must be a key priority of governments, and, supported by a strong, sustainable and committed multilateral strategy, the emphasis must be on achieving a fundamental shift towards a social determinants of health approach to create a healthier, wealthier world for all.

Notes

1. http://www.un.org/millenniumgoals/pdf/mdg2007.pdf
2. Some of the most notable are the South Africa-based 'Treatment Action Campaign' (www.tac.org.za), the US-based 'Health GAP' (www.healthgap.org), Oxfam (www.oxfam.org) and Medécins Sans Frontières (www.msf.org) campaigns.
3. The CSDH website is at http://www.who.int/social_determinants/about/en/.

References

Abboud, B. (2005) Personal Interview (by Mulay) Mississauga, Ontario, 19 October.

Abrahamsen, R. (2004) 'The Power of Partnerships in Global Governance', *Third World Quarterly*, 25(8): 1453–67.

Accenture (2004) 'Global Fund to Fight AIDS, Tuberculosis and Malaria. Briefing Paper on In-kind Donations Project'; Annex 4 to the Report of the Resource Mobilizations and Communications Committee for the 7th Board Meeting (GF/B7/10).

Adeyi, O., O. Smith and S. Robles (2007) *Public Policy and the Challenges of Chronic Noncommunicable Diseases* (Washington: World Bank).

AFL-CIO, Cardin, B. L. and C. H. Smith (2006) *Section 301 Petition [to Office of the United States Trade Representative] of American Federation of Labor and Congress of Industrial Organizations* (Washington, DC: AFL-CIO), http://www.aflcio.org/issues/jobseconomy/globaleconomy/upload/china_petition.pdf

Africa Action (2006) 'Betraying Africa's Priorities: Short Analysis of US Policies on HIV in Africa', 22 May, http://www.africaaction.org/newsroom/index.php?op=read&documentid=1879&type=15&issues=1, date accessed 5 May 2007.

Africa Action (2008) 'HIV/AIDS Campaign Update: PEPFAR Reauthorization Act Passes: The Struggle Continues', 30 July, http://www.africaaction.org/campaign_new/docs/PEPFARREAUTHUPDATE.pdf, date accessed 10 October 2008.

Agarwal P. and P. Saibaba (2001) 'TRIPS and India's Pharmaceutical Industry', *Economic and Political Weekly*, 36: 3787–90.

Ågren, G. (2003) 'Sweden's New Public Health Policy: National Public Health Objectives for Sweden', Report 2003: 58 (Stockholm: Swedish National Institute of Public Health), available at http://www.fhi.se/shop/material_pdf/newpublic0401.pdf, date accessed 20 July 2007.

Aidspan (2004) 'An Updated Analysis of the Equitable Contributions Framework Regarding the Global Fund', www.aidspan.org/gfo/docs/gfo61.pdf, date accessed 5 November 2008.

Aiken, K., J. Swasy and A. Braman (2004) 'Patient and Physician Attitudes and Behaviours Associated With DTC Promotion of Prescription Drugs', Report for US Department of Health and Human Services, FDA and Center for Drug Evaluation and Research, November.

Ainsworth, M. and D. Filmer (2002) 'Poverty, AIDS and Children's Schooling: A Targeting Dilemma', World Bank Policy Working Paper No. WPS2885, September.

Ainsworth, M., Vaillancourt, D. and J. H. Gaubatz (2005) *Committing to Results: Improving the Effectiveness of HIV/AIDS Assistance,* An OED Evaluation of the World Bank's Assistance for HIV/AIDS Control (Washington DC: OED, World Bank).

Aizenman, J. and Y. Jinjarak (2006) 'Globalization and Developing Countries: A Shrinking Tax Base?' NBER Working Paper 11933, National Bureau of Economic Research, Cambridge, MA, http://www.nber.org/papers/w11933, date accessed 8 December 2008.

Akin, J. S., W. H. Dow, P. M. Lance and C. P. Loh (2005) 'Changes in Access To Health Care in China, 1989–1997', *Health Policy & Planning*, 20(2): 80–89.

Altman, D. (1999) 'AIDS and Questions of Global Governance', *Pacifica Review,* 11(2 June): 195–211.

Altman, D. (2003) 'HIV and Security', *International Relations,* 17(4): 417–27.
Anderson, J. E. (1975) *Public Policy-making: An Introduction* (New York: Houghton Mifflin).
Anis, A. H. (2000) 'Pharmaceutical Policies in Canada: Another Example of Federal-Provincial Discord', *Canadian Medical Association Journal,* 162(4): 523–26.
Anis A. H., D. Guh and X. Wang (2001) 'A Dog's Breakfast: Prescription Drug Coverage Varies Widely across Canada', *Medical Care,* 39(4): 315–26.
Annan, K. (2005) 'A More Secure World: Our Shared Responsibility', The Secretary-General's High-Level Panel Report on Threats, Challenges and Change, available in *Population and Development Review,* 31(3 September): 595–600.
Anon (2007) 'Sizzling: The Big Mac Index, Food for Thought about Exchange Rate Controversies', *The Economist,* 384(8536): 74.
Apotex (2008) 'Canadian-Made Life Saving HIV/AIDS Drug Heading to Africa under Canada's Access to Medicines Regime (CAMR)', http://www.apotex.com/ca/en/aboutapotex/pressreleases/20080923.asp, date accessed 31 October 2008.
Appadurai, A. (2000) 'Spectral Housing and Urban Cleansing: Notes on Millennial Mumbai', *Public Culture,* 12(3): 627–51.
Ash, T. (2008) 'One Practical Way to Improve the State of the World: Turn G8 into G14', *The Guardian,* 24 January, p. 33.
Atarah, L. (2005) *Playing Chicken: Ghana vs the IMF* (Oakland, CA: Corporate Watch), http://www.corpwatch.org/article.php?id=12394, date accessed 10 December 2008.
Attaran, A. (2004) 'How Do Patents and Economic Policies Affect Access to Essential Medicines in Developing Countries?' *Health Affairs,* 23(3): 155–66.
Attaran, A. and L. Gillespie-White (2001) 'Do Patents for Anti-Retroviral Drugs Constrain Access to Aids Treatment in Africa?' *Journal of the American Medical Association,* 286(15): 1886–92.
Attawell, K. and C. Dickinson with R. B. Madden, R. Drew, N. Druce, B. Waring and O. Weil (2007) 'An Independent Assessment of Progress of The Implementation of the Global Task Team Recommendations in Support of National AIDS Responses', HLSP Report, UNAIDS/PCB (20)/CRP 4 (London: HLSP), http://data.unaids.org/pub/ExternalDocument/2007/hlsp_gtt_assessment_item4_3_en.pdf, date accessed 14 October 2008.
Babar, Z. (2007) 'Medicalizing Pakistan', 8 January, http://www.chowk.com, date accessed 14 August 2008.
Bamako (2008) 'Global Ministerial Forum on Research for Health', http://bamako2008.org/en/index.shtml0, date accessed 10 November 2008.
Barnett, T. (2006) 'A Long-Wave Event: HIV/AIDS, Politics Governance and "Security": Sundering the Intergenerational Bond', *International Affairs,* 80(5): 931–52.
Barnett, T. and A. Whiteside (2006) *AIDS in the Twenty-First Century: Disease and Globalization,* 2nd edition (Basingstoke & New York: Palgrave Macmillan).
Barnett, T. and G. Prins (2006) *HIV/AIDS and Security: Fact, Fiction and Evidence* (Geneva: UNAIDS).
Barr, D. A. (2007) 'Ethics in Public Health Research: A Research Protocol to Evaluate the Effectiveness of Public-Private Partnerships as a Means to Improve Health and Welfare Systems Worldwide', *American Journal of Public Health,* 97(1): 19–25.
Barrett, S. (2004) 'Transnational Public Goods for Health', Background Paper, International Task Force on Global Public Goods, Johns Hopkins University.
Bartsch, S. (2002) 'Global Public-Private Partnerships as a Mechanism of Global Health Governance', *Nord-Süd Aktuell,* 3: 447–51.

Bartsch, S. (2007) 'The Global Fund to Fight AIDS, Tuberculosis and Malaria' in W. Hein et al. (eds) *Global Health Governance and the Fight against HIV/AIDS* (Basingstoke: Palgrave Macmillan): 146–71.

Bartsch, S. (2008) 'Accountability of Global Public-Private Partnerships: Specifics and Challenges', Paper prepared for the International Studies Association Annual Convention 2008, San Francisco, 26–29 March 2008.

Bartsch, S. and L. Kohlmorgen (2007) 'The Role of Civil Society Organizations in Global Health Governance' in W. Hein, et al. (eds) *Global Health Governance and the Fight against HIV/AIDS* (Basingstoke: Palgrave Macmillan): 92–118.

Bates, I., C. Fenton, J. Gruber, D. Lalloo, A. Medina Lara, S. B. Squire, S. Theobald, R. Thomson and R. Tolhurst (2004) 'Vulnerability to Malaria, Tuberculosis, and HIV/AIDS Infection and Disease. Part II: Determinants Operating at Environmental and Institutional Levels', *Lancet Infectious Diseases*, 4(6): 368–75.

Baunsgaard, T. and M. Keen (2005) 'Tax Revenue and (or?) Trade Liberalization', IMF Working Paper WP/05/112 (Washington, DC: International Monetary Fund), http://www.imf.org/external/pubs/ft/wp/2005/wp05112.pdf, date accessed 10 December 2008.

Beigbeder, Y. (1998) *The World Health Organization, International Organization and the Evolution of World Society*, Vol. 4 (The Hague: Martinus Nijhoff).

Bell, C., S. Devarajan and H. Gersbach (2006) 'The Long-Run Economic Costs of AIDS: A Model with an Application to South Africa', *The World Bank Economic Review*, 20(1): 55–89.

Bennell, P. (2003) *HIV/AIDS in Sub-Saharan Africa: The Growing Epidemic?* ELDIS discussion paper, http://www.eldis.org/fulltext/BennellHIVAfrica.pdf, date accessed 21 July 2007.

Benner, T., W. Reinicke and J. M. Witte (2004) 'Multisectoral Networks in Global Governance: Towards a Pluralistic System of Accountability', *Government and Opposition*, 39(2): 191–210.

Berhe, T., H. Gemechu and A. de Waal, (2005) 'War and HIV Prevalence', *African Security Review*, 14(3), http://www.iss.co.za/pubs/ASR/14No3/EBehre.htm, date accessed 8 December 2008.

Berkley, S. (2004) '15 Minutes with Seth Berkley, President and CEO International AIDS Vaccine Initiative', *Stanford Social Innovation Review*, Winter, http://www.ssireview.org/articles/entry/15_minutes_with_seth_berkley/, date accessed 30 November 2008.

Bernstein, M. and M. Sessions (2007) 'A Trickle or a Flood: Commitments and Disbursement for HIV/AIDS from the Global Fund, PEPFAR, and the World Bank's Multi-Country AIDS Program (MAP)', Center for Global Government, http://www. cgdev.org/content/publications/detail/13029/, date accessed 26 September 2008.

Bettcher, D. et al., (2001) *Confronting the Tobacco Epidemic in an Era of Trade Liberalization* (Geneva: WHO).

Bettcher, D., D. Yach, and G. E. Guindon (2000) 'Global Trade and Health: Key Linkages and Future Challenges', *Bulletin of the World Health Organization*, 78(4): 521–33.

Bhargava, A. and B. Chatterjee (2007) 'Chikungunya Fever, Falciparum Malaria, Dengue Fever, Japanese Encephalitis... Are We Listening to the Warning Signs for Public Health in India?' *Indian Journal of Medical Ethics*, 4: 18–23.

Biehl, J. (2007) 'Pharmaceuticalization: AIDS Treatment and Global Health Politics', *Anthropological Quarterly*, 80(4): 1083–1126.

Bill and Melinda Gates Foundation, http://www.gatesfoundation.org/GlobalHealth/Grantseekers/GH_Strategy/default. htm, date accessed 7 November 2007.

Bill and Melinda Gates Foundation (2005) 'Statement by Bill Gates on the Launch of the International Finance Facility for Immunization', http://www.gatesfoundation.org/GlobalHealth/Pri_Diseases/Vaccines/Announcements/Announce-050908.htm, date accessed 25 August 2007.

BIO (2006) *On the Patent and Trademark's Strategic–2007–2012*, Comment, Washington, 6 October, http://bio.org/ip/domestic/20061006.pdf, date accessed 8 November 2008.

Birdsall, N. (2006a) 'Stormy Days on an Open Field: Asymmetries in the Global Economy', WIDER Working Paper 81, February.

Birdsall, N. (2006b) 'The World is Not Flat: Inequality and Injustice in our Global Economy', 2005 WIDER Annual Lecture (Helsinki: World Institute for Development Economics Research), http://www.cgdev.org/doc/commentary/speeches/Birdsall_WIDERpaper.pdf, date accessed 10 December 2008.

Birdsall, N., D. Rodrik and A. Subramanian (2005) 'How to Help Poor Countries', *Foreign Affairs*, 84(4): 136–52.

Black, D. R. (2006) 'Mapping the Interplay of Human Security Practice and Debates: The Canadian Experience' in S. MacLean et al. (eds) *A Decade of Human Security* (Aldershot: Ashgate).

Bloche, M. G. and E. R. Jungman (2007) 'Health Policy and the World Trade Organization' in I. Kawachi and S. Wamala (eds) *Globalization and Health* (Oxford: Oxford University Press).

Blouin, C. (2007a) 'Can the World Trade Organization Help Achieve the Health Millennium Development Goals?' in A. F. Cooper, et al. (eds), *Governing Global Health: Challenge, Response, Innovation* (Aldershot: Ashgate).

Blouin, C. (2007b) 'Canada and the Global Right to Health' in *The Global Right to Health: Canadian Development Report 2007* (Ottawa: The North-South Institute).

Bond, P. (2004) 'The ANC's "Left Turn" & South African Sub-imperialism', *Review of African Political Economy*, 31(102): 599–616.

Bonita, R., A. Irwin and R. Beaglehole (2007) 'Promoting Public Health in the Twenty-First Century: The Role of the World Health Organization' in Kawachi and Wamala (eds) *Globalization and Health* (New York: Oxford University Press).

Börzel, T. A. and T. Risse (2005) 'Public-Private Partnerships: Effective and Legitimate Tools of International Governance?' in E. Grande and L. W. Pauly (eds) *Complex Sovereignty: Reconstituting Political Authority in the 21st Century* (Toronto: University of Toronto Press).

Bradford, C. I. (2005) 'Anticipating the Future: A Political Agenda for Global Economic Governance' in English et al. (eds) *Reforming from the Top: A Leaders' 20 Summit* (Tokyo: United Nations University Press).

Brando, L. (2004) 'Global Public Goods for Health: Myth or Mantra?' Working Paper 2004–01, UCD Health and Behavioral Sciences (HBSC) Working Paper Series (Denver: University of Colorado at Denver).

Bratton, M. and C. Logan (2006) 'Voters but not Yet Citizens: The Weak Demand for Political Accountability in Africa's Unclaimed Democracies', Afrobarometer Working Paper No. 63, September.

Bratton, M. and M. Sibanyoni (2006) 'Delivery or Responsiveness? A Popular Scorecard of Local Government Performance in South Africa', IDASA Afrobarometer Working Paper No. 62, August.

Bratton, M. and W. Cho (2006) 'Where is Africa Going? Views from Below', Afrobarometer Working Paper No. 60, May.

Broad, R. (ed.) (2002) *Citizen Initiatives for a Just World Economy* (Lanham, MD: Rowman and Littlefield).

Brown, A. (2008) 'AIDS Plan Stronger but Still Flawed, Groups Say', Inter Press Service News Agency, Washington, http://ipsnews.net/print.asp?idnews=43382, date accessed 15 October, 2008.

Brown, G. (2002) 'The Global Threats to Workers' Health and Safety on the Job', *Social Justice*, 29(3): 12–25.

Brown, S. (2006) 'Global Public-Private Partnerships for Pharmaceuticals: Ethical and Procedural Features, Prospects and Challenges', Paper presentation to the Canadian Political Science Association Annual Conference, Toronto, Ontario, 1–4 June.

Brown, T. M., M. Cueto and E. Fee (2006) 'The World Health Organization and the Transition from "International" to "Global" Public Health', *American Journal of Public Health*, 96(1): 62–72.

Bryce, J., Black, R. E., Walker, N., Bhutta, Z. A., Lawn, J. E. and Steketee, R. W. (2005) 'Can the World Afford to Save the Lives of 6 Million Children each Year?', *Lancet*, 365(9478): 2193–2200.

Bujra, J. (2006) 'Class Relations: AIDS and Socioeconomic Privilege in Africa', *Review of African Political Economy*, 33(107): 113–29.

Bull, B. and D. McNeill (2007) *Development Issues in Global Governance: Public-Private Partnerships and Market Multilateralism* (New York: Routledge).

Bull, B., M. Boas and D. McNeill (2004) 'Private Sector Influence in the Multilateral System: A Changing Structure of World Governance?' *Global Governance*, 10(4): 481–98.

Bulmer, M. (1999) 'The History of Philanthropic Foundations in the United Kingdom and the United States: Philanthropic Foundations in Industrial Society' in H. K. Anheier and S. Toepler (eds) *Private Funds, Public Purpose: Philanthropic Foundations in International Perspective* (New York: Kluwer Academic).

Burke, M. and A. de Francisco (eds) (2006) *Monitoring Financial Flows for Health Research 2005: Behind the Global Numbers* (Geneva: Global Forum for Health Research).

Burke, M. and S. Matlin (eds) (2008) *Monitoring Financial Flows for Health Research 2008: Prioritizing Research for Health Equity* (Geneva: Global Forum for Health Research).

Buse, K. (2004) 'Governing Public-Private Infectious Disease Partnerships,' *Brown Journal of World Affairs*, 10(2): 225–42.

Buse, K. and A. Harmer (2007) 'Seven Habits of Highly Effective Global Public-Private Health Partnerships', *Social Science and Medicine*, 64(2): 259–71.

Buse, K. and A. Waxman (2001) 'Public-Private Health Partnerships: A Strategy for WHO', *Bulletin of the World Health Organization*, 79(8): 748–54.

Buse, K. and G. Walt (2000) 'Global Public-Private Partnerships: Part I – A New Development in Health?', *Bulletin of the World Health Organisation*, 78(4): 549–61.

Buse, K. and G. Walt (2002) 'Globalisation and Multilateral Public-Private Health Partnerships: Issues for Health Policy' in K. Lee et al. (eds) *Health Policy in a Globalising World* (Cambridge: Cambridge University Press).

Buse, K. and K. Lee (2005) *Business and Global Health Governance* (London: London School of Hygiene & Tropical Medicine).

Caesar-Katsenga, M. and M. Myburg (2006) *Parliament, Politics and AIDS: A Comparative Study of Five African Countries* (Cape Town, IDASA, 2006).

Caines, K., K. Buse, C. Carlson, R. de Loor, N. Druce, C. Grace, M. Pearson, J. Sancho and R. Sandanandan (2004) *Assessing the Impact of Global Health Partnerships* (London: DFID Health Resource Centre).

Calcagnotto, G. (2007) 'Consensus Building on Brazilian HIV/AIDS Policy: National and Global Interfaces in Health Governance' in Hein et al. (eds) *Global Health Governance and the Fight against HIV/AIDS* (Basingstoke: Palgrave Macmillan).

Canada's Statement to the World Health Assembly, 14 May 2007, Geneva, Switzerland, http://www.dfait-maeci.gc.ca/Canada_un/Geneva clf1/2007-05-14-en.asp, date accessed 20 August 2007.

CIDA (Canadian International Development Agency) (2006) *CIDA Departmental Performance Report*, 31 March.

Carlson, C. (2004) 'Mapping Global Health Partnerships: What They Are, What They Do and Where They Operate', DFID Study Paper 1.

Carment, D. (2003) 'Assessing State Failure: Implications for Theory and Policy', *Third World Quarterly*, 24(3): 407–27.

Castle, S. and M. Landler (2008) 'Hopes of World Trade Deal Collapse', *New York Times*, 30 July.

CCGHR (Canadian Coalition on Global Health Research) (2001) 'Canadian Consultation on Global Health Research Enhancing the Opportunities; Renewing the Vision, Concept Paper (Draft – August 16), http://www.ccrsm.ca/default.cfm?content=renewing_vision&lang=e&subnav=library, date accessed 10 July 2007.

Cerny, P. G. (2000) 'Restructuring the Political Arena: Globalization and the Paradoxes of the Competition State' in R. D. Germain (ed.) *Globalization and its Critics: Perspectives from Political Economy* (Houndmills: Macmillan).

CGPA (Canadian Generic Pharmaceutical Association) (2007) 'The Role of the Generic Pharmaceutical Industry in Canadian Health Care', http://www.canadiangenerics.ca/en/resources/health_care_savings.asp, date accessed 11 October 2008.

Chabal, P. and J.-P. Daloz (1999) *Africa Works. Disorder as Political Instrument* (Oxford: James Currey).

Chan, M. (2008) 'Impact of the Global Financial and Economic Crisis on Health', statement by the WHO Director General, http://www.who.int/mediacentre/news/statements/2008/s12/en/index.html, accessed 9 December 2008.

Chang, K. (1998) 'The Organization of the R&D Intensive Firm: An Application to the Biotechnology Industry', Ph.D. diss., University of Kentucky.

Chapnick, A. (2005) *The Middle Power Project* (Vancouver: UBC Press).

Chaudhuri, S. (2005) *The WTO and India's Pharmaceutical Industry: Patent Protection, TRIPS and Developing Countries* (New Delhi Oxford University Press).

Chaudhuri, S. and M. Ravallion (2006) 'Partially Awakened Giants: Uneven Growth in China and India' in L.A. Winters and S. Yusuf (eds) *Dancing with Giants: China, India, and the Global Economy* (Washington: World Bank).

Chaudhury, R., R. Parameswar, U. Gupta, S. Sharma, U. Tekur and J. S. Bapna (2005) 'Quality Medicines for the Poor: Experience of the Delhi Programme on Rational Use of Drugs', *Health Policy and Planning*, 20 (March): 124–36.

Chen, L., J. Leaning and V. Narasimhan (eds) (2003) *Global Health Challenges for Human Security* (Boston: Global Equity Initiative, Asia Center, Harvard University Press).

Chen, S. and M. Ravallion (2008) 'The Developing World Is Poorer than We Thought, But No Less Successful in the Fight against Poverty', World Bank Policy Research Working Paper WPS4703 (Washington, DC: World Bank).

Cheru, F. (1999) 'Economic, Social and Cultural Rights: Effects of Structural Adjustment Policies on the Full Enjoyment of Human Rights', E/CN.4/1999/50, United Nations Economic and Social Council, Geneva.

Cheru, F. (2000) 'Debt Relief and Social Investment: Linking the HIPC Initiative to the HIV/AIDs Epidemic in Africa: The Case of Zambia', *Review of African Political Economy*, 27(86): 519–35.

Cheru, F. (2001) 'Economic, Social and Cultural Rights: The Highly Indebted Poor Countries (HIPC) Initiative: A Human Rights Assessment of the Poverty Reduction Strategy Papers (PRSP)', E/CN.4/2001/56, United Nations Economic and Social Council, Geneva.

Chirambo, K. (2006) 'Democratization in the Age of HIV/AIDS: Understanding the Impact of a Pandemic on the Electoral Process in Africa', paper delivered at the South African Association of Political Studies' biannual Conference, Cape Town, South Africa, August.

CIA (1990) *CIA Interagency Intelligence Memorandum 91–10005.*

CIDA (Canadian International Development Agency) Canada Fund for Africa, 'Delivering Results', http://www.acdi-cida.gc.ca/cidaweb/acdicida.nsf/En/ANN-76105016-KEG, date accessed 14 August 2007.

CIDA (2006) *CIDA Departmental Performance Report,* 31 March.

CIHI (2007) 'Drug Expenditures in Canada 1985–2007', www.cihi.ca, date accessed 14 August 2008.

CIHR (2007) 'Canadian HIV Vaccine Initiative', http://www.chvi-icvv.gc.ca/about-eng.html, date accessed 17 November 2008.

CIPIH and WHO (2006) 'Public Health: Innovation and Intellectual Property Rights', Report of the Commission on Intellectual Property Rights, Innovation and Public Health (Geneva: World Health Organization).

Cleveland, H. (2005) 'Leadership, Equity, and Global Health' in W. H. Foege et al. (eds) *Global Health Leadership and Management* (San Francisco: John Wiley & Sons, Inc.).

CMH (2001) *Macroeconomics and Health: Investing in Health for Economic Development* (Geneva: Commission on Macroeconomics and Health).

CNW (Canada News Wire) (2003) 'Generics to Parliamentary Committee: End Abuse of Drug Regulations', Canada News Wire, http://www1.newswire.ca/releases/June2003, (Document cnnw000020030603dz63006sp), date accessed 14 August 2008.

Collier, P. (2006a) 'African Growth: Why a "Big Push"?', *Journal of African Economies,* 15(2): 188–211.

Collier, P. (2006b) 'Editorial: Rethinking Assistance for Africa', *Economic Affairs,* 26(4): 2–4.

Collier, P. (2006c) 'Why the WTO is Deadlocked: And What Can Be Done about It', *The World Economy,* 29(10): 1423–49.

Collier, P. (2007) *The Bottom Billion: Why the Poorest Countries are Failing and What Can Be Done about It* (Oxford: Oxford University Press).

Commission for Africa (2005) *Our Common Interest: Report of the Commission for Africa. London: Commission for Africa,* http://www.commissionforafrica.org/english/report/thereport/english/11-03-05_cr_report.pdf, date accessed 23 November 2008.

Commission on Macroeconomics and Health (2001) *Macroeconomics and Health: Investing in Health for Economic Development* (Geneva: World Health Organization).

Community Wealth Ventures (2004) *High-Engagement Philanthropy: A Bridge to a More Effective Social Sector* (Washington DC: Venture Philanthropy Partners).

Connolly, C. (2003) 'FDA Steps Up Enforcement on Drug Imports', *Washington Post,* 30 September, A2.

CP Tech (Consumer Project on Technology) 'Background Information on Fluconazole (Diflucan)', www.cptech.org/ip/health/fluconazole/index.html, date accessed 30 March 2006.

Consumer Protection Network (2006) 'Prices, Availability and Affordability of Medicines in Pakistan', http://www.haiweb.org/medicineprices/surveys/200407PK/survey_report.pdf, date accessed 15 August 2008.

Cook, D. (2006) 'Ways to Fight the AIDS Pandemic (interview with Stephen Lewis, UN Special Envoy for AIDS) *Africa Report*', October, 109–11.

Cooksey, D. (2006) 'A Review of UK Research Funding', London: HM Treasury, December, http://www.hm-treasury.gov.uk/media/4/A/pbr06_cookseyfinal_report_636.pdf, date accessed 20 July 2007.

Cooper, A., J. Kirton and T. Schrecker (2007) 'Governing Global Health in the Twenty-First Century' in A. Cooper et al. (eds) *Governing Global Health*.

Cooper, M. (1998) 'General Pinochet Still Rules: Twenty-Five Years after Allende – An Anti-Memoir', *The Nation*, 266(23 March): 11–23.

Cooper, M. (2006) 'Pre-empting Emergence: The Biological Turn in the War on Terror', *Theory, Culture & Society* 23(4): 113–35.

Corlazzoli, V. and J. Smith (2005), 'The Group of 8' in V. Corlazzoli and J. Smith (eds) (2005) *The G8 and Africa Final Report: An Overview of the G8's Ongoing Relationship with African Development from the 2001 Genoa Summit to the 2005 Gleneagles Summit*, Civil Society and Expanded Dialogue Unit, G8 Research Group, University of Toronto, http://www.g8.utoronto.ca/evaluations/csed/g8africa_050624.html, date accessed 12 December 2008.

Cornia, G. A., R. Jolly and F. Stewart (eds) (1987) *Adjustment with a Human Face, vol. 1: Protecting the Vulnerable and Promoting Growth* (Oxford: Clarendon Press).

Cornia, G. A., S. Rosignoli and L. Tiberti (2008) 'Globalisation and Health: Pathways of Transmission and Evidence of Impact', Globalization Knowledge Network Research Papers (Ottawa: Institute of Population Health, University of Ottawa).

Correa, C. M. (2008) 'Public Health and the Implementation of the TRIPS Agreement in Latin America' in C. Blouin, N. Drager and J. Heymann (eds), *Trade and Health: Seeking Common Ground* (Montréal: McGill-Queen's University Press).

Cox, R. (1981) 'Social Forces, States and World Orders: Beyond International Relations Theory', *Millennium Journal of International Studies*, 10(2): 126–55.

Cox, R. (1999) 'Civil Society at the Turn of the Millennium: Prospects for an Alternative World Order', *Review of International Studies* 25(1): 3–28.

Cox, R. (2000) 'The Way Ahead: Towards a New Ontology of World Order' in R. W. Jones (ed.) *Critical Theory and World Politics* (Boulder: Lynne Rienner).

CSDH (2008) *Closing the Gap in a Generation: Health Equity through Action on the Social Determinants of Health, Final Report of the Commission on the Social Determinants of Health* (Geneva: WHO).

Cueto, M. (2004) 'The Origins of Primary Health Care and Selective Health Care', *American Journal of Public Health*, 94(11): 1864–74.

Cutler, A. C. et al. (eds) (1999) *Private Authority and International Affairs* (Albany: State University of New York).

Cutler, A. C. (2003) *Private Power and Global Authority: Transnational Merchant Law in the Global Political Economy* (New York: Cambridge University Press).

Daar, A., P. Singer, D. Persad, S. Pramming, D. Matthews, R. Beaglehole, A. Bernstein, L. Borysiewicz, S. Colagiuri, N. Ganguly, R. Glass, D. Finegood, J. Koplan, E. Nabel, G. Sarna, N. Sarrafzadegan, R. Smith, D. Yach and J. Bell (2007) 'Grand Challenges in Chronic Non-Communicable Diseases', *Nature*, 450(7169): 494–96.

Dallmayer, Fred (2006) 'Globalization and Inequality: A Plea for Cosmopolitan Justice', *Comparative Studies of South Asia, Africa and the Middle East*, 26(1): 63–74.

Dawkins, R. (2006) *The God Delusion* (London: Bantam Press).

DCD-DAC (Development Cooperative Directorate of OECD's Development Assistance Committee) *Countries and Organizations Adhering to the Paris Declaration*, http://

www.oecd.org/document/22/0,3343,en_2649_3236398_36074966_1_1_1_1,00.html, date accessed 3 October 2008.

Deaton, A. (2003) 'Health, Inequality, and Economic Development', *Journal of Economic Literature*, 41(1): 113–58.

De Vogli, R. and G. L. Birbeck (2005) 'Potential Impact of Adjustment Policies on Vulnerability of Women and Children to HIV/AIDS in Sub-Saharan Africa', *Journal of Health Population and Nutrition*, 23(2): 105–20.

de Waal, A. and A. Whiteside (2003) 'New Variant Famine: AIDS and Food Crisis in Southern Africa', *Lancet*, 362(9391): 1234–37.

de Waal, A. (2003) 'How Will HIV/AIDS Transform African Governance?', *African Affairs*, 102(406): 1–23.

de Waal, A. (2005) 'Issue Paper 2: HIV/AIDS and Democratic Governance', Expert Seminar on AIDS, Security and Democracy, Clingendael Institute, The Hague, 2–5 May.

de Waal, A. (2006a) 'Evidence for the "New Variant Famine" Hypothesis in Africa', *Justice Africa*, http://www.justiceafrica.org, date accessed 16 December 2006.

de Waal, A. (2006b) *AIDS and Power: Why There is No Political Crisis–Yet* (London & New York: Zed Books).

DFAIT (2008) *Canada's Contribution to the Global Fight against Avian and Pandemic Influenza*, http://www.international.gc.ca/pdf/Infosheet-DFAIT-en.pdf, date accessed 13 June 2007.

DFID (2003) *Global Fund Country Case Studies Report* (London: DFID).

DFID (2005) *Why We Need to Work More Effectively in Fragile States* (London: Department for International Development).

DH (Department of Health, UK) (2008) *Global Health Partnerships: The UK Contribution to Health in Developing Countries: The Government Response* (London: DH).

Dicken, P. (2007) *Global Shift: Reshaping the Global Economic Map in the 21st Century*, 5th edn. (New York: Guilford Press).

Dickinson, C. J. Mundy, E. Serlemitos, J. Whitelaw Jones (2008) *A Synthesis of Institutional Arrangements of National AIDS Commissions in Africa*, May 2008, http://www.hlspinstitute.org/projects/?mode=type&id=177782 (London: HLSP), date accessed 5 June 2008.

Dmitrienko, K. and A. Birn (2006) 'Juggling Demands: Canadian Health Aid to Latin America since WWII', *Canadian Journal of Public Health*, 97(6): I2–I7.

Dodgson, R., K. Lee and N. Drager (2002) 'Global Health Governance: A Conceptual Review', Discussion Paper No. 1, Centre on Global Change and Health, London School of Hygiene and Tropical Medicine, and Department of Health and Development, World Health Organization, February, http://libdoc.who.int/publications/2002/a85727_eng.pdf, date accessed 16 July 2008.

Donaldson, L. and N. Banatvala (2007) 'Health is Global: Proposals for a UK Government-Wide Strategy', *The Lancet*, 369(9564): 857–61.

Drahos, P. (2002) 'Developing Countries and International Intellectual Property Standard-Setting', *Journal of World Intellectual Property*, 5(5): 765–89.

Drahos, P. and J. Braithwaite (2002) *Informational Feudalism: Who Owns the Knowledge Economy?* (London: Earthscan).

Dreher, A. and N. Gaston (2008) 'Has Globalization Increased Inequality?' *Review of International Economics*, 16(3): 516–36.

Duffield, M. (2005) 'Getting Savages to Fight Barbarians: Development, Security and the Colonial Present', *Conflict, Security & Development*, 5(2): 141–59.

Dummer, T. J. B. and I. G. Cook (2007) 'Exploring China's Rural Health Crisis: Processes and Policy Implications', *Health Policy*, 83(1): 1–16.

Dunoff, J. L. (1996–97) 'Trade and: Recent Developments in Trade Policy and Scholarship – and Their Surprising Political Implications', *Northwestern Journal of International Law and Business*, Winter–Spring: 759–74.

Dupont, V. (2008) 'Slum Demolitions in Delhi since the 1990s: An Appraisal', *Economic & Political Weekly*, 43(12): 79–87.

Dyer, G. (2004) 'A Laboratory for Globalization: How India Hopes to Reshape the World Drug Industry', *Financial Times*, 14 August.

Economic Times (2006) 'Government Signs Bird Flu Drug Deal', 3 January, https://global.factiva.com, date accessed 14 August 2008 (Document ECTIM00020060102e2130001c).

Economist, The (2006) 'The Birth of Philanthrocapitalism', 378(8466): 9.

Economist, The (2008) 'The Side Effect of Doing Good', 368(8568): 77–78.

Eizenstat, S. E., J. E. Porter and J. M. Weinstein (2005) 'Rebuilding Weak States', *Foreign Affairs*, 84(1): 134–46.

Elbe, S. (2006) 'Should HIV/AIDS be Securitized? The Ethical Dilemmas of Linking HIV/AIDS and Security', *International Studies Quarterly*, 50(1): 119–44.

Elias, P. (2006) 'Biotech Company Gilead Criticized for AIDS Drug Supply', *Associated Press*, posted 7 February, http://lists.essential.org/pipermail/ip-health/2006-February/009078.html, date accessed 10 November 2008.

English, J., R. Thakur and A. Cooper (eds) (2005) *Reforming from the Top: A Leaders' 20 Summit* (Tokyo: United Nations University Press).

Ernst and Young (2007) *Beyond Borders: The Global Biotechnology Report 2007*, www.ey.com/global/content.nsf/International/Biotechnology_Library_Beyond_Borders_2007, date accessed 8 November 2008.

Evans, P. (2005) 'Neoliberalism as a Political Opportunity: Constraint and Innovation in Contemporary Development Strategy' in K. Gallagher (ed.) *Putting Development First: The Importance of Policy Space in the WTO and IFIs* (London: Zed Books).

Evans, R. G. and G. L. Stoddart (1990) 'Producing Health, Consuming Health Care', *Social Science & Medicine*, 31(12): 1347–63.

Evans, R. G., M. L. Barer, and T. R. Marmor (eds) (1994) *Why are Some People Healthy and Others Not? The Determinants of Health of Populations* (New York: Aldine de Gruyer).

Evans, T. G. (2002) *Health-Related Global Public Goods: Initiatives of the Rockefeller Foundation* (New York: United Nations Office of Development Studies). http://www.undp.org/ods/monterrey-papers/evans.pdf, date accessed 10 July 2007.

Evans, T. G. and L. C. Chen (2005) 'Public-Private Partnerships in Global Health', Discussion Paper (Washington, DC: The Rockefeller Foundation).

Falk, R. A. (1996) 'An Inquiry into the Political Economy of World Order', *New Political Economy*, 1(1): 13–26.

Falk, R. A. (2000) *Human Rights Horizons: The Pursuit of Justice in a Globalizing World* (New York and London: Routledge).

Falk, R. A., G. Kolko and R. J. Lifton (eds) (1971) *Crimes of War: A Legal, Political, and Psychological Inquiry into the Responsibility of Leaders, Citizens, and Soldiers for Criminal Acts in War* (New York: Vintage).

Farmer, P. (2003) *Pathologies of Power: Health, Human Rights and the New War on the Poor* (Berkeley: University of California Press).

Feachem, R. G. A. (2001) 'Globalisation is Good for Your Health, Mostly', *British Medical Journal*, 323(7311): 504–6.

Ferguson, N. (2006) 'Poverty, Death and a Future Influenza Pandemic', *The Lancet*, 368(9554): 2187–88.

Fidler, D. (2003) 'SARS: Political Pathology of the First Post-Westphalian Pathogen', *Journal of Law, Medicine and Ethics*, 31(4): 485–505.

Fidler, D. (2004) *SARS, Governance and the Globalization of Disease* (Basingstoke: Palgrave Macmillan).

Fidler, D. (2005) 'From International Sanitary Conventions to Global Health Security: The New International Health Regulations', *Chinese Journal of International Law*, 4(2): 1–68.

Fidler, D. (2007) 'Architecture amid Anarchy: Global Health's Quest for Governance', *Journal of Global Health Governance*, 1(1), 18pp, http://diplomacy.shu.edu/academics/global_health, date accessed 16 July 2008.

Fidler, D. and N. Drager (2006) 'Editorial: Health and Foreign Policy', *Bulletin of the World Health Organization*, 84(9): 687.

Fink, C. and Reichenmuller, P. (2006) 'Tightening TRIPS: Intellectual Property Provisions of US Free Trade Agreements' in R. Newfarmer (ed.) *Trade, Doha, and Development: A Window into the Issues* (Washington, DC: World Bank).

Finnemore, M. and K. Sikkink (1998) 'International Norm Dynamics and Political Change', *International Organization*, 52(4): 887–917.

Fleck, F. (2004) 'News Report: Spending on Neglected Diseases has Increased, Says Report', *British Medical Journal*, 328(7459): 1220.

Flood, C. M., M. Stabile and C. Tuohy (2002) 'The Borders of Solidarity: How Countries Determine the Public/Private Mix in Spending and the Impact on Health Care', *Health Matrix*, 12(2): 297–356.

Foladori, G. (2003) 'Can PPPs in Health Cope with Social Needs?' Section 3, *Knowledge Flows and Knowledge Collectives: Understanding The Role of Science and Technology Policies in Development*, A Project for the Global Inclusion Program of the Rockefeller Foundation, http://nanoandsociety.com/home/cspoideas/know_flows/CSPO_Rockefeller_Vol1.pdf, date accessed 30 October 2008.

Ford, N., A. Gray and W. D. F. Venter (2008) 'Tough Choices: Tenofovir, Tenders and Treatment', *Southern African Journal of HIV Medicine*, 9(1): 8–10, http://fieldresearch.msf.org/msf/bitstream/10144/29474/1/Ford%20Tough%20Choices.pdf, date accessed 11 October 2008.

Fort, M., M. A. Mercer and O. Gish (eds) (2004) *Sickness and Wealth: The Corporate Assault on Global Health* (Cambridge: South End Press).

Foucault, M. (1997) *Society Must Be Defended: Lectures at the Collège de France 1975–1976* (New York: Picador).

Foundation Center (2007) 'Top 100 U.S. Foundations by Asset Size', http://foundationcenter.org/findfunders/topfunders/top100assets.html, date accessed 15 July 2007.

Fourie, P. (2006) *The Political Management of HIV and AIDS in South Africa: One Burden Too Many?* (Basingstoke & New York: Palgrave Macmillan).

Fourie, P. and M. Schönteich (2001) 'Africa's New Security Threat', *African Security Review*, 10(4), http://www.iss.co.za/pubs/ASR/10No4/Fourie.html, date accessed 12 December 2008.

France, T., G. Ooms and B. Rivers (2002) 'The Global Fund: Which Countries Owe How Much?' *Global AIDSLink*, 74(5): 17.

Fukuyama, F. (2004) *State Building: Governance and World Order in the Twenty-First Century* (London: Profile Books).

Fund for Peace (2006) *Failed State Index 2006*, http://www.fundforpeace.org/programs/fsi/fsindex2006.php, date accessed 16 December 2006.

G8 (2001) *Communiqué* (Genoa: G8 Information Centre, University of Toronto), http://www.g8.utoronto.ca/summit/2001genoa/finalcommunique.html

G8 (2002) *G8 Africa Action Plan* (Kananaskis and Ottawa: G8 Summit Secretariat, Government of Canada).

G8 (2005) *Africa* (Gleneagles: G8 Information Centre, University of Toronto), http://www.g8.utoronto.ca/summit/2005gleneagles/africa.pdf

G8 (2006) *Trade* (St. Petersburg: G8 Information Centre, University of Toronto).

G8 (2007) *Chair's Summary* (Heiligendamm: G8 Information Centre, University of Toronto).

Gambardella, A. (1995) *Science and Innovation: the US Pharmaceutical Industry during the 1980s* (New York: Cambridge University Press.

GAO (2008) 'Global HIV/AIDS: A More Country-Based Approach Could Improve Allocation of PEPFAR Funding', Report to Congressional Committees, GAO- 08-480, April, http://www.gao.gov/new.items/d08480.pdf, date accessed 3 October 2008.

Gardiner, E. (2003) 'The Price of Access: Making Drugs Available in Africa', Masters Thesis, Sloan Fellowship Masters Program, London Business School.

Garrett, L. (2005) 'The Lessons of HIV/AIDS', *Foreign Affairs*, 84(4): 51–64.

Garrett, L. (2007) 'The Challenge of Global Health', *Foreign Affairs*, 86(1): 14–38.

Gates, B. (2008) 'Prepared Remarks by Bill Gates', for presentation at the World Economic Forum, 24 January, http://www.gatesfoundation.org/speeches-commentary/Pages/bill-gates-2008-world-economic-forum.aspx, date accessed 17 November 2008.

GAVI Alliance (2008) *GAVI Alliance*, http://www.gavialliance.org/, date accessed 1 March 2008.

Gaynor, C. (2005) 'Structural Injustice and the MDGs: A Critical Analysis of the Zambian Experience', *Trocaire Development Review*, 57–84.

Gellman, B. (2000) 'An Unequal Calculus of Life and Death', *Washington Post*, 27 December, A01.

George, S. (1976) *How the Other Half Dies: The Real Reasons for World Hunger* (Harmondsworth: Penguin).

GFATM (The Global Fund to Fight AIDS, Tuberculosis and Malaria) (2004) 'Country Coordinating Mechanisms. A Synthesis and Analysis of Findings from CCM Case Studies, Tracking Study, GNP and other Surveys' (Geneva: GFATM).

GFATM (2005) *Harmonization of Global Fund Programs and Donor Coordination: Four Case Studies with a Focus on HIV/AIDS* (Geneva: GFATM).

GFATM (2007a) 'Country Coordinating Mechanisms', http://www.theglobalfund.org/en/apply/mechanisms, date accessed 26 March 2007.

GFATM (2007b) *The Framework Document of the Global Fund to Fight AIDS, Tuberculosis and Malaria* (Geneva: GFATM).

GFATM (2007c) *Guidelines on the Purpose, Structure, Composition and Funding of Country Coordinating Mechanisms and Requirements for Grant Eligibility* (Geneva: GFATM), http://www.theglobalfund.org/pdf/5_pp_guidelines_ccm_4_en.pdf, date accessed 15 October 2008.

GFATM (2007d) 'Donors Provide US$9.7 Billion to the Global Fund', Geneva, http://www.theglobalfund.org/en/pressreleases/?pr=pr_070927, date accessed 7 January 2009.

GFATM (2007e) *Partners in Impact. Results Report* (Geneva: GFATM).

GFATM (2008a) 'Lessons Learned in the Field, Health Financing and Governance', The Global Fund Implementer Series, http://www.theglobalfund.org/documents/publications/other/CCM/CCM_report. pdf, date accessed 25 September 2008.

GFATM (2008b) *Distribution of Funding after 6 Rounds* (Geneva: GFATM) http://www.theglobalfund.org/en/funds_raised/distribution/, date accessed 23 October 2008.

Giacomini, M., J. Hurley, I. Gold, P. Smith and J. Abelson (2004) 'The Policy Analysis of "Values Talk": Lessons From Canadian Health Reform', *Health Policy*, 67(1): 15–24.

Giddens, A. (1998) *The Third Way: The Renewal of Social Democracy* (Cambridge: Polity Press).

Gilks, C., S. Crowley, R. Ekpini, J. Perriens, Y. Souteyrand, D. Sutherland, M. Vitoria, T. Guerma and K. De Cock (2006) 'The WHO Public-Health Approach to Anti-Retroviral Treatment against HIV in Resource-Limited Settings', *Lancet*, 368(9534): 505–10.

Gill, S. (2008) *Power and Resistance in the New World Order*, 2nd edn (Basingstoke: Palgrave Macmillan).

Gilmartin, R. V. (2005) 'A New Role for Corporate America: Partners in Global Health and Development' in William H. Foege, et al. (eds) *Global Health Leadership and Management* (San Francisco: Jose-Bass).

Global Forum for Health Research (2002) *The 10/90 Report on Health Research 2001–2002* (Geneva: World Health Organization).

Global Forum for Health Research (2006) *Monitoring Financial Flows for Health Research 2005: Behind the Global Numbers* (Geneva: Global Forum for Health Research).

Global Forum for Health Research (2008) 'The '10/90 Gap Now', http://www.globalforumhealth.org/Site/003__The%2010%2090%20gap/001__Now.php, date accessed 23 July 2008.

Global Fund, www.theglobalfund.org/en, date accessed 14 August 2007.

Global Fund to Fight AIDS, Tuberculosis and Malaria (2007) 'Donors Provide US$9.7 Billion to the Global Fund', Global Fund, Geneva, http://theglobalfund.org/en/media_center/press/pr_070927.asp, date accessed 14 August 2007.

Global Health Council (2008) 'Not Just another Buzzword? Public-Private Partnerships in Action', 35th International Conference, Global Health, http://www.globalhealth.org/conference/view_top.php3?id=702, date accessed 25 July 2008.

GNP+ (The Global Network of People Living with HIV/AIDS) (2003) 'A Multi-Country Study of the Involvement of People Living with HIV/AIDS (PLWHA) in the Country Coordinating Mechanisms', Amsterdam, http://www.synergyaids.com/documents/GNP_Plus_MultiCountryPLWHA_study.pdf, date accessed 5 November 2008.

Godlee, F. (1995) 'The World Health Organisation: WHO's Special Programmes: Undermining From Above', *British Medical Journal*, 310(6973): 178–82.

Goldstein, A. (2007) *Multinational Companies from Emerging Economies: Composition, Conceptualization and Direction in the Global Economy* (Houndmills: Palgrave Macmillan).

Gootnick, D. (2003) 'Global Fund to Fight AIDS, TB and Malaria has Advanced in Key Areas, but Difficult Challenges Remain', Report to the Honorable Jim Kolbe Chairman, Subcommittee on Foreign Operations, Export Financing, and Related Programs, Committee on Appropriations, House of Representatives (Washington: United States General Accounting Office).

Gootnick, D. (2005) 'The Global Fund to Fight AIDS, TB and Malaria is Responding to Challenges but Needs Better Information and Documentation for Performance-based Funding', Report to Congressional Committees, GAO-05-639 (Washington: United States General Accounting Office).

Gootnick, D. (2007) 'Global Fund to Fight AIDS, TB and Malaria Has Improved Its Documentation of Funding Decisions but Needs Standardized Oversight Expectations and Assessments', Report to Congressional Committees (Washington: United States General Accounting Office).

Gore, C. (2004) 'MDGs and PRSPs: Are Poor Countries Enmeshed in a Global-Local Double Bind?' *Global Social Policy*, 4(3): 277–83.

Gosden, R. G. and A. P. Feinburg (2007) 'Editorial: Genetics and Epigenetics–Nature's Pen-and-Pencil Set', *New England Journal of Medicine*, 356(7): 731–733.

Gostin, L. O. (2007a) 'Why Rich Countries Should Care about the World's Least Health People', *JAMA*, 298(1): 89–92.

Gostin, L. O. (2007b) 'Meeting the Survival Needs of the World's Healthy People: A Proposed Model of Global Health Governance', *JAMA*, 298(2): 225–28.

Government of Canada (2004), 'An Act to Amend the Patent Act and the Food and Drugs Act (The Jean Chrétien Pledge to Africa)', Statutes of Canada, Chapter 23, assented to 14 May, http://www2.parl.gc.ca/HousePublications/Publication.aspx?Docid=2331620&file=4, date accessed 23 July 2008.

Grace, C. (2006) *Developing New Technologies to Address Neglected Diseases: The Role of Product Development Partnerships and Advanced Market Commitments* (London: DFID Health Resource Centre).

Grant, R. and R. Keohane (2005) 'Accountability and Abuses of Power in World Politics', *American Political Science Review*, 99(1): 29–43.

Grayson, K. (2004) 'Branding Transformation in Canadian Foreign Policy: Human Security', *Canadian Foreign Policy*, 11(2): 41–68.

Gregson, S., H. Waddell and S. Chandiwana (2001) 'School Education and HIV Control', *Journal of International Development*, Special Issue: Aids and Development in Africa, 13(4): 467–85.

Greene, W. (2007) 'The Emergence of India's Pharmaceutical Industry and Implications for the U.S. Generic Drug Market', Office of Economics Working Paper US International Trade Commission No 2007-05-A, http://www.usitc.gov/ind_econ_ana/research_ana/research_work_papers/documents/EC200705A.pdf, date accessed 11 October 2008.

GTT (Global Task Team) (2005) *Global Task Team on Improving Coordination among Multilateral Institutions and International Donors*. Final report, 14 June (Geneva: UNAIDS).

Gupta, S., B. Clements, M. T. Guin-Siu and L. Leruth (2002) 'Debt Relief and Public Health Spending in Heavily Indebted Poor Countries', *Bulletin of the World Health Organization*, 80(2): 151–57.

Gwatkin, D. R. (2005) 'How Much Would Poor People Gain from Faster Progress towards the Millennium Development Goals for Health?' *The Lancet*, 365: 813–17.

Gwatkin, D. R., S. Rutstein, K. Johnson, E. Suliman, A. Wagstaff and A. Amouzou (2007) *Socio-Economic Differences in Health, Nutrition and Population Within Developing Countries: An Overview* (Washington, DC: World Bank).

Haakonsson, S. J. and L. A. Richey (2007) 'TRIPs and Public Health: The Doha Declaration in Africa', *Development Policy Review*, 25(1): 71–90.

HAI (Health Action International) Europe (2001) *'Public-Private "Partnerships" Addressing Public Health Needs or Corporate Agendas?'*, Seminar Report, http://www.haiweb.org/campaign/PPI/seminar200011.doc, date accessed 24 August 2007.

Hall, R. B. and T. J. Biersteker (eds) (2002) *The Emergence of Private Authority in Global Governance* (Cambridge: Cambridge University Press).

Hamied, Y. K. (1988) 'The Indian Patents Act, 1970 and the Pharmaceutical Industry', National Seminar on Patent Laws, New Delhi, India.

Hanlon, J. (2000) 'How Much Debt Must Be Cancelled?' *Journal of International Development,* 12(6): 877–901.

Harris, G. (2004) 'At FDA, Strong Drug Ties and Less Monitoring', *New York Times*, 6 December, A1.

Hasenclever, A., P. Mayer and V. Rittberger (1997) *Theories of International Regimes* (Cambridge: Cambridge University Press).

Heffler, S., S. Smith, G. Won, M. K. Clemens et al (2002) 'Health Spending Projections for 2001–2011: The Latest Outlook', *Health Affairs* 21(2): 207–18.

Hein, W. (2007) 'Global Health Governance and WTO and TRIPS: Conflicts between "Global Market-Creation" and "Global Social Rights"', in Hein et al. (eds) *Global Health Governance and the Fight against HIV/AIDS*.

Hein, W. and L. Kohlmorgen (2008) 'Global Health Governance: Conflicts on Global Social Rights', *Global Social Policy,* 8: 80–108.

Hein, W., S. Bartsch and L. Kohlmorgen (eds) (2007) *Global Health Governance and the Fight against HIV/AIDS* (Basingstoke: Palgrave Macmillan).

Hein, W., S. Burris and C. Shearing (2009) 'Conceptual Models for Global Health Governance', in Buse, Kent, Wolfgang Hein, and Nick Drager (eds.) *Making Sense of Global Health Governance: The Policy Perspective* (Basingstoke: Palgrave Macmillan): 72–98.

Heinecken, L. (2001) 'Living in Terror: The Looming Security Threat to Southern Africa', *African Security Review,* 10(4).

Held, D. and M. Koenig-Archibugi (eds) (2006) *Global Governance and Public Accountability* (Malden, MA: Blackwell).

Henry, D. and J. Lexchin (2002) 'The Pharmaceutical Industry as a Medicine Provider', *The Lancet*, 360(9345): 1590–95.

HHS (US Department of Health and Human Services) (2001) 'HHS Initiative Prepares for Possible Bioterrorism Threat', August 16, http://www.os.dhhs.gov/news/press/2001pres/01fsbioterrorism.html, date accessed 9 June 2008.

Hill, M. (1997) *The Policy Process: A Reader* (London: Prentice Hall).

Hindustan Times (2008) 'Japanese firm buys Ranbaxy', June 12, 2008, http://epaper.hindustantimes.com/blog/2008/06/japanese-firm-buys-ranbaxy.html, date accessed 11 October 2008.

HIV Implementers (2007) http://www.hivimplementers.org/2007/index.htm.

HIV Implementers (2008) http://www.hivimplementers.org/.

Holbrooke, R. (2000) 'Battling the AIDS Pandemic', *Global Issues: AIDS*, July, http://usinfo.state.gov/journals/itgic/0700/ijge/gj02.htm, date accessed 12 June 2008.

Holm, K. (ed) (2001) 'Public-Private Partnerships for Health and Guaranteeing Drug Delivery Through Health Systems: Issues Needing Further Analysis', Report of a Meeting Hosted by the London School of Hygiene and Tropical Medicine, 27–28 September, London.

Hoover, R. N. (2000) 'Editorial: Cancer–Nature, Nurture, or Both', *New England Journal of Medicine,* 343(2): 135–36.

Howse, R. (2000) 'The Canadian Generic Medicines Panel: A Dangerous Precedent in Dangerous Times', *The Journal of World Intellectual Property,* 3(4): 493–507.

Huckel, C., L. Rieth and M. Zimmer (2007) 'Die Effektivität von Public-Private Partnerships' in A. Hasenclever, K. D. Wolf and M. Zürn (eds) *Macht und Ohnmacht Internationaler Institutionen* (Frankfurt: Campus).

Human Development Report (1997) *Human Development to Eradicate Poverty* (New York, Oxford: Oxford University Press).

Human Development Report (2003) *Millennium Development Goals: A Compact Among Nations to End Human Poverty* (New York, Oxford: Oxford University Press).

Hurley, G. (2007) 'Multilateral Debt: One Step Forward, How Many Back?' European Network on Debt and Development (EURODAD), Brussels.

IAVI (2006) *Imagining a World without AIDS: A History of the International AIDS Vaccine Initiative* (New York: International AIDS Vaccine Initiative).

ICASO (International Council of AIDS Service Organizations) (2004) 'NGO Perspectives on the Global Fund', http://www.hivpolicy.org/Library/HPP000321.pdf, date accessed 4 December 2008.

IDASA (2004) 'Public Opinion and HIV/AIDS: Facing Up to the Future?' Afrobarometer Briefing Paper No. 12, April.

IDASA (2005) 'AIDS and Public Opinion in South Africa', Afrobarometer Briefing Paper No. 14, August.

IDASA (2006) 'The Public Agenda: Change and Stability in South Africans' Ratings of National Priorities', Afrobarometer Briefing paper No. 45, June.

IFPMA (International Federation of Pharmaceutical Manufacturers and Associates) (2006) 'IFPMA Commentary on Oxfam's Report Patents versus Patients: Five Years after the Doha Declaration', http://www.ifpma.org/News/NewsReleaseDetail.aspx?nID=6097, date accessed 25 August 2007.

IMF Staff (2002) *Improving Market Access: Toward Greater Coherence between Aid and Trade* (Washington, DC: International Monetary Fund).

IMS Health Canada (2007) 'Pharmaceutical Market Performance', http://www.imshealthcanada.com/vgn/images/portal/cit_40000873/54/17/83605631IMS%20Charts%20Final%20ENGLISH%20march%2026.PDF, date accessed 29 October 2008.

Indo-Asian News Service (2008) 'Indian Firm, Clinton Foundation Sign Deal on Malaria Drugs', http://www.freshnews.in/indian-firms-clinton-foundation-sign-deal-on-malaria-drugs-33824, date accessed 10 November 2008.

Irwin, R. (ed.) (2001) *Ethics and Security in Canadian Foreign Policy* (Vancouver: UBC Press).

Jenson, J. and D. Saint-Martin (2003) 'New Routes to Social Cohesion? Citizenship and the Social Investment State', *Canadian Journal of Sociology,* 28(1): 77–99.

Jessop, B. (1999) 'Reflections on Globalization and Its (Il)logic(s)' in K. Olds, P. Dicken, P. F. Kelly, L. Kong and H. Yeung (eds) *Globalisation and the Asia-Pacific: Contested Territories* (London and New York: Routledge).

Jessop, B. (2004) 'Multi-Level Governance and Multi-Level Meta-Governance' in I. Bache and M. Flinders (eds) *Multi-level Governance* (Oxford: Oxford University Press).

Jeter, J. (2002) 'The Dumping Ground: As Zambia Courts Western Markets, Used Goods Arrive at a Heavy Price', *Washington Post*, 22 April, A1.

Joint World Bank/IMF Development Committee (2005) *'Note on the G8 Debt Relief Proposal: Assessment of Costs, Implementation Issues and Financing Options',* IMF/World Bank, Washington, DC, http://siteresources.worldbank.org/DEVCOMMINT/Documentation/20656508/DC2005-0023(E)-DebtRelief.pdf

Joseph, S. (2003) 'Pharmaceutical Corporations and Access to Drugs: The "Fourth Wave" of Corporate Human Rights Security', *Human Rights Quarterly,* 25(2): 425–52.

Kapur, V. and K. Basu (2005) 'Drug Coverage in Canada: Who Is at Risk?' *Health Policy,* 71(2): 181–93.

Kaul, I. (2006) 'Exploring the Policy Space between Markets and States: Global Public-Private Partnerships' in I. Kaul and P. Conceicao (eds) *The New Public Finance: Responding to Global Challenges* (New York: The United Nations Development Programme and Oxford University Press).

(Brown) Kaul, I., I. Grunberg and M. A. Stern (1999) *Global Public Goods: International Cooperation in the 21st Century* (New York; Oxford: Oxford University Press).

Kawachi, I. and B. P. Kennedy (2002) *The Health of Nations: Why Inequality is Harmful to Your Health* (New York: New Press).

Kawachi, I. and S. Wamala (2007) 'Poverty and Inequality in a Globalizing World' in I. Kawachi and S. Wamala (eds) *Globalisation and Health* (Oxford: Oxford University Press).

Keen, D. (1994) *The Benefits of Famine: A Political Economy of Famine and Relief in Southwestern Sudan, 1983–89* (Princeton: Princeton University Press).

Kenny, C. and D. Williams (2001) 'What Do We Know About Economic Growth? or, Why Don't We Know Very Much?', *World Development,* 29(1): 1–22.

Kenny, M. (1986) *Biotechnology: The University-Industrial Complex* (New Haven, Yale University Press).

Keohane, R. (2002) 'Global Governance and Democratic Accountability', Paper prepared for Miliband Lectures, LSE, London, http://www.lse.ac.uk/collections/LSEPublicLecturesAndEvents/pdf/20020701t1531t001.pdf, date accessed 5 November, 2008.

Keohane, R. and J. Nye (2001) 'Democracy, Accountability and Global Governance', manuscript, Cambridge, MA, Kennedy School of Government.

Kerry, V. B. and K. Lee (2007) 'TRIPS, the Doha Declaration and Paragraph 6 Decision: What are the Remaining Steps for Protecting Access to Medicines?' *Globalization and Health,* 3(3), http://www.globalizationandhealth.com/content/3/1/3/, date accessed 7 November 2007.

Khalfan, A., J. King and B. Thomas (2003) 'Advancing the Odious Debt Doctrine', CISDL Working Paperm Centre for International Sustainable Development Law, McGill University, Montreal.

Kickbusch, I. (1997) 'New Players for a New Era: Responding to the Global Public Health Challenges', *Journal of Public Health Medicine,* 19(2): 171–78.

Kickbusch, I. (2007) 'Foreword: Governing Interdependence' in W. B. Hein (ed.) *Global Health Governance and the Fight against HIV/AIDS* (Basingstoke: Palgrave MacMillan).

Killick, T. (2005) 'Don't Throw Money at Africa', *IDS Bulletin,* 36(3): 14–19.

Kimotho, E. (2005) 'HIV/AIDS and Governance in Kenya', results of interviews with MPs, Councillors and Electoral Commission, parliamentary staff and activists, Report for Justice Africa, London, December.

Kingdon, G. and J. Knight (2005) *Unemployment in South Africa, 1995–2003: Causes, Problems and Policies*. Oxford: Centre for the Study of African Economies, University of Oxford, http://www.csae.ox.ac.uk/conferences/2006-EOI-RPI/papers/csae/Kingdon.pdf

Kingdon, J. (1995) *Agendas, Alternatives, and Public Policies,* 2nd edn. (New York: Harper-Collins).

Kirk, J. and P. McKenna (1997) *Canada-Cuba Relations: The Other Good Neighbour Policy* (Gainesville: University of Florida Press).

Kirton, J. and J. Mannell (2007) 'The G8 and Global Health Governance' in Cooper, et al. (eds) *Governing Global Health.*

Kirton, J. et al. (2006) 'Gleneagles Final Compliance Report, July 8, 2005, to June 1, 2006', Toronto: G8 Research Group, University of Toronto, http://www.g8.utoronto.ca/2005g8compliance060612c.pdf

Koelble, T. (2004) 'Economic Policy in the Post-Colony: South Africa between Keynesian Remedies and Neoliberal Pain', *New Political Economy* 9(1): 57–78.

Kohlmorgen, L. (2007) 'International Governmental Organizations and Global Health Governance: the Role of the World Health Organization, World Bank and UNAIDS' in Hein, et al. (eds) *Global Health Governance and the Fight against HIV/AIDS.*

Kovach, H., C. Neligan and S. Burall (2003) *Power without Accountability? The Global Accountability Report 2003* (London: The One World Trust).

Krasner, S. and C. Pascual (2005) 'Addressing State Failure', *Foreign Affairs*, 84(4): 153–63.
Krugman, P. (2008) 'Fighting off Depression', *International Herald Tribune*, Tuesday, 6 January, p. 7.
Kumaranayake, L. and S. Lake (2002) 'Regulations in the Context of Global Markets' in K. Lee et al. (eds) *Crossing Boundaries: Health Policy in a Globalizing World* (Cambridge: Cambridge University Press).
Kutty, A. (2000) 'Ranbaxy Thrust on Research and Development', Pharmbiz.com, 19 July, http://www.pharmabiz.com/article/detnews.asp?articleid=11287&sectionid=46, date accessed 14 August 2008.
Labonté, R. and T. Schrecker (2004) 'Committed to Health for All? How the G7/G8 Rate', *Social Science and Medicine* 59(8): 1661–76.
Labonté, R. and T. Schrecker (2005) *The G8, Africa and Global Health: A Platform for Global Health Equity for the 2005 Summit* (London: Nuffield Trust).
Labonté, R. and T. Schrecker (2006) 'The G8 and Global Health: What Now? What Next?' *Canadian Journal of Public Health*, 97(1): 35–38.
Labonté, R. and T. Schrecker (2007a) 'Foreign Policy Matters: A Normative View of the G8 and Population Health', *Bulletin of the World Health Organization*, 85(9): 185–91.
Labonté, R. and T. Schrecker (2007b) 'Globalization and Social Determinants of Health: The Role of the Global Marketplace' (part 2 of 3), *Globalization and Health*, 3(6), http://www.globalizationandhealth.com/content/3/1/6.
Labonté, R., T. Schrecker and A. S. Gupta (2005) 'A Global Health Equity Agenda for the G8 Summit', *British Medical Journal*, 350(7490): 533–36.
Labonté, R., T. Schrecker, D. Sanders and W. Meeus (2004) *Fatal Indifference: The G8, Africa and Global Health* (Cape Town: University of Cape Town Press).
Labonte, R., C. Blouin, M. Chopra, K. Lee, C. Packer, M. Rowson, et al. (2007) *Towards Health-Equitable Globalization: Rights, Regulation and Redistribution, Globalization Knowledge Network Final Report to the Commission on Social Determinants of Health.* Ottawa: Institute of Population Health, University of Ottawa, http://www.who.int/social_determinants/resources/gkn_final_report_042008.pdf.
Lake, S. (2004) 'GFATM Tracking Study: Tanzania', Macroeconomics and Sector background paper, London School of Hygiene and Tropical Medicine, London, http://www.theglobalfund.org/en/files/links_resources/library/studies/IE6_full.pdf, date accessed 2 May 2007.
Lanjouw, J. O. and I. M. Cockburn (2001) 'New Pills for Poor People? – Empirical Evidence after GATT', *World Development*, 29(2): 265–69.
Lee, K. (1999) 'Globalization, Communicable Disease and Equity: A Look Back and Forth', *Development*, 42(4): 35–39.
Lee, K. and J. Collin (eds) (2005) *Global Change and Health* (Maidenhead, UK: Open University Press.
Lee, K., K. Buse and S. Fustukian (eds) (2002) *Health Policy in a Globalizing World* (Cambridge: Cambridge University Press).
Lele, U., N. Sarna, R. Govindaraj and Y. Konstantopoulos (2004) *Global Health Programs, Millennium Development Goals and the World Bank's Role: Assessing Challenges of Globalization: An Independent Evaluation of the World Bank's Approach to Global Programs* (Washington: World Bank Operations Evaluation Department).
Lele, U., R. Ridker and J. Upadhay (2005) 'Health Systems Capacities in Developing Countries and Global Health Initiatives on Communicable Diseases', *Secretariat of the International Task Force on Global Public Goods. Expert Paper Series One: Infectious Disease* (Stockholm: Secretariat of the International Task Force on Global Public Goods), http://www.gpgtaskforce.org/uploads/files/174.pdf, date accessed 16 October 2008.

Levy, M. A. and M. Chernyak (2006) 'Sustainable Development Partnerships', *Environment*, 48: 3–5.

Lewis, J. M. (2005) *Health Policy and Politics: Networks, Ideas and Power* (Melbourne: IP Communications).

Lexchin, J. (1993) 'Pharmaceuticals, Patents, and Politics: Canada and Bill C-22', *International Journal of Health Services*, 23(1): 147–60.

Lexchin, J. (1997) 'After Compulsory Licensing: Coming Issues in Canadian Pharmaceutical Policy and Politics', *Health Policy*, 40(1): 69–80.

Lexchin, J. (2004) 'The Effect of Generic Competition on the Price of Brand-Name Drugs', Health Policy, 68(1): 47–54.

Lexchin, J. (2007) 'No Excuse for Denying Drug Coverage: It's Time to End Canadians' Long Wait for Pharmacare', Canadian Centre for Policy Alternatives Monitor Issue, 1 December, http://www.policyalternatives.ca/monitorissues/2007/12/monitorissue1795/?pa=bb736455, date accessed 3 October 2008.

Loeppky, M. (2005b) '"Biomania" and US Foreign Policy', *Millennium: Journal of International Studies*, 34(1): 85–113.

Loeppky, R. (2005a) *Encoding Capital: the Political Economy of the Human Genome Project* (New York: Routledge).

Löfgren, H. (2007) 'The Global Biopharma Industry and the Rise of Indian Drug Multinationals: Implications for Australian Generics Policy', *Australian New Zealand Health Policy*, 4, 7pp., http://www.anzhealthpolicy.com/content/pdf/1743-8462-4-10.pdf, date accessed 10 November 2008.

Logan, C., T. Fujiwara and V. Parish (2006) 'Citizens and the State in Africa: New Results from Afrobarometer Round 3', Afrobarometer Paper No. 61, May.

Loughlin, K. and V. Berridge (2002) *Global Health Governance: Historical Dimensions of Global Governance* (Geneva: World Health Organization and London School of Hygiene and Tropical Medicine).

Love, J. (2001) 'Compulsory Licensing: Models for State Practice in Developing Countries, Access to Medicine and Compliance with the WTO TRIPS Accord', paper prepared for the LSHTM (London School of Hygiene and Tropical Medicine).

Love, R. (2007) 'Corporate Wealth or Public Health? WTO/TRIPS Flexibilities and Access to HIV/AIDS Antiretroviral Drugs by Developing Countries', *Development in Practice*, 17(2): 208–19.

LSHTM (2003) *Tracking the Global Fund in four countries: an interim report* (London: School of Hygiene and Tropical Medicine).

MacDonald, L. (1997) 'Going Global: the Politics in Canada's Foreign Economic Relations' in W. Clement (ed.) *Understanding Canada: Building on the New Canadian Political Economy* (Montreal: McGill-Queen's University Press).

MacDonald, R. and R. Horton (2008) 'Global Health and the G8 – Is Power Just Too Sweet to Share?' *The Lancet*, 372(9620): 99–100.

Mackay, B. and C. Laurence (2005) 'Putting the "Three Ones" to Work', National AIDS Commissions, Futures Group Briefing, February, http://www.constellafutures.com/Documents/NACs_Final.pdf, date accessed 13 June 2007.

MacLean, S. (2007) 'Health in Development', in A. McGrew and N. Poku (eds) *Globalization, Development and Human Security* (Cambridge: Polity).

MacLean, S. (2008) 'Microbes, Mad Cows and Militaries: Exploring the Links between Health and Security', *Security Dialogue*, 39(5): 543–62.

MacLean, S. and D. MacLean (2008) '(Transnational) Affairs of the Heart: Political Economy and the Globalization of Cardiovascular Disease', *Global Health Governance*, 2(1), http://www.ghgj.org/.

Malena, C. (2004) 'Strategic Partnership: Challenges and Best Practices in the Management of Governance of Multi-Stakeholder Partnerships Involving UN and Civil Society Actors', Background Paper, Multi-Stakeholder Workshop on Partnerships and UN-Civil Society Relations, Pocantico, New York.

Mandel, S. (2006) *Debt Relief as if People Mattered: A Rights-Based Approach to Debt Sustainability* (London: New Economics Foundation), http://www.neweconomics.org/gen/z_sys_publicationdetail.aspx?pid=223.

March, J. G. and J. P. Olsen (1989) *Rediscovering Institutions. The Organizational Basis of Politics* (New York: The Free Press).

Marmot, M. (2003) 'Understanding Social Inequalities in Health', *Perspectives in Biology and Medicine*, 46(3 Supplement): S9–S23.

Marmot, M. and R. Wilkinson (eds) (2006) *Social Determinants of Health* (Oxford: Oxford University Press).

Martens, J. (2007) 'Multistakeholder Partnerships: Future Models of Multilateralism', No. 29, Dialogue on Globalization, Fredrich Ebert Foundation, http://library.fes.de/pdf-files/iez/04244.pdf, date accessed 23 October 2008.

Martin, M. (2004) 'Assessing the HIPC Initiative: The Key Policy Debates' in J. Teunissen and A. Akkerman (eds) *HIPC Debt Relief: Myths and Realities* (The Hague: Forum on Debt and Development).

Matlin, S. et al. (eds) 2008: Health Partnerships Review. Focusing collaborative efforts on research and innovation for the health of the poor. Global Forum for Health Research, Geneva.

Matthews, D. and V. Munoz-Tellez (2006) 'Bilateral Technical Assistance and TRIPs: The United States, Japan and the European Communities in Comparative Perspective', *The Journal of World Intellectual Property*, 9(6): 629–53.

May, C. (2000) *A Global Political Economy of Intellectual Property Rights: The New Enclosures?* (London and New York: Routledge).

May, C. and S. K. Sell (2006) *Intellectual Property Rights: a Critical History* (London: Lynne Rienner Publishers).

McCoy, D. (2007) 'The World Bank's New Health Strategy: Cause for Alarm?', *The Lancet*, 369(9572): 1499–501.

McGrew, A. (2002) 'Liberal-Internationalism: Between Realism and Cosmopolitanism' in D. Held and A. McGrew (eds) *Governing Globalization: Power, Authority and Global Governance* (Cambridge: Polity)

McGrew, A. (2006) 'Globalization and Global Politics' in J. Baylis and S. Smith (eds) *The Globalization of World Politics: An Introduction to International Relations* (Oxford: Oxford University Press).

McInnes, C. and K. Lee (2006) 'Health, Security and Foreign Policy', *Review of International Studies*, 32(1): 5–23.

McKinsey & Company (2003) *Global Health Partnerships: Assessing Country Consequences. A report commissioned by the Bill and Melinda Gates Foundation* (New Jersey: Mc Kinsey & Company).

McMillan, M., Zwane, A. P., and Ashraf, N. (2006) 'My Policies or Yours: Does OECD Support for Agriculture Increase Poverty in Developing Countries?' in A. Harrison (ed.) *Globalization and Poverty* (Chicago: University of Chicago Press for National Bureau of Economic Research).

McPherson, M. (2003) 'Macroeconomic Models of the Impact of HIV/AIDS', Background Paper, Center for Business and Government, Harvard University, http://www.ksg.harvard.edu/m-rcbg/hiv-aids/ksg/McPherson_Macroeconomic.models.pdf, date accessed 21 July 2007.

McQuaig, L. (2007) *Holding the Bully's Coat: Canada and the U.S. Empire* (Toronto: Doubleday Canada).

Medical Research Council (UK) www.mrc.ac.uk/Our Research/Research Portfolios/index.htm, date accessed 8 September 2007.

Menon, D. (2001) 'Pharmaceutical Cost Control in Canada: Does it Work?' *Health Affairs*, 2(3): 92–103.

Milanovic, B. (2003). 'The Two Faces of Globalization: Against Globalization as We Know It', *World Development,* 31(4): 667–83.

Ministers of Foreign Affairs of Brazil, France, Indonesia, Norway, Senegal, South Africa, and Thailand (2007) 'Oslo Ministerial Declaration–Global Health: A Pressing Foreign Policy Issue of Our Time', *The Lancet*, 369(9596): 1373–78.

Moellendorf, D. (2002) *Cosmopolitan Justice* (Boulder: Westview).

Molyneux, M. (2007) *Change and Continuity in Social Protection in Latin America: Mothers at the Service of the State?* (Geneva: United Nations Research Institute for Social Development).

Morgan, S. (2004) 'Drug Spending in Canada: Recent Trends and Causes', Medical Care, 42(7): 635–42.

Morin, J. F. (2006) 'Tripping Up TRIPs Debates: IP and Health in Bilateral Agreements', *International Journal of Intellectual Property Management,* 1(1/2): 37–53.

Morrison, D. (1998) *Aid and Ebb Tide: A History of CIDA and Canadian Development Assistance* (Waterloo, Ont.: Wilfried Laurier University Press in association with the North-South Institute).

Moser, K. A., Leon, D. A. and Gwatkin, D. R. (2005) 'How Does Progress towards the Child Mortality Millennium Development Goal Affect Inequalities between the Poorest and Least Poor? Analysis of Demographic and Health Survey Data', *British Medical Journal*, 331(7526): 1180–82.

Mosley, L. (2006) 'Constraints, Opportunities, and Information: Financial Market-Government Relations around the World' in Bardhan, P., S. Bowles and M. Wallerstein (eds) *Globalization and Egalitarian Redistribution* (New York and Princeton: Russell Sage Foundation and Princeton University Press).

MSF (Médecins Sans Frontières) (2005) 'Untangling the Web of Price Reductions: A Pricing Guide for the Purchase of ARVs in Developing Countries', 10th Edition, http://www.doctorswithoutborders.org/publications/reports/2007/Untangling-the-Web-10th-Edition-July2007.pdf , date accessed 5 November 2008.

MSF, HAI and CPTech (1999a) *An Open Letter to WTO Member States*, http://lists.essential.org/pharm-policy/msg00291.html, date accessed 26 August 2007.

MSF, HAI and CPTech (1999b) *Amsterdam Statement to WTO Member States on Access to Medicine,* http://www.cptech.org/ip/health/amsterdamstatement.html, date accessed 26 August 2007.

Mufunda, J., R. Chatora, Y. Ndambakuwa, P. Nyarango, J. Chifamba, A. Kosia and H. Sparks (2006) 'Prevalence of Noncommunicable Diseases in Zimbabwe: Results from Analysis of Data from the National Central Registry and Urban Survey', *Ethnicity and Disease,* 16(3): 718–22.

Mulay Ndikumana, L. and J. K. Boyce (2003) 'Public Debts and Private Assets: Explaining Capital Flight from Sub-Saharan African Countries', *World Development,* 31(1): 107–30.

Muraskin, W. (2004) 'The Global Alliance for Vaccines and Immunization: Is It a New Model for Effective Public–Private Cooperation in International Public Health?' *American Journal of Public Health*, 94(11): 1922–25.

Murumba, S. (1998) 'Globalizing Intellectual Property: Linkage and the Challenge of a Justice-Constituency', *University of Pennsylvania Journal of International Economic Law,* Summer: 435–60.

Musungu, S. and G. Dutfield (2003) *'Multilateral Agreement and a TRIPs-plus World: the World Intellectual Property Organisation (WIPO)'*, Issue Paper 3 (Geneva and Ottawa: QUNO and QIAP).

Naidoo, J. (2006) 'The Impact of HIV/AIDS on Crime in South Africa', http://www.sarpn.org.za, date accessed on 16 December 2006.

National Intelligence Council (2000) *The Global Infectious Disease Threat and Its Implications for the United States* (Washington DC: National Intelligence Council).

Nelson, J. (2002) *Building Partnerships: Cooperation between the United Nations System and the Private Sector* (New York: United Nations Department of Public Information).

Neubauer, D. (2005) 'Globalization and Emerging Governance Modalities', *Environmental Health and Preventive Medicine,* 10(5): 286–94.

'New Cancer Genes are Low-risk' (2007) *Globe and Mail,* 29 May, p. L4.

NIC (2005) 'Mapping Sub-Saharan Africa's Future', paper summarizing a one-day conference of US experts on Africa convened in January 2005 and sponsored by the National Intelligence Council, CR 2005–02, March.

NIHR (National Institute for Health Research, UK), http://www.nihr.ac.uk/programmes_research_programmes_eme_faq.aspx, date accessed 10 November 2008.

Nishtar, S. (2004) 'Public-Private Partnerships in Health – A Global Call to Action', *Health Research Policy and Systems*, 2(5): 102–6.

Nissanke, M. and E. Thorbecke (2006) 'Channels and Policy Debate in the Globalization-Inequality-Poverty Nexus', *World Development*, 34(8): 1338–60.

Norwegian Ministry of Health and Care Services (2007) 'National Strategy to Reduce Social Inequalities in Health', Report No. 20 (2006–2007) to the Storting (Oslo: Norwegian Ministry of Health and Care Services), available at http://ec.europa.eu/health/ph_ determinants/ socioeconomics/documents/norway_rd01_ en.pdf, date accessed 20 July 2007.

O'Brien, R., A. M. Goetz, J. A. Scholte and M. Williams (2000) *Contesting Global Governance: Multilateral Economic Institutions and Global Social Movements* (Cambridge: Cambridge University Press).

O'Manique, C. (2007) 'Global Health and Universal Human Rights: The Case for G8 Accountability', in Cooper et al. (eds) *Governing Global Health.*

OECD (2005) *Paris Declaration on Aid Effectiveness: Ownership, Harmonisation, Alignment, Results, and Mutual Accountability* (High Level Forum), http://www.oecd.org/dataoecd/11/41/34428351.pdf , date accessed 5 March 2007.

OECD (2008) *Growing Unequal? Income Distribution and Poverty in OECD Countries* (Washington, DC: OECD).

OECD Development Assistance Committee (2007) 'Development Aid from OECD Countries Fell 5.1% in 2006', OECD, http://www.oecd.org/document/17/0,2340,en_2649_201185_38341265_1_1_1_1,00.html.

OECD Development Assistance Committee (2008) 'Debt Relief is Down: Other ODA Rises Slightly', OECD, http://www.oecd.org/document/8/0,3343,en_2649_34447_40381960_1_1_1_1,00.html.

Office of the World Health Organization Representative in China and Social Development Department of China State Council Development Research Center (2005) *China: Health, Poverty and Economic Development,* Macroeconomics and Health Initiative (Geneva: WHO), http://www.who.int/macrohealth/action/CMH_China.pdf

OGAC (2005) 'The President's Emergency Plan for AIDS Relief. General Policy Guidance for All Bilateral Programs' Office of the Global AIDS Coordinator, http://www.state.gov/documents/organization/57252.pdf, date accessed 10 October 2008.

OGAC (2006) 'The U.S. President's Emergency Plan for AIDS Relief HIV Prevention among Drug Users Guidance #1: Injection Heroin Use March 2006', http://www.state.gov/documents/organization/64140.pdf, date accessed 16 October 2008.

OGAC (2007) *The Power of Partnerships: The President's Emergency Plan for AIDS Relief. Third Annual Report to the Congress* (Washington DC: OGAC).

OGAC (2008) *PEPFAR Reauthorization. Fact Sheet*, http://www.pepfar.gov/press/107735.htm, date accessed 29 September 2008.

Okediji, R. (2004) 'Back to Bilateralism? Pendulum Swings in International Intellectual Property Protection', *University of Ottawa Law and Technology Journal*, 1(1/2): 125–47.

Okeke, I., R. Laxminarayan, Z. A. Bhutta, A. G. Duse, P. Jenkins, T. F. O'Brien et al. (2005a) 'Antimicrobial Resistance in Developing Countries', Part I: Recent Trends and Current Status, *Lancet Infectious Diseases*, 5(8): 481–93.

Okeke, I., K. Klugman, Z. Bhutta, A. Duse, P. Jenkins, T. O'Brien et al. (2005b) 'Antimicrobial Resistance in Developing Countries', Part II: Strategies for Containment, *Lancet Infectious Diseases*, 5(9): 568–80.

Okie, S. (2006) 'Global Health–The Gates-Buffett Effect', *New England Journal of Medicine*, 355(11): 1084–88.

Oomman, N., M. Bernstein and S. Rosenzweig (2008) *The Numbers Behind the Stories. PEPFAR Funding for Fiscal Years 2004–2006* (Washington: Center for Global Development), http://www.cgdev.org/section/initiatives/_active/hivmonitor/pepfar data ?print=1 date, date accessed 28 August 2008.

Ooms, G., W. Van Damme, B. Baker, P. Zeitz and T. Schrecker (2008) 'The "Diagonal" Approach to Global Fund Financing: A Cure for the Broader Malaise of Health Systems?', *Globalization and Health*, 4(6), http://www.globalizationandhealth.com/content/4/1/6.

Orbinsky, J. (2007) 'Global Health: Social Movements, and Governance' in Cooper et al. (eds) *Governing Global Health.*

Oscampo, J. A. and L. Taylor (1998) 'Why Trade Liberalisation in Developing Economies: Modest Benefits but Problems with Productivity Growth, Macro Prices, and Income Distribution', *The Economic Journal*, 108 (September).

Ostergard, R. (2002) 'Politics in the Hot Zone: AIDS and National Security in Africa', *Third World Quarterly*, 23(2): 333–50.

Osterholm, M. (2005) 'Preparing for the Next Pandemic', *Foreign Affairs*, 84(4): 24–37.

Ostry, S. (1997) *The Post Cold War Trading System: Who's In First? (*Chicago: The University of Chicago Press).

Owen, J. W. and O. Roberts (2005) 'Globalization, Health and Foreign Policy: emerging linkages and interests', *Globalization and Health*, 1(1), 12pp., http://www.globalizationandhealth.com/content/1/1/12, date accessed 7 June 2008.

Oxfam (2001) 'Patent Injustice: How World Trade Rules Threaten the Health of Poor People', http://www.oxfam.org.uk/what_we_do/issues/health/downloads/patentinjustice.pdf, date accessed 10 October 2008.

Oxfam (2002) 'False Hope or New Start? The Global Fund to Fight HIV/AIDS, TB and Malaria', Oxfam Briefing Paper No. 24, http://www.oxfam.org.uk/what_we_do/issues/health/downloads/bp24_globalfund.pdf, date accessed 5 November 2008.

Palan, R. (ed.) (2000) *Global Political Economy: Contemporary Theories* (London and New York: Routledge).

Paluzzi, J. and P. Farmer (2005) 'The Wrong Question', *Development,* 48(1): 12–18.

Patent and Trademark Office, US Department of Commerce (1994) 'Public Hearing on the Patenting of Biotechnological Inventions', 17 October.

Patrick, S, (2006) 'Weak States and Global Threats: Fact or Fiction?', *The Washington Quarterly,* 29(2): 27–53.

Patterson, A. (2005) 'Weak and Ineffective? African States and Recent International AIDS Policies' in A. Patterson (ed.) *The African State and the AIDS Crisis* (Aldershot: Ashgate).

Patterson, A. (2006) *The Politics of AIDS in Africa* (Boulder: Lynne Rienner Publishers).

Pattison, N., L. Warren and F. Clemente (2003) 'Drug Industry Profits: Hefty Pharmaceutical Company Margins Dwarf Other Industries', *Public Citizen Report,* June.

Payne, A. (2006) 'Blair, Brown and the Gleneagles Agenda: Making Poverty History, or Confronting the Global Politics of Unequal Development?' *International Affairs,* 82(5): 917–35.

Pearce, C., R. Greenhill and J. Glennie (2005) 'In the Balance: Why Debts Must be Cancelled Now to Meet the Millennium Development Goals', Jubilee Debt Campaign, London, http://www.makepovertyhistory.org/docs/inthebalance.pdf, date accessed 7 January 2009.

PEPFAR (2006) 'FY 05 Annual Program Results Partner Count. Country: Tanzania', 24 January, http://www.state.gov/documents/organization/60680.pdf, date accessed 10 May 2007.

PEPFAR (2008) 'Reauthorizing PEPFAR', http://www.pepfar.gov/press/107735.htm, date accessed 29 August 2008.

PEPFAR/WB/GFATM (2006) *Joint Coordination Meeting on HIV/AIDS. January 10–11, Washington DC Report* (Washington DC: Center for Global Development), http://www.cgdev.org/doc/blog/Coordshort.pdf, date accessed 5 June 2007.

Peters, G. (1998) 'Managing Horizontal Government: The Politics of Coordination', *Public Administration,* 76 (Summer): 295–311.

Peterson, S. (2002) 'Epidemic Disease and National Security', *Security Studies,* 12(2): 43–81.

Phadke, A. R. (1998) *Drug Supply and Use: Towards a Rational Policy in India* (New Delhi: Sage Publications).

PhRMA, 'Industry Profile', http://www.phrma.org/2005_industry_profile/9/, date accessed 10 November 2008.

PhRMA, http://www.phrma.org/about_phrma/, date accessed 10 November 2008.

PhRMA (2006) 'Special 301 Submission', Appendix C, 12 January, www.phrma.org.

PMPRB (2007) 'Annual Report 2007', http://www.pmprb-cepmb.gc.ca/english/View.asp?x=1068&mp=91, date accessed 3 October 2008.

Pogge, T. (2002) 'Human Rights and Human Responsibilities' in P. De Greiff and C. Cronin (eds) *Global Justice and Transnational Politics* (Cambridge, MA: MIT Press).

Pogge, T. (2004) 'The First United Nations Millennium Development Goal: A Cause for Celebration?' *Journal of Human Development,* 5(3): 377–97.

Pogge, T. (2005) 'Recognized and Violated by International Law: The Human Rights of the Global Poor', *Leiden Journal of International Law,* 18(4): 717–45.

Pogge, T. (2007) 'Severe Poverty as a Human Rights Violation' in T. Pogge (ed.) *Freedom from Poverty as a Human Right: Who Owes What to the Very Poor?* (Oxford: Oxford University Press).

Poku, N. (2002) 'The Global AIDS Fund: Context and Opportunity', *Third World Quarterly,* 23(2): 283–98.

Popkin, B. (2006) 'Global Nutrition Dynamics: The World is Shifting Rapidly toward a Diet Linked with Noncommunicable Disease', *American Journal of Clinical Nutrition*, 84: 289–98.

Porter, J., K. Lee and J. Ogden (2002) 'The Globalisation of DOTS: Tuberculosis as a Global Emergency' in K. Lee, et al. (eds) *Health Policy in a Globalising World* (Cambridge: Cambridge University Press).

Pradhan, J. P. (2006) 'Global Competitiveness of Indian Pharmaceutical Industry: Trends and Strategies', Working Paper No: 2006/05, Institute for Studies in Industrial Development, http://isidev.nic.in/pdf/wp0605.pdf, date accessed 30 September 2008.

Pratt, C. (2001) 'Moral Vision and Foreign Policy: The Case of Canadian Development Assistance' in R. Irwin (ed.) *Ethics and Security in Canadian Foreign Policy* (Vancouver: UBC Press).

PTI (Press Trust of India) (2006) 'India Pharma Firms Agree to Cut Prices of AIDS Tests', Press Trust of India Limited, https://global.factiva.com (Document PRTRIN0020060114e21d0001k), date accessed 14 August 2008.

Public Health Agency of Canada (2007) 'Global Public Health Intelligence Network', http://www.phac-aspc.gc.ca/media/nr-rp/2004/2004_gphin-rmispbk_e.html, date accessed, 13 June 2007.

Quattek, K. (2000) 'The Economic Impact of AIDS in South Africa: A Dark Cloud on the Horizon', in *HIV and AIDS: A Threat to the African Renaissance?* Konrad Adenauer Foundation Occasional Paper, June.

Radelet, S. (2004) 'The Global Fund to Fight AIDS, Tuberculosis and Malaria: Progress, Potential, and Challenges for the Future', http://www.cgdev.org/doc/commentary/GFATM%20full%20report.pdf, date accessed 5 November.

Radelet, S. and K. Caines (2005) 'The Global Fund to Fight AIDS, TB, and Malaria: Performance and Vision', A Report Prepared for the UK Department for International Development, 17 February (Washington, DC: Center for Global Development), http://www.cgdev.org/doc/commentary/GlobalFundDFID.pdf, date accessed 20 October 2008.

Raghavan, C. (2000) 'EC- Canada Patent Ruling Raises More Questions over DSU', Third World Network, http://www.twnside.org.sg/title/raises.htm, date accessed 16 August 2008.

Ramiah, I. and M. R. Reich (2005) 'Public-Private Partnerships and Antiretroviral Drugs for HIV/AIDS: Lessons from Botswana', *Health Affairs*, 24(2): 545–51

Ranson, K. A., T. Sinha, M. Chatterjee, A. Achary, A. Bhavsar, S. S. Morris and A. J. Mills (2006) 'Making Health Insurance Work for the Poor: Learning from the Self-Employed Women's Association's (SEWA) Community-Based Health Insurance Scheme in India', *Social Science and Medicine*, 62(3): 707–20.

Reddy, S. and T. Pogge (2005) *How Not to Count the Poor*Social Science Research Network, http://papers.ssrn.com/sol3/papers.cfm?abstract_id=893159, date accessed 16 February 2009.

Reich, M. (ed.) (2002) *Public-Private Partnerships for Public Health* (Cambridge: Harvard University Press).

Reid, M. A. and E. J. Pearse (2003) 'Whither the World Health Organisation?', *Medical Journal*, 78(1): 9–12.

Reinicke, W. (1997) 'Global Public Policy' *Foreign Affairs*, 76(6): 127–38.

Reinicke, W., F. Deng, T. Benner and M. Witte (2000) *Critical Choices. The United Nations, Networks, and the Future of Global Governance* (Ottawa: IDRC).

Renz, L. and J. Atienza (2006) *International Grantmaking Update: A Snapshot of U.S. Foundation Trends* (New York: The Foundation Center).

Rice, X., D. Campbell and M. White (2007) 'UK Attacks Kenya over Role in Search for Missing £1bn', *The Guardian*, 1 September.

Richardson, W. and J. Allegrante (2001) 'Shaping the Future of Health through Global Partnerships' in C. E. Koop (ed.) *Critical Issues in Global Health* (San Francisco: Jossey-Bass).

Richey, Lisa Ann (2008) *Population Politics and Development: From the Policies to the Clinics* (New York and London: Palgrave Macmillan).

Richter, J. (2003) *We the Peoples or We the Corporations? Critical Reflections on UN-Business Partnerships* (Geneva: IB-FAN).

Richter, J. (2004) 'Public-Private Partnerships for Health: A Trend with no Alternatives?' *Development*, 47(2): 43–48.

Ricupeiro, R. (2006) 'The Paradoxes and Contradictions of World Trade', *Bridges Monthly Review*, 10(5): 17–20.

Risse, T. (2004) 'Transnational Governance and Legitimacy; paper presented at ECPR Standing Group on International Relations Conference', The Hague, 9–12 September.

Rittberger, V., C. Huckel, L. Rieth and M. Zimmer (2008) 'Inclusive Global Institutions for a Global Political Economy' in V. Rittberger and M. Nettesheim (eds) *Authority in the Global Political Economy* (Houndmills: Palgrave Macmillan).

Robinson, D., T. Hewitt and J. Harriss (2000) 'Why Inter-organizational Relationships Matter' in D. Robinson et al. (eds) *Managing Development. Understanding Inter-organizational Relationships* (London: Sage Publications).

Rockefeller Foundation (1994a) *Bellagio Report – Accelerating the Development of Preventive HIV Vaccines for the World – Summary Report and Recommendations of an International Ad Hoc Scientific Committee* (New York: International AIDS Vaccine Initiative).

Rockefeller Foundation (1994b) *Paris Report – Accelerating the Development of Preventive HIV Vaccines for the World: Summary Report and Recommendations of an International Ad Hoc Scientific Committee* (New York: International AIDS Vaccine Initiative).

Rockefeller Foundation (1995) *New York Report – Accelerating the Development of Preventive HIV Vaccines for the World: Financial and Structural Issues* (New York: International AIDS Vaccine Initiative).

Rockefeller Foundation (2007) 'Product Development Partnerships' http://www.rockfound.org/efforts/partners/partners.shtml, date accessed 10 May 2007.

Rodin, J. (2007) 'Opening Plenary Address: Navigating the Global American South – Global Health and Global Initiatives', University of North Carolina, Center for Global Initiatives, 19 April.

Romanow, R. (2002) *Building on Values: The Future of Health Care in Canada*, Final Report of the Commission on the Future of Health Care in Canada, November (Ottawa: Government of Canada).

Rosenau, J. (2005) 'Global Governance as Disaggregated Complexity' in A. B. and M. Hoffman (eds) *Contending Perspectives on Global Governance: Coherence, Contestation and World Order* (London and New York: Routledge).

Rosenau, J. N. (1997) *Along the Domestic-Foreign Frontier: Exploring Governance in a Turbulent World* (Cambridge: Cambridge University Press).

Rosenau, J. N. and O. Czempiel (1992) *Governance without Government: Order and Change in World Politics* (Cambridge: Cambridge University Press).

Rx&D (2001) 'Bill S-17: A Necessary First Step to Bring Canada's Patent Act to Internationally Competitive Standards', Submission to the House of Commons Standing Committee on Industry, Science and Technology by Canada's Research-Based

Pharmaceutical Companies, 29 May, http://www.canadapharma.org, date accessed 14 August 2008.

Ryan, L., E. Sarriot, P. Bachrach, B. Dude, D. Cantor, J. Rockwood, J. Lissfelt and V. Barnes (2008) *Evaluation of the Organizational Effectiveness and Efficiency of the Global Fund to Fight AIDS, Tuberculosis, and Malaria, Results from Study Area 1 of the Five-Year Evaluation* (Calverton: Macro International Inc), http://www.theglobalfund.org/en/files/terg/TERG_SA1_FullReport.pdf

Ryan, M. P. (1998) *Knowledge Diplomacy: Global Competition and the Politics of Intellectual Property* (Washington: Brooking Institution Press).

Sabatier, P. A. (ed.) (1999) *Theories of the Policy Process* (Boulder; Oxford: Westview Press).

Sachs, J. (1999) 'Helping the World's Poorest', *The Economist*, 14 August, 17–20.

Sachs, J. (2003) 'Achieving the Millennium Development Goals: Health in the Developing World', Speech at the Second Global Consultation of the Commission on Macroeconomics and Health, World Health Organization, Geneva, http://www.earthinstitute.columbia.edu/about/director/pubs/CMHSpeech102903.pdf

Sachs, J. (2005) 'Health in the Developing World: Achieving the Millennium Development Goals' in William H. Foege et al. (eds) *Global Health Leadership and Management* (San Francisco: John Wile & Sons Inc.).

Sachs, J. (2007) 'Beware False Tradeoffs', *Foreign Affairs*, 23 January, http://www.foreignaffairs.org/special/global_health/sachs, date accessed 7 November 2008.

Santa Cruz, M. (2007) 'Intellectual Property Provisions in European Union Trade Agreements: Implications for Developing Countries', Issue Paper 20, International Centre for Trade and Sustainable Development, Geneva.

Sassen, S. (1996) *Losing Control? Sovereignty in an Age of Globalization* (New York: Columbia University Press).

Sassen, S. (2003) 'Economic Globalization and the Redrawing of Citizenship' in J. Friedman (ed.) *Globalization, the State, and Violence* (Walnut Creek, CA: AltaMira Press).

Satterthwaite, D. (2003) 'The Millennium Development Goals and Urban Poverty Reduction: Great Expectations and Nonsense Statistics', *Environment and Urbanization*, 15(2): 181–90.

Satyanarayana, K. and S. Srivastava (2007) 'Poverty, Health and Intellectual Property Rights with Special Reference to India', *Indian Journal Medical Research*, 126: 390–406, http://findarticles.com/p/articles/mi_qa3867/is_/ai_n21279019?tag=artBody;col1, date accessed 25 September 2008.

Saul, J. (2004) 'Africa: The Next Liberation Struggle?' Theme Paper prepared for the workshop 'Socialism, Democracy, Activism', Department of Political Science, York University, Toronto.

Scharpf, F. W. (1999) *Governing in Europe: Effective and Democratic?* (Oxford: Oxford University Press).

Schieber, G., P. Gottret, L. Fleisher and A. Leive (2007) 'Financing Global Health: Mission Unaccomplished', *Health Affairs*, 26(4): 921–34.

Schild, V. (1998) 'Market Citizenship and the "New Democracies": The Ambiguous Legacies of Contemporary Chilean Women's Movements', *Social Politics: International Studies in Gender, State Society*, 5(2): 232–49.

Schild, V. (2000) 'Neo-liberalism's New Gendered Market Citizens: The "Civilizing" Dimension of Social Programmes in Chile', *Citizenship Studies*, 4(3): 275–305.

Schild, V. (2007) 'Empowering "Consumer-Citizens" or Governing Poor Female Subjects? The Institutionalization of "Self-development" in the Chilean Social Policy Field', *Journal of Consumer Culture*, 7(2): 179–203.

Scholte, J. A. (2000) *Globalization: A Critical Introduction* (New York: St. Martin's Press).

Schönteich, M. (1999) 'Age and AIDS: South Africa's Crime Timebomb?' *African Security Review*, 8(4).

Schrecker, T. (2008) 'Denaturalizing Scarcity: A Strategy of Inquiry for Public Health Ethics', *Bulletin of the World Health Organization*, 86(8): 600–5.

Schrecker, T., R. Labonte and D. Sanders (2007) 'Breaking Faith with Africa: The G8 and Population Health Post-Gleneagles' in Cooper et al. (eds) *Governing Global Health*.

Schultz, M. and D. Walker (2005) 'How Intellectual Property Became Controversial: NGOs and the New International IP Agenda', *Engage*, 6(1): 82–98.

Scott-Samuel, A. and E. O'Keefe (2007) 'Health Impact Assessment, Human Rights and Global Public Policy: A Critical Appraisal', *Bulletin of the World Health Organization*, 85(3): 212–17.

Sell, S. (2002) 'TRIPS and the Access to Medicines Campaign', *Wisconsin International Law Journal*, 20(3): 481–522.

Sell, S. (2003) *Private Power, Public Law: the Globalization of Intellectual Property Rights* (Cambridge: Cambridge University Press).

Sepulveda, J., C. Carpenter, J. Curran, W. Holzemer, H. Smits, K. Scott and M. Orza (eds) (2007) *PEPFAR Implementation: Progress and Promise* (Washington DC: Institute of Medicine and The National Academy of Sciences).

Shakow, A. (2006) *Global Fund – World Bank HIV/AIDS Programs Comparative Advantage Study*, http://www.theglobalfund.org/en/files/links_resources/library/studies/GFWBReportFinalVersion.pdf, date accessed 24 February 2007.

Shashikant, S. (2006) 'Indian Opposition to Drug Patents', Third World Network, http://www.twnside.org.sg/title2/health.info/twninfohealth018.htm, date accessed 23 November 2008.

Sidibe, M., I. Ramiah and K. Buse (2006a) 'The Global Fund at Five: What Next for Universal Access for HIV/AIDS, TB and Malaria?' *Journal of the Royal Society of Medicine*, 99(10): 497–500.

Sidibe, M., I. Ramiah and K. Buse (2006b) 'Alignment, Harmonisation, and Accountability in HIV/AIDS: A Comment', *Lancet*, 368(9550): 1853–54.

Singh, M. (2005) personal interview (by Mulay), Delhi, India, 15 December.

(Brown) Smith, R., R. Beaglehole, D. Woodward and N. Drager (eds) (2003) *Global Public Goods for Health: Health Economics and Public Health Perspectives* (Oxford: Oxford University Press).

Sontag, S. (2002) *Illness as Metaphor and AIDS and Its Metaphors* (London: Penguin Classics).

Sørensen, E. and J. Torfing (2007) 'Introduction: Governance Network Research: Towards a Second Generation' in E. Sørensen and J. Torfing (eds) *Theories of Democratic Network Governance* (London: Macmillan).

Sørensen, G. (2002) 'The Global Polity and Changes in Statehood' in M. Ougaard and R. Higgott (eds) *Towards a Global Polity* (London and New York: Routledge).

Spinaci, S., L. Currat, P. Shetty, V. Crowell and J. Kehler (2006) *Tough Choices: Investing in Health for Development* (Geneva: WHO).

Sridhar, L. (2003) 'Handwash or Eyewash? – Selling Soap in the Name of Public Private', India Resources Centre, http://www.indiaresource.org/issues/water/2003/projectwash.html, date accessed 10 August 2007.

Stanford in Washington (2002) 'Health and Genomics R&D: Some Facts and Figures', January 2002, http://www.stanford.edu/class/siw198q/websites/genomics/entry.htm, date accessed 20 July 2007.

Statistics South Africa (2005) *Mortality and Causes of Death in South Africa, 1997–2003: Findings from Death Notification*, P0309.3, 18 February.

Sterckx, S. (2004) 'Patents and Access to Drugs in Developing Countries: An Ethical Analysis', *Developing World Bioethics*, 4(1): 58–75.

Stiglitz, J. (2002) *Globalization and Its Discontents* (London: Allen Lane).

Stiglitz, J. and A. Charlton (2005) 'A Development Round of Trade Negotiations?' in F. Bourguignon, B. Pleskovic and A. Sapir (eds) *Annual World Bank Conference on Development Economics – Europe 2005: Are We on Track to Achieve the Millennium Development Goals?* (New York: Oxford University Press).

Strand, P. (2005) 'AIDS and Elections in Southern Africa: Is the Epidemic Undermining its Democratic Remedy?' ISS Occasional Paper no. 110, July, http://ww.iss.co.za/pubs/papers/110/Paper110.htm, date accessed 9 January 2007.

Strand, P. and K. Matlosa (2004) *HIV/AIDS and Democratic Governance in South Africa: Illustrating the Impact on Electoral Processes* (Pretoria: IDASA).

Streak, J. (2004) 'The GEAR Legacy: Did Gear Fail or Move South Africa forward in Development?' *Development Southern Africa*, 21(2): 271–88.

Strong, K., C. Mathers, J. Epping-Jordan and R. Beaglehole (2006) 'Preventing Chronic Disease: A Priority for Global Health', *International Journal of Epidemiology*, 35(2): 492–94.

Stuckler, D. and M. McKee (2008) 'Five Metaphors about Global-Health Policy', *Lancet*, 372(9633): 95–97.

Summers, T. (2003) *The Global Fund to Fight AIDS, TB and Malaria: A Progress Report* (Washington: The Bill and Melinda Gates Foundation).

Swidler, A. (2006) 'Syncretism and Subversion in AIDS Governance: How Locals Cope with Global Demands', *International Affairs*, 82(2): 269–84.

t'Hoen, E. (2005) Director Policy Advocacy and Research, Médicins sans Frontières Access to Essential Medicines Campaign, 'Presentation to European Parliament Committee on International Trade Hearing on TRIPs and Access to Medicines', Brussels, 18 January.

Tabb, W. (2004) *Economic Governance in the Age of Globalization* (New York: Columbia University Press).

TAC (Treatment Action Campaign) http://www.tac.org.za/Documents/Other/tachist.pdf, date accessed 23 July 2008.

TACAIDS (2006) 'Follow-up to the Declaration of Committment on HIV/AIDS (UNGASS). Country: United Republic of Tanzania', Reporting period January 2003-December 2005, http://data.unaids.org/pub/Report/2006/2006_country_progress_report_tanzaniaen.pdf, date accessed 18 November 2008.

Thomas, C. (2002) 'Trade Policy and the Politics of Access to Drugs', *Third World Quarterly*, 23(2): 251–64.

Thomas, C. and M. Weber (2004) 'The Politics of Global Health Governance: Whatever Happened to "Health for All by the Year 2000"?' *Global Governance*, 10(2): 187–205.

Thompson, A. S. (2005) *Reforming from the Top: A Leaders' 20 Summit*, Policy Briefs No. 2 (Tokyo: United Nations University), http://www.unu.edu/publications/briefs/policy-briefs/2005/L20.pdf#search=%22Thompson%20%22reforming%20from%20the%20top%22%20%22policy%20brief%22%22.

Thompson, K. W. (1972) 'The Green Revolution: Leadership and Partnership in Agriculture', *The Review of Politics*, 34: 174–89.

Thompson, N. (2001) 'Gene Blues: United States Patent and Trademark Office Overloaded', *Washington Monthly*, 33(4): 9.

Tomitova, L. (2005) 'Is the G8 Dealing Justly with Debt? Carnegie Council on Ethics and International Affairs', http://www.cceia.org/resources/articles_papers_reports/5185.html/:pf_printable?

Topol, E. J., S. S. Murphy and K. A. Frazer (2007) 'The Genomics Gold Rush', JAMA, 298(1): 218–21.

Trouiller, P., E. Torreele, P. Olliaro, N. White, S. Foster, D. Wirth and B. Pécoul (2001) 'Drugs for Neglected Diseases: A Failure of the Market and a Public Health Failure?' *Tropical Medicine and International Health*, 6(11): 945–51.

Türmen, T. (1999) 'Making Globalization Work for Better Health', *Development,* 42(4): 8–11.

UK Department of Health and Social Security (1980) *Inequalities in Health: Report of a Research Working Group (Black Report) (*London: DHSS).

UN (2004) *A More Secure World: Our Shared Responsibility. Report of the High-level Panel on Threats, Challenges and Change* (New York: United Nations).

UN (2005) *In Larger Freedom: Towards Development, Security and Human Rights for All: Report of the Secretary-General,* A/59/2005 (New York: United Nations).

UN (2007) *The Millennium Development Goals Progress Report,* New York. Online: http://www.un.org/millenniumgoals/pdf/mdg2007.pdf

UN Department of Economic and Social Affairs (2005) *World Economic and Social Survey 2005: Financing for Development,* E/2005/51/Rev.1, ST/ESA/298 (New York: United Nations).

UN General Assembly (2000) 'United Nations Millennium Declaration', A/Res/55/2, 18 September.

UN General Assembly (2005) *2005 World Summit Outcome,* A/RES/60/1 (New York: UN).

UN Millennium Development Goals http://www.un.org/millenniumgoals, date accessed 14 August 2007.

UN Millennium Project (2005) *Investing in Development: A Practical Plan to Achieve the Millennium Development Goals* (London: Earthscan).

UN Secretary-General (2006) *Report of the Secretary General on Recent Developments in External Debt,* A/61/152 (New York: United Nations).

UNAIDS (2003) *CCM and the Broader Country Level Co-ordination Context* (New York: UNAIDS).

UNAIDS (2005a) 'Rapid Assessment of Implementation status of the "Three Ones" Initiative in Tanzania', May, http://www.tzdac.or.tz/DPG%20Events/three%20ones% 20 report %202.doc, date accessed 5 June 2008.

UNAIDS (2005b) 'Making the Money Work through Greater UN Support for AIDS Responses: The 2006–2007 Consolidated UN Technical Support Plan for AIDS' (Geneva: UNAIDS).

UNAIDS (2005c) 'Implementation of the Global Task Team Recommendations', Update paper 25 August, UNAIDS, Geneva.

UNAIDS (2006a) 'Effectiveness of Multilateral Action on AIDS: Harmonized Support to Scaling Up the National Response', Report for the 18th Meeting of the UNAIDS Program Coordinating Board, UNAIDS/PCB (18)06.6, Geneva, 12 May, http://data.unaids.org/pub/Report/2006/PCB_18_06_6_en.pdf, date accessed 25 April 2007.

UNAIDS (2006b) *19th Meeting of the UNAIDS Programme Coordinating Board; Lusaka, Zambia; 6–8 December 2006*, Follow-up to the 2006 Political Declaration on HIV/AIDS; 2007–2010 Strategic Framework for UNAIDS Support to Countries' Efforts to Move Towards Universal Access, UNAIDS/PCB(19)/06.5, 13pp., date accessed 12 May 2007.

UNAIDS (2006c) *2006 UNAIDS Annual Report. Making the Money Work* (Geneva: UNAIDS).

UNAIDS (2006d) 'AIDS, Security and Humanitarian Response', Report from the 19th Meeting of the UNAIDS Programme Coordinating Board, Lusaka, Zambia, 6–8 December.

UNAIDS (2007) 'Making the Money Work: UNAIDS Technical Support to Countries', 15 October Geneva, http://data.unaids.org/pub/Report/2007/jc1388-makingmoneywork_en.pdf, date accessed 5 August 2008.

UNAIDS (2008a) *2008 Report on the Global AIDS Epidemic* (Geneva: UNAIDS).

UNAIDS (2008b) *UNAIDS Partnership with the Global Fund to fight AIDS, Tuberculosis and Malaria* (Geneva: UNAIDS), http://www.unaids.org/en/Partnerships/Global+Fund+to+Fight+AIDS+TB+and+Malaria/default.asp, date accessed 3 October 2008.

UNAIDS (2008c) *Memorandum of Understanding: UNAIDS and the Global Fund to Fight AIDS, Tuberculosis and Malaria*, http://data.unaids.org/pub/Manual/2008/20080601_global_fund_mou_en.pdf, date accessed 3 October 2008.

UNAIDS (2008d) *New Tool to Improve Coordination of AIDS Technical Support*, (UNAIDS: Geneva) 3 October, http://www.unaids.org/en/KnowledgeCentre/Resources/FeatureStories/archive/2008/20080310_CoATS.asp, date accessed 6 October 2008.

UNAIDS/WHO (2004a) *The Three Ones. Key Principles*, http://data.unaids.org/UNA-docs/Three-Ones_KeyPrinciples_en.pdf, date accessed 10 April 2007.

UNAIDS/WHO (2004b) 'AIDS Epidemic Update', December 2004 (Geneva: UNAIDS/World Health Organization).

UNCTAD/WHO (2005) 'Implementation of the Decision on Paragraph 6 of the Doha Ministerial Declaration on the TRIPS Agreement and Public Health: Progress Report', World Tr@de Net, September, http://www.intracen.org/mts/dda/dda_doc/para6_sept05.pdf, date accessed 23 July 2008.

UNDG (2003) *Guidance Note on Joint Programming* (New York: UNDG), http://www.undg.org/archive_docs/3642-Finalized_Guidance_Note_on_Joint_Programming__complete_.doc, date accessed 16 October 2008.

UNDG (2006) *Proposed Working Mechanisms for Joint UN Teams at Country Level. Guidance Paper* (New York: UNDG), http://data.unaids.org/pub/Manual/2007/jc1325_jointu_teams_ en. pdf, date accessed 16 October 2008.

UNDP (1994) *Human Development Report 1994: New Dimensions of Human Security* (New York and Oxford: Oxford University Press).

UNDP (2002) *Human Development Report 2002: Deepening Democracy in a Fragmented World* (New York and Oxford: Oxford University Press).

UNDP (2005) *Human Development Report 2005 – International Cooperation at a Crossroads: Aid, Trade and Security in an Unequal World* (New York and Oxford: Oxford University Press).

United Nations Country Team Viet Nam (2003) *Health Care Financing for Viet Nam*, Discussion Paper No. 2 (Hanoi: United Nations Viet Nam), http://www.un.org.vn/undocs/healthcare/HealthcareFinancing.pdf

United States Government Accountability Office (2007) *Intellectual Property: U.S. Trade Policy Guidance on WTO Declaration on Access to Medicines May Need Clarification*, GAO-07-1198 (Washington, DC: USGAO), http://www.gao.gov/new.items/d071198.pdf

US Congress (2003) *'United States Leadership on HIV/AIDS, Tuberculosis and Malaria Act of 2003'*, 22 USC 7601 PUBLIC LAW 108-25-May 27, 2003, 108th Congress, http://frwebgate.access.gpo.gov/cgi-bin/getdoc.cgi?dbname=108_cong_public_laws&docid=f:publ025.108.pdf, date accessed 24 February 2007.

US Congress (2008) *Tom Lantos and Henry J. Hyde United States Global Leadership Against HIV/AIDS, Tuberculosis, and Malaria Reauthorization Act of 2008*, http://www.pepfar.gov/documents/organization/108294.pdf, date accessed 15 October 2008.

US Congress, Office of Technology Assessment (1988) *Mapping Our Genes–Genome Projects: How Big? How Fast?* (Washington: U.S. Government Publishing Office).

US House (2001a) 'Recent Developments which may Impact Consumer Access to, and Demand for Pharmaceuticals', Comments of Sherrod Brown, Committee on Energy and Commerce, Subcommittee on Health, 13 June.

US House (2001b) 'Recent Developments which may Impact Consumer Access to, and Demand for Pharmaceuticals', Comments of Janet Woodcock (Director, Center for Drug Evaluation and Research).

US House (2001c) 'Recent Developments which may Impact Consumer Access to, and Demand for Pharmaceuticals', Submitted testimony of Billy Tauzin.

US House (2001d) 'Recent Developments which may Impact Consumer Access to, and Demand for Pharmaceuticals', Statement by Richard Kingham.

US House (2002a) 'Reauthorization of the Prescription Drug User Fee Act', Statement by Chairman Michael Bilirakis, Committee on Energy and Commerce, Subcommittee on Health, 4 March.

US House (2002b) 'Reauthorization of the Prescription Drug User Fee Act', Statement by Lester Crawford. Committee on Energy and Commerce, Subcommittee on Health, 4 March.

US House (2002c) 'Reauthorization of the Prescription Drug User Fee Act', Statement by Sherrod Brown, Committee on Energy and Commerce.

US House (2003) 'NIH: Moving Research from the Bench to Bedside', Committee on Energy and Health, Subcommittee on Health, 10 June 2003.

US Institute of Medicine (1997) *America's Vital Interest in Global Health: Protecting Our People, Enhancing Our Economy, and Advancing Our International Interests* (Washington, DC: National Academy Press).

US Senate (1989) 'The Human Genome Initiative and the Future of Biotechnology', Subcommittee on Science, Technology, and Space, Committee on Commerce, Science and Transportation' (Washington, DC: US Government Printing Office).

US Senate (2007a) 'Follow-on Biologics', Testimony of Senator Charles Schumer, Committee on Health, Education, Labor, and Pensions, 8 March, transcribed by author (Loeppky).

US Senate (2007b) 'Paying Off Generics to Prevent Competition with Brand Name Drugs', Testimony of Billy Tauzin, Committee on the Judiciary, 17 January.

US Senate (2007c) 'Patent Reform: The Future of American Innovation', Testimony of Katherine Biberstein (on behalf of BIO), Committee of the Judiciary, 6 June.

USPTO (2003) *The 21*st *Century Strategic Plan*, Washington, 3 February 2003, www.uspto.gov/web/offices/com/strat21/stratplan_03feb2003.pdf, date accessed 9 November 2008.

USTR (2005) *Special 301 Report*. Washington, p. 10, http://www.ustr.gov/assets/Document_Library/Reports_Publications/2005/2005_Special_301/asset_upload_file195_7636.pdf, date accessed 10 December 2005.

USTR (2007) *Special 301 Report*. Washington, http://www.ustr.gov/assets/Document_Library/Reports_Publications/2007/2007_Special_301_Review/asset_upload_file230_11122.pdf, date accessed 9 November 2008.

USTR (United States Office of the Trade Representative) (1998) *Trade Policy Agenda and 1997 Annual Report of the President of the United States on the Trade Agreements Program* (Washington, DC: USTR).

US Trade Act (2002) US Congress Public Law 107–210, 107th Congress, 19 USC 3801, 6 August 2002.

Utting, P. (2005) 'Corporate Responsibility and the Movement of Business', *Development in Practice*, 15: 375–88.

Utting, P. and A. Zammit (2006) *Beyond Pragmatism: Appraising UN-Business Partnerships* (Geneva: UNRISD).

Valiquet, D. (2006) 'The Patented Medicines (Notice of Compliance) Regulations', http://www.parl.gc.ca/information/library/PRBpubs/prb0614-e.htm, date accessed 11 October 2008.

Vallings, C. and M. Moreno-Torres (2005) 'Drivers of Fragility: What Makes States Fragile?' Department for International Development PRDE Working Paper No. 7.

van Kersbergen, K. and B. Verbeek (2007) 'The Politics of International Norms: Subsidiary and the Imperfect Competence Regime of the European Union', *European Journal of International Relations*, 13(2): 217–38.

Vancouver Sun (2007) '"Landmark Breakthrough" in Breast Cancer Research', *The Vancouver Sun*, 28 May, p. A1.

Vinocur, J. (2008) 'German Comfort Zone: Oblivious and Proud', *International Herald Tribune*, Tuesday, 6 January, p. 2.

von Soest, C. V. and M. Weinel (2007) 'The Treatment Controversy: Global Health Governance and South Africa's Fight against HIV/AIDS', in Hein et al. *Global Health Governance and the Fight against HIV/AIDS*, pp. 202–25.

Watal, J. (2001) *Intellectual Property Rights in the WTO and Developing Countries* (Delhi: Oxford University Press).

Watkins, K. and Fowler, P. (2002). *Rigged Rules and Double Standards*. Washington, DC: Oxfam International, http://www.maketradefair.org/assets/english/report_english.pdf

Weber, T. (2006) 'Who Should Decide What is a Good Cause', British Broadcasting Corporation, 27 January, http://news.bbc.co.uk/1/hi/business/4655908.stm, date accessed 14 August 2008.

Weindling, P. (1997) 'Philanthropy and World Health: The Rockefeller Foundation and the League of Nations Health Organisation', *Minerva*, 35: 269–81.

Wertheimer, A. I., T. M. Santella and H. J. Lauver (2004) 'Successful Public/Private Donation Programs: A Review of the Diflucan Partnership Program in South Africa', *Journal of the International Association of Physicians in AIDS Care*, 3(3): 74–85.

Whiteside, A., C. Andrade, L. Arrehag, S. Dlamini, T. Ginindza and A. Parikh (2006a) *The Socio-Economic Impact of HIV/AIDS in Swaziland*, Report prepared by the National Emergency Response Council on HIV/AIDS (NERCHA), Mbabane, Swaziland, and the Health, Economics and HIV/AIDS Research Division (HEARD), Durban, South Africa.

Whiteside, A., A. de Waal and T. Gebre-Tensae (2006b) 'AIDS, Security and the Military in Africa: A Sober Appraisal', *African Affairs*, 105(419): 201–18.

Whiteside, A., R. Mattes, S. Willan and R. Manning (2002) 'Examining HIV/AIDS in Southern Africa through the Eyes of Ordinary Southern Africans', Afrobarometer Paper No. 21, August 2002.

WHO (2003a) *Treating 3 Million by 2005: Making it Happen: The WHO Strategy* (Geneva: WHO).

WHO (2003b) *Global Defence Against the Infectious Disease Threat,* 15th Communicable Diseases Progress Report (Geneva: WHO).

WHO (2004) *The World Medicines Situation* (Geneva: WHO), http://www.who.int/medicinedocs/en/d/Js6160e/#Js6160e, date accessed 15 August 2008.

WHO (2005a) *Preventing Chronic Disease: A Vital Investment* (Geneva: WHO).
WHO (2005b) 'Accelerating Access Initiative (AAI) – Fact Sheet,' www.who.int/entity/hiv/AAI_fs_4Q2005.pdf, date accessed 18 March 2006.
WHO (2006) *WHO Constitution, Basic Documents, Forty-fifth edition*, October (Geneva: WHO), http://www.who.int/governance/eb/who_constitution_en.pdf, date accessed 13 July 2007.
WHO and WTO (2001) 'Report of the Workshop on Differential Pricing and Financing of Essential Drugs', www.who.int/inf-pr-2001/en/pr2001-20.html, date accessed 15 August 2008.
WHO Media Centre (2007) 'WHO and Manufacturers Move Ahead for Plans for H5N1 Influenza Global Vaccine Stockpile', 13 June, http://www.who.int/mediacentre/news/statements/2007/s14/en/index.html, date accessed 12 August 2007.
WHO/UNAIDS/UNICEF (2007) Towards universal access: scaling up priority HIV/AIDS interventions in the health sector: progress report, April 2007, Geneva.
WHO (2008) 'HIV/AIDS Estimates are Revised Downwards', *World Health Statistics 2008* (Geneva: WHO).
Widdus, R. (2003) 'Public-Private Partnerships for Health Require Thoughtful Evaluation', *Bulletin of the World Health Organisation*, 81(4): 235.
Widdus, R. (2004) 'Why Public-Private Partnerships for Product Development Emerged and How? A Summary' in R. Widdus and K. White (eds) *Combating Diseases Associated with Poverty: Financing Strategies for Product Development and the Potential Role of Public-Private Partnerships* (London: Wellcome Trust).
Williamson, J. (2004) 'The Washington Consensus as Policy Prescription for Development', World Bank Practitioners for Development Lecture series, Institute for International Economics, Washington, DC, http://www.iie.com/publications/papers/williamson0204.pdf, date accessed 16 February 2009.
Willman, D. (2000) 'How a New Policy Led to Seven Deadly Drugs', *Los Angeles Times*, 20 December, A1.
Windfuhr, M. (ed.) (2005) *Beyond the Nation State: Human Rights in Times of Globalization* (Uppsala: Global Publications Foundation).
Winslow, C. (1975) 'Sussex Smugglers' in D. Hay, P. Linebaugh, J. G. Rule, E. P. Thompson and C. Winslow (eds) *Albion's Fatal Tree: Crime and Society in Eighteenth-Century England* (New York: Pantheon).
Wise, T. A. (2004) 'The Paradox of Agricultural Subsidies: Measurement Issues, Agricultural Dumping, and Policy Reform', GDEI Working Paper No. 04–02, Global Development and Environment Institute, Tufts University.
Wolf, K. D. (2001) 'Private Actors and the Legitimacy of Governance beyond the State', Paper presented at the ECPR Joint Sessions, 6–11 April, Grenoble.
Wolff, S. (2006) 'State Failure in a Regional Context', unpublished research report, University of Bath, United Kingdom.
Wollman, H. (2006) 'Coordination in the Intergovernmental Setting' in G. Peters and J. Jon (eds) *Handbook of Public Administration* (London: Sage).
Wong, C., K. Tang and V. Lo (2007) 'Unaffordable Healthcare amid Phenomenal Growth: The Case of Healthcare Protection in Reform China', *International Journal of Social Welfare*, 16(2): 140–49.
Wood, E. (1991) *The Pristine Culture of Capitalism: A Historical Essay on Old Regimes and Modern States* (London: Verso).
Wood, E. M. (1991) *The Pristine Culture of Capitalism: A Historical Essay on Old Regimes and Modern States* (London: Verso).
Woodward, D. and A. Simms (2006) *Growth Isn't Working: The Unbalanced Distribution of Benefits and Costs from Economic Growth* (London: New Economics Foundation),

http://www.neweconomics.org/NEF070625/NEF_Registration070625add.aspx?returnurl=/gen/uploads/hrfu5w555mzd3f55m2vqwty502022006112929.pdf

Woodward, D. and S. Abdallah (in press) *How Poor is 'Poor'? Towards a Rights-Based Poverty Line*, Technical Version (London: New Economics Foundation).

Woodward, D., N. Drager, R. Beaglehole and D. Lipson (2001) 'Globalization and Health: A Framework for Analysis and Action', *Bulletin of the World Health Organization*, 79(9): 875–81.

Woodward, S. (2004) 'Fragile States', paper presented to the 'States and Security' Learning Group at the Peace and Social Justice meeting of the Ford Foundation, Rio de Janeiro, Brazil, 29 November.

Wooley, M., S. M. Propst and E. Connelly (2005) 'United States Investment in Global Health Research', *Global Forum Update on Research for Health: Poverty, Equity and Health Research,* 2 September, http://www.researchamerica.org/publications/articles/Global Forum.pdf, date accessed 16 July 2007.

World Bank (1993) *World Development Report 1993: Investing in Health* (Oxford: Oxford University Press for the World Bank).

World Bank (2000) *World Development Report 2000/2001: Attacking Poverty* (Oxford: Oxford University Press).

World Bank (2006) *World Development Report 2006: Equity and Development* (Washington DC: World Bank).

World Bank (2007a) 'The Africa Multi-Country AIDS Program 2000–2006: Results of the World Bank's Response to a Development Crisis', World Bank report, Washington DC, http://siteresources.worldbank.org/EXTAFRREGTOPHIVAIDS/Resources/717147-1181768523896/complete.pdf, date accessed 31 July 2007.

World Bank (2007c) *Our Commitment: The World Bank's Africa Region HIV/AIDS Agenda for Action 2007–2011,* Advance copy (Washington DC: International Bank for Reconstruction and Development), http://siteresources.worldbank.org/EXTAFRREGTOPHIVAIDS/Resources/WB_HIV-AIDS-AFA_2007-2011_Advance_Copy.pdf, date accessed 31 July 2007.

World Bank (2007d) *Multi-country HIV/AIDS Program,* http://web.worldbank.org/WBSITE/EXTERNAL/COUNTRIES/AFRICAEXT/EXTAFRHEANUTPOP/EXTAFRREGTOPHIVAIDS/0,,contentMDK:20415735~menuPK:1001234~pagePK:34004173~piPK:34003707~theSitePK:717148,00.html, date accessed 4 July 2008.

World Bank (2008a) *ASAP Strategy Support* (Washington: World Bank), http://web.worldbank.org/WBSITE/EXTERNAL/TOPICS/EXTHEALTHNUTRITION-ANDPOPULATION/EXTHIVAIDS/0,,contentMDK:20974001~menuPK:2754898~pagePK:210058~piPK:210062~theSitePK:376471,00.html, date accessed 5 October 2008.

World Bank (2008b) *ASAP Progress Report,* 1 October, http://siteresources.worldbank.org/INTHIVAIDS/Resources/375798-1151090631807/ASAPProgressReportOct12008.pdf, date accessed 13 October 2008.

World Bank Health, Nutrition and Population Program (2007) 'HNPStats', World Bank, http://devdata.worldbank.org/hnpstats.

World Bank Independent Evaluation Group (2006) *Engaging with Fragile States: An IEG Review of World Bank Support to Low-Income Countries under Stress* (Washington, DC: The World Bank).

World Bank List of Economies (July 2005) http://web.worldbank.org/WBSITE/EXTERNAL/DATASTATISTICS/0,,contentMDK:20485916~menuPK:1297819~pagePK:64133150~piPK:64133175~theSitePK:239419,00.html

World Commission on the Social Dimension of Globalization (2004) *A Fair Globalization: Creating Opportunities for All* (Geneva: International Labour Organization), http://www.ilo.org/public/english/wcsdg/docs/report.pdf

World Development Report (2000/2001) *Attacking Poverty.* Washington DC.
World Economic Forum (2005) *Development-Driven Public-Private Partnerships in Health* (Geneva: World Economic Forum).
World Health Organization, 'Regional Office for South-East Asia: Burden of Leprosy.' http://www.searo.who.int/en/Section10/Section20_9888.htm, date accessed 14 August 2008.
WTO (World Trade Organization) (2001) 'Declaration on the TRIPS Agreement and Public Health', adopted 14 November, WT/MIN(01)DEC/2, http://www.worldtradelaw.net/doha/tripshealth.pdf, date accessed 23 July 2008.
Yamey, G. (2001) 'Global Vaccine Initiative Creates Inequity, Analysis Concludes', *British Medical Journal,* 322(7289): 754.
Youde, J. (2005) 'Enter the Fourth Horseman: Health Security and International Relations Theory', *The Whitehead Journal of Diplomacy and International Relations,* VI(1): 193–208.
Young, A. (2005) 'The Gift of the Dying: the Tragedy of AIDS and the Welfare of Future African Generations', *The Quarterly Journal of Economics,* CXX(2): 423–66.
Zacher, M. (1999) 'Uniting Nations: Global Regimes and the United Nations System' in Vayrynen, R. (ed.) *Globalization and Global Governance* (New York: Rowman and Littlefield Publishers).
Zammit, A. (2003) *Development at Risk: Rethinking UN-Business Partnerships* (Geneva: The South Centre and UNRISD).
Zhang, R., K. Eggleston, V. Rotimi and R. Zeckhauser (2006) Antibiotic Resistance as a Global Threat: Evidence from China, Kuwait and the United States', *Globalization and Health,* 2(6), http://www.globalizationandhealth.com/content/2/1/6.
Zuern, M. (2004) 'Global Governance and Legitimacy Problems', *Government and Opposition,* 39(2): 260–87.

Index